Deconstruction and the Remainders of Phenomenology

Deconstruction
and the Remainders of
Phenomenology

SARTRE, DERRIDA, FOUCAULT, BAUDRILLARD

Tilottama Rajan

STANFORD UNIVERSITY PRESS

STANFORD, CALIFORNIA

2002

Stanford University Press
Stanford, California

© 2002 by the Board of Trustees of the
Leland Stanford Junior University.
All rights reserved.

Printed in the United States of America
on acid-free, archival-quality paper.

Library of Congress Cataloging-in-Publication Data

Rajan, Tilottama.
    Deconstruction and the remainders of phenomenology : Sartre, Derrida,
Foucault, Baudrillard / Tilottama Rajan.
        p. cm.
Includes bibliographical references and index.
    ISBN 0-8047-4501-3 (alk. paper) — ISBN 0-8047-4502-1 (pbk. : alk.
paper)
    1. Phenomenology. 2. Deconstruction. 3. Poststructuralism. 4.
Sartre, Jean Paul, 1905- 5. Derrida, Jacques. 6. Foucault, Michel. 7.
Baudrillard, Jean. I. Title.
    B829.5 .R35 2002
    142'.7—dc21   2002006718

Original Printing 2002

Last figure below indicates year of this printing:
11   10   09   08   07   06   05   04   03   02

Designed by Janet Wood
Typeset by Alan Noyes in 11/14 Adobe Garamond.

Contents

Abbreviations

Full bibliographic information can be found in Works Cited.

AK	Michel Foucault. *The Archaeology of Knowledge and "The Discourse on Language"*
BC	Michel Foucault. *The Birth of the Clinic*
BN	Jean-Paul Sartre. *Being and Nothingness*
CS	Jean Baudrillard. *The Consumer Society*
DL	Michel Foucault. *Death and the Labyrinth*
EC	Jean Baudrillard. *The Ecstasy of Communication*
EE	Emmanuel Levinas. *Existence and Existents*
FS	Jean Baudrillard. *Fatal Strategies*
G	Jacques Derrida. *Le problème de la genèse dans la philosophie de Husserl*
GO	Maurice Blanchot. *"The Gaze of Orpheus" and Other Literary Essays*
LE	Jean Hyppolite. *Logic and Existence*
M	Jacques Derrida. *Margins of Philosophy*
NP	Georges Canguilhem. *On the Normal and the Pathological*
OG	Jacques Derrida. *Edmund Husserl's "Origin of Geometry"*
OGr	Jacques Derrida. *Of Grammatology*
OT	Michel Foucault. *The Order of Things*
P	Jacques Derrida. *Positions*
RR	Paul de Man. *The Rhetoric of Romanticism*
RT	Paul de Man. *The Resistance to Theory*
S	Jean Baudrillard. *Seduction*
SED	Jean Baudrillard. *Symbolic Exchange and Death*
SO	Jean Baudrillard. *The System of Objects*

Acknowledgments

This book has been ten years in the making, and although its original goals of desynonymizing deconstruction and poststructuralism and recovering the importance of Sartre for theory have remained part of the project, it has not ended where it began, nor is it finished. Over the years Kristeva dropped out of the book and Baudrillard became unexpectedly important. The interdisciplinarity of deconstruction and its place in a larger history of interdisciplinary organizations of knowledge became an increasingly important background concern and is an area on which I hope to do more work in the future. Graduate classes at the University of Wisconsin, the Center for Comparative Literature at the University of Toronto, where I lectured on this material as Northrop Frye Professor of Theory in 1999, and the Centre for Theory and Criticism at Western Ontario have provided me with an evolving context for this project. The last, in particular, has brought me to think about the importance of interdisciplinarity to both phenomenology and deconstruction. Stanley Corngold read the chapter on Sartre at an earlier stage. David Clark has read the whole manuscript at various stages and has provided sensible advice, constant feedback, support on many interrelated levels, and the invaluable sense of intellectual community that comes from the example and encouragement of his own work. Joel Faflak has not read the whole manuscript, but he has nevertheless understood it all in the ways that only a romanticist who grasps philosophy as psychoanalysis can do. As always, my father Balachandra Rajan has provided the emotional and intellectual support that makes so many things possible. Rebecca Gagan, who helped me prepare the final copy of the manuscript, has dealt unflinchingly with the nightmare of its endnotes and other such technical and technological matters. She has been the best of all research assistants: a practical help, a constant intellectual stimulus, and a hope for the future. Finally, I am also grateful to Helen Tartar for her support of this book and for keeping a place for Theory in a market that seems driven by very different imperatives.

A shorter and different version of Chapter 6 was published as "The Phenomenological Allegory: From Death and the Labyrinth to The Order of Things" in *Poetics Today* 19:3 (1998): 439–66. Chapter 3, "The Double Detour: Sartre, Heidegger, and the Genealogy of Deconstruction," has also appeared in a slightly shorter version in *After Poststructuralism: Writing the Intellectual History of Theory*, edited by myself and Michael O'Driscoll (Toronto: University of Toronto Press, 2002). I am grateful for permission to reprint this material.

Preface

I.

This study explores the place of phenomenology in the early and subsequent careers of theorists who can loosely be described as deconstructive or poststructuralist, terms that were first used synonymously in the North American reception of French theory. I begin with two hypotheses. Poststructuralism—with its narrowed emphasis on sixties linguistic and structural models—developed from deconstruction, but it is not identical with deconstruction. This earlier deconstruction is linked to a phenomenology (particularly that of Jean-Paul Sartre) whose seminal place in French theory has been neglected as a result of the swerve away from a philosophy concerned with consciousness, perception, and being to a discourse centered on representation and the sign. One of the things attempted here is thus a "desynonymizing" of deconstruction and poststructuralism. Equally important, I argue that French deconstruction as it emerges in the early sixties, far from being an approach focused on literature, is an interdisciplinary attempt to rethink *philosophy* in relation to the threat posed by the human sciences. As a unique attempt to approach cultural phenomena and disciplinary fields in terms of the relation between being and knowledge, deconstruction still has much to tell us even (and particularly) after the current paradigm shift to cultural studies, which itself emerges from a continuation of the epistemic crisis that first saw the reconfiguration of philosophy as deconstruction.

The book takes the form of a "narrative" that allows for a reflection

xi

on the blindnesses and insights of three linked areas: phenomenology, deconstruction, and poststructuralism. Focusing on Jacques Derrida, Michel Foucault, Jean Baudrillard, and at points Paul de Man, I trace the displacement in their work from a deconstruction that comes out of phenomenology to a poststructuralism that refigures deconstruction so as to abject a vocabulary of consciousness in favor of what Peter Dews calls an "imperialism of the signifier."[1] Thus, while deconstruction makes language an occasion for a broader reflection on the relations between ontology, epistemology, and culture, poststructuralism (to adapt Foucault's description of a classicism that he links to structuralism) confines signs "within . . . representation . . . in that narrow space in which they interact with themselves in a perpetual state of decomposition and recomposition" (OT: 67). Poststructuralism is mobilized by a return to Saussure after structuralism, but it is also a belated response to developments in technology that Friedrich Kittler has traced as far back as the invention of the typewriter and the resulting exteriorization of writing as a mechanical prosthesis. In the form studied here ("negative" and ascetic rather than "affirmative"), poststructuralism registers the trauma of technology and structure in its submission to a "postmodern" world of depthless surfaces. This subjection is expressed as a nominalism that refuses to posit anything outside discourse (in Foucault), media simulation (in Baudrillard), or rhetoric (in de Man). The particular theoretical corpus explored here—texts written roughly between the mid-forties and the mid-eighties—thus also provides a scene of reading in which we can reflect critically on the more affirmative direction given to the term *poststructuralism* today.

Accordingly, I focus on three distinct theory types that I attempt to relate to the situation of theory today. The first is phenomenology, insofar as it provides a series of pre-texts for deconstruction. I consider the work of Edmund Husserl, Martin Heidegger, and Maurice Merleau-Ponty wherever relevant in the chapters on contemporary theorists. But I give particular attention to one aspect of the prehistory of deconstruction that has been neglected: the work of Sartre before his political turn in the late forties, particularly *Being and Nothingness* (1943). In locating phenomenology as the site at which deconstruction first emerges, I am not so much arguing for a return to phenomenology as tracing the genealogy of its effacement. My aim is to situate poststructuralism in a way that allows it to be read against its own margins and silences. A second area of concern is thus poststructural-ism itself, as exemplified by the later work of Foucault (and de Man), more resistantly Baudrillard, and more intermittently Derrida (as poststructural-ism in his work gives way to a post-Heideggerianism that is by no means un-problematized). Commenting on Foucault's fascination with textualized sur-faces, Maurice Blanchot writes that *The Archaeology of Knowledge* marks Foucault's search for "discursive practices that were virtually pure, in the sense of referring only to themselves."[2] Blanchot merely hints at what is be-hind this desire for purity and rigor. But we can speculate that the obsession with surfaces and suspicion of depth is an ascetic response to the reification that characterizes advanced capitalism and that the self-discipline of the lin-guistic turn is in certain moments part of a search for autonomy. It is, in other words, a search for what Sartre calls a being in-itself emancipated from the contingency and vulnerability of the for-itself. In the terms Derrida takes over from Jean Hyppolite, it is a search for a "structure" without "gen-esis" that curiously repeats in its turn away from phenomenology the very psychotropology that Derrida had discerned in (Husserlian) phenomenology.

If the poststructural turn provides this study with its narrative center, its normative center is to be found earlier in the history of French theory. As my references to Sartre, Hyppolite, and Derrida imply, deconstruction emerges in a symbiotic relationship with existential (as distinct from tran-scendental) phenomenology, wherein deconstruction's unworking of lan-guage has already been prefigured in phenomenology's unworking of con-sciousness and perception. Thus finally and most importantly I also argue that after phenomenology but before poststructuralism there existed a third theory-type more constructively engaged with phenomenology, which can be discerned in the work of Emmanuel Levinas and Blanchot in the forties, in the early work of de Man, in Foucault's work up to and including *The Order of Things* (1966), in Derrida's studies of Husserl culminating in *Speech and Phenomena* (1967) and other work of that period, and in Baudrillard's work up to the ambiguous turning point marked by *Symbolic Exchange and Death* (1976).

This deconstruction is more interdisciplinary than the purely literary or "Yale" version with which the term is sometimes equated in North America. While partly generated by the cross-fertilization of philosophy and litera-ture, it deploys its notions—of unworking (Blanchot), *différance* (Derrida), the semiotic (Julia Kristeva), or anti-matter (Baudrillard)—across what Derrida calls "the human sciences of writing" (OGr: 10), thus attempting to close the breach, created by Sartre after his political turn, between prose and a more purely literary poetry. In this sense deconstruction, I argue, emerges as a continuation of the phenomenological project in a period when philosophy in France was increasingly threatened by the human sciences as renewed and reconceived by structuralism. The space for this continuation is opened up, among others, by Merleau-Ponty and Lyotard, who argue for the continued relevance of phenomenology to psychology, sociology, and history. In *Of Grammatology* and "The Discourse on Language," Derrida and Foucault will extend this project to information theory, thus creating a further space for the work of Baudrillard.

Foucault's own deployment of this space (in the last section of *The Order of Things*) is more deeply self-reflexive than anything envisioned by Lyotard. Foucault uses phenomenology and literature to rethink the various other disciplines in terms of a philosophical (psycho)analytic. But he also radically rethinks philosophy, through the "quadrilateral" of self-reflexive figures introduced at the end of *The Order of Things*, in terms of and as "non-philosophy"—a term to which I return. Still, it is important to distinguish deconstruction from poststructuralism if we are not to misrecognize it through the initial moment of its Anglo-American translation. For in its own context it is a reinvention of philosophy rather than a form of criticism whose "linguistic" origins made it easily assimilable into literary criticism as well as sufficiently scientific to be respectable in an increasingly technobureaucratic academy.[3] It is correspondingly important to desynonymize *poststructuralism* and *deconstruction* if we are not to miss the pathos of its renunciatory turn to linguistic and discursive models (since I argue that poststructuralism is not just an Anglo-American mistake but a fortuitously accurate description of a tendency in French theory).

Finally, it is important to recover the seminal role of *phenomenology*—and particularly of Sartre—in the conjugation of deconstruction: not simply "to do justice to" phenomenology (to evoke Derrida's essay "To Do Justice to Freud" in *Resistances of Psychoanalysis*), but also to bring deconstruction back into dialogue with an age of postmodern media(tiza)tion and to raise larger questions of the relation of modernity to postmodernity.

II.

With these concerns in mind the first two chapters deal with the interrelations among the theory types explored here. Chapter 1 focuses on how to think the relation of phenomenology and deconstruction. I begin with Derrida's dismissal of phenomenology in *Positions* as a deliberate forgetting of the complexity of phenomenology and specifically of the difference between existential and transcendental phenomenology that is the condition of possibility for his own early work. But the prestructuring of deconstruction by phenomenology is not just a matter of parallels and influences, many of which have been documented. What is at issue is a style of thinking, a certain relation of thought to its language, which makes deconstruction a continuation of the process whereby phenomenology "descends into its own substratum" by unworking transcendental through existential phenomenology. The phrase is Merleau-Ponty's, and the essay in which it occurs—a discussion of the missed encounter between phenomenology and psychoanalysis—provides a useful approach to the correlation between bodies of thought. Merleau-Ponty suggests that the consonance of phenomenology and psychoanalysis does not lie in the one saying "clearly" what the other said "obscurely," but rather in the way each "aim[s] toward the same latency."[4] It is in this latency, I argue, that the early work of Sartre is important: both because he breaches the disciplinary purity of philosophy in Husserl and Heidegger and because (although he may not theorize them) Sartre's writing is organized by the (non)structures of aporia, chiasmus, *différance*, and the supplement.

Deconstruction emerged from phenomenology in the mid-forties in ways I trace both here and in Chapter 3—through a transposition of phenomenological concerns into the field of "writing" that is best exemplified by the work of Blanchot. But in the mid-sixties it took a much more interdisciplinary direction as a response to the rising power of the human sciences under the aegis of structuralism. Both deconstruction and poststructuralism, at a certain point, are responses to structuralism, with the difference that the first counters structuralism with a phenomenology that the second claims to reject. Poststructuralism is an Anglo-American coinage that, tied up as it is with antihumanism, reflects both a replacement of organicist and/or ontological with structural or technological models, and a problematizing of structure. Chapter 2 thus attempts a genealogy of poststructuralism similar to the one attempted in the previous chapter with respect to deconstruction. I trace the phenomenon it names from the early work of Jacques Lacan and Roland Barthes, through its cathexis with the events of 1968, to its usage in more recent theory. In the process I distinguish between a negative, ascetic form of poststructuralism and a more affirmative version in the work of Barthes and Deleuze/Guattari. It is the latter that survives today and that has provided a foundation for cultural studies, but the more negative version is the focus of this book. As exemplified in this chapter by the late work of de Man, its submission to structures that are no longer rational or intelligible is shaped by what Judith Butler calls a "constitutive loss": the loss of phenomenology and deconstruction. To speak of loss may seem to cast this book in the mode of mourning. But this is true only if we recognize with Derrida that mourning is a form of affirmation and a kind of cultural memory and that memory is the return of the past as future.[5]

Returning to deconstruction, Chapter 3 takes up the contribution of Sartre to the reconfiguration of French theory, a contribution that is both conceptual and affective, intangible. Chapter 3 thus begins with Sartre's exclusion from the canon of theory due to his supposed misreading of Heidegger. I suggest, however, that the difference between Sartre and Heidegger provides the space within which deconstruction emerges as an attempt to use each philosopher to think through and against the other. As is well known, the French reading of Heidegger was mediated by Sartre, and this "error" was constitutive for deconstruction as the resistance, synthesis, and/or cathexis between multiple, intersecting phenomenologies. This chapter therefore explores Sartre's deterritorializing of phenomenology, including his uprooting of his own dialectic between the *pour-soi* (or for-itself) and the *en-soi* (or in-itself) in the sections on the body and the viscous in *Being and Nothingness*. If the Sartrean dialectic is an element in deconstruction, these sections are the unassimilable excrement of that project that returns in the late Baudrillard's account of a society that is *de trop*, obese. Chapter 3 then traces, with reference to different theorists, three forms taken by the transference of phenomenology into deconstruction. Briefly, they involve a crossing or chiasm between one philosopher and another; a resistance or aporia between them; and a dialogical overlapping and supplementation of one by the other. Focusing on the last of these tropes, this book gives a particular emphasis to Foucault's use of phenomenology to (de)construct knowledge through its unthought in *The Order of Things*. A similar convergence of different phenomenologies in an affirmative deconstruction can be found at many points in the work of Derrida and Baudrillard. But this is not to say that the work of any one theorist can be reduced to a single form of transference. Rather each theorist's work is overdetermined by more than one form of transference, which is why the "synthesis" of an affirmative deconstruction may be no more than an imaginary resolution of underlying contradictions.

The remaining chapters concentrate on the work of Derrida, Foucault, and Baudrillard, with occasional attention to de Man. They trace the emergence of deconstruction from phenomenology in the work of each theorist studied, with particular emphasis on questions of disciplinarity and on the attempt (however reticent) to recover a place for philosophy in the aftershock of what Husserl calls "The Crisis of European Sciences and Transcendental Phenomenology." They also analyze the turn away from this affirmative deconstruction to its displacement, disciplining, or renunciation in poststructuralism. In the process they provide what is in effect a phenomenological psychoanalysis of the latter in its unique theoretical pathology.

Chapter 4 traces Derrida's work on Husserl from his still untranslated *Problem of Genesis* to *Speech and Phenomena*. While Derrida at this stage claims to critique phenomenology, my argument is that he provides a deconstruction of transcendental phenomenology from the perspective of existential phenomenology, in a radicalization of the interpretive models used by Levinas and Hyppolite in their studies of Husserl and Hegel respectively. The deconstruction of Husserl also entails epistemic issues having to do with the way Husserl imagines philosophy and language on the model of mathematics. "The Ends of Man" signals a turn from or, at least, a modification of Derrida's earlier work, marked by an attack on Sartre that repeats Heidegger's "Letter on Humanism." Combined with the framing role of "Structure, Sign, and Play in the Human Sciences" in the Anglo-American reception of Derrida, "The Ends of Man" suggests why Derrida is often loosely labeled a poststructuralist or associated with a form of ultratextualism. But while Derrida does briefly valorize terms such as *science, structure,* and *system,* the turn he makes (although never decisive) is better described as post-Heideggerian. Chapter 4 concludes with a brief discussion of the complicity between poststructuralism and this post-Heideggerianism that both is and is not a return to phenomenology.

Chapters 5 to 7 trace the similar but different unfolding of Foucault's work from his early phenomenological studies to *The Archaeology of Knowledge* (1969) and contemporaneous work. Publishing *The Birth of the Clinic* (1963) on the same day as his study of the proto-structuralist writer Raymond Roussel, Foucault sets up subterranean connections—with implications for the onto-psychology of knowledge—between literature and science, sociology, and psychoanalysis. Foucault's study of Roussel is a cryptic psychoanalysis of the evasions that inhabit the latter's "formalism." Taking their cue from *Raymond Roussel* (translated as *Death and the Labyrinth*), these chapters in part offer a phenomenological psychoanalysis of Foucault's own (post)structuralism. Chapter 5 focuses on the internal differences that organize *The Birth of the Clinic* as an opening of the cogito to its "unthought" that works on two levels: disciplinarity or the organization of knowledge and method or theory. I therefore read *The Birth of the Clinic* in terms of the "allegorical" or "folded" structure also traced in the next chapter. Thus the text is first of all a breaching of the cogitos of medicine and sociology by ontological issues. And it is secondly a chiasmatic linking of phenomenology and structuralism, wherein each is used to unsettle the other. In the process Foucault also develops a unique way of engaging philosophy with cultural phenomena that is very different from his approach in *Discipline and Punish*. Indeed his earlier model serves as a valuable alternative to those used by cultural studies today, some of which derive from Foucault's later work.

The Birth of the Clinic is a limited case study that prefigures the much more ambitious exploration of similar issues in *The Order of Things* across the entire range of the *Geisteswissenschaften* from the Renaissance onward. Accordingly Chapter 6 focuses on *The Order of Things* and follows this same "fold" along historical, theoretical, and disciplinary paths. Literally speaking, Foucault's text is an ordering of knowledge that proceeds—more dialectically than he admits—from the Renaissance, through classicism, to modernity. But it also allegorizes a phenomenology of theoretical styles in which a renaissance associated with Merleau-Ponty yields to a classicism explicitly linked to structuralism and thus to the replacement of language with a

purely nominalist discourse. This history culminates in Foucault's third period with the return of language in the more negative mode of literature. On
an allegorical level, then, the history allows Foucault to rethink phenomenology as "deconstruction" through a dialectical encounter with structuralism. Working in the space between various phenomenologies, Foucault develops a deconstructive method that he uses in the final section to reorgan-
ize the various disciplines in terms of a dialogue between the cogito and its
unthought. This deconstruction is his implicit response to a university in
ruins and hints at a new interdisciplinary curriculum anchored in a reconfiguration of philosophy.

In *The Order of Things* Foucault finds a role for philosophy as deconstruction. But 1968 marks a turning point in his career, as also—however
obscurely and indeterminately—in Derrida's. Accordingly in *The Archaeology of Knowledge* Foucault moves away from a deconstruction linked to phenomenology. Chapter 7 traces this turn in *The Archaeology of Knowledge*, its
aesthetic addendum *This Is Not a Pipe*, and, more briefly, *Discipline and
Punish*, so as to explore both the public and the private faces of poststructuralism. On the one hand we can approach poststructuralism as a self-discipline that claims the reward of an autonomy anchored in rigor and science. On the other hand we can see it as an "apathetic formalism," to borrow Rodolphe Gasché's description of de Man's later work, which is also a
subject of this chapter. Apathetic formalism allows us to see poststructuralism as part of the figural economy of "stubborn attachments" analyzed by
Judith Butler, in which subjectification (as subjection) is founded on a
bonding with the means of one's subordination that conceals a "constitutive
loss."[6] In this case poststructuralism's attachment to structuralism conceals
the loss of phenomenology. For Foucault's silence towards the ontological issues that had preoccupied him in the early sixties is what now allows him to
speak as a genealogist. In so doing he wrests from the apophatic, self-negating style of *The Archaeology of Knowledge* a position as a public intellectual.
But "position," as de Man suggests, is a trope for the "zero." And to return
genealogy to its vanishing ground in *The Archaeology of Knowledge*, by reading Foucault with de Man as I do here, is to put in question a whole series
of tropes that underwrite the North American academy's valorization of a
"post"structuralism that has gone beyond deconstruction. These include the
very replacement of de Man by Foucault as an academic master, the

transference of nothingness into being and "position," of philosophy into cultural studies, and of theory into practice.

Foucault's turn from philosophy to sociology sets the stage for Baudrillard's return from sociology to philosophy. Chapters 8 and 9 thus trace Baudrillard's extension of the debate between philosophy and the social sciences into the postmodern technosciences. Gianni Vattimo's identification of the "society of generalized communication" with the social sciences provides a convenient way of demarcating two stages in Baudrillard's career: his concerns first with the modern and the postmodern and then with the positivism of the mediatized human sciences and that of the increasingly cyberneticized media. Chapter 8 follows Baudrillard's work up to *Symbolic Exchange and Death* (1976). The early Baudrillard, like the early Foucault, is engaged in an analysis of the hegemony of the social sciences (specifically economics and sociology studied at the site of advertising) from the perspective of an antiscience variously invested in poetics, psychoanalysis, philosophy, and anthropology. Where Derrida rethinks philosophy itself, Baudrillard's affirmative deconstruction creates a space for an antisociology that results in a philosophically grounded cultural studies. But, beginning in the mid-seventies, Baudrillard turns from commodification to simulation, escalating his critique from the social sciences to their hyperconsummation in the media. Baudrillard in his later work thus assumes the failure of deconstruction and the end of philosophy in ways that specify culturally a postmodern trauma already present at the end of *Being and Nothingness*. In the process he systematically abjects his earlier concerns with ontology and psychoanalysis. Even so, what he offers is a phenomenology of media culture: a Juvenalian and provocative (psycho)analysis of the mode of consciousness of technology in a time when the very category of consciousness is passé.

Baudrillard's turn both resembles and differs from the one traced in other parts of this study. He too turns from deconstruction to its dissipation in a poststructural world of depthless surfaces. He likewise responds to the demise of the subject by seeking the autonomy of objectivity, through such fatal strategies as seduction, apathy, and irony (which are homologous with apathetic formalism). His turn recalls what Sartre had much earlier confronted as a kind of death drive: the desire of the *pour-soi* to become *en-soi*. But if Baudrillard seeks to evade finitude through a self-hardening of theory, he is at once actor, victim, and analyst of this process. He does not execute so much as *perform* the turn so as to bring out what Butler calls its "bodily remainders."[7] Correspondingly he himself figures his career in terms of a turning and returning—a "double spiral" that negates and continues his earlier commitments (EC: 79). The double spiral images a postmodern vertigo and yet contains the trace of a negative dialectic. Accordingly Chapter 9, while tracing Baudrillard's poststructural turn, also finds in his later work a performative, cryptic deconstruction.

Baudrillard sees himself as a theorist of the sign form, and not just of the commodity or object form. Sign and symbol, metaphor and metonymy, are recurrent topics of his texts. There is thus a further dimension or "fold" to his work. While Derrida, Foucault, and de Man make language the basis of analysis, Baudrillard is unique in considering the language of theory itself, following the work of Henri Lefebvre, who saw structuralism as responsible for the implantation of a technocratic society. Baudrillard more systematically and agonistically develops Lefebvre's critique into an antiscience of the sign form. His own work is thus a "political economy of the sign," but also a phenomenology of structuralism and more silently, as I argue in Chapter 9, of poststructuralism as reification. Recognizing structuralism and poststructuralism as modes of consciousness, it is concerned with the sign system as a form of social organization and also with the psychological and ethical effects of this system. Baudrillard thus allows us a unique vantage on the linguistic paradigm, and in that sense he provides an appropriate culmination for this study.

Deconstruction and the Remainders of Phenomenology

First Matters

CHAPTER ONE

Phenomenology and/as Deconstruction

Desynonymizing Deconstruction and Poststructuralism

The terms *deconstruction* and *poststructuralism* surface simultaneously in the early stages of the Anglo-American assimilation of French theory.[1] They are used interchangeably to refer to the same general group of theorists, though they are also indexed separately, reflecting an untheorized awareness of their difference. In books published in the eighties deconstruction is most often identified with Derrida and de Man and sometimes more extensively with the *Tel Quel* group and the American Heideggerians William Spanos and Joseph Riddel.[2] As such it may name an operation—of dismantling, unworking, or desedimentation—that is transportable to the work of other theorists not specifically called deconstructive (such as Foucault).[3] Or it may refer not just to a critical activity but to a certain view of language as *écriture* that privileges literature as what de Man calls "the most advanced and refined mode of deconstruction."[4] Hence the view, polemically proclaimed by Habermas, that deconstruction involves the "leveling of the genre distinction" between philosophy and literature, and then between criticism and literature, in "one comprehensive, all-embracing context of texts. . . . a 'universal text'."[5] The term *poststructuralism* has a wider provenance, being used to describe the work of Lacan, Foucault, Deleuze and Guattari, and on occasion that of Michel Serres, Paul Ricoeur, and Gerard Genette, as well as more recently Baudrillard and Lyotard.[6] On this basis we could describe deconstruction as an approach that, while not confined to literary theory, privileges the philosophical category literature, as Blanchot uses the term. This usage is most sympathetically glossed by Foucault, who notes that the word *literature* "is of recent date" as is the isolation, after romanticism, of a "'literary'" language increasingly "differentiated from the discourse of ideas . . . [and] the values that were able to keep it in general circulation." Literature in this sense is left with nothing "to do but to curve back in a perpetual return upon itself, as if its discourse could have no other content than the expression of its own form" (OT: 300).

Poststructuralism, we could then say, is a broader interdisciplinary movement that exceeds this separatism of literature, thus holding out possibilities of escape from the prison-house of language with which deconstruction is often associated.[7] But there are at least two problems with this distinction. First, Derrida is also referred to as a poststructuralist, even when he is being criticized for an ultratextualism that privileges the category "text/textuality" if not exactly literature.[8] Derrida, who uses the term *deconstruction* but not the Anglo-American term *poststructuralism*, is also placed under the second heading because of the initial gateway status of "Structure, Sign, and Play in the Human Sciences" in the translation of his work from France to North America.[9] Similarly the evolution of Barthes's work as an overturning of his earlier structuralism leads him to be described as poststructuralist, even though his interest in textuality leads him to be discussed in books on deconstruction.[10] When both terms are used to describe the same theorist, then, it would seem that poststructuralism (or ultra-, neo-, or superstructuralism)[11] names a relationship to structuralism that is not foregrounded in the term *deconstruction*.

Second, it is incorrect to tie deconstruction's focus on *écriture* to a privileging of the literary; on the contrary deconstruction is arguably not a development internal to literary studies but to philosophy. Indeed, the literariness of deconstruction, and hence a certain taint of formalism that has led to its overthrow by new historicism and now cultural studies, are largely North American phenomena—results of the brief hegemony enjoyed by "Yale" deconstruction[12] and even more so of its temporary co-optation into an apparatus of pedagogical reproduction that has been described by John Guillory in *Cultural Capital*. Deconstruction in America is associated with the privileging of literary studies; in fact its institutional impetus in France comes from an attempt to rethink philosophy in the face of the rising power of the social sciences.[13] For his part, Derrida disavows any exclusive focus on literature; he speaks of his "first desire . . . to go in the direction of the literary event," towards Mallarmé and Blanchot, but then of the necessity "not to close oneself up in philosophy as such or even in literature."[14] Moreover, if we can, indeed, divide Derrida and de Man as exemplars of deconstruction from Foucault as a practitioner of poststructuralism, we must ask why literature is also important to the early Foucault, not to mention to Baudrillard.[15] Either the distinction between the two terms is untenable, or there is a difference between them that cannot be so easily aligned with a division of theorists.

Because *poststructuralism* is an Anglo-American term, or at least because it does not originate in France,[16] we could simply conclude that the duplication of terms is careless. I suggest, however, that we see it as what Stanley Corngold, commenting on de Man, calls an "error." Whereas mistakes are "without true value. . . . the skew of error implies a truth": "Error functions as a movement informing both human existence and the thought adequate to existence that is literary language. The notion of error is implicated in the very definition of the trope."[17] Thus the duplication of deconstruction as poststructuralism is not simply wrong. Rather, the redundant coinage of the second term points to an aspect of the Anglo-American appropriation of French theory not accounted for by the term *deconstruction*. Conversely, this duplication also points to a resistance of deconstruction to being economized within "poststructuralism." In short, it points to a palimpsestic history within this theory that the doubled terminology helps to unpack and that is covered over by the asymmetry between the time of the appearance of the works discussed in this study (which spans five decades) and their condensed, achronological translation into English. Among the peculiarities of this translation, the history of which would require a different kind of study, it is worth mentioning two examples. One is the translation of Baudrillard, which has proceeded backward from the later to the earlier work.[18] The other is the framing of early translations of Derrida and Foucault by the discovery of Saussure and structuralism, whilst the translation of Blanchot and Levinas has had to wait till much later.

While the doubling of deconstruction and poststructuralism occurs in the Anglo-American commentary, my interest is in its heuristic value for reading French theory itself. In other words, this error discloses a difference within a theoretical corpus that was too rapidly mediated to the English-speaking world for the genealogical entanglements that are perhaps still overlooked in France as well to be fully grasped. Poststructuralism combined with the American appropriation of Derrida into literary studies to cover over certain aspects of deconstruction that this study explores. The term names the fact that deconstruction in England and America was perceived almost entirely as a problematizing of or emancipation from structuralism, which retained the latter's dismissal of phenomenology and its rhetoric of the end of man. In commentaries of the eighties, Derrida is invariably approached through Saussure. When it is recognized that his work began with Husserl and not Saussure, phenomenology is metonymized with structuralism as a thought reducible to Husserl and a naive foil to deconstruction. In the process we forget one part of the intellectual context in which deconstruction emerged as a return of a phenomenological project—a "humanisme de l'autre homme" in Levinas' phrase[19]—that acquires renewed urgency if we return to it through deconstruction.

The Linguistic Turn of Phenomenology: Sartre, de Man, and the Image

In the early work of de Man, we can see that the linguistic turn we associate with structuralism also occurs as a radicalization of phenomenology.[20] De Man is often viewed as Derrida's American "disciple," but as Lindsay Waters points out his career developed quite autonomously until they met in 1966 (when de Man was forty-seven).[21] De Man's early work is an unusually pure case of the emergence of deconstruction from phenomenology. Although Derrida's linguistic turn can be seen as early as the *Origin of Geometry* and arguably develops from Blanchot, at a certain stage (in *Of Grammatology*) it becomes caught up and energized by a critique of Saussure and structuralism. In de Man's early work there are few references to structuralism; indeed, his marginalization of Derrida's discussion of Saussure in his review of *Of Grammatology* (1970) shows his disinterest in linguistics, even though he is everywhere concerned with language.[22] In *Allegories of Reading* de Man does indeed refashion himself as a poststructuralist by building his work around a linguistics of tropes and speech-act theory. But as I argue elsewhere, at this point he is systematically rewriting his earlier "vocabulary of intent and desire" in a "more linguistic terminology."[23] The terms *presence/absence, immanence/transcendence* and the Benjaminian pair *symbol/allegory* are thus translated into a vocabulary of figure/reference and metaphor/metonymy that claims a greater technical rigor.[24]

The importance of Heidegger for de Man is well known, though by 1955 de Man already expresses reservations about him similar to those of Derrida in the "Ends of Man" (1968).[25] Less well known, however, is that de Man's theory of the intentional structure of the romantic image—which predates *Of Grammatology* by seven years—draws strongly on Sartre's theory of the image in *Imagination* and *The Psychology of Imagination*, as well as on his division between the *pour-soi* and the *en-soi*. Sartre ontologizes intentionality so as to make it part of the "destruction" of the cogito. Intentionality as a "mode of existence of consciousness," in Levinas's phrase, means simply that consciousness is conscious *of* something and thus "in contact with the world." For Husserl it is simply "an animating act which gives to the hyletic phenomena a transcendent meaning." In this act the subject is constituted through a subject-object relationship in which the amorphous world of sense available to the pre-thetic consciousness is focused and given a sense (as meaning). Intentionality, in other words, is a way of knowing linked to the postulate of an ego.[26] But for Sartre intentionality strikes at the very core of human being. To be conscious of something means that consciousness is *not* that of which it is conscious; that it is not means that it is lacking in relation to an in-itself that *is*. This in-itself has being, while consciousness as intentionality is a nothingness that desires being.

The "consequences for images are immediately apparent," Sartre says: "An image, too, is an image *of* something" that it is not, a lack of presence. Imagination is thus radically different from "perception."[27] Following Sartre de Man also embarks on a "phenomenology of poetic language" as negativity—a phrase he later edits out of "The Intentional Structure."[28] For de Man too there is a radical difference between consciousness as *pour-soi* and the natural object as *en-soi*, wherein the latter as an object of "nostalgia" is also a temptation to "permanence" and "lethargy."[29] The natural object does not originate by imitation or desire; it is defined by its "identity," "safe in its immediate being" (RR: 4). The image by contrast is pure nothingness, "always constitutive, able to posit regardless of presence but . . . unable to give a foundation to what it posits except as an intent of consciousness" (RR: 6).[30] Language is a form of unhappy consciousness: "Critics who speak of a 'happy relationship' between matter and consciousness" forget that the constitution of this relationship in "language indicates that it does not exist in actuality" (RR: 8). This nonbeing (*non-être*) of language is what accounts for the "annihilating power" (*l'action destructive*) of thought (RR: 6, 8), which in turn makes the theory of consciousness the site of an ethics as well as an ontology. The "demands of consciousness" (RR: 8) require a constant vigilance against the bad faith that mistakes words for things; or as Derrida later says: "Writing is dangerous from the moment that representation there claims to be presence and the sign of the thing itself" (OGr: 144).

De Man grows critical of Sartre for abandoning the "theoretical poetics" of his early work for a positivist investment in "experience." Whereas Sartre had once insisted on the "radical distinction between perception and imagination," he later fails to separate "direct experience and the knowing of this experience." This is why de Man praises Heidegger for leading "the problem of history back" from "the naive forms it had taken in the interior of activisms and political determinisms" to "the ontological level."[31] But in fact de Man's work up to *Blindness and Insight* (1971) is a classic case of filtering Heidegger through the pre-Marxist Sartre, as described in Chapter 3. De Man turns to Heidegger to avoid Sartre's "unphilosophical undertaking" in *What Is Literature?* yet finds in Heidegger the complacency that also disturbs Levinas. Analyzing the convergence of metaphors of building and vegetation, he sees Heidegger as succumbing to the "temptation to permanence,"[32] the phrase he later uses in "The Intentional Structure" to describe the natural object as in-itself (RR: 4, 6). As such Heidegger's thought involves a "beatitude that properly speaking is a lethargy."[33] Inasmuch as *Dasein* approximates the lethargy of being in-itself, the "demands of consciousness" require, in Sartre's words, a subject that is not what it is and is what it is not (BN: 28). Indeed, de Man's "vigilance" leads him to criticize the bad faith of Heidegger and Malraux in specifically Sartrean terms. The temptation to permanence consists in "the death of the mind," in refusing to think the negation and in assimilating it to death pure and simple, in refusing the effort and the pain of interiorizing the exterior negation that is organic death."[34] For this reason, in leading the problem of literature back from an "empirical" to an "ontological" level in his own criticism, de Man adopts a

Sartrean vocabulary that refuses the shelter of being: a vocabulary of "absence," "nonbeing," "nothingness," and the "void."[35]

De Man's early work suggests that the critique of representation, as a refusal of presence, largely precedes the advent of structuralism. Indeed, it takes place through a distinction between imagination and perception that derives from Sartre, not Saussure, albeit intensified by Blanchot. But this genealogy is by no means confined to de Man, who himself notes that a "grounding in phenomenology" was seminal for Foucault in *The Order of Things*.[36] Indeed, we also find in *Of Grammatology* a similar Sartrean vocabulary of "void," "emptiness," and the "abyss of representation" associated with the supplement as "lack" (OGr: 145, 163, 184). We find the same posing of "imagination" as "at bottom the relationship with death" against "the thing itself," "immediate presence," and "originary perception" (184, 157) and the same insistence on the radical division between imagination and perception (SP: 44). And we likewise find a deconstruction of representation that occurs as much at the site of the "image" as of the "sign" (OGr: 144–51, 182–87). This analysis is, moreover, mobilized by a Sartrean psychoanalytic that sees the "imaginary" (*l'imaginaire*) as a form of bad faith: hence the "danger" and "seducti[veness]" of the image (151), which takes the sign for the real, and hence also what Derrida calls auto-affection or what Sartre calls the "shut . . . consciousness" of the Imaginary.[37]

In the remainder of this chapter I begin by tracing the compatibility of phenomenology with deconstruction as a general style of thinking so as to suggest why it matters that we distinguish deconstruction from poststructuralism. Deconstruction is a transposition of phenomenological into linguistic models that retains the ontological concerns of the former. Those concerns derive not only from Heidegger but also from Sartre via Levinas and Blanchot. When Derrida speaks of language he speaks of death, as he repeatedly makes clear: "Death is the movement of difference to the extent that that movement is necessarily finite" (OGr: 143); and again death is the "master-name for the supplementary series" that keeps language in motion as a process of "metonymic substitutions" (183). Death here entails not just an ontology but an ethics that has to do with the "dispossession" we experience through language (166, 142). These ontological and ethical concerns are not ones admitted by structuralism. They are elided by poststructuralism[38] whether in the liberatory surpassing of "metaphysics" I discuss in the next chapter or in the ascetic, resistant forms more fully explored in this book. De Man's later work exemplifies the second case. When he writes that "death is a displaced name for a linguistic predicament" (RR: 81) he reverses Derrida; he affiliates himself with a poststructuralist refusal of interiority that, because of its own history, virtually solicits its own deconstruction.

To forget deconstruction's links to phenomenology is to disconnect it from this analytic of finitude at the core of its focus on language. This forgetting partly explains why the linguistic turn has been taken for a "critical aestheticism." Reading Derrida through his "American followers," William Spanos associates deconstruction, as well as structuralism and the New Criticism, with "spatial form" and with an "antitranscendental transcendental literary rhetoric:"

> Because of its commitment to the textuality of texts—the absolute absence of reference in the signifier, the deconstructive mode . . . transforms all texts into self-canceling, free-floating signifying systems that hover above time . . . into an undifferentiated global anti-Book . . . a universalist discourse in reverse.[39]

Spanos's comments do not fully do justice to Derrida. They do describe a tendency in certain forms of poststructuralism, though they neglect the pathos that often attends the loss of temporality. But to complicate things further, the meaning of the term *poststructuralism* has also changed since it first surfaced in the early seventies. While it once carried the taint of ultra-textualism and a loss of agency, it has now become a general term for oppositional presentisms that reclaim precisely this rhetoric of agency. In this refashioning of poststructuralism, the neglect of a deconstruction linked to phenomenology has also played a crucial role.

Beyond Husserl: The French Connections of Phenomenology

Derrida, as I suggest in Chapter 4, plays a key role in turning phenomenology towards deconstruction. Indeed, he himself describes his work as "radicaliz[ing] phenomenology in order to go further even than the structuralist objection."[40] Yet curiously the proscription of phenomenology in the late sixties has much to with influential statements by Derrida. In "Semiology and Grammatology" (1968) he characterizes "phenomenological meaning" as disconnected from any materiality that cannot be contained within the "concept" (P: 22):

> Meaning is the phenomenality of the phenomenon. . . . This layer of pure meaning, or a pure signified, refers . . . to a layer of prelinguistic or pre-semiotic (preexpressive, Husserl calls it) meaning whose presence would be conceivable outside and before the work of *différance*. . . . Such a meaning . . . given to consciousness in perceptive intuition—would not be, from the outset, in the position of a signifier. (30, 32)

As is well known, Derrida further associates phenomenology with voice as the pure interiority of consciousness and thus with a pneuma without psyche or a presence freed from the trace: "the voice is consciousness itself. When I speak, not only am I conscious of being present for what I think, but I am conscious also of keeping as close as possible to my thought, or the 'concept'" (22).

Derrida's view, however, rests on a "reduction" of phenomenology to Husserl that forgets its diversity as "the sum," in Ricoeur's words, both of "Husserl's work and of the heresies issuing from it."[41] To begin with Derrida neglects a difference that is seminal to his own work: between transcendental and existential phenomenology or, in Foucault's version, between "a philosophy of knowledge, of rationality and of concept" represented by Husserl and one of "experience, of sense and of subject" exemplified by Sartre and Merleau-Ponty.[42] Transcendental phenomenology, as Ricoeur says, studies "the conditions of the appearances of things to the structure of human subjectivity"; it is thus a form of neo-Kantianism that will prove curiously complicit with structuralism in the figural economy of the careers studied here. One need not be surprised, then, that in "Semiology and Grammatology" Derrida places this "phenomenology" in metonymic proximity to Saussurian linguistics. But, as Ricoeur says, the phenomenology "termed 'existential' . . . becomes a method and is placed in the service of a dominating problem-set, namely, the problems concerning existence" and the "investigation of the various aspects of man's insertion in the world." Derrida is not unaware of this difference (P: 32–4), already highlighted by Levinas in the thirties.[43]

Ricoeur's use of the term *method* in connection with existential phenomenology is significant in that it cuts through the conventional privileging of transcendental phenomenology on the grounds that the latter alone is sensitive to the rigor of method. By 1969 Foucault, for instance, has come to see existential phenomenology as a subjectivism and a positivism that avoids the rigor of method,[44] although earlier he had seen its emphasis on "actual experience" in more complex terms that are perhaps inflected by Georges Bataille's notion of "inner experience."[45] Foucault's later dismissal of existential phenomenology rests on its conflation with "existentialism," which is not a phenomenology but an applied ethics or pragmatic anthropology. For this reason Jean Wahl prefers the term "philosophies of existence" to describe a range of anti-idealisms from Schelling to Levinas.[46] Method in these cases is precisely the condition of possibility for a disclosure of the idealism of method. Thus Levinas's work on Husserl criticizes transcendental phenomenology on the very grounds of "method." He complains that Husserl brackets ontology for epistemology when a method is always "deep[ly]" implicated in "an ontology."[47] Husserl's autonomization of method becomes the spur to an existential counter-method that criticizes the technical as self-certainty. Method is likewise the basis on which Jean Hyppolite's *Genesis and Structure in Hegel's Phenomenology of Spirit* (1946) shifts Hegel from the transcendental to the existential side. And both Levinas and Hyppolite were important early models for Derrida's own work in intellectual history up to *Speech and Phenomena.*

Derrida's dismissal of phenomenology as a philosophy of consciousness also rests on a second metonymic reduction that assumes the identity of consciousness with what he later calls "spirit." Yet as Sartre says, the "being of consciousness" is a "being such that in its being, its being is in question" (BN: 120). This nonbeing of consciousness has to do precisely with the term *presence*, which Sartre in the section of *Being and Nothingness* on "Presence to Self" foregrounds some twenty-five years before Derrida. As Christina Howells points out, "presence" for Sartre is "'a way of *not coinciding with oneself*, of escaping identity'. It is not *plenitude.*"[48] Presence "supposes that an impalpable fissure has slipped into being. If being is present to itself, it is because it is not wholly itself" (124). Moreover, Sartre rigorously refuses to positivize nonpresence or difference as the space between two terms that can be "apprehended in themselves and include as such elements of positivity" (125). If we ask *what it is* which separates the subject from himself, we are forced to admit that it is *nothing*. Ordinarily what separates is a distance in space, a lapse of time, a psychological difference, or simply the individuality of two co-presents—in short a *qualified* reality. . . . [But the] separation which separates [consciousness] from itself can not be grasped or even conceived in isolation. If we seek to reveal it, it vanishes. . . . The fisssure within consciousness is a nothing [that has] being only as we do not see it. (124–25)

Indeed, what Sartre describes here exceeds the opposition presence/absence and beckons towards a new vocabulary: Derrida's gram, in which nothing is "simply present or absent" because there are only "differences and traces of traces" (P: 26).

In short, Derrida's absorption of consciousness into the "series" spirit/mind/ego[49] neglects the care taken by French phenomenology to desynonymize these various terms. Sartre separates consciousness from being as well as from the "transcendental ego." Ricoeur distinguishes it from spirit in terms of phenomenology's already doubled genesis in Hegel and Husserl. "Spirit" names the being-in-itself that consciousness lacks; it "is not directed toward another who is lacking to it" but claims to be "entirely complete within itself." In effect Ricoeur uses the term *consciousness* to problematize the spirit that Derrida takes consciousness to be. Unlike spirit, "consciousness aims at another that it is not, another placed before it, outside it." To be sure, Husserl speaks of consciousness in the ways Derrida suggests. But, as Ricoeur argues, Husserl's is "a phenomenology of consciousness that is raised above itself into a phenomenology of mind," whereas Hegel's is a "phenomenology of spirit in the element of consciousness. . . . The theory of *Geist* continues to be a *phenomenological* description [emphasis mine] because spirit is identical to itself only in the final moment. . . . All the earlier developments . . . [are] only consciousness and not yet spirit."[50] Or as Ricoeur says elsewhere, Hegel (and here we could also read Sartre) introduced into the field of phenomenological analysis the "negative" experiences of disappearance, contradiction, struggle, and frustration that impart the tragic tone to his phenomenology. This tone is utterly foreign to Husserl's works.

Ricoeur's partition of consciousness from spirit, his reference to "the suppression of consciousness by spirit,"[51] obviously draws on the French Hegelians' shift of focus from the *Logic* to the *Phenomenology* and, within this shift, on the prominence given by the *Phenomenology's* translator Jean Hyppolite to the unhappy consciousness. And here it is important to distinguish Hyppolite's commentary on Hegel, *Genesis and Structure Of Hegel's Phenomenology of Spirit*, from Alexandre Kojève's lectures on the *Phenomenology*, given in the thirties but not published till 1947. Kojève was a Stalinist; Hyppolite, though always left-leaning, was more cautious in relating philosophy to politics—and much closer in this respect to Foucault, Derrida, and Lyotard. Kojève, despite his emphasis on man as a "negating-negativity," directs the negative outward as an aggressive "anthropogenetic" desire; he focuses on Hegel as a thinker of history and on, in particular, the Battle of Jena and the Napoleonic period as inaugurating the famous "end of history." Correspondingly, he emphasizes the master-slave relationsip so as to recuperate negativity within an "anthropology."[52] As Judith Butler says, Kojève maintains a "dualistic ontology that severs human beings into natural and social dimensions;" on this basis he makes negation into "an action of human origin that is applied externally to the realm of the nonhuman" so as to transform the natural into the social.[53] In effect, Kojève follows the Kantian division of "pragmatic" from "physiological" anthropology that gave "anthropology" a bad name in French theory after the war. Physiological anthropology, according to Kant, is concerned with "what Nature makes of man," whereas pragmatic anthropology "aims at what man makes, can, or should make of himself as a freely acting being" or with man as "his own ultimate purpose." In this binary, the pragmatic as the basis of civil society is used to protect human freedom from the entire realm of what later came to be called the "unthought."[54]

Hyppolite also accepts the Hegelian formulation that "human beings are what they are not and are not what they are." But whereas Kojève "infers from this non-coincidence a dualistic world" in which negation is a creative power exerted by the free subject upon an external object, Hyppolite—and Sartre in *Being and Nothingness*—internalizes negation so as to establish "duality (inner-negation) as a monistic principle."[55] This radical difference between the two is evident in Hyppolite's emphasis on the unhappy consciousness rather than the master-slave relationship. It is also evident in the way the two thinkers position Hegel and philosophy. Kojève frames Hegel's career against the Battle of Jena. For him philosophy is the philosophy of history; in fact it *is* history, destiny. For Hyppolite, whether "Hegel was conscious of it or not" the *Phenomenology* conveyed "not a completed system but the history of [its] own philosophical development," its own autobiography in which the commentary on Hegel is also implicated within its "own philosophical journey,"[56] the work on Hegel being the unworking of both Hegel and his critics. Foucault will later refer to the seminality of this method for his own generation: "Instead of conceiving philosophy as a totality ultimately capable of dispersing and regrouping itself in the movement of the concept, Jean Hyppolite transformed it into an endless task, against the background of an infinite horizon, . . . uncertain, mobile all along its line of contact with non-philosophy" (AK: 236).

For Hyppolite, then, consciousness, and, indeed, the very cogito of philosophy, are imbued with nonpresence. "Consciousness," he writes, "is not a thing, a determinate Dasein; it is always beyond itself; it goes beyond, or transcends itself." And again: "Self-certainty cannot be in-itself without losing itself and becoming a thing. It is a perpetual transcendence toward a never given adequation with itself. Consciousness is never what it is."[57] To say that consciousness is nonidentical is perhaps nothing new; for instance Peter Dews, following Manfred Frank, has traced an intellectual history linking deconstruction and post-Kantian idealism in ways that arguably normalize the former.[58] But we could go further and argue that "consciousness" is the site at which French philosophy first encounters the (non)structures of aporia, supplementarity, chiasmic exchange, and *différance* later named within the field of writing. Foucault does, indeed, make this claim for the originality of Hyppolite as not simply conceptual but as having to do with his relation to writing. Foucault's words can be adapted to Sartre and "the alterations he worked, not within [phenomenology], but upon it, and upon philosophy" as previously conceived in its Husserlian separation from "non-philosophy" (AK: 236). For instance, although Sartre may not use the term *aporia*, the aporia is at the heart of his intellectual syntax. This syntax constantly puts its own statements under erasure in doubled, self-reversing formulations, such as the famous description of the *pour-soi* as "being what it is not and not being what it is" (BN: 28) or the vertiginous account of consciousness as a "reflection-reflecting" caught in a perpetual circle, "circuit," or "*dédoublement*" (214–15). Sartre's way of writing in *Being and Nothingness* makes it impossible for him to say anything without unsaying it. Again, although Sartre does not speak of a *supplement*, it is prefigured in the way he conceives the relation between the *pour-soi* and *en-soi*, which is un-like anything in Hegel. For it is not simply the case that nothingness "needs being" to posit itself as negation, whereas being is self-sufficing.[59] On the contrary, the for-itself is also the "nothingness whereby 'there is' being" (251). Or, as Sartre later puts it, lacking difference and distance, the in-itself as absolute identity cannot "found" itself or become "present" to itself; in "a project to found itself" it must therefore "g[i]ve itself the modification of the for-itself" (789–90), thus supplementing itself with its own supplement.[60]

Sartre likewise encounters, in the famous scene in the park in which he meets the Other, "a decentralization of the world which undermines the centralization" effected by the cogito (343). That he apprehends this "disintegration" or "original dispersion" (343, 215) phenomenologically as an ungraspable experience rather than as what de Man calls "a linguistic predicament" (RR: 81) does not mean that it is any less a "decentering" of the cogito (BN: 83) than the one effected by language. Indeed, the Sartrean consciousness has a profoundly linguistic structure as spacing and reference. The *pour-soi* is a "reference to itself" that can never escape "from the chains of this reference" to become a "*seen* reference" or a "reference which is what it is" (216). As "distance" and difference (125) the *pour-soi* has no referent and does not "refer us elsewhere to another being," but is "only a perpetual reference of self to self" (125–26). This latency of the linguistic as the basis for a deconstruction of self-consciousness and perception is disseminated throughout Sartre's text, even if he does not systematically thematize it.[61] There are, for instance, his discussions of perception as figure, which unravel the collusion of *Gestalt* psychology with structuralism (42, 466).[62] There are also his frequent accounts of consciousness as a "reflected-reflecting" that "refers to a reflecting without there being any object of which the reflection would be the reflection" (178–79)—accounts that rely for their unsettling of a classical reflectionism on aporias of grammar.[63] Sartre's brief but pregnant discussion of language as the discourse of the other,[64] which culminates a much more extensive discussion of the subject as a barred subject divided between the Symbolic and the Real, is equally important.[65] In short the transposition of phenomenological into linguistic insights in deconstruction occurs because in some sense the linguistic is already embedded in phenomenology.

Levinas's Critique of Phenomenology

Derrida's generation is not alone in ignoring the radicality of existential phenomenology. One of the major sources for his view is Levinas, who also defines "consciousness" as the suppression of alterity and "an adequation between thought and what it thinks."[66] Levinas associates phenomenology as a philosophy of consciousness with the twin motifs of light and intentionality. Although intentionality was to become a major locus for phenomenology's self-deconstruction in the work of Sartre, Levinas reads it strictly through Husserl.[67] Intentionality is "an animating act, which gives to the transcendent phenomena a transcendent meaning."[68] As "consciousness of" something, it is not, like Merleau-Ponty's "perception," a nonthetic connection in which the self is exscribed upon the world; it is rather a directed, focusing activity in which the predication of an object constitutes the subject. On this basis Levinas associates intentionality with the "sphere of intelligibility" and "vision:" "the structure of a *seeing* having the *seen* for its object" (TO: 97). Moreover, because an epistemology always conceals an ethics, intentionality as "aiming" is a "moment of egoism or egotism" (97–98): in "thought understood as vision, knowledge, and intentionality, intelligibility thus signifies the reduction of the other to the Same" (99).

Light, which Derrida evokes as "the *phenomenological* metaphor" (M: 131), is Levinas's figure for this clarity or phenomenality of cognition that he also associates as early as 1940 with "representation":

> Every intention is a self-evidence being sought, a light that tends to make itself known. To say that at the basis of every intention—even affective or relative intentions—representation is found, is to conceive the whole of mental life on the model of light. . . . The theory of intentionality in Husserl, linked so closely to his theory of self-evidence . . . identifies mind with intellection, and intellection with light.

Light, intention, and representation form a matrix that allows Levinas to see phenomenology as blind to the unthought: "phenomenology describes [only] that which appears." While it may deal with states (*états d'âme*) such as fear and anguish that are nonpredicative or "without an object,"[69] a "descriptive phenomenology" always grasps them phenomenally in their coming to light rather than materially in their unintelligibility. And for Levinas phenomenology is always descriptive; as such, it "stages *personages*" and "presupposes an ego" (EE: 66). This process of hypostasis explains why light is also related to "property" and (self)possession. Light is "a condition for phenomena" and "makes objects into a world, that is, makes them belong to us. . . . Illuminated space all collects about a mind which possesses it. In this sense it is already like the product of a synthesis. Kant's space is essentially a lit up space: it is in all its dimensions accessible, explorable" (48).

Levinas's criticisms of Husserl in the thirties are undertaken from what he sees as a Heideggerian perspective. Yet in the forties he comes to see Heidegger too as a philosopher of light, opposing him to Blanchot as a figure for "night."[70] As Derrida later says, in spite of everything it leads us to "question, and to redistribute, [Heideggerian] *Dasein* still occupies a place analogous to that of the transcendental subject."[71] Inasmuch as Heidegger had provided Levinas with the means to criticize Husserl, the condensing of the two conveys Levinas's dismissal of the entire phenomenological tradition, both transcendental and existential. With this identification of the Germans Levinas claims to leave phenomenology behind, therein also modelling Derrida's exit from all Western philosophy, metonymically reduced to logocentrism and ontotheology. In Levinas's case this condensation of phenomenologies also takes the form of a placement of both "knowledge" and "experience" under the heading of "intention." Experience is "assimilable to a knowledge [*savoir*]" and is constructed through "protentions" and "retentions." Levinas's dismissal of experience—and his reading of this category through Husserl—is all the more significant, given that in 1929 it was experience that had allowed him to critique Husserl, by insisting on the reinsertion of the "phenomenon" into "consciousness" or "the individual and affective life of which [it] is the object."[72]

"To Do Justice" to Phenomenology

Yet there are several points to make. First, it is not clear why Heidegger's complicity with transcendentalism should be grounds for dismissing experience, an area Heidegger himself tries to avoid by dividing the ontic from the ontological. Existential phenomenology can only be partly attributed to

Heidegger. We must also include under this rubric Bataille's radical attempt to rethink the terms *existence* and *experience* as "inner experience" so as to push beyond Heidegger's thinking of *Dasein* as "*determined by knowledge.*" If Bataille's work transgresses Heidegger's, it is precisely on the grounds of "experience" as that which "tear[s]" one's being "into shreds." In this sense Bataille takes up a concern with inner experience that he attributes to "*phenomenology,*" so as to develop a philosophy of existence that is not limited by the coupling of experience with knowledge as Levinas defines it. As I suggest in Chapter 3, experience of this kind—extreme, unassimilable to reflection—is at the heart of Sartre's encounters with the body and the viscous, even if it is disavowed by his dialectic of negative freedom.[73]

But, second, the author of *Sein und Zeit* is not identical with the more transcendental Heidegger of the *Kehre.* Or, if he is, Levinas's misreading of the German philosopher before the war nevertheless generates a valuable way of reading transcendental thought in terms of a materiality that disrupts its phenomenality. Interestingly Levinas departs from Heidegger's own self-fashioning in "The Letter on Humanism" to describe Heidegger's prewar work as "existential," or at any rate he allows that what he got from Heidegger before the *Kehre* was an existential method.[74] As I argue in the fourth chapter, Derrida's early work on Husserl radically reworks this method—tentatively prefigured by Levinas—as a deconstructive method,[75] which uses "against the edifice the instruments or stones available in the house" itself (M: 135). However, deconstruction in this methodological sense of a philosophy's unworking of its past as a simultaneous unworking of *itself* through this past, first occurs in the autobiography of phenomenology—as the unworking of transcendental by existential phenomenology. Inasmuch as this self-criticism can always be taken further, Levinas's development, beyond his own deconstruction of Husserl by "Heidegger" to a deconstruction of Heidegger himself, models a vigilance that Derrida and de Man will also take over as the structure of their corpus. But this vigilance is part of phenomenology; indeed, Levinas will later speak of his 1947 text that rejects phenomenology as a phenomenology. And he will also attribute his disappointment with Heidegger's work after the *Kehre* to "the disappearance in it of phenomenology properly speaking."[76]

Moreover, phenomenology, especially by the sixties, cannot be confined to Husserl or even Heidegger. Husserl, as Ricoeur says, "abandoned along the way as many routes as he took," so that his work has multiple nontotalizable effects as the unfolding, beyond him, of his own "errors."[77] We could think of phenomenology's influence rhizomatically as well as historically or genealogically. But even this formulation does not quite capture its particular hospitability to deconstruction. Phenomenology, both in its method and in its history, is a thought that returns upon itself. Merleau-Ponty points to this quality when he argues that as a "study of essences [that] puts essences back into existence," phenomenology's own essence "is accessible only through a phenomenological method" that, in effect, risks putting it under erasure. It is because of this perpetual folding of phenomenology back on itself that Merleau-Ponty can speak of its "unfinished nature" and the "inchoative atmosphere surrounding it"[78] or that Lyotard can speak of its "essential incompletion" and avoidance of "hypostasis."[79]

This incompletion, Lyotard argues, can be seen by "approach[ing] phenomenology through its history."[80] Lyotard sees this history as still to come, hinting at a paradigm for intellectual history that is later developed by Derrida and Nancy. But Foucault sees it more recursively, in terms of the perpetual doubling that he describes as "the return and retreat of the origin" (OT: 328) and that arises from phenomenology's split genesis as a thought that is aporetically empirical and transcendental. Thus, on the one hand, "the naive discourse of a truth reduced wholly to the empirical" leads phenomenology to "restore the forgotten dimension of the transcendental" as that which exceeds experience (321). Foucault here uses the "transcendental" to signify finitude and as the "unthought" of the empirical "cogito" (322). On the other hand, given a different sense of the transcendental as self-certainty, it is precisely the empirical that interrupts the positivity of the transcendental ego: "the phenomenological project continually resolves itself . . . into a description—empirical despite itself—of actual experience, and into an ontology of the unthought" that "short-circuits the primacy of the 'I think'" (326). This unworking of empiricism has to do with the "mixed nature" of the category "actual experience." For in phenomenology as empiricism "the possible objectivity of a knowledge of nature" is thwarted by "the original experience of which the body provides an outline" (321)—an aporia we already find in Hegel's *Philosophy of Nature*, where the attempt at a science of nature ends darkly with an analysis of illness that may well have influenced Foucault in *The Birth of the Clinic*. In this way Foucault sees both the empirical and the transcendental as internally doubled. And, in his most sympathetic account of phenomenology, he presents it as constantly unworking itself in an ongoing traversal of its split genesis.

In short, as Merleau-Ponty suggests, phenomenology at its limits *is* its own deconstruction, which "descends into its own substratum." Merleau-Ponty himself provides a model for such a descent, which makes Husserl the object of the deconstruction that is implicit in phenomenology. In his 1960 preface to Hesnard's book on Freud, Merleau-Ponty approaches Husserl in terms of a missed encounter with the body of his own thought. In so doing he shifts the ground of interpretation from philosophy to psychoanalysis—arguably the most profound hermeneutic shift that will be made by deconstruction. His comments are worth citing at length:

> The more that one penetrates phenomenological thought, and the more familiar one becomes with Husserl's enterprise, thanks to the publication of his hitherto unpublished works, the better one can distinguish phenomenology from the new *philosophy of consciousness* which it took itself to be at first. A superficial reading of *Ideas I* could lead one to believe that . . . philosophy will never have anything to describe but transparent correlations between acts of thought and objects of thought. . . . [But] as Husserl proceeded to the execution of his program, he brought to light fragments of being which disconcerted his frame of reference: neither the body, which is "subject-object"; nor the passage of interior time . . . nor the other person . . . nor history, which is my life in others and the life of others in me. . . . None of these allow themselves to be brought together under the correlation of consciousness and its objects, of the noesis and the noema. Philosophy ceases to be an exact knowledge, a pure regard on pure objects.[81]

The point here is not the connections between Husserl and later thought, most of which are now well known. The point is Merleau-Ponty's procedure; for rather than engineering the unity of Husserl's work, he deterritorializes it by retrieving it as "fragments" that "disconcert" its containment as a self-present body of thought. It is as just such a bricolage that Merleau-Ponty's own last text, *The Visible and the Invisible*, was published in the form of a philosophy that includes its own margins as "working notes." Interestingly Merleau-Ponty still describes this way of assembling a corpus as a bringing to "light," even as Derrida later uses the trope of "visibility" for what his reading lets appear in Husserl's discussion of signs (SP: 3). Similarly,

when Merleau-Ponty proceeds to his main concern, which is the shared terrain of phenomenology and psychoanalysis, the point is not—or not only—
what they share conceptually. Merleau-Ponty also opens the phenomenality
of philosophy to its materiality by allowing psychoanalysis to have an impact on phenomenology that is physiological rather than conceptual. Merleau-Ponty is careful to insist that the "accord of phenomenology and psychoanalysis should not be understood to consist in phenomenology's saying
clearly what psychoanalysis had said obscurely." On the contrary, "it is by
what phenomenology implies or unveils as its limits—by its *latent content* or
its *unconscious*—that it is in consonance with psychoanalysis." One could
also say conversely that this consonance—or coupling in Derrida's terms—
cannot consist in psychoanalysis saying clearly what phenomenology had
missed in the restriction of consciousness to light and intention, yet
glimpsed in its exploration of sense and the prereflective and tacit cogitos.
On the contrary, it is through a certain way of being with respect to language that the chiasmus of the two arises: "Phenomenology and psychoanalysis are not parallel: much better, they are both aiming toward the same
latency."[82]

Psychoanalysis is in fact one of the many "hinges" between phenomenology and deconstruction, to evoke Derrida's figure, in his essay on Foucault's
relation to Freud, for the simultaneous "opening" and "closing" off of one
body of thought by another.[83] As I suggest in Chapter 6, psychoanalysis is
what allows Foucault to inscribe knowledge or "science" in a doubling of the
cogito by its unthought that takes Merleau-Ponty's vocabulary of the visible
and the invisible towards its own unconscious. But, more broadly speaking,
phenomenology itself stands in relation to deconstruction in the position of
a hinge. Interestingly, Derrida brings back this notion of the hinge precisely
in connection with reading the past or, we might say, intellectual history. In
Of Grammatology the hinge was associated with the trace, with the "becom-
ing-absent and the becoming-unconscious of the subject" that makes all
thought nonpresent to itself as writing (OGr: 66–69). This "*brisure*" was the
aperture in past thought that released us—if not entirely—from its mystifi-
cation. But in *Resistances of Psychoanalysis* Derrida brings back the hinge
(*charnière*) in the context of "vigilance and greater justice."[84] The last essay,
"To Do Justice to Freud," is a re-vision of Derrida's earlier "Cogito and the
History of Madness." Whereas earlier Derrida had attacked Foucault for not

recognizing Descartes's complex relation to madness, now he admits that what was really at issue was Foucault's relation to psychoanalysis. To begin with Derrida thus reflects on his own as well as Foucault's discourse; he allows that in speaking of one thing one is often speaking tropologically of another. But secondly he also rethinks the reinscription of deconstruction in what it seeks to undo, recognized as early as "The Ends of Man," in terms of "justice" rather than of unavoidable complicity. The section on the hinge is tellingly entitled "The Hinge—Today." In the historical urgency of "The Ends of Man" the interimplication of past and present had brought to an impasse the "necessity for a 'change of terrain'" (M: 135) raised by philosophy's responsibility to its political margins. This, in turn, surrounded Derrida's project with a certain presentism. In the intellectual history practiced in the essay on Foucault, it is more a question of grasping the past in its complexity so as to grasp reciprocally the complexity of the present.

To do justice to phenomenology would be to rethink its place in an intellectual genealogy through the terms that Derrida now reintroduces as hermeneutic, not just deconstructive, figures, namely, the hinge, the copula, and the "multiple chiasmus that organizes [the] interpretative scene." Merleau-Ponty had suggested just such a "coupling" of phenomenology and psychoanalysis, not unlike Derrida's "conjugat[ion]" of the opposites Nietzsche and Freud.[85] Deconstruction is, in this sense, conjugated, rather than derived, from phenomenology. And indeed, in his many recent attempts at justice, Derrida, who has always been fair to Husserl and Heidegger, has also gone back to Sartre in "Il courait mort," a letter written for the fiftieth anniversary of *Les Temps modernes*. Given the occasion, Derrida confines himself to Sartre's essays in that journal. But because his dismissal of Sartre's philosophy as "anthropology" in "The Ends of Man" was based on a criticism of his role as a public intellectual, doing justice to Sartre's politics now speaks figuratively to more than this politics.[86] Derrida recognizes what is important for our purposes: the almost intangible presence of Sartre for his time as a "taste" or flavor whose presence requires one to think intellectual history in affective as much as conceptual ways. He admits that he came to Blanchot, Ponge, and Bataille, even to Husserl and Heidegger, by way of Sartre. These others are tinged with the flavor of Sartre—a point that is crucial to my argument in the third chapter.

Derrida locates Sartre's impact in his dis-ease with the positions he took, in his way of "passing to the other side" to take in the thought of his adversary, and "above all [in] the ruptures (interior and exterior) which marked the history and sculpted the landscape" of the Sartrean milieu.[87] To suggest Sartre's place in the future he borrows Sartre's image of the marathon runner who continued to run after his death, announcing the Greek victory when he was already dead. As important as the fact that the runner lives after his death is his uncanny ability to speak, perhaps *because* he is dead. For the messenger is not a figure for immortality but a "revenant," a return of something not yet present in the past and not quite grasped in the present:

> This forgetting [of Sartre], which must happen to me more often than I am sometimes aware afterwards, is at bottom the theme of this letter: a strange transaction between amnesia and anamnesis in the heritage that makes us what we are and which has already given us what we have not yet thought, as if our heritage was always a spectre to come, a spirit which runs before us [*un revenant qui court devant nous*], after which we strain, running in our turn to our death.

Interestingly Derrida adds one detail to Sartre's image; he makes him headless (*acéphale*).[88] He thus alludes to Bataille's figure of the acephalic body, a precursor of Deleuze and Guattari's body without organs. Without necessarily invoking Deleuze and Guattari's as the only model for intellectual history, we might mention their notion of the "*names* of history," in which names are not identities but "zones of intensity on the body without organs."[89] A traditional approach to a corpus would require that it be grasped under certain headings. In this vein Levinas can say that the very "nerve" of Sartre's thought is to be found in the *topoi* of freedom, engagement, and the project as the basis for an "intentional thinking."[90] By contrast the idea of a name as a field allows a theoretical corpus to be deterritorialized into multiple nonsynthesizable effects. This is what Derrida does when he makes Sartre a headless messenger, thus freeing us not to approach *Being and Nothingness* under the heading of the political turn that led Sartre to be guillotined by theory. Interestingly Kristeva too has recently taken up the work of Sartre, arguing that his emphasis on the negativity of consciousness and the difficult freedom of the imaginary as negation, disavowal, and fantasy, lead (despite Sartre) to psychoanalysis.[91] Indeed, it is because he is dead that Sartre can return outside the Bloomian agon of identities in which he was anxiously configured at the height of his reputation. For the names of history must be minority figures. And Sartre, perhaps unlike Heidegger, is now minor.

Deconstruction, the Human Sciences, and the Crisis of Philosophy

This book is not about phenomenology per se. It is rather about the "fragments" of phenomenology that produce deconstruction and continue to disconcert both deconstruction and its permutation into poststructuralism. For this reason, although phenomenology was so dominant as to exert an anxiety of influence by the sixties, I have tried to present it as unfinished. Derrida refers to the Sartrean milieu as a "landscape" rather than a territory to be mapped (OG: 125n), while Jean Wahl refers to phenomenology as a "climate."[92] As such metaphors suggest, phenomenology is neither spatially nor temporally closed. It cannot be identified with the work of a single philosopher or fully grasped even as a set of oppositions between them. Rather its work continues in the spaces between philosophers. Lyotard's 1953 study *Phenomenology* proposes to disclose this quality of being still "in process" by "approach[ing] phenomenology through its history" so as then to "leave it in its debate with history."[93] Deconstruction is, I suggest, a further stage in this history that conjugates philosophy as theory both by philosophically radicalizing phenomenology and by taking it in a more interdisciplinary direction. And Lyotard's book is itself a part of this third stage[94] in that it explores not just the problems and aporias internal to (post)Husserlian philosophy but also their pertinence to the "human sciences" of psychology, history, and sociology.

Lyotard's book, which was reprinted ten times, does not trace this history; it focuses on Husserl and mentions his successors only in passing, though it notes that there are "*many*" phenomenologies.[95] Yet Lyotard opens the *space* of the history explored here not by allowing Husserl to be unworked through his successors but by engaging phenomenology with the various regions for which Husserl had given phenomenology as "first philosophy" the task of providing a "universal" "eidetic ontology." From these areas that Husserl mentions in his Freiburg lecture,[96] Lyotard chooses the "human sciences" of psychology, sociology, and history (though not anthropology or semiotics, which achieved prominence later). "It is above all with respect to the human sciences," he writes, that phenomenology "claims our attention." Lyotard is not critical of Husserl, whose work he reads as always beginning, "correcting itself, erasing itself." But a great distance has been travelled between his and Levinas's attempt to render unto "Husserl that which is Husserl's."[97] While Levinas deals only with Husserl's philosophy, Lyotard is concerned with its relation to other disciplines. This pressure to bring phenomenology into dialogue with the human sciences is also evident in Merleau-Ponty's work from 1942 onward. Merleau-Ponty reads Husserl as an emergently interdisciplinary thinker who in this respect was far in advance of Heidegger; Husserl recognized "the actual being of the philosopher in the world," whereas Heidegger "remained fixed" in an "opposition between philosophy and the sciences of man . . . the ontological and the ontic."[98]

While Lyotard's and Merleau-Ponty's interdisciplinarity is not yet Derrida's and Foucault's attempt to explore the "margins of philosophy," their work is an important link in the process traced here. On one level Lyotard continues from Husserl in seeing philosophy as the eidetic foundation of the empirical disciplines. Yet the "infrastructures of thought" it provides are the existential categories of the body, community, and historicity. The result is a "decentering of the transcendental ego in favor of the Lifeworld" and a consequent breaching of "intentional analysis" in Husserl's sense. Lyotard's book has not yet caught up with this insight, and it is closer to Bourdieu's joining of phenomenology and structuralism fifteen years later than to the work of the theorists studied here. He still places phenomenology, if not in a founding position, then as one partner in a dialogue of bounded areas: subject and structure. In this dialectic the social "is grasped as lived experience," but only on the basis of "data" that require its "prior objectivation," so that each is held responsible to the other.[99] Still the formulation maintains phenomenology and the human sciences as "opposed," not "exposed," to one another, in Jean-Luc Nancy's terms.[100] Thus what philosophy brings to the human sciences is not an analytic of finitude or a thought of the outside but a positivity of the human quite foreign to deconstruction. Yet we can sense in Lyotard's use of the word *decentering* and in the historical concerns he introduces at the end a pre-text for the return of more recent French philosophy to issues of justice, community, and historical disaster.[101] This work—by Blanchot, Nancy, and Lyotard himself—represents a survival of deconstruction even after its displacement by poststructuralism, an unworking and re-working of the work begun by phenomenology and begun again by deconstruction in the early sixties.[102]

Because Lyotard raises the question of the human sciences, he opens a space for deconstruction's particular transformation of phenomenology. For deconstruction tries to renew philosophy in the face of the challenge, even more the menace, of the "human sciences." The issue of the human sciences is ubiquitous in the sixties and is linked to the rise of structuralism and the decline of philosophy. The urgency of relating philosophy to "nonphiloso-phy" can be seen in a course Merleau-Ponty gave in 1961.[103] While certainly not aligned with structuralism, the student radicals of the sixties were often hostile to philosophy; one notes, for instance their contempt for Ricoeur, then Rector at Nanterre.[104] Nanterre, where both Bourdieu and Baudrillard were trained, was the academic home of Henri Lefebvre, who taught phi-losophy, but as Marxism, and was a leading force in the uprising there. The Nanterre experience was the beginning of Bourdieu's turn from philosophy to sociology and anthropology, though Baudrillard—trained in sociology—returns to philosophy, admittedly in his own way and outside the academy.

François Dosse provides a useful account of this disciplinary turmoil, which begins with Lévi-Strauss in the fifties, comes to a head in the mid-six-ties, and survives the overthrow of the structuralism that had initiated it by its displacement of phenomenology. Indeed, thirty years later we are ar-guably still in the same "crisis." Central to it are the growing power of the social sciences, of a postcolonialism then housed in anthropology and now also in literature departments, and the extension of the human sciences par-adigm, by way of structuralism, into a literary criticism also anxious for sci-entific and technobureaucratic legitimation. While the social sciences were a flashpoint because they were particularly vulnerable to manipulation by the state apparatus, we can distinguish between the "critical" and "the or-thopaedic human sciences (i.e. those aiming at adaptation and readjustment within the system)." The Sorbonne liaison committee, which made this dis-tinction, proclaimed the need for a "pluridisciplinary . . . critical university of Human Sciences." Thus contesting boundaries between fields, the Sorbonne students nevertheless defined the interdisciplinarity of the critical human sciences as the marginality of philosophy: "This university destroys the opposition between the place of work and the place of theory. . . . Every practitioner must also be a student. Each teacher and every researcher must also be a practitioner." These developments, while they are far from having overthrown an aging phenomenological professoriate as Dosse argues, are intertwined with the articulation of deconstruction from the sixties to the eighties.[105] Indeed, deconstruction's breaching of disciplinary boundaries both resists and responds to the absorption of interdisciplinarity into a pragmatic anthropology exemplified by the Sorbonne committee. From a deconstructive viewpoint, pragmatic anthropology (as Kant defines it) is what structuralism and the "affirmative" poststructuralism I describe in the next chapter have in common, even if the former is orthopaedic and the latter critical.

The challenge posed to philosophy is noted in the mid-sixties by Heidegger in "The End of Philosophy and the Task of Thinking," where he assails cybernetics as "the theory of the steering of the possible planning and arrangement of human labor." Cybernetics is "the determination of man as an acting social being and corresponds to what Gianni Vattimo calls "the human sciences of communication, which transform "language" into a positivistic "exchange of news" and information.[106] As such cybernetics is the emancipation of these sciences from philosophy: "the independence of psychology, sociology, anthropology as cultural anthropology . . . and semantics," all of which Husserl had sought to keep under the umbrella of philosophy in the first stage of the "crisis" of philosophy's interdisciplinarity.[107] Heidegger continues on the subject of "the end of philosophy": "The sciences are now taking over as their own task what philosophy in the course of its history tried to present in certain places . . . that is, the ontologies of the various regions of beings (nature, history, law, art). . . . 'Theory' means now supposition of the categories which are allowed only a cybernetic function, but denied any ontological meaning."

Heidegger's essay was first published in France in 1966 at a point when the social sciences, theoretically renewed by structuralism, were taking over the university. As the "technology" by which man "establishes himself in the world by working on it in the manifold modes of working and shaping," these sciences of pragmatic anthropology were turning philosophy itself "into the empirical science of man."[108] This positivism, critiqued by Foucault in *The Order of Things*, is deeply paradoxical given the antihumanist rhetoric that attends the French term *sciences humaines*. For as against Dilthey, who coined the term *human sciences*, the emphasis here is not on the human but on the scientific—not on the functioning of these disciplines as hermeneutic rather than naturalistic, but on the fact that man is known scientifically, as an effect of structure. And yet perhaps there is no paradox here. For in the absorption of the human into science, as in the theoretical formations that emulate science in their technicality and rigor, there is, as Levinas recognizes, a metaphysics of the "end of metaphysics." The "human sciences" place man entirely "outside." In this absolute exteriority there is, to be sure, a destruction of the absolute interiority of the "me identical with itself." But there is also a new claim to "totality" in the form of a knowledge "without folds or secrets."[109]

In the early sixties this antihumanist totality faced a variety of challenges. One is provided by Henri Lefebvre, whose *Position: contre les technocrates* is a seminal pre-text for Baudrillard's *Consumer Society*. Lefebvre writes as a traditional Marxist concerned to redeem everyday life from its transformation under capitalism into a completely mediatized existence. Coining the phrase "société de consommation," he introduces Baudrillard's major themes: the "bracketing" of relations of production by the commodity form; the shift to reification through the economizing even of alienation itself under the forms of codified nostalgia and "anodine revolt"; and the further subsumption of the commodity into the sign/image and thus the introduction of "chains of signifiers detached from signifieds." Structuralism as a "discourse about discourse" is deeply complicit in this technobureacuratization, with the "systematic character of language" furnishing "the general model of the System" as well as of its autoreferentiality. As part of the state apparatus, structuralism makes common cause with the human sciences, which collaborate in the division of labor and the autonomization of fields, under the cover of science as the emancipatory "end of ideologies." Most important is Lefebvre's sense that with structuralism and the human sciences we are entering a new age: that of the "cyberanthrope," which is the end product of what Vattimo will name—less critically—the society of generalized communication. The cyberanthrope is not the robot, safely placed "outside the human species," but the very transformation of man himself into a prosthesis. Entirely outside, this new man with his infallible memory knows nothing of "the analytic of finitude:" of death, failure, or forgetting.[110]

Where Lefebvre poses a nostalgic Marxism against the structuralism of Althusser and Lévi-Strauss, Lyotard had earlier made phenomenology the supplement of the human sciences. As we have said, Lyotard at this stage sets up a somewhat positivist dialogue between two bounded areas. Or, put differently, while it is precisely the positivism of the human sciences that he questions, he conceives the structure of their relation to phenomenology in positivist, indeed, humanist terms.[111] By contrast deconstruction approaches this relation in terms of what Nancy calls "being-exposed." Writing on the work of Heidegger as a hinge, Nancy notes that the thinking of being, death, and *Mit-Sein* "determined the essence of the *Dasein* outside of subjectivity . . . in a being-exposed . . . to others" of which conventional philosophy has "been, despite everything, the denial." Yet "the assignation of this *Dasein*" in the form of an individuality "as much opposed as exposed to other individualities" keeps this work in a "sphere of autonomic, if not subjective, allure." In *Phenomenology*, despite Lyotard's embrace of a "philosophy eliminated as a separated existence," and despite his reference to a consciousness "which 'bursts outward' [*qui 's'éclate vers*]," both philosophy and the human sciences retain their "autonomic" identities.[112]

By contrast, *exposure* marks the way that deconstruction thinks about the relationship between disciplinary subjectivities. Deconstruction in the sixties is constituted by a double gesture: on the one hand the "exposition"[113] of the human sciences passes through the detour of philosophy; on the other hand philosophy itself is exposed to its margins. The second move is foregrounded by Derrida, the first by the early Foucault, though both are interrelated. In *The Order of Things* the human sciences and indeed all positivisms are exposed to their finitude by means of a quadrilateral of conceptual procedures. Foucault names these the analytic of finitude, the empirical and the transcendental, the cogito and its unthought, and the return and retreat of the origin. The point here is not that philosophy adds something to knowledge as science; rather it withdraws or chiasmatically suspends something. Lyotard already speaks of this exposure of philosophy to nonphilosophy, albeit in more ecstatic terms than Foucault. Interestingly he evokes Sartre's concept of intentionality when he writes that "in place of the traditional consciousness which 'digests,' or at least ingests . . . phenomenology reveals a consciousness which 'bursts outward' (Sartre) . . . [and] *is* nothing if not a relation to the world."[114] Foucault takes up this challenge when he writes of the "articulation of thought on everything within it, around it, beneath it which is not thought, yet . . . not foreign to thought" (OT: 324). His *Birth of the Clinic*, as we shall see, is just such an exposition of one discipline (the sociology of medicine) by the trace, not the oppositional challenge, of its others (including history, language, and psychoanalysis).

Deconstruction as practiced by Derrida and Foucault brings to fruition the goal, outlined by Merleau-Ponty in 1961, of engaging the cogito of philosophy with nonphilosophy:" "another order" that is not beyond philosophy but on "this side," as a "double." In the background of Merleau-Ponty's discussion of nonphilosophy, which deals with Marx and Hegel, may be Trân Duc Thao's attempt to relate phenomenology to Marxism, which had acquired a new urgency ten years later. Whereas this attempt requires that nonphilosophy be positivized as "historical reality," the nonphilosophy of which Foucault speaks in "The Discourse on Language" (AK: 236–37) is what Hyppolite calls "non-knowledge" (LE: 3, 9–10). Marx had critiqued "philosophical Denken for remaining at home in what is other than self" and for understanding this other "from the outside, without experience." But any positing of nonphilosophy in another discipline will be equally "contained in itself," hence the profound reservations of deconstructive thinkers about political discourses and their need to think of the relations between disciplines in terms of a chiasm or fold that results in the inside always becoming outside as thought is touched by its unthought.[115]

Deconstruction, then, is a way of thinking that began to germinate well before the sixties, though it acquires a particular interdisciplinary inflection in the sixties. Its effect is to rethink knowledge as science: internally, through its grammatological unworking; vertically, through its reinscription in a retreating past; and horizontally, through a redistribution of the disciplines along zones of contact rather than confrontation. Foucault translates this phenomenological attempt to eliminate philosophy as a "separated existence" into the disciplinary debate of the sixties. For *The Order of Things* deconstructs the human sciences through the countersciences of ethnology, psychoanalysis, and literature—the last two being closest to (non)philosophy.[116] But *Of Grammatology* too is part of this project. Derrida's text is a complex, ambivalent work: a theoretical intersection. On the one hand it is a poststructuralist overturning of a Saussurean, Husserlian, and structuralist past, affirmatively oriented to the future. This affirmation is evident when Derrida announces that "the science of writing—*grammatology*—shows signs of liberation all over the world" from the tyranny of the *logos* (OGr: 4). It is picked up in such books as Gregory Ulmer's *Applied Grammatology*, in a futurism that short-circuits the darker rhetoric of deconstruction. But *Of Grammatology* is as much a deconstruction of the preeminent human science, ethnology—anxiously privileged by Foucault a year earlier—through a folding back of the present (Lévi-Strauss) into the past (Rousseau). Derrida takes aim at an "ethnocentrism *thinking itself* as anti-ethnocentrism, an ethnocentrism in the consciousness of a liberating progressivism" (120). In so doing he does not aim to correct Lévi-Strauss politically—which would be to fall into the positivism of "critique"; he rather seeks to question all positivisms.

The Unavowable Community of Deconstruction

This questioning is at the heart of deconstruction: in the grammatological form of the trace and in the intellectual-historical form of a cautioning of the present by the past. Whereas affirmative poststructuralisms are marked by their presentism, deconstruction is the retroversion and introspection of thought in a return and retreat from its origins. Yet *Of Grammatology* often affiliates itself with a liberating progressivism, even though in "The Ends of Man" Derrida is aware that such claims to "absolute" difference reinstate "the new terrain on the oldest ground" (M: 135). It is for this reason that de Man in his two early pieces on *Of Grammatology*—his review (1970) and his essay "The Rhetoric of Blindness" (1971)—tries to turn Derrida's work back upon itself. De Man privileges the discussion of Rousseau in Part II over the discussion of the sign in Part I; interestingly he also stresses the continuities of this analysis with the phenomenological work of Starobinski. In his review he asks whether Derrida finds the trace of deconstruction in Rousseau himself, or whether it is a "Nietzschean . . . violence done to Rousseau by a more radical hermeneutics than his own."[117] Such a violence will inevitably be caught in the "*trompe l'oeil* perspective" that Derrida himself describes as "blindness" (M: 135). Thus de Man in "The Rhetoric of Blindness" turns Derrida's insights back onto his own futurist hubris by insisting that the undoing of language, presence, and community had occurred before Derrida, in Rousseau.[118] De Man's two discussions of *Of Grammatology* try to retrieve the insights of deconstruction from the blindnesses of poststructuralism through a "supplementary" reading. In so doing they exercise the same vigilance toward Derrida that Levinas had practiced on phenomenology. Indeed, this vigilance is at the heart of Lyotard's and Merleau-Ponty's conception of phenomenology's "essential incompletion"[119] as a thought that is never closed within the work of a single subject, but is rather the work of a "community."[120]

It is worth recalling briefly the themes of community, exposure, and incompletion in French philosophy of the eighties as a way of grasping both deconstruction in the sixties and its continuity, by way of Bataille and Levinas, with phenomenology and the philosophies of existence. For Lyotard's *Phenomenology*, as a book yet to come—*un livre à venir* in Blanchot's phrase—creates a space for phenomenology as a thought yet to come. Lyotard's text is full of references to the incipience of phenomenology or to Husserl's thought—even after his death—as only *"having begun."* Whereas poststructuralism adopts a rhetoric of the "end" and of a liberating progressivism, Lyotard speaks of a "philosophy which is never finished with the question of a "'radical beginning.'"[121] Inasmuch as Derrida from the eighties—along with Blanchot and Nancy—has picked up this focus on beginning and re-turning, he has disengaged himself from the poststructuralist progressivism sometimes present in *Of Grammatology* and his earlier demystifying studies of intellectual history.

Lyotard's notion intimates the place of phenomenology as the radical beginning of deconstruction. Radical beginning as an attempt to grasp the past as future is a potentializing rather than a "destruction" of the past. But the particular temporality of ideas that it assumes can also be understood by way of Lyotard's later discussion of the *après-coup*, which draws on his notion of figure and discourse. The *"double blow,"* Lyotard writes, includes "a first excitation, which upsets the apparatus" but "is not registered." It remains "potential, unexploitable and thus ignored by the apparatus," though this "absence of form and of transformation is essential to the unconscious affect" recovered in the second blow that repeats the first.[122] From this perspective, and in Lyotard's own career, phenomenology is the first blow to philosophy, which, having failed to register, is repeated by deconstruction in the sixties. This deconstruction has itself failed to register and has been historically un-thematized; it has been subsumed either into structuralism in France or poststructucturalism in North America. The current interest in so-called post-Heideggerian French thought can thus be seen as a further repetition, or return, of something missed in the thought of the early sixties.

In this context we can also think of deconstruction as the work of a com-munity, which is to say that it is the constantly traversed difference between various thinkers from the forties to the eighties. Community, as Nancy de-fines it, is not "fusion into a body, into a[n] . . . identity that would no longer be exposed." It is what we have "*in* common," which is our "'*lack of identity*.'" This "finitude" of "existence" or "existing in common" does not allow community to be posited. Rather it involves "the retreat" or "subtrac-tion of something" by a difference or transcendence that forms a commu-nity around the continuous unworking of its work; this occurs in the pres-ent, but also through an unfolding into a future that must always be folded back into its past. That Nancy evokes the term *existence* is no accident be-cause deconstruction unfolds from the philosophies of existence. As Wahl says, these philosophies do not subscribe to a "body of doctrines," but rather share "an atmosphere, a climate that pervades all of them."[123] We can think of them as "existing in common" and as forming an "unavowable commu-nity" with deconstruction. Indeed, community is the form in which Lyotard thinks phenomenology when he speaks of leaving it in its debate with his-tory. And it is also a way of describing Levinas's vigilance toward phenome-nology, which becomes the very basis of deconstruction. For Levinas is not trying to dismiss phenomenology but rather to continue beyond it.

The emergence of community as a concern and a mode of writing in the eighties thus discloses something of what deconstruction and phenomenol-ogy have in common. Derrida, Blanchot, Nancy, and Agamben write texts to each other on community and friendship, while Nancy himself returns to Bataille.[124] Moreover Derrida's returns to various past disputes rethink intel-lectual history under the framework of community rather than demystifica-tion or supercession. His tribute to *Les Temps modernes* recognizes both the friendship between Merleau-Ponty and Sartre, as well as the acephalic com-munity formed around the journal. His revisiting of his dispute with

Foucault likewise reconceives opposition as friendship. Moreover, by "doing justice" to Freud, Derrida makes intellectual history itself into a community that enfolds not just Foucault but also Heidegger and Freud. Deconstruction exposes these theorists to each other in their radical incompletion. Indeed, its exposition of one theorist through another (for example, Hegel through Freud) is often the beginning of this mutual exposure. This is not to deny that some theorists from the tradition surveyed here—Heidegger, for instance—are (self)fashioned as master-thinkers.[125] But insofar as Heidegger contributes to *deconstruction* via Nancy and others, it is his incompletion that is the condition of his seminality.

As the exposure of theorists to each other across history and as the exposition of discourses and disciplines through one another, deconstruction is part of a radical—though not Habermasian—modernity.[126] Whether it is viable in a postmodern culture is thus an open question. As I suggest intermittently deconstruction as outlined here cannot economize all the remainders of phenomenology. Indeed, phenomenology, even conceived as an "infinite" community,[127] cannot account for everything written under the heading of "phenomenology." Sartre's early work in particular exceeds both his own attempts to contain its trauma, and the conjunction with that of Heidegger worked out in the next chapter. From *Nausea* to the conclusion of *Being and Nothingness* Sartre powerfully anticipates what Slavoj Žižek calls "the obscene object of postmodernity." The postmodern, Žižek argues, has no place for a vocabulary of lack and absence that governs deconstruction from Sartre to Derrida; it is rather the fullness of "an inert, obscene, revolting *presence*."[128] Neither deconstruction, nor what David Simpson calls "the *academic* postmodern" confront this obscene presence of contemporary culture brought on, Baudrillard suggests, by the end of man in cybernetics. Poststructuralism in the negative versions explored here does take account of it, though only obliquely. In this sense poststructuralism, though I subject it here to a deconstruction, is perhaps also the trauma of this very deconstruction.

CHAPTER TWO

Poststructuralism: Emancipation and Mourning

Poststructuralism deserves elucidation since there are various versions and shades of this term. Whereas deconstruction is an earlier form of thought that acquires a name and a new force in the early sixties, poststructuralism became a significant body of thought only in the late sixties. The term is an Anglo-American coinage, a way of seeing French theory that selects certain aspects of a more amorphous and contradictory field. The French at the time did not use the term, subsuming the entire field under *structuralism*. *Poststructuralism* marks the limits of calling Derrida and Foucault (or Lacan) structuralist, as does *deconstruction*. But because *deconstruction* is used by Derrida but rarely by others and because I see poststructuralism as a legitimate way of framing certain aspects even of Derrida's work, I employ *deconstruction* for heuristic purposes as well, marking as it does the survival of a phenomenological problematic.

Poststructuralism entered the American academy in 1966 with "Structure, Sign, and Play in the Discourse of the Human Sciences." But Derrida's début is also framed by his delivery in 1968 at the Johns Hopkins University of the celebrated lecture on "The Ends of Man" and in 1971 of "Signature, Event, Context" at a colloquium in Montreal. These three lectures combined to configure Derrida as a poststructuralist and to efface his phenomenological beginnings. Since the first lecture was delivered at a colloquium called Critical Languages and the Sciences of Man, the perception of Derrida as poststructuralist brings together the themes of intellectual radicalism, the human sciences, and the end of metaphysics under the emancipatory headings of antihumanism and the linguistic turn. This colloquium framed poststructuralism (though the word was not yet used) as a repudiation of phenomenology (Sartre and Merleau-Ponty) and as both a surpassing of structuralism and also its continuation by effecting "a cold and concerted destruction of the subject . . . [and] of origin." The phrase is Deleuze's and is cited by Richard Macksey and Eugenio Donato in their reissue of the proceedings of the Hopkins conference as *The Structuralist Controversy*, where they also frame poststructuralism as post-Nietszchean rather than post-Hegelian.[1] But what does it mean to denounce or renounce origin? Or put differently, given that poststructuralism (unlike structuralism) is still—at first—a form of philosophy, what does it mean to rethink philosophy not as a counterscience but as itself one of the (post)human sciences?

Affirmative Poststructuralism: Antihumanism and 1968

In this context we can distinguish two kinds of poststructuralism: an affirmative variety unconcerned with phenomenological issues and a negative, ascetic version in which the loss of phenomenology constitutes a Real in Lacan's sense: a traumatic core. The latter will be my focus in discussing the poststructuralist turn in the careers of Foucault, Baudrillard, and (briefly) de Man. The former, still influential today, warrants a preliminary discussion.

As indicated thus far, deconstruction and poststructuralism can be separated for theoretical purposes, but they intertwined and became confused in the sixties. Consequently, as there are exemplars of deconstruction who encounter the linguistic paradigm only much later if at all,[2] so too there are poststructuralists who are unconcerned with the ontological problematic that deconstruction inherits from phenomenology. Barthes's dismantling of totalities comes strictly in the wake of his own structuralism, in a turn that occurs in his work in the late sixties in such essays as "The Death of the Author" (1968) and "From Work to Text" (1971) as well as *S/Z* (1970). Although Anglo-American commentators sometimes group him with Derrida under the heading of deconstruction, the term is useful only in describing Barthes's fondness for binary oppositions that privilege dissemination, such as work/text, author/scriptor, or readerly/writerly. Indeed, it is notable that Barthes constructs rather than deconstructs these oppositions, as do Deleuze and Guattari in their numerous parallel pairs such as root and rhizome, royal and nomad science, striated and smooth space. Deleuze and Guattari's relationship to phenomenology is more complex than Barthes's because of Deleuze's extensive work on intellectual history. But for them too poststructuralism is the emancipatory overturning of structuralism as reflected in the re-vision of the machine as an assemblage. Technology is thus freed from the state apparatus, dis-assembled, and made available for a postmodern pragmatic anthropology.

Affirmative poststructuralism thus has several interrelated characteristics. Most important, it uses deconstruction only as a tool. For while it may use the techniques of deconstruction, it deploys them against systems and structures, but not against itself (except in the anaestheticized form of play). Indeed, its procedures are better described as destruction, to borrow the Heideggerian term that Deleuze uses, but differently. For this reason, affirmative poststructuralism is curiously binary, as well as presentist or futurist. It is deeply invested in a rhetoric of the "end" that, as Thomas Pavel suggests, amounts to "an ontological degradation [of] the sequence supposedly ended," that relegates it "to the level of passive material lacking the right and the ability to react."[3]

These liberatory claims led Terry Eagleton to associate poststructuralism with 1968, though the date must be treated with caution.[4] Eagleton too conflates deconstruction and poststructuralism but his comments are best confined to the latter: "Post-structuralism was a product of that blend of euphoria and disillusionment, liberation and dissipation, carnival and catastrophe, which was 1968. Unable to break the structures of state power, post-structuralism found it possible instead to subvert the structures of language."[5] Eagleton's account is relevant to Kristeva's work in the *Tel Quel* period, to Barthes, and to Deleuze/Guattari. It is far from adequate as an account of Derrida or Foucault (not to mention Lacan, who enters the 1968 matrix both directly and via Althusser). Eagleton isolates two key aspects of affirmative poststructuralism: language and emancipation. But he implies a third aspect that limits the adequacy of his description for most French philosophy and that characterizes not only affirmative poststructuralism but also his critique of it for its vicarious revolutionism. This is the Anglo-American transference of philosophy (or literature) into practice.[6] Indeed, it is this emphasis on practice that now retroactively characterizes a cathexis between theory and the sixties. For in a curious mutation poststructuralism in the nineties has been popularly simplified to take up a shift in French theory it-self from language to desire or power.[7] In this version poststructuralism is simply the unscrutinized foundation for "oppositional practices" such as postcolonialism or "poststructuralist anarchism"[8] that borrow its antihu-manism, progressivism, and "destruction" of the past, but not its intensive scrutiny of language. Poststructuralism of this kind locates itself in the crit-ical human sciences, which are "post"-structuralist only in overthrowing the orthopaedic human sciences, whose commitment to pragmatic anthropol-ogy they still maintain. Correspondingly, content, not language, is the target of these academic postmodernisms that, by eliding language, magically re-claim the agency whose loss proved so troubling when poststructuralism was first brought over from France in the sixties.[9]

I will not be concerned here with this loose use of *poststructuralism* to sig-nify any kind of oppositional criticism. For the American putting of post-structuralism into practice is more rigorously exemplified by a book such as Gregory Ulmer's *Applied Grammatology*, which draws directly on Derrida's linguistic revolution. Ulmer consciously ignores the side of Derrida's work emphasized by de Man: his reflexive study of intellectual history. Instead he approaches Derrida "not in terms of deconstruction . . . but in terms of grammatology" as a "new organization of cultural studies" responsive to the current "era of communications technology." Whereas deconstruction leads to an analytic, grammatology is a practice, even if still "only at the level of theory" in Derrida's own work. As "a science that functions as the decon-struction of the concept of science," grammatology facilitates new "tech-nologies" of writing that, as science, are allied with progress.[10] Ulmer's work exemplifies several aspects of affirmative poststructuralism, including the re-tention of the term *science* and the reconfiguration of philosophy as the new human science of cultural studies. His project has a French parallel in the work of Deleuze and Guattari, which also turns away from phenomenology and crosses philosophy with mathematics and science. These theorists are concerned less with representation than with what Friedrich Kittler calls "mediality," in his transference of the thought of Foucault in *The Order of Things* and Derrida in *Of Grammatology* from the domain of epistemology, ontology, and linguistics to that of practices.[11] If Ulmer theorizes cultural work as applied grammatology, John Mowitt provides a genealogy linking the affirmative poststructuralism of the sixties to cultural studies in the nineties. Like other American pragmatists, Mowitt evokes Foucault to explode rather than to submit to discipline. The *Tel Quel* notion of the semiological text, he argues, "reaches into the organizing structure of disciplinarity as such." Text as an antidisciplinary force thus creates the conditions of possibility for the destruction of boundaries between high and low in the replacement of literary with cultural studies.[12]

In this form poststructuralism is very much a postmodern phenomenon. Richard Harland points to its late-capitalist context in coining the term *superstructuralism* to include structuralism and its aftermath. Superstructuralism inverts our ordinary base/superstructure models so that language, the symbolic, and the superego take "precedence over what we used to think of as basic," namely, experience, the individual, and affect.[13] In one sense this loss of the material is a form of transcendence that, by annihilating metaphysics, clears the way for a new pragmatism of thought as technology. As Levinas suggests this, antihumanism of structure can then operate by a sleight of hand, whereby truth is sought in the "objectivity" of structures instead of man, and yet this objectivity is grasped through the mediation of "scientific man."[14] And this covert anthropologism becomes all the more powerful when structures are reconfigured as practices or as agency in the guise of system.

Negative Poststructuralism: "Inhumanism"[15]

But this is not the whole story. For one thing poststructuralism was not born after 1968; only the term was. As Dews points out Lacan was a poststructuralist at the height of structuralism, though it took the late sixties to mark the borders between the two approaches and to polemicize their difference.[16] In the *Discours de Rome* (1953) Lacan's interest shifts from the relations of the ego and the imaginary to the precedence of the symbolic. Since the imaginary is a phenomenological and Sartrean concern whereas the symbolic derives from Lévi-Strauss, Lacan's work also moves at this point from putting phenomenology under erasure to a similar internal analytic of structuralism.[17] Barthes is another theorist who in *Writing Degree Zero* (1953) is poststructuralist at the height of his own structuralism. If structuralism perpetuates systems by describing them, *Writing Degree Zero* deploys the notion of poetic speech as "inhuman" to effect a *destruktion* of bourgeois values that does not allow a return to pragmatic anthropology. Barthes's antihumanism is anchored in his promotion of Robbe-Grillet's *chosisme*—his displacement of interest from the subject to the object—in essays from 1954–62, where Barthes refers to Heidegger and rejects "metaphor" and "pathos" in order to "destroy" or " 'kill' meaning." Robbe-Grillet in turn critiqued metaphysics in "Nature, Humanism, Tragedy" (1958), which is not an apologia for structuralism but rather dismantles a cluster of terms that are later the target of poststructuralism, namely, humanism, interiority, transcendence, lack, and also metaphor and anthropomorphism.[18]

Thus poststructuralism can be said to exist in the fifties but to reemerge in the sixties through a cathexis with 1968 that is itself highly overdetermined. In one form the linking of structure with revolution creates a space for an antiscientific science, a technology beyond technology. And yet poststructuralism had existed before this emancipation as a submission to structure that forgoes both the intelligibility of structure and the transgressiveness of its displacement. Lacan subverts the subject through a structure that is itself decentered; though he uses structuralism to mortify phenomenology, he also questions its claims to decode linguistic messages through the application of a formal system. For Lacan, to disclose the unconscious as a language is thus to create a doubly barred subject: barred from subjectivity and objectivity. In this sense poststructuralism's alleged transcendentalism[19] is strictly limited in ways already delineated by Georg Lukacs's analysis of its favorite figure. Lukacs writes (critically) on Kafka's choice of allegory over realism: allegory is, he says, a form of transcendence, but it is "the transcendence of Nothingness."[20]

Poststructuralism in this second form also returns with renewed poignancy in the late sixties. The words *asceticism* and *rigor* are often used to describe the later work of de Man, Althusser, Lacan, and Foucault.[21] These theorists all privilege the superstructural in the name of rigor—whether as rhetoric, law, the symbolic, or discourse. Indeed, Althusser and Foucault after 1968 converge in approaching subjectification as subjection. Baudrillard is a different case, but he too accepts the power of structure as technology and the code. While this second form of poststructuralism also adopts a rhetoric of antihumanism and science, there is no yield of pleasure in its subversion of the subject by a Kafkan structure. Indeed, science does not connote knowledge but only the stoical rigor of an absolutely technical, apathetic formalism. To be sure, asceticism and rigor allow these theorists to claim a mastery that substitutes for the illusory totality of antihumanism.[22] But as Starr points out, Lacan himself is keenly aware both of the pathology of science and of his own analogously "psychotic rigor." Lacan describes science as "that which holds itself together, in its relation to the real, thanks to the use of little letters."[23] What is true of Lacan's use of linguistics can also be said of the technicality of de Man's turn to rhetoric in the mid-seventies. In short, poststructuralism is inscribed within a relationship to the Real that is unknown to the purely symbolic order of structuralism. And, indeed, Lacan speaks to this relationship when he defines "logic" as "the science of the real because it places access to the Real in the mode of the impossible."[24] Science is, in the end, not mastery but the pathological site of the subject's barring from the symbolic as absolute self-consciousness.

The Near End of Man: Hyppolite's Logic and Existence

Lacan's comment in 1975 on the subject of logic reverts ironically to Hyppolite's turn to antihumanism by way of Hegelian logic in the early fifties, which is picked up by Derrida in "The Ends of Man." In *Logic and Existence* (1952), his second book on Hegel, Hyppolite reverses his privileging of the *Phenomenology* over the *Logic*. He executes several turns that are important for the philosophical (as distinct from cultural) poststructuralism discussed in this study: from phenomenology to logic, from existential to a kind of transcendental phenomenology, and from a radicalized anthropology to a disciplined antihumanism. However, Hyppolite (who participated in Lacan's seminars in the fifties) presents a complex argument whose potential can be unpacked on several levels. Hyppolite's text, in other words, is highly overdetermined. Briefly, he transposes onto the *Logic* something like his analysis of the *Phenomenology* in *Genesis and Structure*; yet this is not just an extension of his earlier work but a renunciation that abandons the *Phenomenology* to resituate the deconstructive project in the asceticism of the *Logic*.

Hyppolite can be contrasted with Kojève, who reads existence as logic and not logic as existence. Kojève articulates a logic of history that is worked out through the *Phenomenology* rather than the *Logic* only so that totality can be manifested as an anthropology. Whereas Kojève reads phenomenology as anthropo-logic, Hyppolite reads logic as phenomenology. In returning to the *Logic* Hyppolite, on one level, does not seek to transfer the desire for totality to transcendental structures. He opposes what we conventionally associate with the *Logic*: a claim to absolute knowledge as the elimination of "non-knowledge [and] of a transcendence essentially irreducible to our knowledge" (LE: 3). Hyppolite's deconstruction of the *Logic* proceeds through the work of Heidegger after the *Kehre*. Thus he introduces two concerns: logic or logos as language and sense as the materiality of the phenomenon. Language is the "Dasein" of thought or "the existence of the essence." In short, it is because logic is logos/language that it is *existence*: the "words of language" are "the 'I' outside of itself, finding itself there before actually being there," "as one is already in life when alive" (26, 47). This relationship between logic and existence is encapsulated in the notion of *sense* in the double sense also given it by Derrida in *Speech and Phenomena* and Nancy in *The Sense of the World*. As Hegel himself says in Hyppolite's citation: "Sense is this wonderful word which is used in two opposite meanings. On the one hand it means the organ of immediate apprehension, but on the other hand we mean by it the sense, the significance . . . the universal underlying the thing" (24). But for Hyppolite this is not a paradox but the aporia of a "sense" that is inextricable from the "sensible" that it must negate so as to "turn into sense" (28). If one sense of sense is inextricable from the other, then thought cannot be separated from language or expression from indication:

> To say that language is prior to thought means that thought is not a pure
> sense which could exist somewhere else, outside of its expression. . . .
> Thought is only by already being there, only by preceding itself . . . in this
> speech which precedes the understanding by means of its grammatical
> structure, sketching in a way, at times prolifically, at other times insuffi-
> ciently, the understanding's forms. This speech, in which the sensible sign
> disappears so that we hear the signification, is still in its form submerged in
> the sensible. (43)

What this means is that the dialectic is "the becoming of sense" or that the Absolute "exists as the Logos only in language" and as finitude (26, 42).

As described so far, Hyppolite finds in the *Logic* an analytic of finitude consistent with deconstruction. Yet there is another strain in this book that speaks against "anthropologism" and "humanism" and that is picked up by Foucault's "Discourse on Language" (AK: 235–37) and Derrida's "Ends of Man." Through its foregrounding of language in the context of antihumanism, *Logic and Existence* becomes a key episode in the emergence of philosophical poststructuralism. As such its importance is symptomatic as well as enabling. For granted that logic is existence, it is fair to ask why a philosophy of existence must be experienced as *logos*. Why is finitude stubbornly attached to "grammatical structure[s]" (LE: 42)? The immediate answer lies in Hyppolite's desire to disaffiliate himself from the Kojèvian "deification of Humanity" (177) and the politics of humanism (or in Lacan's terms ego psychology). One might think that this difference was already established by *Genesis and Structure*. But the years 1946–47 also saw the actual publication of Kojève's lectures, which took on new resonances in the light of the Second World War and the Marshall Plan, of Sartre's *What Is Literature?* and Merleau-Ponty's *Humanism and Terror*, and thus the delegitimation of philosophies of existence through their confusion with existentialism and naive positivisms. In all these ways phenomenology had become compromised by its history, as Hegel's phenomenology of mind had itself been usurped by his philosophy of history. A clearer separation from this context was needed, and how better to effect it than by turning from phenomenology to logic via Heidegger—yet at the site of "Hegel," given the postwar need to say something about *history* in the guise of ontology and given the ambiguities surrounding "Heidegger."

In making this turn Hyppolite gives up the interiority of phenomenology for the symbolic ascesis of a logic that is also denied any fantasies of transcendence because it unfolds in language and not in the Concept. And yet this is not wholly so because the sacrifice of humanism *is* accompanied by a claim to totality through "the Absolute's self-knowledge across man" (177). Such "self-comprehension is not a plan similar to a human plan" yet possesses its own kind of "self-certainty" (188, 41–2). This perhaps answers our earlier question as to why the demystification of humanist illusions is enforced by logic. Why is Hyppolite attached to logic, which as language generates an analytic of existence, but which as logos is connected with a (nonhuman) plan? Judith Butler has analyzed such stubborn attachments to the means of one's subordination with reference to Foucault; Foucault's theory of power is an explanation of the emotional paradox of subjectification and his stubborn attachment to his own subjectification through a power that leaves its "bodily remainder" in the form of a "constitutive loss."[25] In *Logic and Existence* logic still founds a subject even though it is the loss of the subject. For as Levinas says—in examining the complicity between the human sciences, Hegel's logic, Heidegger, and antihumanism—the "system of being" or language simply takes the place of the subject[26] as a "universal self" (LE: 41). In this way, to evoke Butler again, logic (and more generally language and semiology for Derrida) is "a destruction on the basis of which a subject is formed": a destruction (in a Heideggerian sense) of phenomenology.[27]

The Imaginary End of Man: Derrida's German Transference

Lacan uncovers this illusion of logic as mastery, albeit not the mastery of a cogito, in his comments on logic's relationship to the Real. And it is through Lacan that we can read "The Ends of Man" as an uneasy claim to poststructural progress that contains the pathos of a destruction. Hyppolite enters this theoretical matrix by way of Derrida's "implicit reference" to him in "The Ends of Man."[28] In other words, the story of why *Genesis and Structure* becomes *Logic and Existence* has something to say about why deconstruction in the sixties and seventies is disciplined as poststructuralism. Like Hyppolite Derrida turns against anthropologism by returning to Hegel and to a *Phenomenology* read against the grain of French Hegelianism through the *Logic*. To be sure he differs from Hyppolite, picking up only the antihumanist and not the deconstructive side of the latter's argument. Indeed, these two sides of *Logic and Existence* are not really compatible.[29] On the surface Derrida's essay, dated "May 12, 1968," is also much more political than either Hyppolite's study or Heidegger's "Letter on Humanism." Derrida refers to the "margins" of philosophy: the Algerian crisis, the Vietnam war, and the student uprising (M: 113–14). At the end, in discussing two forms of deconstruction, he raises the question of intellectual praxis through the issue of a revolution in critical language. The political frame of the essay might lead one to read it in terms of affirmative poststructuralism. And yet the body of the essay is curiously disembodied and abstracts itself from any political immediacy through a discussion of German philosophy. In connection with Vietnam, Derrida cautions against taking state tolerance of intellectual protest as a simulacrum of material progress (113–14). At the end, as he reflects on breaks with the past, he sees all such "transgressions" as caught in a logic of recuperation. Though Derrida refers to Heidegger here, he must also have in mind the student revolution when he says that those who claim "an absolute . . . difference" inhabit "more naively than ever . . . the inside" they declare they have "deserted" (135). Moreover, he had begun the essay by speaking of philosophic nationalities (111–12). Given that the paper is presented in the United States by a Frenchman uneasy with French philosophy, it would seem that Derrida is also indicating an unease with the progressivism of the American academy and its emphasis on agency and practice.

The essay thus cautions against a covert reaffirmation of poststructuralism as a humanism. And yet Derrida situates himself on the verge of a "trembling" and does claim a " 'change of terrain' " that he refuses to posit (134–35). He too uses a rhetoric of the end that submits the past to an ontological degradation. His progressivism involves not revolution but a disciplined shift to science: a shift from existential to transcendental phenomenology, which allegorizes a more unreadable, nonhumanist form of poststructuralism. The interpretation of Hegel becomes the prefigurative scene of this shift. Following Hyppolite, Derrida insists that the French reading of Hegel was a "mistake" and that the *Phenomenology* has nothing to do with "man." Instead Hegel is a proto-structuralist, if not a herald of something beyond structuralism: "As the science of the experience of consciousness, the science of the structures of the phenomenality of the spirit . . . [the *Phenomenology*] is rigourously distinguished from anthropology" (117). Indeed, the central part of Derrida's essay is a perverse history of phenomenology as poststructuralism recovered through the eradication of French mistakes. For the French reading of Husserl via Heidegger is also dismissed as produced by a misreading of Heidegger to which I return in the next chapter. Hegel, Husserl, and Heidegger are thus all transferred from the side of existence to that of logic, "transcendental structures," and a "consciousness without man." These structures have nothing to do with "man's society, culture, or language," let alone his " 'soul' or 'psyche' " (118).

In effect Derrida resynonymizes consciousness with spirit, though importantly it is a spirit that does not follow "a human plan" (LE: 188). But because the history of spirit is a process without a subject, Derrida can maintain a transference onto a neo-Kojèvian theory of history by not benefiting from it anthropologically.[30] What is at work here is thus a process of interpellation by rigor. Interestingly Hyppolite had already analyzed the substitutive structure of this object(ivity), in which "consciousness alienates its being-for-itself" and transforms "itself into a thing," so as to gain "a much higher truth. In posing itself as a thing, through asceticism, obedience, and the alienation of its own particular will, consciousness discovers—or we discover for it—that the thing is a manifestation of the self and that the self is universal self."

But Hyppolite also reminds us that asceticism is a stage of the unhappy consciousness and thus a form of bad faith. This unhappiness is what Butler discerns when she argues that subjectification is achieved by a "figure of turning . . . even a turning on oneself."[31] For Derrida's history of philosophy involves a profound self-mortification, given his framing concern with philosophic nationalities and the role he assumes as a representative of France at an international colloquium. Derrida speaks for France by turning on it; he seems bent on returning phenomenology to Germany, dismissing all French readings as mistaken. The *Phenomenology*, he says cuttingly, "had only been read for a short time in France" (M: 117). Even Derrida's criticisms of Heidegger serve the purpose of this transference onto German philosophy because, as Ferry and Renaut observe, they outdo Heidegger out of fidelity to the "Heideggerian inheritance."[32]

Nor can the French readings be limited to those Derrida names and reduces (by Henri Corbin, Kojève, Sartre, and Merleau-Ponty). They include the wider tendency of French thought to make logic answerable to existence and to turn phenomenology towards psychoanalysis. Indeed, if we read Derrida's history in terms of philosophic nationalities, we remember an earlier history: Germany's occupation of France, set against France's occupation of German thought from Levinas to Nancy. Lyotard describes this intertextuality between the two countries as the "darkening" of "Enlightenment" that the French have persistently effected by taking responsibility for "what every representation misses." But in "The Ends of Man" Derrida casts aside this history. This is all the more surprising given his return to the issue of philosophic nationalities in *Of Spirit*, where Heidegger is put back into a "Franco-German chronicle" that includes Hegel and Husserl.[33] Yet it is also not surprising because, in the libidinal economy of "The Ends of Man," the submission to the German superego in the essay's middle is rewarded by the intellectually opaque, but rhetorically jubilant, dance with the Nietzschean superman at the end (135–36).

Corpus: De Man's Phantom Body

To remember this earlier history is to see the poststructural subject as constituted by a "destruction," a "nihilation" (in Sartre's terms), that reintroduces nothingness into the heart of its intellectual positions. This loss is masked by the triumphalism of "The Ends of Man," which proceeds through various "near ends" (M: 119) and cautionary delays to a climax earned by such rigor. But its effects can be felt elsewhere in the poststructural corpus, particularly in the work of de Man. De Man's work after *Blindness and Insight* is often analyzed in terms of rigor and the pursuit of a technical language that links it to science. On the one hand, this rigor is often critiqued. On the other hand, it is often read affectively and sympathetically in terms of its "bodily remainder[s]"; like the body in Foucault that, as Butler says, "substitute[s] for the psyche," so too language in de Man is the scene at which we are disciplined or punished into accepting the psyche's foreclosure. Both readings ring true.[34] For de Man's work performs his interpellation into poststructuralism yet increasingly defaces even this identity in essays that auto-graphically take up the mechanisms of this interpellation. These include his essays on Kleist, Shelley, and autobiography. In this sense we should approach *Allegories of Reading*, one of only two books "authored" by de Man, from within the margins of his post-1976 essays edited under the signatures of others.[35]

Allegories of Reading follows the pattern traced here with reference to negative poststructuralism: a turn against the past associated with rigor, in which rigor itself is a turning upon oneself. De Man's later work renounces romantic Idealism and the "vocabulary of consciousness and temporality."[36] Whereas his earlier work had emerged in the aftermath of phenomenology, he now places himself after linguistics and speech act theory. To perform this turn de Man rewrites the term *allegory* (and *rhetoric*)—as we will see Foucault rewriting *archaeology*—by forgetting its phenomenological and Benjaminian resonances in "The Rhetoric of Temporality." The word *allegory* is now virtually illegible within any normal system of meaning. Still it is in this "twisting" of the word, to evoke Butler again, that a subject is "tropologically inaugurated." This subject claims an authority that derives from de Man's formalization of rhetorical analysis. Formalization will be the object of his critique in the essay on Kleist; as he himself says, formalization makes teaching possible (RR: 270–72). And in *Allegories of Reading* de Man creates a curriculum for ascetic education by articulating deconstruction with an epistemological discourse; by deploying a rhetorical terminology that is eminently reproducible; and by naming second and third "degrees" or "powers" of deconstruction, as if gesturing towards systematicity. Moreover, he also identifies a structural matrix for his work when he claims that the "paradigm for all texts consists of a figure (or a system of figures) and its deconstruction." In this sense Guillory is right to see *Allegories* as interpellated by the form of science, even if this form is radically at odds with its content.[37]

Allegories of Reading contains all the conceptual elements of de Man's "glimpse" into "terror" after 1976 (RT: 37).[38] We already find the idea of language as "inhuman" (92) in the account of its "machinelike systematicity." Like Hegel's logic this system does not follow a human plan but "programs a relationship between [terms], and lets mere syntax take its course." Nor is there anything liberating in this antihumanism. We also find the idea of language as an arbitrary positing or performativity.[39] But the "violence of position" (RR: 118) is now dissociated from the freedom of the imaginary, where it had resided in "The Intentional Structure" (6) and is located in the disruptive autonomy of language. For this reason language is no longer reinteriorized in terms of lack. It is an insane system: "texts engender texts as a result of their necessarily aberrant semantic structure,"[40] which will eventually lead de Man to speak of "the *uncontrollable* power of the letter as inscription" (RT: 37; emphasis mine). Nevertheless *Allegories of Reading* is protected by its formalization from the "absolute negation . . . or *denegation*" de Man confronts in his last essays.[41] As a book it is a gathering together of related essays within a defined space. Moreover it is a book *by* de Man in that it elaborates a way of reading rather than being written in the margins of work by others, like *Critical Writings* or *Blindness and Insight*. As such it can be approached in terms of the phenomenology of property and space that Levinas associates with position and having a face. "Illuminated space," he writes, "all collects about a mind which possesses it" as "property" through a Kantian "synthesis"

(EE: 48). *Allegories of Reading* is such a synthesis, whereas *Resistance to Theory* and *Aesthetic Ideology* are unified through an editorial prosopopeia: a conferring of "face" through the voicing back into life of an "absent, deceased, or voiceless entity" (RR: 74–75).

That the last essays exceed any formalization is evident in their increasing use of the terms *disfiguration, defacement,* and *dismemberment.* These terms do not occur in *Allegories of Reading,* which deploys the word *deconstruction.* De Man does not use deconstruction in the same way as Derrida (RT: 118); he does not unwork systems so as to open up other "possibilities of arrangement"[42]; he instead traces a process of endless referential aberration. Still, he shares with Derrida a sense of deconstruction as a "technical" procedure that distinguishes it from the more "negative" term *destruction.*[43] Disfiguration is closer to destruction but forecloses any possibility of a clearing. Its violence is reflected in the trope of catachresis, which enters de Man's vocabulary in 1978 along with the related figure of anthropomorphism (RR: 240–41). Catachresis, unlike any previous figure evoked by de Man, is the eruption of something "monstrous." Catachreses (like the "leg" of a table) are hybrids that abuse metaphor by confusing substances. By "dint of the positional power inherent in language" they "dismember the texture of reality and reassemble it in the most capricious of ways."[44] Catachresis also defaces the technicality of rhetoric and of the systematization of aporia around which *Allegories of Reading* is constructed. In this system logic, rhetoric, and grammar mutually disrupt each other; but "rhetorizations of grammar" are always balanced by a "grammatization of rhetoric" that yields a science of aporias.[45]

What is significant about catachresis is its mixed status; it is a prosthesis that grafts a body back onto the nonhuman. For de Man's examples—the "*face* of a mountain or the *eye* of a hurricane" (RT: 44)—figure the upsurge of the human in the nonhuman, which is the upsurge of nothingness in being. Body and machine are clearly distinguished in *Allegories of Reading.* Through the latter de Man "suffers the loss of the illusion of meaning" yet maintains the self-sufficiency of the inhuman; the machine is "systematic in its performance" even if it is "arbitrary in its principle, like a grammar." The machine has a "logical code" and is a figure for logic as well as grammar.[46] To be sure this logic is without sense. For de Man follows Hyppolite's account of Hegel in seeing formal language as a "blind thought, for which we could substitute a machine": thought "ends up losing all sense and being reduced to a calculus which is an exterior manipulation of symbols. These symbols can, indeed, designate or signify something, but they are treated only as sensible elements external and indifferent to one another" (LE: 45). Moreover, for de Man any logic is always interrupted by another grammar with its own aberrant logic, which is what makes him a grammato-logical rather than structuralist thinker. Yet in *Allegories of Reading* this grammatology is always taken up into further levels of vertiginously structural description. In short *Allegories of Reading* is not deconstruction in the sense explored here, but superstructuralism, that is to say, the infinitization and hyperrealization of structure.

And yet through catachresis, the trope that "gives face to the faceless" in the moment of its defacement (RT: 44), de Man confesses that his own critical machine—which is a kind of aesthetic ideology—can be disfigured by the return of a phantom body. In retrospect the technicality of rhetorical analysis appears as a way for theory to hold itself together in relation to the Real thanks to the use of little letters. Indeed, when de Man speaks of the "uncontrollable power of the letter as inscription," he uses *letter* not in a linguistic and formal way but in the Lacanian sense elaborated by Serge Leclaire, of a socially inscribed mark on the psychic body (the sense in which Lyotard uses the term *figure*). Lacan's letter is a catachresis that assimilates machine and body by figuring the unconscious in terms of cybernetics: "the primordial and primitive language," Lacan says, is "the language of the machine."[47] Derrida develops this notion affirmatively when he hints that cybernetics can lead the machine of language beyond phonetic writing to create new possibilities of "information retrieval" (OGr: 10). In "applied" grammatology the machine is thus opened up by the psyche. But for de Man the uncontrollable power of the letter lies in the machine's foreclosure of the psyche that it inscribes traumatically upon an absent body.

De Man's late work is thus an allegory of poststructuralism: first as a transference onto the linguistic paradigm for purposes of scientific legitimation and then as a disfiguration of its own relapse into an aesthetic ideology. This disfiguration occurs through a catachresis; the terms *dis*figur*ation*, *dis*member*ment*, and *de*face*ment* are anthropomorphisms for *deconstruction* that disclose its bodily remainders. For as Derrida suggests in "White Mythology" catachresis is a *disclosive* and not just an "abusive" trope. As the "violent, forced . . . imposition of a sign upon a meaning" that lacks its "proper sign in language," it brings to light something that is "already in the mind like a grid without a word" but that "could not have been retraced, tracked down . . . without the force of a twisting" that appears as an "infraction" (M: 255–57). And de Man allows catachresis to have this role in his work—the role Derrida assigns it, of causing "irreparable damage" to the restricted economy of rhetoric, even his own rhetoric (270). For Derrida catachresis is both inside and "completely apart" from the system of "classical rhetoric" (256–58). It is the "extra metaphor" that, by "extract[ing]" itself from "the field that it allows to be circumscribed," ensures that "the taxonomy or history of philosophical metaphors will never make a profit" (220). *Allegories of Reading* is organized in terms of this "tropic supplementarity" (M: 220). Further turns are always added to the binary system of a figure and its deconstruction, so that in practice rhetorical analysis is not "repeatable, like a grammar." Thus the "allegorical narrative" is superimposed on a "primary deconstructive narrative," only for this dyad to be displaced by the addition of a "tropological narrative" that may or may not be the original deconstructive narrative.[48] Nevertheless de Man's rhetorical and conceptual figures, though they are not recontained "in" the texts he discusses, seem to be "in [de Man's] philosophical text" (M: 258). For this reason *Allegories of Reading* appears to profit from the system of rhetoric, and its excess is a grid without a word.

But, as Derrida says, "metaphor is less in the philosophical text" than this text "is within metaphor" (258). By disclosing the excess masked by the science of *Allegories of Reading*, the final essays put de Man's own text within metaphor or, rather, figure. They do so by focusing on tropes that disrupt the relation of literal and figural: anthropomorphism, prosopopeia, and catachresis. As de Man uses them, these tropes are unlike metaphor, which forgets the material in the spiritual. By contrast, anthropomorphism "is not just a trope but an identification on the level of substance" (RR: 241), what Leclaire calls a letter that incorporates the material with the figural. These tropes mark the return of the literal within a discourse that purports to unmask the literal as a moment of figure, and they thus break open the containment of de Man's work within the closure of the figural. Thus in "Shelley Disfigured" the argument appears to work metaphorically by making the "shape all light" a figure for trope. Metaphor is the mode of Derrida's similar deconstruction of light and bringing to light through the "heliotrope" in "White Mythology" (M: 245–57). But de Man's translation of the Shape into his own allegory of figure is framed within the pathos of an anthropomorphism: the surfacing of Shelley's dead body in the manuscript as the irruption of something "not present in [the] . . . articulated meaning" of the text or the critical commentary on it (RR: 120).

The last essays are haunted by an anthropomorphism that feels the cost of the inhuman. From the perspective of these essays we glimpse in superstructuralism a response to a specifically postmodern trauma that de Man figures through the machinelike cyberneticization and power of language: a mechanized inscription detached from the hand. This archaeological shift has numerous effects among which are an emphasis on exteriority, an autonomization of systems, and a dehumanization of transcendence. For as Žižek argues, postmodernism is distinguished by a reification that puts even deconstruction under the sign of modernism. We are not dealing here with a loss of presence but with a superfluity in which the "empty place, is always already filled out by the inert . . . *presence*" of the Thing. Thus where modernism is constituted by a dialectic of lack that sees the emptiness of structures in terms of "an 'absent god,'" postmodernism does not function in terms of the pair presence/absence and the related dialectic of *pour-soi* and *en-soi*. Instead it involves a "nondialecticizable" "nauseous" presence that Sartre names the *en-soi* and that Žižek calls the superego. In de Man's case it is the machine of language that becomes what Žižek calls this "*incarnated, materialized emptiness*" of dead Spirit.[49]

And here we can read de Man alongside Kittler. For *Discourse Networks 1800/1900* is a historical rather than a pragmatist account of shifts in the technology of language, which feels the cost of epistemic change. The network of 1800 is based on "alphabetization" as the continuation of orality into writing and reading under "the name of the author." That of 1900 is based on the separation of interiority and inscription by the typewriter and on the redirection of words from memory and temporality into a "countable, spatialized supply." One could see this mechanization of inscription as freeing a manipulable technology from the metaphysics of origin; this is how Gregory Ulmer and Mark Poster view it. Instead Kittler focuses on the "inner experience" of technology as felt by one of poststructuralism's founding fathers. Nietzsche, he suggests, was the first philosopher to confront the "inhuman" exteriority of language. Nietzsche's madness is an anthropomorphism for the trauma of his philosophy. Nietzsche sees in language a "pure materiality:" "writing and writers as accidental events in a noise that generates accidents."[50] Likewise for de Man the machine is the "anamorphosis of a form detached from meaning and capable of taking on any structure whatever." Moreover, this logos or logic, which conceals the murdered trace of Hegelian Spirit, is "ruthless in its inability to modify" its structural design for other than structural reasons.[51] It is what Sartre calls a "thing-like, blind in-itself" (BN: 120), indifferent to the human.

But to name this in-itself language is a catachresis that discloses the very for-itself it forecloses. For as Sartre says one can name the inhuman only by an "anthropomorphi[sm]" (29). Or as Georges Canguilhem argues, "monstrosity"—so much an affect of de Man's late work, as Clark points out—is only possible within the frame of the human; there is no monstrosity for machines.[52] What this means is that the definitive closure of poststructuralism within the linguistic is itself a figure or symptom. That death is the "name for a linguistic predicament" (RR: 81) or that our "predicaments" are "linguistic" and not "ontological"[53] is itself poststructuralism's predicament. For poststructuralism's debarment from the ontological makes it the unhappy consciousness of antihumanism. This is clear in "Shelley Disfigured," where de Man evokes Levinas—not just linguistics or speech act theory—to destroy the "shape all light" as a figure for trope. For Levinas, light facilitates shape as "that by which a thing shows itself," and this phenomenality is the condition of property: "light makes objects into a world [and] makes them belong to us" (EE: 47–48). De Man's disfiguration of trope follows Levinas's unworking of Husserl, whom de Man also links to light (RT: 112). At issue in the loss of face—face in French being "*figure*" (100)—is thus property and self: the "*private* existence" of terms such as romanticism that now return "to an undifferentiated background" (EE: 57–58).

De Man analyzes this dispossession linguistically as the subjection of figures like metaphor, which contain a "phenomenal" and "representational" element, to purely material "tropes such as grammar and syntax." The latter function only "on the level of the letter without the intervention of an iconic factor" and yet are the unavoidable ground of "linguistic organization." In Shelley's poem this inherence of a blind mechanism in the very process that shapes the poem as "measure" and music is figured by the way the Shape itself "trampl[es] out" "the poetic and philosophical light" (RR: 113–15). The repetitive erasures that constitute the poem thus expose us to what Levinas calls being in general (EE: 56). But the further blow that de Man sustains is that he cannot think this disaster through a philosophy of existence. On the contrary, he uses Levinas only to abuse him; for the displacement of "being in general" by the violent "positional power" of language defaces the nonviolence of Levinas's thought. And yet the point is that de Man remains a "metaphysician" and not a "technician" of discourse (RT: 110). For his sustained linkage of light, face, and position confesses that the "undoing of the representational . . . function of figuration by the play of the signifier" is after all an ontological predicament (RR: 114).

Poststructuralism's cryptic link to phenomenology is intimated by Foucault in the "Discourse on Language" (1970), which ends with a tribute to Hyppolite. Indeed, the title is deliberately ironic given a point I discuss later: the desynonymizing of language and discourse in *The Order of Things* and the narrowed focus on discourse in *The Archaeology of Knowledge*. Briefly, *discourse* is a neostructuralist term that refers to a field ordered by exclusion and limitation, whereas *language* is at first sense (or what Merleau-Ponty calls the sensible) and then, more darkly, Levinas's "being in general." As a supplement often printed with *The Archaeology of Knowledge* Foucault's "Discourse on Language" might seem to be its official summation were it not that he begins by wanting to disappear in "words," even as he had begun *The Archaeology of Knowledge* by wanting to have no "face" (AK: 215, 17). The "Discourse on Language" thus de-figures archaeology as a particular discourse on language, on a speech or "murmuring" (236) that cannot be reduced to this discourse.

Foucault figures this excess of philosophy's language in relation to the archaeological discourse through his "debt" to Hyppolite's work on Hegel. By 1970 Hyppolite, who had recently died, belonged to a past phase of theory. But Foucault makes two points with regard to Hyppolite and, one could add, phenomenology. He suggests that breaks with the past are caught in what they try to "escape" and also—as Derrida did not yet say in "The Ends of Man"—that this past runs ahead of us to return "from a different angle." More specifically, Foucault sees *Logic and Existence* as prophetic in connecting philosophy with "non-philosophy" at a point when the very "*raison d'être*" of philosophy was in doubt. Thus Hyppolite drew into the ambit of philosophy "psychoanalysis, with its strange logic of desire; mathematics and the formalisation of discourse," and "information theory and its application to the analysis of life." By inscribing these discourses within an analysis of Hegel, Hyppolite showed that these new logics are always still about "questions of logic and existence" (AK: 235–37).

The reference to the last of these cultural logics indicates what is explicit in Baudrillard's work but veiled in that of Lacan, de Man, and Foucault, namely, the impact of information theory on notions of code and archive, the gram and the unconscious. Indeed, it is this new "mode of information" as Poster calls it—whether it was born with cybernetics or in 1900—that produces the twisting of deconstruction into poststructuralism. The antihumanist logics of poststructuralism either imitate or mimic the obscene object of postmodernity. Yet, as Foucault intimates, in the latter case logic knows itself as a form of existence; thus in de Man's late work the logic of poststructuralism becomes the "inner experience" of this technology. In this sense the poststructuralism discussed here is still within the horizon of phenomenology.

CHAPTER THREE

The Double Detour: Sartre, Heidegger, and the Genealogy of Deconstruction

Sartre against Heidegger

This chapter begins with Sartre's supposed mistranslation of *Being and Time* as *Being and Nothingness* and traces its legacy for a deconstruction that emerges in the crossing over of phenomenology from Germany to France. That the French understanding of Heidegger was mediated by Sartre is well-known. French intellectuals such as Jean Beaufret came to Heidegger *à travers* Sartre, as Sartre himself came to Husserl via Levinas, or as Lacan came to Hegel through Kojève. Correcting this misprision, younger theorists such as Derrida recovered a place for Heidegger in deconstruction, so that Sartre, once a key figure, was displaced as philosophically incorrect by Heidegger. As is often noted, the eclipse of Sartre was the condition of possibility for the linguistic turn as well as for the rise of Heidegger.[1] Though the influence of the two is irreducibly intertwined, "Heidegger" has come to figure what can be kept and purified from the phenomenological pre-text of deconstruction, while the "naive" parts of this legacy have been condensed in "Sartre."

But this history of the relationship between phenomenology and deconstruction conceals two mistranslations. To begin with, Sartre's appropriation of Heidegger is not (as often alleged) the "mistake" of a second-rate philosopher who pillaged Heidegger without understanding him. The rendering of "Eigentlichkeit" as "authenticité" and of "Dasein" as "réalité humaine" by Heidegger's first French translator, Henri Corbin, may be a mistake.[2] But Sartre's appropriation of Heidegger is more like what Corngold calls an "error": a carrying over or troping constitutive for subsequent theory.[3] As important, this error has itself been covered over by a further polemical misprision: Heidegger's representation of Sartre, which in its subsequent acceptance has generated a second error. For when Heidegger "corrects" Sartre, he reduces the latter's work metonymically to *Existentialism Is a Humanism*, thus eliding the difference between Sartre's existentialism and his phenomenology, his political self-popularization and his philosophical work. Indeed, Heidegger, it seems, never read *Being and Nothingness*.[4] Depicting Sartre as straightforwardly "anthropological," Heidegger's misreading thus sets the stage for the second phase of French theory: its turn from a deconstruction that develops its understanding of language from a radicalization of phenomenology's focus on consciousness to a poststructuralism that sees language and consciousness as irreducibly opposed.

Heidegger's claim in "The Letter on Humanism" (1947) that he had been misrepresented by Sartre is well-known, particularly as repeated by Derrida in "The Ends of Man." Alluding to Corbin's translation of *Dasein* as *réalité humaine* and then implicating Sartre too in this "monstrous" mistranslation (M: 115), Derrida speaks of the continued usefulness of phenomenology, "but not—especially not—in the versions proposed by Sartre or by Merleau-Ponty."[5] Briefly, Heidegger's criticisms converge on the issues of anthropology and nihilism, which will continue to haunt deconstruction's anxiety about Sartre's precursory influence. Arguing that there is no essence without existence, Heidegger accuses Sartre of treating existence in Hegelian fashion as the immanent working out of essence, instead of understanding it in terms of ek-static temporality. Sartre is said to misread Heidegger's terms *ek-sistence* and *projection*, thus recentering the latter in his own notion of the project as "a representational positing" that is "an achievement of subjectivity."[6]

Sartre's nihilism, Heidegger complains, is likewise a consequence of his emphasis on man rather than being. Sartre sees the structures of being and consciousness, or the *en-soi* and *pour-soi*, as fundamentally incommensurable. As the fullness of matter, the in-itself or *en-soi* is a plenitude, while the for-itself or *pour-soi* is a void (*néant*) that lacks being. Constructing a dualism that divides existence between extended and thinking matter as being and nothingness respectively, Sartre "pitch[es] everything that does not stay close to the . . . positive into the previously excavated pit of pure negation."

This negation "negates everything, ends in nothing, and so consummates nihilism." Most importantly, Sartre misrecognizes nihilation as something that unfolds "in the existence of man" rather than in "Being itself." He therefore excludes the human as infinite absolute negativity from the world as an undialectical and nonhuman positivity.[7]

That Sartre enlisted Heidegger on the side of existentialism is as puzzling as his own self-vulgarization in *Existentialism Is a Humanism*—though Sartre had always seen Heidegger as a kind of humanist, and with reason (BN: 128). But it is clear three years earlier in *Being and Nothingness*, when politics is not the issue, that Sartre—after an initial enthusiasm for Heidegger in the mid-thirties—does not misunderstand him so much as radically disagree with him. Sartre borrows from Heidegger's "What Is Metaphysics" the terms *nothing* and *nihilation*. But his phenomenology of negativity translates the latter's postmetaphysical idealism only in the sense that Heidegger himself uses the word *translation* to denote a process by which one cultural experience is transferred into "a different way of thinking"[8]—in this case, French, not German.

Far from mistaking *Dasein* for his own *réalité humaine*,[9] Sartre draws attention to the difference between the two, as the difference between spirit and consciousness, being and existence. Heidegger, he observes, begins "with the existential analytic without going through the *cogito*," thus conveniently sidestepping existence. The Sartrean cogito is not to be conceived on the models provided by Descartes, Kant, or Husserl. Husserl "has shut himself up inside the *cogito* and deserves—despite his denial—to be called a phenomenalist rather than a phenomenologist" (BN: 119). Yet in avoiding what Foucault calls this "sovereign transparency" of the phenomenal cogito (OT: 322), Heidegger brackets the cogito altogether so as to engage in his own transcendental reduction. Insofar as it "does not and never can lead to self-consciousness," *Dasein* thus tends towards what Foucault, echoing Sartre, will call "inertia" (322). Similarly Sartre writes that since *Dasein* "has from the start been deprived of the dimension of consciousness, it can never regain this dimension. Heidegger endows human reality with a self-understanding. . . . But how could there be an understanding which would not in itself be the consciousness (of) being understanding? This eksta[sis] . . . will lapse into a thing-like, blind in-itself" (BN: 119–20; cf. also 134).

At issue is the subject as vulnerability—a vulnerability also disclosed by

Hyppolite when he translates the German Hegel of the *Logic* into the French Hegel of the *Phenomenology* and the unhappy consciousness. Writing on Husserl, Levinas marks the difference between logic and phenomenology: logic "which deals with the general form of being can say nothing of its material structures" and thus "lies outside of any psychology."[10] Despite his early allegiance to Heidegger, Levinas will go on to discern a continuity between Husserlian logic and Heideggerian being as philosophies of light. That "nihilation unfolds . . . in Being" and not in the existence of man thus means, for Sartre, that nothingness does not happen *to* anyone and thus does not happen materially or psychologically. Nothingness, by not being grounded upon a subject as "negative being," becomes a form of "transcendence" (BN: 53).

To put it differently Sartre retains the cogito not as a positive term but as a moment of responsibility: "In truth the *cogito* must be our point of departure . . . but it leads us only on condition that we get out of it." As Sartre explains, his ontology and ethics have as their goal precisely this exit: to "question the *cogito* about its being" by furnishing the "instrument that would enable us to find in the *cogito* itself the means of escaping" it (120). Sartre's phrase strikingly anticipates Derrida's definition of deconstruction as "using against the edifice the instruments . . . available in the house" (M: 135). Indeed, Sartre seeks to deconstruct the cogito by disclosing its aporetic structure as "being what it is not and not being what it is" (BN: 28). But he also insists that this deconstruction must be known and felt by a "cogito" if it is to have any urgency. As we shall see in Derrida's rethinking of Husserl through Sartre, to "depart" from the cogito is to deconstruct it, but this deconstruction must occur as part of the autobiography of philosophy if it is to be ethical and not simply logical. In short, one returns to the cogito as a "point of departure," which is to say sensitivity.

Insofar as he short-circuits this cogito, Sartre sees Heidegger as recontaining nothingness—or otherness and difference—in a being closer to spirit than to the unhappy consciousness. This vicarious reunification of the self through the figure of being is a displacement to which Levinas will also point when he notes the complicity of Heidegger's seemingly nonviolent ecstasis with appropriative knowledge: whereas in the latter "the object is absorbed by the subject," "in ecstasis the subject is absorbed in the object and recovers itself in its unity. All these relationships result in the disappearance of the other" (TO: 41).[11] Sartre makes the same point four years earlier, when he describes Heideggerian transcendence as "a concept in bad faith." Sartre further comments that "undoubtedly" *Dasein* "'exists outside itself.' But this existence outside is precisely Heidegger's definition of the *self*" (BN: 336). For Sartre, then, the reduction or putting under erasure of the cogito in ecstasis is an idealization that restores the subject as spirit redeemed from consciousness.

This idealization, in turn, opens Heidegger to a second criticism from Sartre: that "the characteristic of [his] philosophy is to describe *Dasein* by using positive terms which hide the implicit negations" (52). Sartre's aim, then, is to deconstruct Heidegger's thinking by unearthing these negations: "*Dasein* is 'outside of itself, in the world'; it is 'a being of distances'; . . . it is 'its own possibilities,' etc. All this amounts to saying that *Dasein* 'is not' in itself, that it 'is not' in immediate proximity to itself, and that it 'surpasses' the world inasmuch as it posits itself as *not being in itself* and as *not being the world*" (52). In this vein Sartre systematically critiques Heidegger on a range of issues including negativity, temporality, *Mit-sein*, death (697–98), ethics (128), the other (333–37), and the whole question of the "clearing" or the phenomenon as the showing of being (8–9) as against what for Sartre is the opacity of being as solid or "massif" (28).

Sartre notes that the essential structure of Heidegger's thought is positive or that the "nothing" is no more than the "ground" upon which *Dasein* appears (251–52). In effect he finds in Heidegger—but in terms of ontology rather than linguistics—what Derrida analyzes as a metaphysics of presence. Indeed, Sartre is one of Heidegger's earliest critics in this regard, breaking with Levinas's early reading of Heidegger as an existential phenomenologist and foreshadowing his later criticisms of the German philosopher.[12] Sartre admits that Heidegger may indeed seem to move to a "concrete apprehension of nothingness" (50). *Dasein* "rises up as an emergence of being in non-being," even as "the world is 'suspended' in nothingness. Anguish is the discovery of this double, perpetual nihilation" (51). Still, insofar as nothingness is only that "by which the world receives its outlines," Sartre (whether correctly or not) argues that Heidegger renders nothingness marginal: "Here then is nothingness surrounding being on every side and at the same time expelled from being" (51). This in turn has to do with its transcendental, merely theoretical character. For "if I emerge in nothingness *beyond* the world, how can this extra-mundane nothingness furnish a foundation for those little pools of non-being which we encounter each instant in the depths of being" (53)?

The Language of Nothingness

> "Nothingness has defied Western thought."
>
> —*(Levinas)*[13]

These little pools of nonbeing, by contrast, are the concern of Sartre, who finds them in the very microphysics of perception and language. Sartre's resistance to theory is often located in an insensitivity to language, of which Merleau-Ponty is seen as more aware. To be sure, unlike Merleau-Ponty in the fifties, Sartre in the period 1938–43 does not mention Saussure. Yet he finds in *consciousness* the same difference and nonidentity that deconstruction later finds in language. Moreover, Sartre does not entirely bypass language, which he prophetically analyzes as the discourse of the other (BN: 464, 485–87). He discerns the negative in language not by focusing on the diacritical nature of the sign but by analyzing ordinary language so as to deconstruct logical positivism. One could say that he engages with language as it was thought in his time. And as we shall see, even his analysis of perception, drawn from *Gestalt* theory, is organized by what becomes for de Man a linguistic model of "figuration."

For Sartre nothingness is everywhere. Considering a line segment, he argues that the "positive attribute" of length is also "distance" and "intervenes here by virtue of the negation of an absolute . . . proximity." If one considers length as the bridging of distance, then "the negation, expelled from the segment and its length, takes refuge in the two *limits*" of a line that "*does not* extend beyond this point" (54). Sartre seems compelled to find the negative in every situation, however one sees it. Nothingness, he says, "lies coiled in the heart of being—like a worm" (56). Sartre writes of negation, nothingness, nonbeing, and nihilation. As if these terms are inadequate he invents a further term, *négatités*, to signify the "transcendent" or primal nature of nothingnesses that nevertheless arise only in situations of engagement "in the world" (59). Though he sometimes relapses into a hypostasis of nothingness, Sartre is deeply aware that it is neither a substance nor a structure: "One does not *find*, one does not *disclose* nothingness in the manner in which one can find, disclose a being" (126). Sartre's legacy to theory is thus the way he "exscribes" a nothingness that cannot be logically contained or "inscribed" within the text. As Nancy explains, in exscription "meaning spills out of itself, like a simple ink stain on a word": "the exscribed is exscribed . . . not as an 'inexpressible'" but "as writing's opening, within itself . . . to its own inscription as the infinite discharge of meaning." But "discharge" in the present context is less a bursting into presence than an opening into abjection that Nancy also signals by evoking Bataille. By trying vainly to "inscribe" and internalize nothingness through so many synonyms, Sartre thus "exscribe[s] the presence of what withdraws from all significations," only to erupt in his final discussion of the viscous as the "torment" of an "inner experience" that is neither inside nor outside because it has breached the boundaries between them.[14]

We shall consider just one example of *négatité*: Sartre's famous appointment with Pierre in the café. In the first part of the scene Sartre seems to entertain the claims of the positive, as he describes the café with "its mirrors, its light" as "a fullness of being." Pierre's anticipated presence is also a "plenitude": "We seem to have found fullness everywhere." Yet Sartre observes that

> in perception there is always the construction of a figure on a ground. . . . When I enter this café to search for Pierre, there is formed a synthetic organization of all the objects in the café, on the ground of which Pierre is given as about to appear. This organization of the café as the ground is an original nihilation. Each element of the setting . . . attempts to . . . lift itself upon the ground constituted by the totality of the other objects, only to fall back once more into the undifferentiation of this ground. . . . For the ground is that which is seen only in addition, that which is the object of a purely marginal attention. . . . Thus the original nihilation of all the figures which appear and are swallowed up . . . is the necessary condition for the appearance of the principal figure, which is here the person of Pierre. (41)

In other words, thetic consciousness, as an act of focusing, eliminates that penumbra of difference sensed by the prereflective cogito. These other objects, moreover, are not simply marginalized; they are "nihilated," in a positing that Blanchot sees as a form of "murder" (GO: 42) and that Derrida and de Man will refer to as "violence" (WD: 147; RR: 116–19). When Pierre fails to appear this nihilation is redoubled. He is not absent from "some precise spot" but "from the *whole* café," which is consumed by his absence (BN: 42). Nihilation, moreover, attacks not only the ground but the very possibility of figuration, which is not positing but a double erasure:

> the café remains *ground* . . . [but] slips into the background; it pursues its nihilation. Only it makes itself ground for a determined figure. . . . This figure . . . is precisely a perpetual disappearance; it is Pierre raising himself as nothingness on the ground of the nihilation of the café. . . . It is the nothingness of the ground, the nihilation of which summons and demands the appearance of the figure, and it is the figure—the nothingness which slips as a *nothing* to the surface of the ground. (42)

We cannot fail to recall here de Man's traumatic reading of the "positional power of language" as a repetitive, "arbitrary" erasure. In "Shelley Disfigured" de Man writes that "language posits and language means . . . but language cannot posit meaning" because it describes "the emergence of an articulated language of cognition by the erasure, the forgetting of the events this language in fact performed" (RR: 116, 118). The trace is not retention, as in Derrida's Husserlian version of the concept. It is rather what Sartre calls a "nihilating thesis" (BN: 62): an erasure of what is already an erasure, a forgetting of the "knowledge achieved by the forgetting that precedes it" (RR: 119).[15]

Sartre, as we have seen, coins the word *négatité* to describe the unconcealing of "original" nothingness in the commonalities of daily life. Because "they are dispersed in being" these *négatités* cannot be "throw[n] . . . back into an extra-mundane nothingness," as Sartre says Heidegger does (BN: 55–56); instead they are "constituted in immanence as transcendences." In other words, they are "secondary," existentially concrete "nihilations" that disclose an "original" "nothingness" (84). They are also transcendent in the sense that in their very immediacy (or immanence) they nevertheless escape us. As we have suggested, Sartre also finds these *négatités* not only in everyday life but also in ordinary language. And here it is useful to approach him through one of his most astute readers. Blanchot's "Literature and the Right to Death" (1947) is often taken as a rebuke to Sartre's contemporaneous and highly political *What Is Literature?* (1947). But as I argue later, it is also an extension of Sartre's texts on imagination and ontology: a radicalization of a Sartre whose earlier work was already among the most radical contributions to what Blanchot calls "the powerful negative contemporary movements responsible for this volatizing and volatile force which literature seems to have become" (GO: 23).

Whether Blanchot read Saussure is unclear, yet he seems peripherally aware of him, in a way that may also indicate Sartre's residence in the intellectual environment that led to deconstruction. Referring to the notion that there are no positive terms in language, Blanchot comments on the diacritical nature of signs as a missed encounter with original nothingness. Thus the image, he says, does not "designate the thing, but rather, what the thing is not; it speaks of a dog instead of a cat." "Common" language recontains this negation by making it the ground against which predication appears; it accepts that "once the nonexistence of the cat has passed into the word, the cat itself comes to life again . . . in the form of its idea." By contrast, literary language returns us not "to the absent thing, but to absence as presence" (GO: 44–45), to the very phenomenon of nothingness rather than to its intentional correlate in the object designated as absent (44–45; cf. 85–88). Literary language turns from a merely logical to an ontological reading of the negative.

Finding absence not just in literature but at the very heart of ordinary language, Sartre similarly plays with the logical option. He allows that the mind may possess "the *not* as a form of sorting out and separation": I find "1300 francs in my wallet" because there are 1300 and not 1500 or 1100 francs (BN: 43); or I see a cat, which means that I do not see a dog. But as against the negative judgment that is the basis for an affirmation, Sartre would rather say, "I find only thirteen hundred [francs]" (38). He would rather point to a disappointment, to the "non-being that always appears within the limits of a human expectation" (38). This nonbeing is not a logical "category" but an "irreducible and original event" (43). It is, moreover, irreducibly human, since it is only through man that "*nothingness comes to things*" (57). Things cannot feel the negative, which pertains to them only as a mechanism of sorting. Things are separated by an "external" relation "established between two beings by a witness:" "When I say, for example, 'A cup is not an inkwell,' . . . the foundation of this negation is neither in the cup nor in the inkwell. Both of these objects are what they are and that is all. The negation stands as a categorical . . . connection which I establish between them . . . without enriching them or impoverishing them" (243). But man, by contrast, is traversed by an "internal negation." By this "we understand such a relation between two beings that the one which is denied to the other qualifies the other at the heart of its essence—by absence" (243). In this form of negation the very being of the one is put under erasure by the other, as the two terms "constitute" each other, either through lack (135) or through the "collapse" of a positivity onto its internal bond to "what it denies" (243, 245).

Sartre's move from the negative as a form of sorting and identification to a "negative synthesis" through which the nonidentity of each term appears "within and upon the being which it is not" (243, 245) prefigures what Derrida will later do with Saussurian linguistics. For Derrida too departs from structuralism's repositivizing of difference to claim that signs are connected by internal negation such that "no element can function as a sign without referring to another element which itself is not simply present" (P: 26). In the 1968 interview with Kristeva from which this statement is taken Derrida uses the terms *différance, gram,* and *trace.* That these terms build on *négatité* is, however, apparent in his earlier account of indication as "the process of death at work in signs" (SP: 40). Derrida's phrasing recalls Sartre's account of the Other as "the death of my possibilities in so far as I live that death as hidden in the midst of the world" (BN: 354). By transferring "death" from the transcendental sphere of being to the ordinary sphere of language Derrida marks its inescapability, its imperceptible penetration of our daily existence through the signs by which we live in the world.

Indeed, Sartre's notion of *négatité* casts light on what many see as a Derridean aporia, namely, that *différance* is at once transcendent and inescapably immanent. *Différance* is a transcendence constituted in immanence.[16] As transcendence it is the disclosure, within the particular, of "an essential relation . . . to the world," a "rubric . . . which presides over the arrangement and the redistribution of great masses of being in things" (BN: 59). But as immanence it cannot be thrown back into the theoretism of being a category: it is "hidden in the midst of the world" as the underlying condition of all our "relations of instrumentality" (59). Sartre speaks of "an infinite number of realities" that are thus "*inhabited* by negation" (55; emphasis mine). Like the death that Derrida discerns in signs, Sartre locates these pools of nonbeing throughout mundane life: in a visit to a café or a meeting with a stranger in the park.

No Exit: The Double Bind of Nothingness

We could say that a world thus "affected with non-being" (BN: 59) is the product of a certain projection. And indeed Sartre admits this because it is man who brings death into the world, thus disclosing more about his relation to being than about being itself. We could then partition the field of being and nothingness and allow Heidegger to speak for this "Being" that Sartre neglects. However, we are concerned here not with philosophical equity, but with unfolding the errors constitutive for a certain phase of theory. In this context, Sartre's power as a contemporary thinker lies not only in his disclosure of the negative but precisely in his radical, even unreasonable foreclosure of any exit to Being.

Sartre's early work, "when existentialism was not yet a humanism,"[17] is an unrelenting, unremitting deconstruction of the transcendental and Being. French commentators on *Nausea* saw, in Roquentin's encounter with the sheer superfluity of things in the public garden, a thematization of Heideggerian *Dasein*. But here it is a question not of *Dasein* as the being-there of "man" but of the being-there (*être-là*) of things in their fullness and redundancy. In other words, Sartre dehumanizes the relation to Being; he deliberately rereads *Dasein* as the nauseating abject of a materiality that is *de trop* so as to close off any escape into Spirit through what Heidegger calls "the original openness of beings."[18]

In *Being and Nothingness* Sartre similarly unworks but then *also* disfigures both Being and the identity with itself that Being represents for the human. First he unworks the *en-soi* as a positive term, recasting it diacritically. The *en-soi* is linked to the *pour-soi* in a relationship of internal negation such that it discloses the radical contingency of consciousness but without functioning as Being in any conventional sense. On the one hand the for-itself, it is true, stands in a seemingly binary relation to the in-itself as a nothingness that lacks being. It is from this opposition that the self derives its nihilating structure as a "being that is not what it is and is what it is not." Yet the relation of the terms is structured more by supplementarity than by opposition. For the in-itself is itself a lack of negativity, which for Sartre is the internal distance and difference that generate possibility. Being is absolute identity; it "is not a connection with itself. It is *itself*" (27). Lacking the structure of the *pour-soi* as "reference" and transcendence (or noncoincidence), being for Sartre is an "immanence which can not realize itself . . . an activity which can not act, because it is glued to itself" (27–28). It is "opaque to itself precisely because it is filled with itself" in a "synthesis of itself with itself" (28). Or, put differently, being"knows no otherness; it never posits itself as *other-than-another-being*. It can support no connection with the other. It is itself indefinitely. . . . From this point of view . . . it is not subject to temporality" (29).

But, second, as these cloying descriptions suggest, Sartre does not stop at a supplementary relation between the *en-soi* and *pour-soi* that is still phenomenally intelligible in terms of a dialectic, albeit an aporetic one. He describes the *en-soi* in language that is at once philosophical and brutally material. As "immanence" the in-itself does not simply put an end to transcendence or noncoincidence; it is "glued to itself," filled with its own "obesity" as Baudrillard puts it (FS: 27–32). Indeed, it is "inhuman," in de Man's terms (RT: 96), or "obscene" in the terms of Žižek, who picks up Sartre's imagery of the viscous in his own figure of a "repelling" and "sticky" excess.[19] The *en-soi* is the corpse of being, through which Sartre defaces any possibility of being except as what Foucault describes as an "inertia . . . that does not and never can lead to self-consciousness" (OT: 322).

On an ontological level, then, Sartre radically de-idealizes Heidegger. He renounces the possibility of a "clearing" by transposing the phenomenality of *Dasein* into the materiality of the *en-soi*. Being thus becomes that deliverance from desire and lack that Lacan parodies as the phallus and that Sartre himself describes as "massif" (BN: 27). But while he thus seals off any escape from existence to spirit, Sartre does sometimes fall back into a negative hypostasis of the very *pour-soi* that he also deconstructs as "un néant qui veut être." From this double bind there arises the self-negating and aporetic anthropology we associate with Sartrean existentialism: a supplementary recuperation of what is really (in Bataille's terms) an "unusable negativity" through a nihilating "freedom" that is always already in bad faith. Nothingness as freedom is of course Sartre's "exit," which Levinas criticizes when he argues instead for a "being without nothingness," an "irremissible being," which "leaves no hole and permits no escape" (TO: 50). The problematic nature of Sartrean freedom helps explain the turn to Heidegger after the war. Still, it is not enough to dismiss Sartre by pointing out that French theory turns away from him to a radicalized Heidegger. As late as 1962 the same Derrida who later excoriates Sartre also speaks of the latter's "breakthrough" (*trouée*). Remembering Sartre's ontology rather than his politics, Derrida attributes to him the deconstruction that "has so profoundly unbalanced— and then overthrown—the landscape of Husserl's phenomenology and abandoned its horizon" (OG: 125n). In effect, Derrida—as he also does in his comments to de Man (RT: 119)—admits the seminal role of the prewar Sartre in the genealogy of contemporary theory.

This seminality has two aspects. One is Sartre's difference from Heidegger as "something between mistake and error" and hence "capable of dialectical development."[20] To trace this difference is to incorporate Sartre into the corpus of theory, as much of this book attempts to do. But the other aspect of Sartre's legacy is less easy to set aside or take in, as he himself never fully digested it. We can describe it in Blanchot's words as a sense of that "unformed nothingness pushed towards us by the residue of being that cannot be eliminated" (GO: 80)—a nothingness precipitated by being and not by man and uncontainable even in a radicalized anthropology. For Sartre's experience of the negative is profoundly split. On the one hand, the emptiness of the *pour-soi*, its interior distances, and its vicious circularity as a "reflected-reflecting" (BN: 122) are all the condition of possibility for its freedom. Negativity is thus productive, even if more contingently than in Hegel. On the other hand, the human project is constantly menaced, not by its own hyperreflection, but by the inhuman as that which irrevocably resists reflection.[21] Put differently, the very dialectic by which the *pour-soi* as emptiness makes itself different from being's repellent fullness is itself figurally constituted by the repression of a being that, as "transphenomenal" (9), cannot actually be figured. In the last section of *Being and Nothingness* this being returns excessively, decentering Sartre's argument. It returns not as the in-itself that is "the condition of the sharpness of [the for-itself's] outlines" but as the viscous or slimy, which is neither solid nor liquid, and thus indifferent to any difference between *en-soi* and *pour-soi* (55, 774–76).

In the following section I suggest that this materiality or transphenomenality of being is what places Sartre's thought so much ahead of the step he is accused of not taking in *Nausea*. As we have seen, Žižek characterizes the postmodern in terms of presence and the foreclosure of the absence that permits *différance* and the trace. Postmodernism is the "obscene" presence of the Thing, made visible in its "indifferent and arbitrary character," whereas modernism lets us grasp this "emptiness" in terms of a distance that keeps desire in being. Modernism thus proves that "the intersubjective machine, works as well if the Thing is lacking, if the machine revolves around an *emptiness*."[22] According to Robbe-Grillet in "Nature, Humanism, Tragedy," his influential critique of *Nausea* as still complicit with metaphysics, Sartre remains on the modern side of this division by converting emptiness into the "interior distance" of a "solitude." But Robbe-Grillet's own *chosisme* of hard, contoured objects keeps the inhuman safely on the outside. Similarly Levinas implicitly criticizes Sartrean "nothingness" for eliding the sheer "materiality" and "presence" of the there is. And yet his own figuration of this presence as "night" makes it invisible (EE: 58–60) and stops short of where Sartre goes, namely, towards Žižek's "inert presence" that precludes any residue of an "innaccessible, absent, transcendent agency."[23] To be sure, *Being and Nothingness* retains the concepts of lack, difference, transcendence, and reflection that Baudrillard, well before Žižek, also associates with modernity (CS: 187–93). These concepts preserve the subject in the mode of alienation. But Sartre is at once a modern and a postmodern thinker and exists in the traumatic gap between the two. In this gap lies his importance for deconstruction, poststructuralism, and the aporia between them.

The Obscene Object of Being: Nausea, the Slimy, and Levinas's "Horror"

Sartre comes face to face with this obscenity of the postmodern in his discussions of the body and the viscous. For the viscous is a new kind of being that is the catalyst for a different experience of nothingness. Whereas the *en-soi* is hard or solid, the viscous is the disintegration of this self-containedness that the *pour-soi* projects as its transcendent (im)possibility. As long as being was in-itself, it was alien but comprehensible; as Levinas says, a world "made up of solids" is "stable;" it "shows itself to us and is open to our grasp" (EE:

42). But the viscous is this in-itself that the for-itself could be, always already draining away into the "hole" of the for-itself. At the same time it is also, absurdly, the for-itself becoming in-itself, as if in a double disintegration both of being-in-itself and of its supplementary replacement by a being that is at least, negatively, for-itself. Thus Sartre writes of the primal scene of the slimy: "there is a sticky thickness in its liquidity . . . a dawning triumph of the solid over the liquid—that is, a tendency of the indifferent in-itself, which is represented by the pure solid, to fix the liquidity, to absorb the for-itself which ought to dissolve it" (BN: 774).The viscous is the radically other, not a human, but a thingly alterity. It is "an indifferent exteriority . . . [a] foundationless existence" (776). Yet as a nonself, it will not stay outside, but "sticks to me, draws me, sucks at me" (776). In effect, it is neither one thing nor the other but rather a Kafkan *metamorphosis*" (777), a horrible confusion of categories: the material "combined with the psychic" (771), outside with inside, being with nothingness. The viscous congeals thought. Anticipating Kristeva's abject as the disintegration of the difference between subject and object necessary to predication, Sartre says that the viscous is the disappearance of difference into the same; it "presents a constant hysteresis in the phenomenon of being transmuted into itself," "everywhere fleeing and yet everywhere similar to itself" (775–76). Herein lies the nothingness with which it afflicts his text: the impossibility of any differentiated and thus human being.

But the viscous is the catachresis of a hysteria that progressively preoccupies the text, working against the grain of its attempts to economize the negative. Thus, much earlier Sartre had already spoken of the "fresh blood [and] excrement" that "make us vomit" (445), interrupting the phenomenality of his argument with other lurid figures such as drain-holes and hemorrhages (343–45). These catachreses, in turn, literalize a viscosity in the text's very concepts. For example, there is the famous scene in the park that introduces the dialectic of the look. Modelled on the master-slave relation—and more specifically on Kojève's channeling of negativity into a competitive, anthropogenetic desire in the first chapter of his reading of Hegel—this scene seems to reconfirm the founding difference of the *pour-soi* and *en-soi* as a dialectic of self and other, culminating in the unstable negation of one or other entity. But it seems this anthropogenesis is a conceptual figure used to contain a more diffuse panic, even as the other is himself a figure covering over an inexplicable "disintegration of the universe" (344). One remembers that it was in another park that Roquentin discovered, in the trauma of things unmoored from their names, what Levinas calls the "horror" of a "*there is* [that] resists a personal form,"[24] "an existing that occurs without us, without a subject" (TO: 45). In *Being and Nothingness* Sartre apprehends this existing in the "closed 'Gestalt'" of the Other, in order to have " a full object . . . to grasp." But at "the heart of this solid, visible form" the Other "makes himself a particular emptying . . . [and] flight," "a fixed sliding of the whole universe." Moreover, the very word "makes" is no more than a phantasmatic figure of agency, an anthropomorphism that the passage itself de-faces. For it seems that the world is "perpetually flowing off" through "a kind of drain hole in the middle of its being" and that the Other is no more than a way of "determin[ing]" this "internal hemorrhage" through a prosopopeia that gives it a face (BN: 343–45).

Let us take a second example, namely, the very distinction between *pour-soi* and *en-soi*. On the surface consciousness and things, though connected by internal negation, are still protected by a Cartesian separation (26). In other words the *pour-soi*, despite its structure as self-nihilating, aporetic reflection, at least functions in identifiable opposition to the *en-soi*. There is even a reciprocity in their supplementarity. Thus the *pour-soi* is "a lack of being in the face of being" (127), and yet the *en-soi* as "the synthesis of itself with itself" (28) lacks this internal difference and distance; the in-itself "in a project to found itself" must therefore "g[i]ve itself the modification of the for-itself" (790). This reciprocity permits a dialectic, granted that it is also an impasse. In short, Sartre seems to separate *pour-soi* and *en-soi* so as to direct and determine nothingness as human "possibility." The *en-soi* is indifferent and thus without possibility; it is inert, "glued to itself," and also safely outside (27–28). The *pour-soi* in its self-cancelling nothingness is at least dynamic and dissolves the inert—later the practico-inert; it is thus a kind of negative "spirit."

Yet this "absolute interiority" of consciousness (404) is disrupted by its own exteriority through the breach made by the body. For the body is constructed from the outside in. It is not known inwardly through intuition but only by analogy with the other's body; it is even given to us in language by and for the other, for example by the scientist who identifies and assembles its parts (410, 464).[25] Alternatively it is disclosed to us by things: "Far from the body being first *for us* and revealing things to us, it is the instrumental-things which . . . indicate our body to us." My body is therefore outside: "on the chair, in the whole house" (428). It passes over into the body of the other: "When a doctor takes my wounded leg and looks at it" there is no difference "between [my] visual perception . . . of the doctor's body and . . . my own leg" (402). Moreover this body, though externally given, is not a to-tality because one receives it in bits and pieces, as a leg prosthetically emerg-ing from the doctor's body or a "dead eye in the midst of the . . . world" (403). Nor is it really external like a chair because "I exist my body" as the "perpetual 'outside' of my most intimate 'inside'" (460–61). Put differently, the body is "what . . . consciousness *is*." For although Sartre tries to make it "a conscious structure of my consciousness," he ends by saying that con-sciousness "is not even anything except body" (434). The body thus unrav-els the difference between *pour-soi* and *en-soi*; it is an inside that has been wrenched outside, even as it is also an outside that has appeared inside. As Sartre concedes, anticipating his description of the viscous, it "is the in-it-self which is surpassed by the nihilating for-itself and which reapprehends the for-itself in this very surpassing" (409). This indistinguishability of sub-ject and object accounts for the nausea, the threat of nothingness, that punctuates this section (445, 450–51, 468).

It is worth pausing again over this aporia of nothingness, which goes to the heart of Sartre's relation to anthropology, as well as to the thought that instead follows a Heideggerian turn to "ontology."[26] On the one hand, Sartre is conventionally linked to Hegel via Kojève, with whom he shares an emphasis on freedom, death, and the master-slave relationship. These affini-ties explain why Sartrean nothingness is so often taken as the ground for a Hegelian, Kojèvian anthropology that makes man the end of history and the source of nothingness. Kojève writes, for instance, that "Man is essentially *Negativity*, for Time is *Becoming*—that is the *annihilation* of Being or Space. Therefore Man is a Nothingness that nihilates and that preserves itself in (spatial) Being only by *negating* being, this Negation being Action."[27] In his postwar work Sartre will indeed emphasize negation as a nihilating position, thus strengthening and politicizing the negative anthropology that first emerges in *The Psychology of Imagination* before it resurfaces in *Being and Nothingness* in the specification of the "negation as being" (64). But as we have seen this negativity is constantly uprooted by a different kind of nothingness, more like that described by Levinas in *Existence and Existents* (1946)—a text that shares more with Sartre than does Levinas's subsequent work and that Levinas describes as a "phenomenology."[28] Here Levinas speaks of a general reversion "to nothingness," which he also describes as "being in general": "the *there is*, inasmuch as it resists a personal form, is 'being in general'." Levinas cannot define the there is except apophatically, as what it is not. It is not being in-itself or for-itself, but the absence of any such identity: "We have not derived this notion from exterior things or the inner world—from any 'being' whatever. For *there is* transcends inwardness as well as exteriority; it does not even make it possible to distinguish these" (EE: 57). As the impossibility of distinguishing outside and inside, the *il y a* also abolishes the difference between being and nothingness. It is not being in any positive sense, even that of Heidegger, as Levinas indicates by using the words "night" and "absence" against the "light" he associates with Heidegger (47–51). And yet it is not nothingness, at least not the nothingness that "ought" to dissolve Sartre's viscous (BN: 774). For the *il y a* as the disappearance of all existents—things or persons—leaves behind an excessive residue of materiality: "The disappearance of all things and of the I leaves what cannot disappear, the sheer fact of being in which *one* participates, whether one wants to or not. . . . Being remains . . . like a heavy atmosphere belonging to no one, universal, returning in the midst of the negation which put it aside, and in all the powers to which that negation may be multiplied" (EE: 58). Indeed, it is through this *materiality* of being that Levinas achieves a thinking that abandons subjectivity, whereas Heidegger's immateriality of being-as-light reassimilates such thought into what Derrida calls the metonymic series reason:consciousness:spirit:subject.[29]

But this excessive materiality is precisely what Sartre also confronts in *Nausea* and in the section on the slimy. To be sure, Levinas is at pains to mark his difference from Sartre, whom he cannot avoid evoking, if not by name. Levinas thus insists on the term *horror* rather than *nausea*: "'Nausea,' as a feeling for existence, is not yet a depersonalization; but horror turns the subjectivity of the subject . . . inside out. It is a participation in the *there is* which returns in the heart of every negation . . . [and] that has 'no exits'" (61). But if nausea differs from horror, it is not on the ground identified here, namely, its sublation into the "negation." There is no exit in Sartre's novel into the negation; like horror, nausea is "immediately there" and cannot be "grasp[ed] through a thought" (58). Indeed, as Blanchot recognized in his review of *Nausea* (1938), Sartre "takes the novel to a place where there are no longer any incidents, any plot, any particular person; to that site where the mind sustains itself" by focusing on "existence and being" and on the nausea of "exist[ing] without being."[30]

It is no accident that Blanchot uses Levinasian terminology, even before Levinas himself had fully theorized that existence without existents in which "all beings, things, and persons, revert to nothingness" (EE: 57). Interestingly Levinas had written extensively on nausea in *De l'évasion*, three years before the publication of Sartre's novel on which, however, Sartre was working much earlier. *Nausea* is the term both theorists use to rethink Heidegger's enlightenment of being within the particular ethos of a prewar Europe that Levinas, like Blanchot, figures by the word *night*. For Levinas, nausea involves the disappearance of all existents and points of orientation. Inasmuch as it is an indeterminate *mal-aise* irreducible to a precipitating object, nausea is not, as Levinas later says, a "quality of an object" correlatively linked to a subject (EE: 58). On the contrary, it is precisely what he later describes as horror. Nausea is the suffocating and "revolting presence of ourself to ourself"; it is "the nudity of being in its plenitude and in its irremmissible presence" that causes one to be "riveted to oneself." In nausea we come up against the "pure being" that Levinas later calls the *il y à*.

As Jacques Rolland explains, this pure being radically recasts the relation of being and nothingness—a turn signaled by the replacement of the Heideggerian term *anxiety* with *nausea* as the mood or *Stimmung* for what Heidegger calls the "slipping away of beings" into nothing.[31] For Heidegger (as Sartre too observes) "the nothing" is simply a background for being(s) and thus a night symptomatically described as "clear." Heidegger writes: "In the clear night of the nothing of anxiety the original openness of beings as such arises: that they are beings—and not nothing. . . . The essence of the originally nihilating nothing lies in this, that it brings Da-sein for the first time before beings as such."[32] In other words, though "human existence" can understand beings "only on the ground . . . of the nothing," by "being held out into the nothing" this existence "emerges . . . from the nothing" and "relates itself to beings" (103) through "hypostasis" (EE: 65–72; TO: 51–54). But, as Rolland argues, for Levinas—and also Sartre—being(s) cannot be distinguished from nothing; nausea is rather the *return* of the nothingness disclosed by being, the "coming-upon-us" of the nothing, or of "the nothing *as return*."[33] Levinas's images for this return of the nothing are precisely "sticking" (*adhérence*) and vomit; vomit is the attempt to expel what returns (from) inside us as a foreignness that suffocates us from within.[34] Nausea is the impossibility of the hypostasis that Heidegger's ontology still allows.

By 1946 Levinas wants to distance himself from Sartre, even at the cost of giving up a term he himself had favored. By then Sartre had moved from an anthropology riveted to its unthought to one that felt obliged to be pragmatic. Yet the earlier Sartre enters *Existence and Existents* as an ellipsis that Levinas marks when he attributes to the war "the absence of any consideration of those philosophical works published, with so much impact, between 1940 and 1945" (EE: 15). It is surely these works in their unthematized historical urgency that create a space for a thought "inspired" by Heidegger but "governed by a profound need to leave the climate of that philosophy" (19). Sartre and Levinas both read Heidegger in the years before the Occupation, which became the preoccupation of the thought of being with an unspecifiable nothingness. It is for this reason that Derrida echoes Levinas when he describes Sartre's relation to another German philosopher whom Levinas also associates with light. For Derrida, we recall, also writes of Sartre's philosophy as a deterritorialization that overthrew "the landscape of Husserl's phenomenology" thus abandoning "its horizon" (OG: 125n).

Sartre's encounter with the there is as the defacement of his own project first unfolds in the scene in *Nausea* where Roquentin picks up a pebble that is flat and dry on one side, humid and muddy on the other. This experience begins a series of antiepiphanies about "changes" in the structure of objects that reciprocally unravel the *pour-soi*. As a figure for the *en-soi* the pebble discloses that the being of things is not in-itself, accessible within the order of sight and light. Things are oppressively material, unusable, excessive. And yet one cannot turn from the outside to the inside as in conventional models of alienation that Sartre is accused of following by Robbe-Grillet. For the inside of the pebble is unassimilably slimy; it is this exteriority of inner experience that evokes the feeling of "disgust" or nausea.[35] Sartre, in other words, does not ascribe being to things, nor does he derive it from the inner world. And yet he is concerned with thinking being because in the section on the viscous nothingness derives precisely from "being in general" or from what Sartre, anticipating Levinas, already calls the "there is" (BN: 770, 773).

But Levinas is right to distinguish himself from Sartre even for the wrong reasons. "Nausea," Levinas writes, "is not yet a depersonalization" (EE: 59) because it registers a feeling. Likewise the viscous, as a "quality" (BN: 770), is a human perception, which is why Levinas struggles to avoid thinking the negative as "the quality of an object" (EE: 58) any more than as the feeling of a subject. Of course Levinas does not really get rid of affect; his "empiricism" is, in Wahl's words, a particular "metaphysical" empiricism that character-izes the "philosophies of existence" and combines facticity with affectivity.[36] Horror also is not really a depersonalization. Indeed, Levinas's break with Sartre is less radical than he thinks. For one thing, in descriptions of insom-nia, eating, and fatigue he does not entirely abandon "descriptive phenom-enology" (EE: 66). Levinas would of course argue that phenomenology "pre-supposes an ego" capable of capturing the phenomenenon through descrip-tion (66), and indeed, this is true enough of the "regional" or descriptive phenomenologies outlined by Husserl as subdivisions of transcendental phe-nomenology. But Sartre's descriptions, in particular of corporeal phenomena such as eating "oysters or raw eggs," aim to bring out precisely their "transphenomenality" (BN: 770, 779). In addition, Levinas's emphasis on "physiological psychology" recalls Sartre, not Husserl or Heidgger. In emo-tion—Sartre's subject in *Sketch for a Theory of the Emotions* (1939)—the body overwhelms us, impeding our hypostasis as mind or spirit. Emotion "puts into question not the existence, but the subjectivity of the subject; it pre-vents the subject from gathering itself up, reacting, being someone" (EE: 70). Despite this shared territory, Levinas nevertheless differs from Sartre in what Derrida calls his "nonviolence" (WD: 146). He lets being be; he ap-proaches it nonviolently through "anonymous vigilance" (EE: 66). Levinas's withdrawal of all attributes from being is a letting-go or ascesis. By contrast Sartre evokes the absolute unacceptability of a being defined by superfluity, rather than by subtraction, detachment, and renunciation. And it is here that he is both behind and beyond Levinas.

Sartre anthropomorphizes the encounter with being by surrounding it with his own projections. But this does not mean that he preserves the sub-ject, for nausea is the double defacement of being and the human by each other. Let us take as an example the bizarre introduction of the viscous as an elaboration of "existential psychoanalysis" (BN: 764), to which Sartre has al-ready devoted several more conventional pages. In his earlier monograph on

the emotions Sartre draws on Husserl and Heidegger to rethink psychoanalysis as "phenomenological psychology." Sartre's study, including his
turning of phenomenology towards "anthropology," sketches a theoretical
basis for the more practical work of existential psychoanalysis done by Ludwig Binswanger, R.D. Laing, and others. Sartre writes that for "human reality, to exist is, according to Heidegger, to assume its own being in an existential mode of understanding." Existential psychoanalysis studies pathological behavior as the "showing" of something authentically human; in
other words it effects a humanization (though not normalization) of the
strange.[37] Yet in the section on the viscous, Sartre disembowels his project of
rethinking psychology across phenomenology by confronting humanism
with "ek-sistence." Evoking Bachelard, whom he had earlier credited with
an internal critique of phenomenology (428), Sartre attempts a "psychoanalysis of things" (765)—an estrangement of the human into a thing analyzed as human. Moreover, this psychoanalysis is not an anthropology; it
does not "bring to light . . . the subjective choice" by which we become
"person[s]" (734). It is rather an ontology concerned with "a certain way
which being has of giving itself" (764).

Through this mutant form of existential psychoanalysis, which parodies
rather than resembles other work by that name, Sartre con-fuses the human
and thingly, the psychic and the physical (771). It is as though mind is stuck
in matter or as if "material substances have a psychic meaning which renders them repugnant, horrifying" (772). What this confusion, or abjection,
threatens is a reversal in which man and thing exchange places. Indeed, this
last section is a *mise-en-abîme* of the larger text that disfigures its tenuous
anthropology through what Merleau-Ponty calls an "ontological" rather
than existential psychoanalysis.[38] But "ontological" is also a misnomer because Bachelard's "psychoanalysis of things" becomes in Sartre's hands a catachresis, a trope for what cannot be named. In this context, the "upsurge of
the for-itself in being," as the grotesque presumption to psychoanalyze
things, is an "appropriation" unveiled as "flight" and reabsorbed by the materiality it seeks to avoid (779). This defacement of humanism, with its disclosure of the tropological structure of "appropriation," seems virtually to
be staged by the text as a scene of self-reading. Sartre seems to be speaking
of his own text when he writes,"the slimy offers a horrible image; it is horrible in itself for a consciousness to *become slimy*. . . . A consciousness which

became slimy would be transformed by the thick stickiness of its ideas"
(778). Through the viscous Sartre does indeed think "being" just as much
as Levinas or Heidegger do, but with this difference: he cannot approach it
nonviolently. Because it is the for-itself that "exists" being (778) and because without this for-itself being would not *exist* but only be, being cannot simply be left to itself and in itself. Being unfolds "across human reality," a phrase Sartre is not alone among French thinkers in retaining even
after the turn from anthropology in the late forties (see LE: 17, 179). And
here it is worth asking what Sartre actually means by "human reality," a
term he does indeed use throughout *Being and Nothingness* in revisionary
proximity to *Dasein*. Human reality is not a reality controlled by the human, but a pathos, a pathology. As Sartre says in his *Wartime Diaries*, human reality does not mean "that man is anterior to the meaning of things."
Rather the term suggests that being, in its transphenomenality, signifies—
or perhaps utterly fails to signify—*for man*. But man is not a cogito; he is
"transcendence" (BN: 767), which is to say that his being escapes him. As
Hyppolite explains, transcendence is what is "irreducible to our knowledge"; it is the "unthought" or "non-knowledge" that escapes the concept
(LE: 3, 7). What being signifies for man is in part his missed encounter
with (his) being.

In *The Wartime Diaries* Sartre's example of human reality is precisely the
viscous, which he offers as the first in an inventory of "real categories," including elasticity and flakiness "whence man comes slowly to himself" as to
his own radical exteriority.[39] These phenomena-phenomena in the sense that
they cannot be grasped noumenally but only as they appear for consciousness—are yet not "phenomenally" knowable by the understanding in any
Kantian sense; they are material and tactile, not visible and legible. They do
not "show" themselves except as a "quality," which is to say "a symbol of a
being which totally escapes us" (BN: 770). In other words, "quality as a revelation of being" (765) indicates an opacity in the way being gives itself to
man, allegorically rather than in its essence. Moreover, a quality such as the
slimy is a trope, an anthropomorphism. In this sense what is disclosed by
the being of things, or by being as a thing, is precisely *Dasein* as "this human
reality that we do not even understand is ourselves."[40]

Human reality, then, includes a certain transphenomenality of the
human as the Real that eludes symbolic recognition or imaginary identifica-

tion. It is this insistence of the Real that gives rise to what Sartre calls nausea. And while the last section sees an uncontrollable eruption of nausea, it is also present elsewhere, notably in the strange, cyborg descriptions of the body as the exteriority of the inside, its parts detaching themselves as hallucinatory "figure[s] on the body-as-ground" (470, 466). This exteriority of the inside is what Bataille, writing at the same time as Sartre, describes as "inner experience." For Sartre I "exist" this pre-thetic body without organs before it is named and returned to me as "sign [and] identification" through the "alienating, cognitive stratum" of the "Other's concepts" (466). But this synthetic totality does not allow me to "possess" my experience through language and concept; rather it constitutes experience as a transcendence that "escapes me" (466). The Sartrean subject "ek-sists" but cannot "gather itself up." Early in the text Sartre admits that the *pour-soi* is produced by a relation of figure and ground. The for-itself, he says, is founded through a repression of the in-itself that, "engulfed and nihilated . . . remains at the heart of the for-itself as its original contingency" (130).

To disclose this Real that resists symbolization, Sartre seems driven to dismember figuration and perception as the phantasmatic supports of conventional notions of experience, knowledge, and self. He begins and ends the section on the body with the scene already mentioned, where he imagines an "arrangement of the sense organs such that a living being could see one of his eyes while the eye which was seen was directing its glance upon the world" (402). Like Bataille, who disfigures the body so as to question "the horizontal axis of vision" that founds the cogito,[41] Sartre imagines bits of the self "outside in the midst of the world"—his eye, his eyelid, the doctor's ear; hands or arms "without synthetic connection with the corporal totality (402, 420, 462, 454). At other points he sees the inside of his body on a screen during a radioscopy (402) and sees the body as a corpse (456–58), the corpse being both literal and a figure for all that the body figures, from the past self to language (434). As Blanchot says, perhaps remembering Sartre, the corpse figures what cannot be embodied, what is "not in its place," the "remains" (GO: 81, 84).

In the section on the body Sartre tries to absorb these descriptions into a theory of contingency that becomes the basis for existentialism. Yet they obsessively exceed their place in the argument that, instead of a philosophical system, becomes a wartime diary of phenomenology thought at its very limit. They recall the dis-figurations of surrealism that were so seminal for deconstruction and which Foucault associates with "the tortured body [and] the flesh" as the "materiality" of "unthinkable thought" (OT: 381–82). Interviewed in 1983, de Man is evasive about his debts to phenomenology as traditionally understood, but speaks of the powerful influence on him of "Surrealism, specifically Bataille, Blanchot, even . . . Bachelard" (RT: 118–19). But in the sections on the body and the viscous, and in the discussions of figuration as (self)nihilation that run like a leitmotiv through the text, Sartre comes close to this sur-realization of phenomenology, which will also be attempted, less cruelly, in Merleau-Ponty's *Phenomenology of Perception* (1945).

These sections are Sartre's uncanniest contribution to theory—one that returns in de Man's work and in Kristeva's notion of the abject. They approach the conjunction that Merleau-Ponty later projects between phenomenology and psychoanalysis. In 1960 Merleau-Ponty writes, "it is by what phenomenology implies or unveils as its limits—by its *latent content* or its *unconscious*—that [it] is in consonance with psychoanalysis."[42] In its most radical moments *Being and Nothingness* unveils this inner experience of phenomenology. This is Sartre's breakthrough (*trouée*)—aptly linked by Derrida to Sartre's favorite image of the hole—by which he so unbalances the landscape of phenomenology as to prepare a space for deconstruction.

The Dead Runner: Three Revisionary Ratios[43]

Recognizing Sartre's role in 1962 Derrida, as we have seen, evokes the split genesis of deconstruction. Yet from the late sixties on he simplifies and abjects Sartre in a turn to Husserl, Heidegger, and sometimes Hegel. In the process certain properties of Sartre are transferred to "Heidegger" so as to legitimate the forgetting of the one in the other. This is particularly evident in "Différance" (1968), which displaces the Sartrean subtext of *Speech and Phenomena* (1967) that I explore in the next chapter with a celebration of Heidegger that strains beyond the greater cautiousness about the German philosopher in "The Ends of Man." What is repressed in this new version of deconstruction and still not fully registered in French deconstruction of the eighties is a complex genealogy masked by the current idealization of Heidegger, his "turning," and turnings that disavow the past. What is put to rest is Sartre's remains—his tortured, aporetic cogito, but even more the unpalatable, viscous nothingness of nausea.

Chiasm: Blanchot between Heidegger and Sartre

But this is not what happens in an earlier deconstruction. For in returning to Heidegger, French theory after the war turned not to Heidegger but to an undoing of the metaphysics of identity read aslant Sartre. The early Blanchot, for instance, moves away from Sartre's anthropological emphasis to what seems a more Heideggerian concern with a thrownness and essential solitude that unworks even Sartre's negative, deferred hypostasis of the cogito. Yet Blanchot is interested not in the work of art but in worklessness, not in Being but in the nothingness of a being de-posited in a Literature that is not a "shelter" but "a sojourn devoid of *place.*"[44] Blanchot is Heidegger with a minus sign. As Levinas says, despite "many points of perfect agreement," he shifts the space of literature from "day" to "night," from "light" to "a black light . . . that undoes the world": "In Blanchot, the work uncovers, in an uncovering that is not truth, a darkness."[45] Lyotard has said that the critique of Heidegger is "a "French" affair" and that from Rimbaud to Beckett it is what the French "call 'writing' that reveal[s] . . . what every representation misses." Lyotard could be speaking of Blanchot when he writes that French literature and philosophy have found themselves "in charge of . . . [an] irremediable darkening" of "Enlightenment."[46] Blanchot's work is just such a darkening of Heidegger even as it is a "writing" that opens Sartre to his own subtexts.

We cannot trace Blanchot's relationship to Sartre extensively, except to note with Michael Holland that at a certain stage his thought "is so close to Blanchot's own as to pose a serious challenge to it," as is evident in Blanchot's review of *La Nausée* (1938) and his essay "The Novel Is a Work of Bad Faith" (1947). In the former Blanchot praises Sartre for a literature that strips away subject and plot to confront the nausea of "exist[ence] without being."[47] Blanchot's critical kinship with Sartre is, however, most evident in his essay "Literature and the Right to Death" (1947). For this essay, often taken as a repudiation of Sartre, is Blanchot's own theoretical autobiography: a return of and retreat from the Sartrean origins that inaugurate his distinctive vision of literature as the (un)working of the negative. The essay is indeed a critique of Sartre's *What Is Literature?* (1947), the manifesto of Sartre's political conversion. But it is also an unworking of this Sartre through a working back to an earlier Sartre whose focus on "nothingness" had much in common both with Bataille's "inner experience" and with what Foucault calls Blanchot's "thought of the outside."

Sartre's presence in the essay can be felt in its opening references to the "nothingness" that the writer ex-scribes as he seeks identity through his work. As Blanchot details the process of writing from intention to finished text, he discloses little pools of nonbeing at every moment of this process. Literature reveals the "emptiness inside" (*ce dedans vide*), and, even as the author becomes one with his work, he becomes other than himself through its reading (GO: 22, 24, 26). As a "nothingness working in nothingness, to borrow an expression of Hegel's" (24), the writer confronts a negativity that is the very essence of language: "A word may give me its meaning, but first it suppresses it. For me to be able to say 'This woman,' I must somehow take her flesh and blood reality away from her, cause her to be absent, annihilate her [*la rende absente et l'anéantisse*]. The word gives me the being, but it gives it to me deprived of being. The word is the absence of that being, its nothingness [*néant*]" (42). This disclosure of the word as absence is at the heart of the turn given by Derrida to Saussure's view that language has no positive terms or, as Blanchot puts it, that the image "does not directly designate the thing" but "what the thing is not" (45). Blanchot in turn draws this idea of the word as (an)nihilation from Sartre, who writes: "Poets are men who refuse to *utilize* language. . . . Nor do they dream of *naming* the world . . . for naming implies a perpetual sacrifice of the name to the object named, or, as Hegel would say, the name is revealed as the inessential in the face of the thing which is essential."[48] Sartre's theory of naming takes up his earlier analysis of perception as a positing constituted on the trace of what it nihilates. The earlier Sartre was less interested in the positing than in the "nihilation" it disclosed. Nihilation is at the heart of positing as is "effacement" for Blanchot and "erasure" for de Man.[49] In *What Is Literature?* Sartre draws back from this nihilation; he takes up the task of Hegel, thus eliding nothingness to reaffirm negation as predication. But his theory of naming is a linguistic development of his early account of perception in which predication occurred only through the nihilation of a difference that marked position as imposition. And it is to this earlier account that Blanchot returns when he speaks of the word as awakening to the absence of the being it restores.

As important in establishing a dialogue with Sartre is the description of literature as divided along two "slopes": "meaningful prose" and poetry (48, 51–52). The distinction recalls *What Is Literature?* where Sartre too partitions prose from poetry. Whereas prose for Sartre is instrumental, poetry "considers words as things and not as signs," thus replacing the annihilating knowledge of "things by their name" with a "silent contact," a "suggestion of the incommunicable." Both forms of literature are linked in a "common front" against bourgeois society, but while the prose writer is "*in a situation* in language," the poet is "outside of language . . . meeting the word as a barrier as he comes toward men." The poet seeks to become one with his nothingness through a "defeat" that "returns him to himself in his purity."[50] Likewise for Blanchot there is a productive negativity, "turned toward the movement of negation by which things are separated from themselves and destroyed in order to be known, subjugated, communicated." Such negation does not stop at words but reads through them: "Hence its distrust of words, its need to apply the movement of negation to language itself and to exhaust it by realizing it as that totality on the basis of which each term would be nothing" (48–49). Then there is another literature, also turned towards the negation of "day" and light, but as a letting-appear, an "endless resifting of words without content" that is a "concern for the . . . unknown, free, and silent existence" of things (49–50).

Blanchot places himself on the second slope. Literature, he says, by "turning itself into the inability to reveal anything," becomes "the revelation of what revelation destroys" (47). But in moving away from Sartre, Blanchot turns, not to poetry as Heidegger sees it, but to a space of literature he compares to Levinas's *il y a* (51n). The *il y a* rewrites *Dasein* in the aftermath of disaster. Blanchot turns to Levinas, but the strange thing in this turn from Sartre is the proximity of the two slopes. For the two slopes differ from other binaries deployed by Blanchot, such as his "two versions of the imaginary," which divide ordinary from literary perception. The first slope is *not* "ordinary language," which "encloses the absence in a presence" and accepts that "once the nonexistence of the cat has passed into the word" the cat "comes to life again" as "its idea" (59, 44). It is not the instrumental language chosen in *What Is Literature?* but the activity of negation covered over by instrumentality.

In short, rather than drawing on the Sartre of 1947—the year in which Raymond Queneau also edited Kojève's lectures—Blanchot goes back to an earlier Sartre who is interested less in positing than in the nihilation or blindness that makes it possible. To be sure, Blanchot has conflated the philosopher of the war years with the postwar man of action, and to do so he has gone back to Sartre's theory of the image as (an)nihilation in his even earlier *Psychology of Imagination*.[51] Blanchot's "Sartre" claims a certain agency for language as a principle of "deferred assassination" that "enters the world and carries out its work" of infinite absolute negativity (43, 34). "Sartre" seeks to grasp the "ideal[ity]" of the negation and, instead of accepting the "fragmentary, successive results of this movement of negation," seeks to grasp it in its totality (43, 49). Yet Blanchot is a more astute reader of Sartre than is Heidegger, who sees him only as a negative Cartesian. Blanchot recognizes in Sartre an endless circling back to the problem of the negative. He sees the Sartrean nihilation as the most radical encounter yet with the nothingness at the heart of language. For this reason his essay is no simple critique but rather a remembering and working through of a Sartrean moment that he finds fascinating, enabling, and problematic. Hence the curious movement of the essay, which deconstructs through retention, holding back on its rejection of Sartre until the very end when it divides negativity between the two slopes. Indeed, the very figure of the slopes suggests a difference that begins from or returns to a joining, a hinge. For the two slopes "do not lead toward distinctly different works . . . [and] an art which purports to follow one slope is already on the other" (51). "Sartre" is already on a slope that leads ineluctably to "Blanchot."

Blanchot's difference from Sartre is that he transfers nothingness from man to writing, thus laying the basis for a Derridean *écriture* that likewise contains the trace of Sartre. In displacing nothingness away from its human origin, Blanchot aims to unwork any illusion of agency in relation to nothingness because he does not recognize Sartre as having already problematized this agency. Yet Blanchot deconstructs the subject only as agency and not as affectivity. Blanchot's term for writing is the verb *écrire*, not the noun *écriture*, which suggests that writing happens *to* us if not *by* our agency. This residual subject is what Levinas hints at when he associates "solitude"—perhaps Blanchot's "essential solitude"—with "hypostasis."[52] Replacing the in-itself of identity, not with the *pour-soi*, but with something closer to what Levinas calls the *sans-soi* (TO: 49), Blanchot still retains a quasi-subject. For he locates his anonymous "vigilance," not in a "being without nothingness," but in language as a "situation where an existent is put in touch with its existing" (TO: 50–51).

Aporia: De Man's Repetition of Sartre

Transferring nihilation to language instead of man or Being, Blanchot translates Heidegger into a typically French form of thinking also exemplified by de Man. On the surface de Man's career proceeds from "Sartre" to "Heidegger." His first major essay follows Sartre both in deconstructing consciousness through the image and in retaining a negative hypostasis of the subject as "intentionality" (RR: 1–17). While for Husserl intentionality cofounds subject and object, for Sartre it is tied to lack; to be conscious of something is to be aware that I am not, or do not have, that of which I am conscious. Moreover, intentionality for Sartre is already bound up with representation. For his deconstruction of Husserl is also influenced by another translation: Levinas's distinction in his book on Husserl between intuition, which "reaches its object," and "signifying acts," which do not "possess" but only "think" their object. A "signifying intention" is characterized by its "emptiness" and "need for the fulness . . . [of] intuition." It is "unrealized," "unsatisfied": an "expectation" threatened by "disappointment," as Levinas suggests in quoting Husserl, but to produce an affective reading of his texts against their exegetical grain.[53] First encountering Husserl through Levinas, Sartre bypasses the exegesis in Levinas's third chapter of how intentionality founds the Husserlian ego and is struck instead by his more radical account of *signifying* intentions, which assimilates intentionality into a potentially deconstructive problematic of signs, the image, and representation.

De Man likewise makes intentionality into the hollowing out of the subject as a lack of being discerned when the French Hegelians deconstruct spirit through consciousness. At the same time, by locating nothingness within the circuit of an unhappy consciousness, both de Man and Sartre remain on the side of what Levinas calls "hypostasis." As consciousness, nothingness becomes a "'something that is'" and appears in a "situation where an existent is put in touch with its existing" (TO: 51). On the surface, then, de Man's later work seems mobilized by the desire to purge this Sartrean residue. De Man therefore follows a general turn from Sartre to Heidegger in transferring man's radical contingency from consciousness to language, described as the "uncontrollable power of the letter as inscription" (RT: 37). As is well-known it was Heidegger's emphasis on language as that which speaks man that led to his popularity in the heyday of structuralism. But Heidegger, as Sartre suggests, always positivizes the negative, or, as de Man says, he recuperates "non-being" as "forgotten Being."[54] Indeed, the continuing appeal of Heidegger's antihumanism lies in its religiosity, what Tom Rockmore calls his "postmetaphysical humanism."[55] And de Man closes off this tropological substitution; for him language permits no transfer of residence from the human to Being. It is rather a process of dismemberment and terror caught in the "darkening of . . . Enlightenment" that Lyotard finds characteristically French.

De Man discloses this terror when he likens the "materiality of the letter" to "the worst phantasms of dismemberment" in Schreber's *Denkwürdigkeiten eines Nervenkranken*. Writing on Saussure's hypogram, he anthropomorphizes it as a "proper name" cut up into "discrete parts and groups" and dispersed as a form of chaos or "infra-text" that disrupts any stable, phenomenal meaning (RT: 89, 36–37). For de Man the experience of language is a loss of face, person, and property (RT: 44). As Hollier observes, this terror of existence without existents is encapsulated in Blanchot's recognition that to "write . . . is to give up saying 'I.'" Indeed, Blanchot had already compared literature to the "Reign of Terror" in "Literature and the Right to Death" (GO: 41–42) and in a review of Jean Paulhan's book on language and terrorism (1942). But as Hollier also notes, Sartre's own fascination with terrorism and the transcendence of the ego, in his wartime literary texts, is one of "the earliest experiments" with this "deprivatization of existence."[56] Evoking the notion of literature as terror in the violence he associates with language, de Man comments that "it is not at all certain that language is in any sense human" (RT: 87, 96). The materiality of the letter, far from conveying proximity to Being, returns to the primal scene experienced by Sartre when he confronts in the *en-soi* an utter alienness to human projects. Likewise language for de Man is "not natural," and "not phenomenal, in the sense that . . . no knowledge about man" can be derived from it, and it is "not really temporal either, because the structure that animates it is not a temporal structure" (RT: 92). What Foucault, evoking Heidegger, calls the "being of language" (OT: 43, 300) is thus not Being in a Heideggerian sense, at least not for de Man. It is rather what Sartre calls the "transphenomenality of being" as that which cannot be made cognitively, phenomenally present (BN: 9).

In a 1983 interview de Man admits Sartre's enormous influence on his generation. Sartre's work was "for many of us . . . the first encounter with some kind of philosophical language which was not just academic" but engaged with literature and the political. Insisting that he "felt closer" to Heidegger in the "Letter on Humanism," de Man still has more to say about Sartre (RT: 119). Indeed, he invokes Heidegger only to defer Sartre—a role he then assigns to the Surrealists and Blanchot who are complexly intertwined with Sartre.[57] "I felt myself . . . more on the side of Blanchot," de Man says, in "the slight opposition which became visible" between Sartre's and Blanchot's views of literature (RT: 119). This "slight" disagreement can be attributed to the way de Man, like Blanchot, sees Sartre's relation to the terror of language. For Sartre literature is terror(ism): an attempt to deal with the inhuman by appropriating its terror. This, at least, is how Blanchot portrays him in his account of the writer as terrorist (GO: 37–43)[58] and in his rejection of a writing that instead of accepting the fragmentary results of "negation . . . wants to grasp the movement itself" (GO: 38–43, 48–49). Blanchot's portrait of Sartre will be confirmed by Sartre's own political development of terrorism in his *Critique of Dialectical Reason.*[59] Unlike Blanchot's Sartre, de Man cannot take charge of negation so as to claim that "literature becomes history" (GO: 40). For him the terror of writing and criticism consists rather in a mimesis of the (non)being of language: a submission to its machinelike power, through a deprivatizing ascesis that "substitutes a process of formal elaboration for a referential reading" (RT: 37, 36).

Yet as we have seen, Blanchot himself reads Sartre's work on the nothingness of imagination in two ways: teleologically, as completed by his postwar Kojèvian anthropology, and archaeologically, as leading back to a potential proximity to the work of Blanchot and Levinas. For Blanchot, the second slope is the turn Sartre failed to take. But this view telescopes *The Psychology of Imagination* with the postwar work, thereby ignoring Sartre's intervening "phenomenological essay on ontology," which leaves the earlier work still divided between two slopes. For *Being and Nothingness* hinges upon the aporia between negation and nothingness, anthropology and ontology. On one level it develops the idea of the negation as freedom, which will connect *The Psychology of Imagination* to the *Critique of Dialectical Reason*. Yet it also disfigures this freedom through a traumatic materialism in excess of any pragmatic anthropology.

This materialism in its abjected, aporetic relation to anthropology returns in de Man's work after 1976. As he suggests, the decline of Sartre's reputation had to do with his too direct turn to the political after the texts that engaged de Man's generation: "*L'imaginaire, L'être et le néant*," and the literary essays (RT: 119). But if de Man is "closer" to Heidegger in mistrusting the political, they diverge in terms of what Heidegger calls that "other thinking that abandons subjectivity."[60] The "lurid figures" that characterize de Man's descriptions of language hearken back to a cathexis of literature and terror that French theory never quite works through. This cathexis, which in the *Critique of Dialectical Reason* becomes Sartre's missed encounter with his own earlier ontology, returns inversely in de Man's corpus as his own missed encounter with the political. As Neil Hertz argues, despite de Man's eschewal of the term *consciousness*, his texts are punctuated by "drama[s] of subjectivity" played out at a primal scene of linguistic violence associated with key moments in romantic literature. In these episodes, which focus on hanging and physical defacement, what surfaces is a quasi-subject afflicted with the "pathos of uncertain agency: "A subject is conjured up—perhaps a killer, perhaps only the discoverer of the corpse who can serve as a locus of vacillation: did I do it? Or had it already been done?"[61]

This hypostasis, as in Sartre, reflects a sense that nothingness cannot simply happen. The nihilation that is language happens to or through someone, who is responsible to or for it, even in his utter helplessness. Thus we can ask which slope de Man actually takes. Would he say with Blanchot that "by turning itself into an inability to reveal anything" literature tries "to become the revelation of what revelation destroys" (GO: 47)? And, if so, what does it mean that he discovers not the "unknown, free, and silent existence" of things (49) but that "the original was already dead" (RT: 84)? Or does de Man seek the more "murder[ous]" negativity which Blanchot finds in Sartre and Hegel: that of language as "deferred assassination" (GO: 42–43,

45)? De Man's own "murder" of texts, wherein he seeks to get beyond words by "apply[ing] the movement of negation to language itself" (GO: 42) recalls this negativity, but only as the corpse of a Sartrean anthropology that was already dead in 1943.

Yet the dead never wholly die, and de Man repeats Sartre's aporias even where he most resists him. De Man's work is actuated by a fear of "bad faith"—from "The Rhetoric of Temporality," where he refers to Sartre's notion,[62] to the chapter on "Excuses" in *Allegories of Reading*. Indeed, this element has allowed his deconstruction to be misrecognized as a form of critique,[63] although like Sartre, de Man does not believe in the possibility of good faith, only in a vigilance that sees good faith as the most insidious form of bad faith. Although de Man's work is therefore not critique in any positivist or pragmatist sense, it still feels an unfulfillable responsibility to anthropology. For vigilance requires a critical subject, even though de Man is deeply suspicious of reintroducing the subject, even to negate its mastery.

This tension leads to a counterplot in de Man's work that some see as Heideggerian. He is fascinated with language not as a critical tool but as the site of a radical ecstasis figured as the inhuman. The inhuman, according to de Man, is "linguistic structures, the play of linguistic tensions . . . possibilities which are inherent in language" and that operate "independently of any intent . . . or desire" of the subject (RT: 96). To yield to this language would be to elude the fallacies and also the responsibilities of the subject, as Foucault briefly does through the figure of "the end of man." At the close of *The Order of Things* Foucault flirts with a temptation to permanence—albeit one that is bleaker than Heidegger's—as he reflects on man's imminent erasure, "like a face drawn in sand" (OT: 387)—the same image that plays a key role in de Man's "Shelley Disfigured" (RR: 99–100). Sartre analyzes this temptation with reference to Mallarmé, whom he reads through Heidegger, in the same year as Foucault writes *The Order of Things*: "Through Man's very disappearance," Sartre writes, "being [is] restored in all its purity. . . . If Being is dispersion, man, in losing his being, achieves an incorruptible unity."[64] De Man, however, is closer to Sartre. He cannot cease to "think the negation"[65]: as an ethics of reading in the essays before 1976 and, thereafter, as it affects "human reality"—itself a catachresis for the irruption of the Real in the human.

Hiatus: Foucault, the Human Sciences, and Literature

Much deconstruction, then, emerges as a difference or resistance between Sartre and Heidegger as well as other theorists who connect them. This genesis shapes the field in three ways: as a passage of Heidegger through Sartre in which the former returns more negatively; as an internal negation in which a later theorist reworks the aporias of the past only to be doubly bound by them; and finally as a tension between epistemic strands that can be brought into dialogue. This dialogue, unlike the chiasm described in the first case, does not cathect two bodies of thought at an affective level, folding and entwining them, but explores their difference. We have seen how Blanchot reworks Heidegger through Sartre, touching one with the other. While de Man also works between them, he exemplifies a second revisionary ratio that is not so much a darkening of one by the other as a resistance within and between the two. The third structure of influence occurs in the work of Foucault and can be described by a term he uses to intimate his relation to Hyppolite: "hiatus." Foucault speaks of the openings in Hyppolite's work, which transform philosophy "into an endless task, against the background of an infinite horizon." In this context he refers to "that hiatus—where I feel at once his absence and my failings" (AK: 236–37). Hiatus is a more enigmatic term than "clearing," suggesting a space that opens up thought but cannot really be (dis)closed. Hiatus as gap and opening is, moreover, the temporal gap in which the past returns to supplement the future created by what it left unfinished. Thus it is also the framework for Derrida's recent attempts at doing justice and for Nancy's revisiting of Bataille's work on community.

If de Man probes the aporias of Sartre and Heidegger, the early Foucault uses this hiatus more constructively to open up the vexed question of anthropology. Heidegger's later hostility to anthropology can be explained by his association of it with technology as a triumph of the subjective will. This notion was already implicit in Kant's concept of "pragmatic" anthropology in the text on which Foucault wrote his *thèse complémentaire*. Pragmatic anthropology, as man's domination of the Other in the self-service of civil society, sums up everything that French philosophy after the war rejects in anthropology. But as Tom Rockmore points out, *Being and Time* leaves a space for a more radical use of anthropology.[66] Indeed, even Levinas in the 1930s had associated Heidegger with "philosophical anthropology"—a project still at the forefront in the early sixties.[67] Foucault intimates what this anthropology might be in his first work, a monograph on the Heideggerian analyst Binswanger. In *Dream, Imagination, Existence*, Foucault picks up on the side of anthropology Kant tries to set aside; he turns "physiological anthropology" in a more philosophic direction, promising to relocate it "within the context of an ontological reflection whose major theme is presence-to-being, existence, *Dasein*." Thus he speaks of inflecting "phenomenology toward anthropology" in a movement beyond Husserl's transcendentalism and yet of rethinking anthropology through an articulation of "human being . . . upon an analytic of existence." This double gesture allows him to conceive an anthropology opposed to "any type of psychological positivism claiming to exhaust the significant content of man by the reductive concept of *homo natura*."[68] In other words, Foucault develops precisely the method called for by Ferry and Renaut when they critique Heidegger's "one-dimensional" assault on humanism by referring to the nonessentialist humanism of Sartre.[69]

Arguably Foucault does not create this dialogue in his first text, which remains too Heideggerian, though on the strange ground of psychology—a discipline that did not interest the German philosopher but strongly inflected French translations of phenomenology.[70] Nor does Foucault achieve this dialogue in his other text of 1954, *Mental Illness and Personality*, whose Marxist conclusion is marred by a Sartrean pragmatism that led him to suppress it.[71] Yet an anthropology that remembers being remains the stimulus for both *The Birth of the Clinic* (1963) and *The Order of Things* (1966). Unlike *Discipline and Punish*, *The Birth of the Clinic* is not simply a genealogy and archaeology of institutions. It constitutes a new theory type that moves between what Foucault calls the cogito and the unthought by using the study of institutions to reflect on a fundamental nonbeing mediated and disclosed by structure. This nonbeing is unconcealed at the very end when Foucault refers to Nietzsche and a tradition of writers charged with darkening the Enlightenment of science. In disciplinary terms the text crosses (intellectual) history with ontology and literature. Methodologically it constructs a hinge between phenomenology and structuralism, disclosing each as the unconscious of the other. As I suggest in Chapter 6, *The Order of*

Things is an encyclopedic expansion of *The Birth of the Clinic* that makes explicit the philosophical hiatus in which it is implicated. The earlier text had constructed a genetic structural phenomenology: a "noetic" analysis of the medical gaze and a "noematic" analysis of the social world upon which it is articulated—to use the terms Foucault himself borrows from Husserl.[72] *The Order of Things* is a metahistory of several such "positivities" (or "discourses") against the margins of what is not reflected in the cogito. In the penultimate section of the text Foucault analyzes man's doubled and duplicitous relation to knowledge in terms of "four theoretical segments" (OT: 335) with profoundly phenomenological resonances: the analytic of finitude, the empirical and the transcendental, the cogito and the unthought, and the return and retreat of the origin. He thus questions the present "order" that privileges the human sciences from the perspective of the "countersciences" of ethnology, psychoanalysis, and literature. In so doing he constructs an anthropology responsible to being, a theory type that prefigures such later work as that of Nancy and Agamben on community.

Foucault could be seen as following the early Heidegger, given the room left in *Being and Time* for philosophical anthropology. Still, by the early sixties, Heidegger's thought had been definitively distinguished from philosophical anthropology, so that the invocation of this crossing actually puts Foucault's work in the space created by an earlier error: the conflation of Sartre and Heidegger. Indeed, it is questionable whether the hybridizing of phenomenology and anthropology was not always strategic as much as mistaken. Foucault's attempt to combine them may allude to a turn already made by Binswanger in "The Case of Ellen West," subtitled "An Anthropological-Clinical Study" (1944). As a German speaker, Binswanger would not have been corrupted by Sartre's "monstrous mistranslation" and is quite clear about differing from Heidegger in his correspondence with the latter even before "The Letter on Humanism."[73] Binswanger writes:

> Existential analysis (*Daseinanalyse*, as we speak of it) must not be confused with Heidegger's analytic of existence (*Daseinanalytik*). The first is a hermeneutic exegesis on the ontic-anthropological level, a phenomenological analysis of actual human existence. The second is a phenomenological hermeneutic of Being understood as existence, and moves on an ontological level. The similarity of the expressions is justified by the fact that the

anthropological or existential analysis relies throughout on that structure of existence as being-in-the-world which was first worked out by the analytic of existence.[74]

Binswanger indicates what is also a difference between Heidegger and the early Sartre: that for Sartre the ontological does not simply show itself in the ontic or mundane but is reconstituted by it. Though Binswanger is not critical of Heidegger, he allows us to see what so troubled Sartre, namely, that Heideggerian "existence" covers over a transcendentalism that withdraws actual existence into "Being."

Foucault's monograph allies itself with the "analytic of existence" and is Heideggerian in its search through dream for a "Being understood as existence." His goal is not any kind of therapy. Still, the fact that Binswanger provides him with his first enunciative positioning is symptomatically significant. Foucault too must think the ontological through the ontic, through an archaeology of the human sciences. Thus it is appropriate that his definition of "the modern *cogito*" places itself between Heidegger and Sartre. For in a section often misunderstood because we assume that no contemporary theorist would speak of a cogito, Foucault argues that man can "neither posit himself in the immediate and sovereign transparency of a *cogito*" nor "inhabit the objective inertia of something" that does not "lead to self-consciousness" (OT: 322).

This formulation echoes Sartre's criticism of *Dasein* for eliding consciousness, even as it evokes Hegel rather than Heidegger. The *modern* unlike the Cartesian cogito constitutes "Man" as a "mode of being which accommodates that dimension" that extends from "the unthought" to "the act of thought by which he apprehends" the unthought (OT: 322). Foucault's reworking of the *Geisteswissenschaften* through a Nietzschean counterphenomenology of mind differs from the work of Heidegger and Merleau-Ponty in locating this unthought not simply in perception or Being but in the "density of the historic." But it differs from Sartre and more especially Hegel in making "man" answerable to his "being" through the language in which he is articulated. In this sense Foucault, while still using the word *man*, continues Heidegger's task of a "thinking that abandons subjectivity," yet without seeking any proximity to Being. For Foucault reinscribes Heidegger after Sartre, Blanchot, Bataille, and Artaud. He thus turns not to Being but to "counternature, death, [and] the dark underside of disease" (BC: 195).

Supplement: Literature and the Dead End of Ontology

The revisionary ratios outlined here are only suggestive. They do not exhaust the ways phenomenology, itself a multiple field, returns in later theory in disparate, nontotalizable forms. As important, the relation between a given theorist and his precursors cannot be subsumed into a single structure of influence. It is overdetermined by the fact that influence is not purely a relation between individuals but involves fields, sometimes more than one field. Moreover, there can be multiple conflicting points of contact between one corpus and another even within a single text such as "Literature and the Right to Death" where there is more than one Sartre in play. A name too is the site of a dispersion, and we are always dealing with more names than are actually named.

Indeed, *The Order of Things* provides an example of this ir-resolution that disturbs any attempt to provide a simple history of influence. As suggested, by focusing synchronically on the order of knowledge Foucault constructs at the near end of his text, one discerns a dialogue between positivity and negativity in the difference between the human sciences and the "counter-sciences" of ethnology, literature, and psychoanalysis. This dialogue brings together Heidegger and Sartre, ontology and anthropology or a radicalized epistemology, given that the concern with knowledge and the relation between the ontological and the ontic actually derives from Heidegger, while the (non)being to which science must attend has been filtered through Sartre. In other words the hiatus between Sartre and Heidegger contains further crossings between the two that make the relationship difficult to schematize. Still, we can read Foucault's text under the general figure of hiatus as opening.

Yet if we focus on the diachronic movement of Foucault's text through its near end to its end and then place it in his corpus, the Sartre/Heidegger relation becomes one of aporia. For Foucault's epistemic history involves a darkening of his own enlightenment through a Nietzschean dialectic that moves from the Renaissance through classicism to the modern. In this process a language intermingled with "the prose of the world" (OT: 17) is covered over by the nominalism of classical discourse, then returning as literature in the late nineteenth century. Literature is a specific form of language folded back on "the enigma of its own origin" so as to grow "progressively more differentiated from the discourse of ideas" and enclosed in "a radical intransitivity" (300). As Foucault loses faith in ethnology and psychoanalysis, he is left with literature as the only "counter-science" (379). Thus isolated, literature is not dialogically engaged with science or knowledge but is a form of pure ontology; it "has nothing to say but itself, nothing to do but shine in the brightness of its being" (300). As we have seen, Sartre, who first deals with this literature (or poetry) in *What Is Literature?* later links it to Heidegger via Blanchot's work on Mallarmé. For Sartre, literature as the will to failure seeks the inertia that Levinas finds in Heideggerian being when he says," in ekstasis the subject is absorbed in the object and recovers itself in its unity" (EE: 41). Through literature Foucault finds himself borne towards the end of man and returns to a being rewritten as nonbeing after the disaster.

And here it is useful to compare Foucault with Derrida, whose early work also takes up the hiatus described in the last section and who is also thought to privilege literature. Whereas Foucault's literature finds itself on the slope of (non)being, *écriture* works at the hinge of the two slopes that Blanchot, like Sartre, cannot bring together. For what Derrida calls arche-writing is a language not specialized as literature but present throughout discourse in the "prose of the world." In other words, *écriture* is not "detached from all the values that . . . keep it in general circulation" before the nineteenth century (OT: 300). On the contrary, Derrida works across the Sartrean bifurcation of prose and poetry that Foucault accepts after the classical period. Thus Derrida rarely deals with literature as separate from philosophical or anthropological texts. In short, he opens the aporia between prose and poetry so as to permit a dialogue between epistemology and ontology. On the one hand, *écriture* is "the process of death at work in signs" (SP: 40) and thus an unravelling of knowledge into its finitude. On the other hand, Derrida's deconstruction is not the prelude to a negative ontology; it is always epistemic, which is to say "affirmative." A deconstruction, he suggests, always concerns "systems," with a view not to bringing them down but of opening onto other "possibilities of arrangement."[75]

On one level, Foucault too works in this opening, as I suggest in Chapter 6. Through language as "the prose of the world," he unravels the complicated cosmological structures fabricated by the Renaissance. Though it is covered over in the classical period, Foucault still uses language to expose the positivity of discourse to its limits. Finally the return of language offers the hope of a language not confined to literature but put to work within the human sciences through psychoanalysis and ethnology. In this sense Foucault does not wholly reject Kant; indeed, as James Miller points out, his early work on the *Anthropology* is "the seed" of *The Order of Things*.[76]

But these disciplines are disappointments and fall back into various kinds of positivism. Indeed, their potential as means of access to the unthought can be realized only by using them to deconstruct one another, which was not the path taken by ethnology, renamed anthropology in the university of the sixties. Thus the hiatus unravels back into an aporia between ontology and epistemology that spells the collapse of Foucault's attempt to make phenomenology the source of an affirmative deconstruction. Language, instead of being a process at work in signs, becomes restricted to literature as a negative absolute. Nowhere is this more evident than in Foucault's monograph on Blanchot, also published in 1966. Blanchot, as the epitome of literature, is associated with a negative theology.[77] This nonbeing, which is so enigmatically in-itself, constitutes both the fascination and the dead-end of a certain phenomenology. This may be why Foucault in his later work rarely writes on literature. And yet his turn to the poststructural social sciences after 1968 is still a return to Sartre, this time another Sartre. For Foucault's role as a disengaged public intellectual is a curious sub-version of Sartre's postwar "*engagement*," which is also mobilized by the aporia between ontology and the prose of the world. Even in its exit from phenomenology, poststructuralism and its current continuations do not escape the problems left unresolved by phenomenology.

PART TWO

Revisions and Remainders

CHAPTER FOUR

Existence and Method: Derrida's Early Texts on Husserl

Derrida's Early Project: Grammatology as Existential Historiography

To locate Derrida within phenomenology may seem surprising given his criticisms of Husserl and even more of Merleau-Ponty and Sartre. In his 1971 interview with Kristeva Derrida identifies phenomenology with the view that meaning is "given to consciousness" in an "intuition" free of difference (P: 32). He associates phenomenology with pure meanings purged of material residue, which confer on consciousness a similar presemiotic purity. To be sure, he recognizes phenomenology's negative value as the origin of the aporias that continue to "organize" deconstruction.[1] But he has little positive to say about a philosophy committed to the "reduction" of writing in the transcendental subjectivity of "living speech" (P: 24–25). Yet such antithetical simplifications mask not only the complexity of Derrida's relationship to phenomenology before 1968 but also the elisions in which it is inscribed thereafter. As already noted, the comments in *Positions* refer only to transcendental phenomenology, while the three texts that inaugurate Derrida's career are all critiques purely of Husserl. In these texts Derrida makes silent use of existential phenomenology and praises Sartre for having "unbalanced—and then overthrown—the landscape of Husserl's phenomenology" (OG: 125n). He sees phenomenology as generated by a series of such "unbalanc[ings]" (WD: 157). Indeed, up to 1967 Derrida's work could be described as a deconstruction of transcendental phenomenology that draws on existential phenomenology so as to work towards "a thought of the trace" that is irreducible to phenomenology but still a part of it (OGr: 62).

Derrida's rethinking of phenomenology between 1953 and 1967 recognizes both the divergence and the dependence between its transcendental and existential versions. Despite this very precise sense of the differences within phenomenology as creating a clearing for some kind of postphenomenology, Derrida later seems content to use Husserl as a metonym for phenomenology in general. At the same time in "The Ends of Man," after fifteen years of taking apart Husserl, he praises him for unveiling "transcendental structures" that inscribe a "consciousness without man" (M: 118). Whereas Husserl's resistance to psychologism had earlier been an object of criticism (SP: 11, 30), anthropology and "intraworldly being" suddenly become more dangerous than the "phenomenality of the spirit relating to itself" (M: 117–18). This imaginary identification with Husserl in 1968 is at odds with the continued criticism of him in 1971. But it is repeated in 1980 in "The Time of a Thesis" when Husserl is again used to polarize two directions in phenomenology that were once "inseparable and dialectically linked" (G: 256–57).[2] In "The Ends of Man" Derrida had already constructed Sartre in opposition to anything salvageable in phenomenology. In 1980 he expands this abjection of French phenomenology when he writes that phenomenology was invaluable to his early work, but "not—especially not—in the versions proposed by Sartre or Merleau-Ponty which were then dominant."[3]

A study focused on Derrida would provide a symptomatic reading of his relationship to phenomenology across his career. But this chapter is limited to the three early books on Husserl that provide his most complex engagement with phenomenology. The period 1968–71 marks a shift in Derrida's understanding of phenomenology, which is also a turn against the very approach he had used to rethink it from within. Hereafter he increasingly displaces his attack on phenomenology from transcendental to existential phenomenology, while exempting the original object of his deconstruction from radical criticism. But it is important to remember that before this turn Derrida's energies are directed only against a certain kind of phenomenology. In "'Genesis and Structure' and Phenomenology" (1959) he observes that Husserl's early work emerged "at the same time as the first structuralist projects." Indeed, Derrida is careful to demarcate a "first phase of phenomenology" that, "in its style and its objects, is structuralist" because "it seeks to stay clear of psychologism and historicism" (WD: 159). Derrida's early work takes apart only this "positivist" phenomenology (155) from the perspective of a second phase to which he bears a unique and radical relationship.

The importance Derrida gives to Husserl may seem puzzling until we recall that "Husserl" was a site for assessing the very renewability of phenomenology. The French reading of Husserl parallels that of Hegel in focusing not on his ends but on the tools and means to those ends by which his text reads itself against the grain. Without deconstructing him, as Merleau-Ponty says, it thus "recommenc[es] Husserl's efforts instead of simply repeating what he said."[4] As already indicated, Merleau-Ponty sees Husserl as opening the topics of the body, temporality, alterity, and history. As he "proceeded to the execution of his program" Husserl's epistemology thus "brought to light fragments" of an ontology that "disconcerted his frame of reference." In Merleau-Ponty's "intentional" as distinct from "empirical history"[5] the transcendental and existential versions of phenomenology that Ricoeur distinguishes for heuristic purposes are dialogically present in Husserl himself, as a hiatus disclosed through the Heideggerian readings his work later elicited. In addition to Merleau-Ponty's work, Levinas, Ricoeur, Lyotard, and Trân Duc Thao also wrote major studies of Husserl. Except for Thao's Marxist critique, these studies attributed to Husserl himself the radical opening of the transcendental into the existential brought about by his French readers, thus simultaneously deconstructing him and reconfirming the authority of the parent through a reverse filiation. Often this radicality was located in the last texts. Thus Ricoeur traces the deepening sense of "constitution" as genetic rather than static, and notes a "new concern for history" linked to "the consciousness of crisis." Merleau-Ponty similarly argues for a new attitude to language: while the earlier Husserl thinks of language only as a "substitute, [or] memorandum" for thought, in Husserl's later writings "language appears as an original way of intending certain objects, as thought's body," and thus as a "quasi-corporeal" element in which thought is "enveloped and situated."[6]

By contrast Derrida sees an underlying consistency between Husserl's first and last writings (OG: 25, 78). He denies that there is any real "opening [of] the phenomenological parentheses to historical factuality" in the texts of *The Crisis of European Sciences and Transcendental Phenomenology* or that there is any relinquishment of what Merleau-Ponty calls Husserl's "eidetic of language" (OG: 116, 78).[7] Derrida would not have devoted three books to Husserl if he too did not appreciate the possibilities Husserl created in introducing temporality, alterity, and "life" into the sanctum of transcendental idealism (SP: 6). Of particular importance for him (as for Sartre and de Man) is Levinas's radicalizing of Husserlian intentionality so as to show it as perilously balanced on the tension between "intuitive acts" that "reach" their object and "signifying acts" that only "aim" at it.[8] Derrida grants that phenomenology is "tormented, if not contested from within, by its own descriptions" of what it theorizes (SP: 6). Or, as Foucault puts it, phenomenology "despite itself" becomes a "description . . . of actual experience" and thus "an ontology of the unthought that automatically short-circuits the primacy of the 'I think'" (OT: 326). But for Derrida, to adapt Thao, it is important not to rewrite Husserl's "theoretical principles" according to his "concrete analyses." He recognizes that "the profound intention of [Husserl's] work *strove for* an idealism" even if this idealism "was *actually expressed* as a realism."[9] To reduce the difference between the transcendental and existential is to miss the radicality of what Derrida describes as a "*trouée*" and not just an extension. His more thoroughgoing critique of Husserl thus outlines the "historical *closure*," if not the "*end*" (OGr: 14) of a thought whose horizon must be abandoned if one is to push further Merleau-Ponty's vision of a "phenomenology which descends into its own substratum."[10]

In what follows I argue that Derrida develops a new way of thinking in the hiatus between transcendental and existential phenomenology and that he does so as part of a larger epistemic project outlined in *Of Grammatology*. Derrida's critique of Husserl would not have been possible without the work of Ricoeur and Merleau-Ponty, including the latter's 1951 paper on "The Phenomenology of Language," published in 1960 in *Signs*. As Derrida himself admits, it is the problems that surface within phenomenology (rather than those raised by structuralism) that have continued to organize his work up to the present. Indeed, though phenomenology is often accused of eliding the problem of language, Derrida's recasting of the relation between expression and indication radicalizes Merleau-Ponty's account of the relation between "*complete* expression" and the "second-order language" it conceals. This "indirect" language is one where signs "lead the vague life of colors, and in which significations *never free themselves completely from the intercourse of signs.*" Derrida's readings of Husserl also begin from Merleau-Ponty's discussions of the "fundamental" role of language in "The Origin of Geometry."[11] Both in his deconstruction of Husserl and in his own theory of language and consciousness, Derrida thus draws considerably on existential phenomenology. In this sense it is worth noting that before 1968 he is critical of Husserl, but never of Merleau-Ponty and Sartre.

But it is also notable that Derrida rarely names his precursors and that the word *existential* disappears after his first book on Husserl. Derrida's work draws on the second stage of phenomenology for its method and ethics, but it is not conceptually reducible to it. One senses the trace of the existential in "Violence and Metaphysics," where he opposes Levinas to "the two Greeks named Husserl and Heidegger" in terms of the way Levinas's texts seek "to be understood from within a *recourse to experience itself*" (WD: 83). Paradoxically in the same essay Derrida also complains that the "concept of experience" is always "determined by the metaphysics of presence" (153). Yet he links experience to an irremediable difference, to "that which is most irreducible within experience: the passage and departure toward the other; the other itself as that which is most irreducibly other within it" (83). Derrida's ambivalent relationship to the vocabulary of existential phenomenology explains why he submits it to what Bloom calls an "askesis," or deployment through curtailment and reduction.[12] By confining his precursors to an allusive subtext, he avoids encumbering his text with accounts of similarity and difference, of how experience can be "irreducibly other" when it is also the "encountering of an irreducible presence" (152), and of why he uses terms that he also criticizes. In addition Derrida does not explicitly mention existential phenomenology because he finds transcendental thinking, with its emphasis on method and rigor, a useful way of curtailing an existential involvement that ended in the mistaken political engagement of Sartre and Merleau-Ponty. As Herman Rapaport points out, Derrida rarely takes up a position in relation to other writers because he resists "the notion of a thesis . . . as a position that stays the same." Instead he parcels out the "critique of presence" among several figures so that this critique cannot be recovered as "a position which is present to itself as itself."[13]

Derrida's existential-transcendental method is both the correlate of and the ethical frame for a theory of *écriture* and *différance* that eventually emerges from his historiographical analysis of Husserl. After 1967 Derrida's theory of writing and his focus on method increasingly displace historiography, with the result that the landscape of the later texts is very different from that of the early work. Indeed, Kristeva restricts *grammatology* to Derrida's own theory of language,[14] when initially he uses the term to refer to the entire history of "the science of writing," which finds its "end" in his own theory (OGr: 4). Thus it is worth pointing out that the early Derrida develops his analysis of *différance* largely through commentaries on other thinkers from Plato to Bataille and that his use of commentary is not simply an effect of his novitiate status. For at this point Derrida does not pursue grammatology for its own sake, but in conjunction with another project that Habermas, writing of Foucault, describes as an "erudite-positivist historiography in the form of an antiscience."[15] In this sense, "deconstruction" is ultimately part of an (anti)dialectic that rethinks what Derrida (following Foucault's mentor Georges Canguilhem) calls the dominant "rationality" (10).

In *Of Grammatology* Derrida sees his work as focused on three areas: writing, (intellectual) history, and science (3). Outlining the genesis of his concerns from his earliest work on Husserl's philosophy of mathematics, he explains that writing is not only "an auxiliary means in the service of science" but also "the condition of the possibility of ideal objects"—of all idealizations—and thus of the very "*epistémè*" itself (27). Insofar as writing is the "medium of the great metaphysical, scientific, technical, and economic adventure of the West" as well as of the "cultural areas" on which it imposes its "laws," grammatology is the general economy within which the restricted economies of specific disciplines must be approached so as to rethink their very grounds. By grammatology Derrida means the history, epistemology, and ontology of a phonetic writing now being reconfigured through "cybernetics" so as to create new spaces for what had been the "'human sciences' of writing" (10).

At this stage Derrida's elevation of writing into a metacategory does not connote a "reduction" to the signifier; instead, a global "liberation" occurs as various restricted economies are rethought within the general economy of grammatology (4). Moreover, the reference to the human sciences also indicates a theorist very different from the one described by Tim Clark, who identifies Derrida with an exclusively post-Heideggerian focus on literature as a way of thinking Being. Separating Derrida's work on literature from his studies of philosophers, Clark reinstates the division between the "two slopes" that I argue Derrida avoids. For Derrida himself speaks of his "first desire . . . to go in the direction of the literary event," but then of the necessity "not to close oneself up in . . . literature" or for that matter philosophy.[16] Derrida's work thus grows out of the third phase of phenomenology, which is characterized by an expansion of philosophy towards the sciences of the *Lebenswelt*. Commenting on this expansion, which also provides the axis of Lyotard's *Phenomenology*, Merleau-Ponty evokes the names of Max Scheler, Binswanger, and Eugene Minkowski. As usual he attributes this expansion to Husserl, whom he sees as intensely concerned in *The Crisis of European Sciences and Transcendental Phenomenology* with the "interdependence" of all knowledge and thus the relationship of philosophy to the "sciences of man (psychology, sociology, history)." But Husserl is better seen as defending philosophy against the "psychologism" of the human sciences. Instead it is Merleau-Ponty himself, in such essays as "Phenomenology and the Sciences of Man" and "The Philosopher and Sociology," who questions philosophy's status as the disciplinary symbol of the mind's "autonomy" and who explores the "*reciprocal envelopment*" of philosophy and the social by each other.[17] We must add, of course, that this envelopment can also be found much earlier in theorists such as Hegel and Simmel.

The grammatological project is first conceived within the larger economy of this "reciprocal envelopment" between the disciplines. But whereas Foucault partly preserves historiography as genealogy, Derrida retreats from the ambitious intellectual-historical project outlined in 1967, at least in the sense that he never writes an *Order of Things* and prefers the modes of the literary essay and the philosophical exegesis. That his work can be read alongside Foucault's as an attempt to rethink the disciplines in terms of an analytic of finitude will nevertheless be clearer if we begin from his first book, *The Problem of Genesis in the Philosophy of Husserl*, where the framing of philosophical concerns within issues of history and historiography is more evident than in *Speech and Phenomena*. As already indicated this interdisciplinarity is "postphenomenological" in several ways. First, the historiographical project itself is post-Hegelian; in addition, existential phenomenology provides Derrida with a context from the outside of which he can rethink transcendental idealism from Hegel to Husserl; and finally existential thought also provides the underlying orientation for returning the linguistic to life and the life of signs in society. But the dialogue of philosophy and the social—instituted by the "third" phase of phenomenology—sometimes risks falling back into positivism, which is why *deconstruction* lays so much emphasis on literature as the unthought of epistemology. Derrida's studies of literature (which cannot be confined to the literary) are outside the scope of this chapter, but at this stage they are mostly found in *Writing and Difference* (1967), which contains essays on Jabès, Levinas, Artaud, Bataille, and others. To have a sense of how his work in the sixties inhabits the hiatus between disciplines, it is necessary to place the two later exegeses of Husserl within the broader framework of the *The Problem of Genesis in the Philosophy of Husserl* and *Of Grammatology*, but then to fold them into the inner experience of writing explored in *Writing and Difference*.[18] Only then can we see how close Derrida's early work is to that of Foucault prior to *The Archaeology of Knowledge*.

The Problem of Genesis in the Philosophy of Husserl: Derrida's First Study of Husserl

The Problem of Genesis in the Philosophy of Husserl was published only in 1990 but written in 1953–54. In what follows I suggest that this study, more "panoramic" than Derrida's subsequent philosophical work (G: vi) that adheres more strictly to the discipline's emphasis on exegesis, allows us to see these very exegeses in a different perspective, as part of the Foucaultian project previously outlined. In his "Advertisement," Derrida locates in the *Genesis* the same "logic" that organizes his later works: an "originary complication of the origin" and a "law of differential contamination" that undoes the opposition between the pairs "transcendental/worldly, eidetic/empirical, . . . active/passive, present/non-present . . . originary/derived, pure/impure" (v–vi). Yet he is also uneasy with the text, not only because its style has failed to catch up with his thinking (v), but also because of its emphasis on *dialectic*. This term, which sums up what distinguishes the *Genesis* from the subsequent studies of Husserl that Derrida can more comfortably see as inaugurating his career (vii), also names a neglected and continuing strand in his corpus. For the *Genesis*, I suggest, is not just a shadowy type of future truths but an arche-type for procedures more reticently present in Derrida's texts of the sixties. Together these texts rethink the relations among the disciplines as configured by Husserl in *The Crisis of European Sciences and Transcendental Phenomenology* through what Derrida calls an "originary dialectic" that retains the trace but not the presence of Hegel and Marx (vii). To be sure, Derrida has not quite found the voice of this dialectic, any more than Foucault in 1953 has managed to work out an analytic of finitude in ways not overshadowed by Heidegger and Sartre. Still, what the text discloses is precisely the genesis of Derrida's deconstruction in the early sixties.

Like the problems of origin and language in Derrida's two subsequent books on Husserl, that of genesis here serves as a "conducting thread" (2) for a range of other concerns. Unlike the later studies, however, this one takes in Husserl's corpus from the *Philosophy of Arithmetic* to the late essay on "The Origin of Geometry." Genesis is thus its mode as well as its subject. It not only deals with Husserl's anxieties about genesis as the crack through which philosophy falls back into the life of "a real historical subject" (46); it is itself a genetic study of the subject "Husserl" and the temporality of his corpus. This no doubt is why Hyppolite urged Derrida to publish it (vi). The motif of genesis is behind a "disquietude" that haunts Husserl's entire work; it is the "essential motivation" of his thought and the moment of a dilemma that "without respite, Husserl seems to have repressed or dissimulated" (35). Without as yet using tropological language, Derrida analyzes the Husserlian corpus in terms of the evasions and substitutions used to protect the philosophical gaze from an empirical and historical outside to which it opens itself. We shall return to why he stops short of the openly historicist critique of transcendental phenomenology provided by Trân Duc Thao in a study Derrida cites as a major influence on his generation. Nevertheless the *Genesis*, though often an "internalist" critique of Husserl on his own (philosophical) ground, is also Derrida's most "historical" work. It begins by emphasizing that philosophy is inseparable from (its) history (1). It concludes with what verges on a cultural critique of Husserl's last work that emphasizes the latent Hegelianism of *The Crisis of European Sciences and Transcendental Phenomenology*. And Husserl, as Derrida later says, "has always associated 'Hegelianism' with 'romanticism' and with 'historicism,' to which romanticism is led when 'belief' in its 'metaphysics of history' has been lost" (OG: 103n).

The crux of Derrida's argument is his discussion of the relation between passive and active genesis in the constitution of the transcendental subject.

At this point it is useful to turn to Thao who, despite their differences, also foregrounds this tension. For Derrida's choice of genesis rather than intentionality or the lived body as the site at which to read Husserl against the grain has much to do with his later "malaise" over this "student work" (v–vi). As he complains, perhaps too harshly, it reflects a mistaken critique of Husserl via Thao and Cavailles rather than Levinas, Sartre, and Merleau-Ponty (vii)[19] and thus a complicity with an enlightenment project that Derrida will later renounce. Briefly, genesis is Thao's "respectful" (vii) and oblique way of introducing history as the effaced ground of Husserl's phenomenology. This move opens the "pure description of lived experience" to a critique of its "values." Moving from "static" to "genetic" constitution and then between active and passive genesis, Thao traces a series of displacements in which Husserl creates openings only to close them off, following the logic of the hinge that Derrida himself later articulates. To begin with, Husserl focuses on static constitution, which analyzes significations that have already been posited. Whereas static analysis focuses on "structure" and assumes an "ideal object . . . capable of being understood" identically by everyone, genetic analysis defines the very conditions "of the act that produces" structure. Insofar as it goes beyond the simple "appearing" of objects to the "*origin* of the meaning that dominates them," genetic analysis thus concedes that structures can only be understood "in a *history*."[20] Indeed, in the period after Thao's *Phenomenology and Dialectical Materialism* the terms *genesis* and *structure* (already introduced by Hyppolite) were to assume increasing importance in an attempt to redefine the relationship between phenomenology and history.

Yet for Husserl, as Derrida says in his 1959 essay on this subject, there was never a "'structure-genesis' problem" (WD: 156). According to Thao, Husserl avoids the contamination of history in two ways. First, genesis is not concerned with actual causes but with "the primordial act that is *always present* in the actuality of intellectual life" or with a becoming that is not within history since it already is.[21] As Derrida puts it, Husserl is not interested in the empirical genesis of geometry in Euclid but in the "very sense of [its] founding," (OG: 38) or in its "transcendental" genesis. Just as language is the infinite repeatability of the different as the same, so also this "primordial concrete essence of geometry" exists "only once," no matter how often it originates empirically (160, 52). Through the sleight-of-hand of a "transcendental" origin, Husserl thus resists the aporia implicit in genesis, of a constituting source that "turns out to be something constituted as well."[22] Secondly, in Thao's view, this protection of the transcendental from the empirical is facilitated by the emphasis on a "*passive genesis* that occurs in the naiveté of an '*anonymous*' life in which the self is not conscious of its creative activity." A merely passive genesis allows the subject not to be responsible for its acts. At the same time the passive is no more than a trope, being possible "only as the *retention* of a primordial act in which the meaning was created by . . . an *active genesis*" which "progressively became weaker and so fell, finally, into the '*unconscious.*'"

Passive genesis, moreover, is inherently conservative. As Thao says, it refers to a "*first creation* that it does nothing but perpetuate," recalling a meaning "that is continuously and passively reproduced in the unconscious." As Ricoeur says, it thus permits "the maintenance of former acts of the ego in new acts."[23] Indeed, it is Husserl who first develops the notion, more critically theorized by Bourdieu, that makes passivity the condition of possibility for the active constitution of the ego in the *habitus*. In the third section of the *Genesis*, Derrida continues this analysis of the figural construction of an empirical subject as transcendental through the misrecognition of the active as passive: "In effect . . . no transcendental activity would be possible if the unity of the object were totally constituted by a passivity"; rather, the "history supposed by passive genesis" is "the intentional linkage of significations, the series of moments in which the passive synthesis 'animated' by an active synthesis is 'recognized' as a passive synthesis" (G: 233–35).

But there is a crucial difference between Thao and Derrida. Thao faults Husserl for failing to theorize *active* genesis and thus the possibility of history. But Derrida, while agreeing that Husserl ostensibly privileges the passive, complains that he actually "brackets" it by making it a mere "substratum [couche inférieure]" for active genesis and by using it only as a figure for the latter (231–32). Derrida thus faults Husserl for failing to theorize *passive* genesis. This valorizing of a "passivity in the interior of the 'vigilant' and active I" (239) is prophetic of Derrida's subsequent, post-Heideggerian work, as he suggests in later linking it to "the question of time and of the other."[24] It also signifies his resistance to Thao's materialist dialectic, which remains "the prisoner of a metaphysic" (257n). For to privilege active genesis is to assume an agency that reinscribes the very transcendental subject Derrida critiques in the fourth section and whose empirical origins mark Husserl's betrayal of genuine "transcendental" thought. Derrida's interest in the passive aligns him with theorists such as Merleau-Ponty, whose phenomenology of perception develops Husserl's comments on pre-predicative experience towards a displacement of the Cartesian by the tacit cogito. As important, it links him to Levinas and Nancy. When Derrida claims that "with passive genesis, we have introduced historical time into the transcendental sphere" (240), he thus assumes that meaning emerges in a "movement of production that is 'implied as *sedimented history*'"[25] or that history is an archive, a site of traces that exceed the self-production of the subject. In other words he assumes a history very different from that of Thao.

That Derrida should link pre-predicative experience to *history* is nevertheless significant. On one level passive genesis lays the groundwork for grammatology. Yet the emphasis on *history* distinguishes Derrida's first two works from a text such as "Differance" (1968), which also radicalizes Husserl's "retention" and "protention" (SP: 142–43) but in a manner that verges on transcendental analysis in investigating the "primordial" essence of *différance* in the very sense of its founding as a "nonsimple 'origin'" (SP: 143, 141). The significance of "history" surfaces in the word *dialectic*—a term that explains not only Derrida's later discomfort with this text but also why history is not simply a synonym for temporality. And here it is worth noting that dialectic is what Kristeva later accuses grammatology of foreclosing through its Husserlian emphasis on the trace as retention.[26] By *dialectic* Derrida does not intend the "purely 'mundane'" dialectic of Marxism but rather a process in which "being . . . takes account of the necessity of dialectic as of its original finitude" (G: 257). But conversely, by using this term Derrida also distinguishes his references to finitude and temporality from those of Heidegger, whose emphasis on authenticity, being-towards-death, and "the absolute purity of 'anguish', suspends the dialectic of originary temporality" (257n).

Attempting to return philosophy to history, Derrida concludes by analyzing the misrecognition of active as passive in the genesis of Husserl's own corpus. Husserl's *Crisis* and the associated "Vienna Lecture," written between the wars and in the wake of various imperialisms, are his most polemical and Eurocentric texts. Picking up on his much earlier "Philosophy as a

Rigourous Science" (1911), Husserl sees philosophy as a "rigorous" if not "exact" science and connects its loss of rigor to the "sickness" of Western man. He reasserts philosophy's place as the master-discipline among the human sciences against the damage done by thinkers from Hegel to Dilthey. Much of Husserl's career is a reflection upon the identity of philosophy that starts from Dilthey's distinction of the human (or reflexive and hermeneutic) sciences from the natural sciences. Repeating this distinction in his own critique of naturalism, Husserl also reverses it by allying naturalism with psychologism, including the hermeneutics of Dilthey. By thus sublating and discarding Dilthey, Husserl thinks he has delivered philosophy from the errors of both the humanities and science. He avoids the disadvantages of science as empiricism, while reclaiming a figurally scientific status for philosophy. By thinking it through the metonyms of arithmetic and geometry, he places it on the side of logic rather than psychologism. By *psychologism* Husserl means any reduction of the mind's workings to something outside it, whether through sociology, history, or psychology proper. In his unceasing battle against this contamination, Husserl first defines the subject as logical rather than psychological and finally settles on the term *transcendental* as a way of avoiding both anthropologism and naturalism. But *The Crisis* is not just a formulation of transcendental phenomenology; it is also an account of its (historical) genesis intended to intimate the (psychological) urgency of a rigorous philosophy. As such it is the crisis of Husserl's own career, the revenge of a history "ostracized" by a phenomenology that turns out to be "dans le monde" (247, 251).

Though focusing on *The Crisis*, Derrida begins by citing the subject of his next study, "The Origin of Geometry," as a paradigm for Husserl's very constitution of philosophy (260). To begin with, geometry, as one of those "ideal objects of science" that we can produce "by identifying acts, as 'the same'" (OG: 25), is part of the sphere of "ideal Objectivity" that vicariously gives its identity to the philosophy that studies it. As important, through such study philosophy emerges as the discipline that "grasp[s], at its very birth, the transcendental origin of a historical product of consciousness" (260). Husserl is thus able to construct philosophy as an *anamnesis* that paradoxically forgets the difference between the transcendental and the historical. As Robert Cumming points out, it is noteworthy that Husserl uses mathematics as an analogue for philosophy, whereas Merleau-Ponty and

Heidegger think philosophy through painting and poetry.[27] For Husserl, the study of geometry figures the very Idea of philosophy as "phenomenology," as Universal Reason, and as the synthesis of the transcendental and the empirical in a *"material* eidetics" that deals with concrete things without the contamination of the sensible (OG: 123).

But in Husserl's last period "history itself breaks through into phenomenology" (29). For in order not to immobilize it "in a concept" and to maintain it as an "infinite task" (G: 277–81), this "most nonhistorical . . . of philosophers," to quote Ricoeur, gives philosophy a history.[28] In the process Husserl creates several problems. By putting philosophy within history, he exposes it to "failure," "crisis," and the loss of its transcendental identity (277–81). Its "origin" proves hard to locate because "universal" philosophy comes into being only with Galileo and then only too imperfectly. Moreover, Husserl clearly identifies philosophy as a European idea, and though he claims that "Europe" is an "eidetic" term (250) he also defines it in relation to the empirical entities of India and China, which lack an "immanent teleology." Husserl's project, in other words, founders on an unanswerable question: if the Idea of phenomenology is anterior to *"homo europeanus,"* why does this Idea appear "so belatedly" and only "in the history of Europe"? And contrarily, if "ideal objectivities" exist a priori, why is there any need for them to develop historically (272)? In exposing the aporetic construction of a "transcendence" that has a "genesis," Derrida also returns Husserl's own "transcendental" Idea to its origins in occidental prejudice. He traces the process by which a regional idea of philosophy is naturalized through the troping of assumptions actively constituted by a certain culture as passively given.

Derrida's analysis marks a profound break in Husserl studies. Indeed, it can be contrasted with Ricoeur's "Husserl and the Sense of History" (1949), on which Derrida draws extensively, but which uneasily recuperates Husserl by arguing that his awareness of history finally effects a "profound transformation of the sense of philosophy itself."[29] Nevertheless it is questionable whether Derrida's analysis in the last pages of *Genesis* quite realizes his own sense of dialectic. It is too much an application of his critique of passive genesis to Husserl himself, which is to say that it comes close to forms of positivist cultural critique that historicize the past only to substitute the interpreter as transcendental subject. One problem is that Derrida brilliantly analyzes the *habitus* of Husserlian phenomenology, thus considering how the passive serves the purposes of the active. But he stops short of any autonomous elaboration of the passive itself as the site of the unthought. In this sense he too brackets the passive—a further reason why he is later uncomfortable with the "voice" of this study (v).

Instead, as we shall see, it is the early work of Foucault that best exemplifies the deconstructive development of genetic phenomenology towards a dialectic of finitude rather than enlightenment, in which the sedimentations of history open the cogito to its unthought. Foucault's archaeology develops Ricoeur's passing suggestion that we can displace *sedimentierte Geschichte* as "settled" history by "renewing contact with the sense 'buried' under the 'sedimentations,'"[30] thus transforming passivity from a conservative to a deconstructive element. But if Derrida's critique of Husserl falls midway between archaeology and what Bourdieu calls political ontology, his *theoretical* description of the dialectic of finitude a decade before Foucault is worth citing in full. In his closing pages he calls for a "new ontology" that

> far from ignoring the essential and unsurpassable moment of eidetic phenomenology will show, through the deepening addition of a phenomenology of temporality, that, at the level of originary temporal existence, fact and essence, the empirical and the transcendental are inseparable and dialectically linked. . . . The human existence in which being becomes dialectically a subject 'for-itself' [*pour-soi*], in which it assumes an originary temporality and takes account of the necessity of dialectic as of its own original finitude, is the point of departure for an ontological reflection. (256–57)

It is important to grasp the precise philosophical location of Derrida's project. Derrida takes account of the *supplementary* relationship between the transcendental and the empirical disclosed throughout the *Genesis* by arguing for a "deepening" of transcendental by existential phenomenology. This new hybrid does not abandon a transcendental thinking that requires the subject to have an ek-static relation to itself; rather, Derrida anticipates Foucault's distinction of "transcendental reflection in its modern form" as an openness to the "*not-known*" from Kant's inscription of the transcendental motif in a "science of nature" (OT: 323), which is continued in Husserl's identification of philosophy with the philosophy of science. The Heideggerian resonances of this passage are unmistakable and are consistent with Derrida's description of his approach as an "existential analytic" (G: 251). Yet by connecting this analytic to a "dialectic," Derrida also allies himself with the project of "enlightenment," which for Christopher Norris marks deconstruction as modern rather than postmodern. Derrida, like Foucault, would undoubtedly question *Kantian* Enlightenment and would identify truth with "that level of contingent events or shifts . . . revealed through a jointly 'archaeological' and 'genealogical' approach."[31] Consequently, by the time of *Speech and Phenomena* he might also share Foucault's dissociation of enlightenment from "humanism" and his transposition of the site for a "permanent critique of ourselves" from the body politic to art (or *écriture*) as the terrain of "conscience."[32] Still, *dialectic* signifies a set of concerns completely foreign to Heidegger.

Thus it is significant that Derrida evokes Sartre in referring to a "*human existence* in which *being* becomes dialectically a subject '*for itself*'" (emphasis mine). Sartre had criticized Heideggerian Being for ignoring consciousness, thus allowing man to give up responsibility for himself in a reabsorption of active by passive genesis. Whereas Sartrean Being is *en-soi* and devoid of genetic links to an empirical history or an intending subject, consciousness is a *pour-soi* that deconstructs both this simulacrum of Being and its own empirico-transcendental doubling as "un néant qui veut être." The *pour-soi* thus involves a permanent self-critique in which reason becomes "conscious of its finitude" (G: 281). Throughout the *Genesis* Derrida echoes Sartre's critique of the *en-soi*, his emphasis on intentionality, and on the supplementary dependence of essence on existence. Though the reduction claims to reveal essences that are *en-soi* (36), Husserl's concern with genesis discloses them as constituted within existence, thus raising the question of their link to "empirical reality" and to a "subject who makes himself responsible for [them] in a transcendental adventure" (OG: 42). Genesis confronts Husserl with the aporia of the relation between the *pour-soi* and *en-soi*: "if psychological subjectivity could not of itself produce objective laws, one also asks how these laws that are purely autonomous and 'en-soi' can function and be recognized as such by a subject" (G: 49). Given this aporia one concludes that essences have "no foundation 'in-themselves,' independently of the intentional acts that aim at them" (36). Indeed, in the final section Derrida deconstructs Husserl's own constitution of the *eidos* with reference to its cultural intention.

The Sartrean allusions provide a context for Derrida's otherwise puzzling description of his "existential analytic" as an "'anthropology' . . . in the heideggerian sense" (251). By 1953 Heidegger had dissociated himself from "anthropology," which he equated with "humanism." Derrida's awareness of Heidegger's *Kehre* is evident when he emphasizes that the "existence" he opposes to "being" is not "that of Heidegger" (257n). A "heideggerian" anthropology is thus a convenient shorthand for the distinct theoretical formation produced in France through a double detour in which Heidegger and Sartre are read aslant of each other. This approach involves a "permanent critique of ourselves" from the vantage point of *fundamental* anthropology—a term Derrida still uses with reference to Heidegger in 1993, which has a certain warrant in *Being and Time* but which Heidegger himself might have repudiated. As opposed to more regional anthropologies located in particular cultures and disciplines, fundamental anthropology is the ontological foundation for such studies of man in his "appearing" at the ontic level. As such, and because, as Derrida says in *Aporias*, the "request . . . for the conditions of possibility often speaks the language of methodology," fundamental anthropology is also the interrogation of *anthropology* from a more "fundamental" perspective.[33]

Regardless of Derrida's later ambivalence about a term linked to humanism and enlightenment, *fundamental anthropology* is a convenient label for the approach invoked in 1953, which shares nothing "with the mundane science rejected by Husserl" (G: 251). At the same time, the existential analytic of the *Genesis* differs from that of *Aporias* in its more dialectical character. Heidegger's analytic "does not want to know anything" about the ontic and "derivative disciplines" of psychology or ethnology[34] to which Foucault was exposed as Professor of the History of Systems of Thought. But the early Derrida and Foucault both envision a dialectic of finitude in which "the empirical contents of knowledge" are not transcendentally reduced, yet "necessarily release, of themselves, the conditions that have made them possible" (OT: 322). The result is what Habermas calls "an erudite-positivistic historiography" that is also an "antiscience."[35] Or, in Foucault's words, the disciplines are still theorized and practiced as the "positive forms" in which man learns "his finitude" (OT: 314). But the dialectic they generate is recursive rather than teleological, moving constantly between a "part of [man] not reflected in a *cogito* to the act of thought by which he apprehends that part" (322).

More specifically this "double movement" responds to the emergence of man as "an empirico-transcendental doublet" pulled in contrary directions

(324, 322). For post-Kantian philosophy is caught in a "confusion of the empirical and the transcendental" and thus in a reflection that "is mixed in its levels" (341). Indeed, phenomenology itself, according to Foucault, exhibits this mixture in which the empirical stands for the transcendental, thus contaminating the very concept of the transcendental (341). This aporetic movement is also Derrida's concern. In analyzing Husserl's *Philosophy of Arithmetic*, he shows how the (transcendental) concept of numbers is constructed on the ground of the empirical; the "existent" thus paradoxically becomes the "primitive foundation" of essences (G: 74–75). Derrida's discussions of origin and genesis likewise focus on a reflection stalled by the supplementary relation between the transcendental and the empirical. On the other hand, it is because of its self-supplementing character that phenomenology has "always been led to questions" (OT: 326), and this is why Derrida can also describe it as "born" from its "initial failure" to reconcile structure and genesis (WD: 157).

In locating this failure in the "first phase" of phenomenology (159), Derrida assumes a second phase and perhaps a beyond of phenomenology. This beyond emerges in the clearing created by a new cartography of failure. Husserl failed, not because he did not reconcile the empirical and the transcendental, but because he did not respect the hiatus between them. Likewise the human sciences for Foucault are duplicitous because they try to conceal their problematic self-doubling. The early work of Derrida and Foucault weaves this doubling into the very fabric of a deconstruction in which epistemic analysis becomes the place where man learns his finitude. It is arguable that the *Genesis* is not yet deconstruction and that it repeats the mixture of the transcendental and the empirical as a gap between its own theory and practice. Derrida has not yet found a form of writing adequate to his thought. On a theoretical level, however, the direction he was beginning to take is clear.

The Cogito of Geometry

Whereas genesis is strongly privileged in Derrida's first study of Husserl, in "'Genesis and Structure' and Phenomenology" (1959), he refuses to choose between genesis and structure or, by extension, existential and transcendental phenomenology (WD: 154–68). Correspondingly Derrida's next study, *Edmund Husserl's "The Origin of Geometry": An Introduction*, is, at least on the surface, more structural than genetic in style. Focusing on only twenty pages, it lacks the range of the *Genesis* or *The Order of Things* and anticipates the close deconstructive analysis of the later work. Moreover, this exegetical "reduction" is repeated in the text's rigorously philosophic mode, which stylistically brackets the larger considerations that surface at the end of *Genesis*. The text's ascetic self-confinement reflects Derrida's sense that he had misrecognized the dialectic of finitude in yoking it to the infinite ambitions of cultural criticism. Nevertheless he alludes to Husserl's "The Origin of Geometry" in the *Genesis* and returns to *The Crisis of European Sciences and Transcendental Phenomenology* in the *Origin*, and this intertextuality frames his two earliest studies in a certain continuity.

In the *Genesis* Derrida speaks of a history of the "successive appearance of rational structures, of 'consciousnesses' (in the sense in which Sartre uses the word)," and an analysis that discloses the "dependence of . . . all philosophic intention" on "its historical moment" (G: 2). He thus allies himself with the study of "rationalities" undertaken after the war by Cavailles and Canguilhem (vii) and culminating in the early work of Foucault. As a historian of science, Canguilhem had begun to question the equation of science with truth when he shifted from the hard sciences as a metonymy for knowledge to the soft sciences. Foucault moves beyond his mentor by expanding the history of science into a history of reason in *The Order of Things* that doubles as an "antiscience" or "critique of reason."[36] He uses the human sciences to unmask the claims of all science to be in-itself and thus interrogates the structure of knowledge across the entire *Geisteswissenschaften*. It is against this backdrop that we can place Derrida's contemporaneous work up to *Of Grammatology* as a more limited attempt to rethink the cognitive subject of philosophy and linguistics. Derrida begins with Husserl because of Husserl's equation of philosophy with rigorous science via the metaphor of geometry. *Speech and Phenomena*, which inscribes this philosophy in its assumptions about language, allows Derrida to shift his analysis of the empirico-transcendental doubling of the subject from geometry to language theory and from Husserl to logocentrism in general. In the process Derrida begins to develop the grammatology that evolves into his own theory of language. But his subsequent path should not obscure our sense of his initial project. This project is epistemic rather than linguistic, concerned not with Derrida's autonomous theory but with rethinking intellectual history as a critique of reason in which knowledge is held responsible to its conditions of possibility.

The *Origin* deals with "transcendental" genesis and its attendant notions of a nonempirical "historicity," "origin," and "tradition" at the specific site of Husserl's attempt to construct geometry as an "ideal object" "independent of sensible spatiotemporality" (OG: 25–26, 90). As a pure science, geometry seems free from "factual existence" and thus from any reference to "*experience*" (44). As we shall see, however, the doubling at the heart of the philosophical-geometrical project is already foreshadowed, prior to any genesis, in the very structure of geometry as Derrida sees it. For geometry and the disciplines it represents are "*material* eidetics" whose "purpose is the thingly." These disciplines then behave as "*abstract* material sciences" by treating only "certain eidetic components of corporeal things in general, disregarding their independent and concrete totality" (123). Geometry already displays the mixed epistemic behavior that Foucault attributes to the human sciences—as forms that need and eschew an empirical ground for the transcendental. This doubling only continues as Husserl traces the "origin" or genetic constitution of geometry, its recourse to history as the medium in which the *eidos* "(in one and the same movement) . . . discloses and lets itself be threatened" (142).

Derrida's analysis thus hints at what Husserl repudiates, namely, a "psychogenetic" analysis of Husserlian phenomenology as produced by "a subject who makes himself responsible for it in a transcendental adventure" (26, 42). Derrida intimates the desire behind the privileging of mathematics at the outset of the *Origin*: "the mathematical object is *ideal*. Its being is thoroughly transparent and exhausted by its phenomenality. Absolutely objective, i.e. totally rid of empirical subjectivity, it nevertheless is only what it appears to be. Therefore, it is always reduced to its phenomenal sense, and its being is, from the outset, to be an object for a pure consciousness" (27). The seduction of the mathematical object is like that of Hölderlin's flowers in de Man's analysis of the gap separating consciousness from objects; it is a being whose existence coincides at all times with its essence (RR: 4). As pure phenomenality, "mathematical space no longer knows what Sartre calls *transphenomenality*" (OG: 136); it is without material remainder, without that excess that inscribes the cogito in an ek-static relation to itself. The mathematical object thus signifies the bracketing of the natural and historical realms by which Husserl felt so profoundly threatened because they inscribed the cogito in the contingency of "empirical subjectivity."

In what follows, Derrida, though naming him only twice, hints at a Sartrean analysis of the mathematical object as an *en-soi* constructed by a *pour-soi* to simulate its own autonomy. By describing the ideal object as an "object for a pure consciousness," and by later personifying the philosophy of science as a "gaze," he discloses in the very institution of knowledge a transference in which the ideal object vicariously gives its identity to the philosophy that studies it. If the "Idea" of philosophy has a *psychological* genesis in "the act of a concrete consciousness" (42), Derrida also points towards its *historical* genesis. As in *Genesis*, this Idea, it is hinted, is a "bound ideality" that is fundamentally Eurocentric though troped as "universal" (131), and its "coming to consciousness" institutes a Hegelian history that aims at "a universal teleology of Reason" (131, 145).

Origin, though written eight years later, resembles *Genesis* on the level of *content* and *can* be read as a "critique." It abounds with references to "history," and whole sections (9 in particular) assume Derrida's earlier analysis. Yet there is a curious difference in the *form* of the later text, a certain reticence not unlike that analyzed with reference to Foucault in Chapter 7. Derrida seems willing to treat the universalism of science as a "cultural formation" (58) but does not actually do so. He creates a space for reading Husserl's work in terms of its psychological and historical genesis, but he does not provide the details of such a reading. In fact he insists that "we will always be guided by [Husserl's] own intentions, even when we get caught up in certain difficulties" (27). Derrida's critique thus occurs only obliquely. He continually reminds us of what Husserl brackets, introducing other methodological possibilities even as he brackets them. Moreover, he often attributes to Husserl a radicality at odds with his own characterization of him and more consistent with the readings of Ricoeur and Merleau-Ponty. Husserl, for instance, is credited with the Sartrean view that "every ideal objectivity is produced by the act of a concrete consciousness" and has "a history which is always already announced in that consciousness" (42). The terms for a critique are made available in Derrida's text. But the use of those terms is left to the reader, who finds him- or herself in a dilemma. If we read Husserl according to his own statements, we are "caught up in certain difficulties;" if we do not, we are in a sense ignoring "his own intentions."

The delegation or dispersal of critique into the space of reading is a new stage in Derrida's technique. To begin with, it attempts to make his practice more consonant with his theory. For the last section of *Genesis* reconceives intellectual history within an existential analytic only to fall back into an empiricism at odds with the project of a *fundamental* anthropology. This section allows transcendental thinking to be usurped by practical reason. In *Origin*, Derrida withdraws from constituting himself as the subject who performs a critique, and he thus enacts a mode of analysis in which the contents of knowledge are made to "release, of themselves, the conditions that have made them possible" (OT: 322). This concern with conditions allows epistemic analysis to occur in a fundamental rather than regional way. At the same time, because Derrida is not firmly present as a subject presumed to know, critique cannot constitute itself as an alternative form of knowledge and is itself drawn into the analytic of finitude. This is true as much of our critique as of Derrida's because our self-constitution of ourselves as enlightened subjects finds no support in the voice of the author.

In other words, Derrida's elusiveness in this text is inscribed in a new concern with *method*. Here it is worth citing the final pages, where Derrida speaks of method as response and responsibility. Phenomenology's "Method of Discourse" is

> *Selbstbesinnung* and *Verantwortung*, the free resolution to "take up one's own sense" . . . in order to make oneself accountable, through speech, for an imperilled pathway. This speech is historical because it is always already a *response*. Responsibility here means shouldering [*se charger de*] a word one hears spoken, as well as taking on oneself the transfer of sense, in order to look after its advance [*cheminement*]. In its most radical implications, then, Method is not the neutral preface or *preambulatory* exercise of thought. Rather, it is thought itself in the consciousness of its complete historicity. (OG: 149)

This passage in fact exemplifies Derrida's curious approach of using Husserl to ventriloquize the terms of his own deconstruction. Ostensibly the passage describes *Husserl's* method, Husserl's sense that the *Endstiftung* of phenomenology lies in "a concrete *consciousness* which is made *responsible* for it despite the finitude of that consciousness" (141). Yet if the "radical responsibility" to method is Husserlian (141), the method itself is not. Rather Derrida, who was reading Levinas at the time, emphasizes the ethics rather than the logic of method, thus linking method to the finitude rather than the infinite ambitions of philosophy.

We shall return to this new "care" for method, which is Kant's and Heidegger's as well as Husserl's. Suffice it to say that it emerges here as the very site and stimulus for the existential analytic. Karl Jaspers describes the asceticism of method in Kant, who "forgoes richness of content, because he wishes to convey a pure consciousness of the 'forms.'" Jaspers specifically discusses the role of formalism in transcendental thinking: "Forms are superior to philosophical embodiment, because, if I think them through, they make me produce my thinking. They act upon my non-objective inwardness, my freedom."[37] Derrida's displacement of commentary by method is likewise designed to make us produce our thinking on a fundamental level. But the role of method in the analytic of finitude that *Genesis* had failed to develop is equally important. At the heart of this analytic is the relation between reading and "tradition," which for Husserl is an "open chain" in which "each investigator not only feels himself *tied* to all the others by the unity of an object or task" but also feels himself constituted as an individual by this "total subjectivity" (60–61). Husserl's notion of tradition does *not* suggest a *Selbstbesinnung* responsible "through speech" for the transcendental adventure in which his project has its genesis. Rather, as Derrida also says, such tradition is "the ether of historical perception" (49). Derrida's reading of Husserl is a "response" that takes on the transfer of sense differently, in its *différance*, so as to situate Husserl in the imperilled path of his own history. Derrida thus advances Husserl's concern for method towards a more radical responsibility for itself as an ethics of method, though by taking up a burden hidden in Husserl's own words. In this advance Derrida's response is also accountable to its own historicity—a responsibility he does not so much state as repeat through his reader. For his elusiveness forces readers to shoulder the words of his text, to take up their own sense through the text, and to place their own reading in the "imperilled pathway" of their own history.

At this point we notice a curious crossing of two kinds of "phenomenology." Derrida's concern with method is that of Husserl rather than Merleau-Ponty and Sartre and marks his commitment to transcendental thinking. But this self-reflection of transcendental thinking is also described as an "existential act" (G: 281). A transcendental thinking not tied to logic had already been practised by Heidegger, who similarly focuses on the finitude of human being as *Dasein*. Derrida's language of responsibility and free resolution, however, is specifically existential and not simply Heideggerian. Some of this vocabulary can be traced to Levinas, though one should not forget that Levinas's difference from Heidegger on the ground of *ethics* has in a sense passed through Sartre's sensitivity to bad faith and is a form of existentialism-though freed from practical reason. But Levinas cannot account for Derrida's emphasis on taking up one's own sense and on *choice* as the very site of finitude. It seems clear, then, that Derridean deconstruction at this stage is less an overturning of phenomenology than an analytic of finitude produced by the mutually supplementary relationship among various kinds of phenomenology.

From this perspective it is appropriate that a certain *aphanisis*, a (dis)appearance of Derrida's own voice in *Origin*, leaves the nature of his relationship to phenomenology undetermined. Unlike Ricoeur and Merleau-Ponty, Derrida does not want to recuperate the late Husserl, and indeed this is what makes his reading deconstructive. But since this deconstruction is done with terms borrowed from Husserl himself (not to mention Sartre and Heidegger), Derrida may not be as different from Merleau-Ponty as he claims. It is clear at any rate that he does not stand outside phenomenology in the manner of Thao, perhaps because he cannot be as sure as Thao about what phenomenology is. Sometimes Derrida's difference from Ricoeur and Merleau-Ponty seems decisive, and sometimes it does not. One could argue that he breaks with them on the matter of Husserl's openness to history but finds much of value in Husserl's method, except that method and history cannot be separated. The early Derrida leaves the precise nature of the difference between deconstruction and phenomenology, indeed of the deferrals and relays operating between them, deliberately obscure. In this sense he might not disagree with Lyotard that this difference, like phenomenology itself, is still "'in process.'"[38]

Speech and Phenomena *or Logic as Existence*

Published five years after *Origin*, Derrida's third study of Husserl reflects a shift in content but an intensification of *Origin*'s form and method. *Speech and Phenomena* continues the disciplinary project of questioning philosophy's claim to purity. But it transfers the analysis of man's empirico-transcendental doubling from the aporia of genesis and origin to that of writing. In fact it expands a section of *Origin* that deals with language as the Achilles's heel of Husserl's attempt to posit a realm of ideal objectivities. In this foregrounding of *écriture*, history and cultural formations disappear from the Derridean analytic; at this same moment, Sartre is writing the introduction to Frantz Fanon's *Wretched of the Earth*. It would be all too easy to see this occlusion as evidence of the linguistic turn and to read *Speech and Phenomena* as dismantling phenomenology. But in fact Derrida's concern with the "existential constitution of the theoretical attitude" (G: 259) is clearer than ever before, although the methodological ascesis of a discourse on the sign seems designed as a further refinement of the existential analytic.

In *Origin*, Derrida isolates language as a key element in Husserl's representation of geometry as a form of universal knowledge. Ideal formations must be fully "expressible in discourse and translatable . . . from one language into another" (OG: 66). For Husserl this is not problematic because he conceives language in terms of logic, as "an immediate eidetic" that assumes "a spontaneous neutralization of the factual existence of the speaking subject" (67). Yet, for Derrida, Husserl's project is shipwrecked by language, which "offers the most dangerous resistance to the phenomenological reduction" by exposing "transcendental discourse" to an "ambiguous worldliness" (67–69). Thus the paradox in which Husserl is caught is that science is only possible through "a reduction of all language" (75) in an "inner life" that has no need of "communication" (SP: 70, 38). At the same time this "pure expression" needs the representation from which it retreats because "ideality" becomes objective only in acquiring "linguistic flesh" (SP: 38; OG: 75–76).

Expanding this discussion of language, Derrida deconstructs transcendental phenomenology through its dependence on language, as he had earlier disclosed the finitude of philosophy through its supplementary need for embodiment in history. More specifically he takes apart the illusion of language as pure expression. Because language always depends on indication and because indication refers to the world, the transcendental is "contaminated" by the psychic, as spirit becomes consciousness. (SP: 20, 30). Thus, Derrida's concentration on the sign only seemingly anticipates the poststructuralist reduction of the empirical to the linguistic. In fact his linguistic turn must be read with his statement that no concept can be "isolated" from the "ontology" and the approach to life that it contains (WD: 118). His thematization of language therefore involves a double gesture in which the Derridean reduction can be unfolded into what it infolds. For, as Derrida explains, "the whole future problem of the reduction and all the conceptual differences in which it is articulated (fact/essence, worldliness/transcendentality)," and thus the very "enigma of Husserl's phenomenology," are metonymically present in the difference "between two kinds of signs" (SP: 30). In this sense Derrida repeats the reduction only to analyze it. Or, put differently, the turn to language returns on itself in an unforgetting of the use of language to forget being, which will once again be forgotten by poststructuralism.

Speech and Phenomena was written before Derrida's return to Husserl in "The Ends of Man." To adapt his own figure, it can be "stapled" (P: 4) into the essays folded between the texts on Husserl—specifically the two on the Jewish writers Jabès and Levinas. In his essay on Jabès's *Le Livre des questions* Derrida already inscribes the problem of history in that of writing in order to decouple it from a "Hellenic" temporality of nostalgia for origins and to displace it into the "Hebraic" space of exile. The Judaizing trope of writing thinks history in existential terms rather than in the still transcendental terms of Heideggerian temporality. The founding text for the "exchange between the Jew and writing" is Walter Benjamin's *Origin of German Tragic Drama*, which Derrida echoes when he describes how "writing is itself written, but also ruined, . . . within [Jabès's] book, which infinitely reflects itself and which develops as a painful questioning of its own possibility" (WD: 65). As ruin or allegory, writing gives history its structure as an involution,[39] a "painful folding of itself" in which it "reflect[s] itself as it ciphers itself" (64). History, then, only seems to disappear; instead, writing becomes the crypt where Derrida maintains and renounces an identification with "historic anxiety" (76). Moreover, writing is described as a state of consciousness; it is a "dissimulation of [the] Face" of God as Logos, a "cry" that stands in place of speech, and a "tearing of the self toward the other within a confession of infinite separation" (67, 73, 75). The term *écriture* is charged with complicating links to Judaism, Schelling, Hegel, and Artaud. In this sense it is less a poststructuralist than a postphenomenological motif, as Derrida admits when he writes that the "Jewish consciousness is indeed the unhappy consciousness," and Jabès's book is "the poem inscribed just beyond the phenomenology of the mind" (68).

If the essay on Jabès is important in grasping what is cathected onto *écriture*, then the one on Levinas is crucial to understanding both Derrida's method and his unsettling of Husserl's method. Levinas had virtually founded Husserl studies in France, and Derrida's argument with phenomenology is thus closely intertwined with Levinas. The early Levinas is not overtly critical of Husserl, whom he reads through Heidegger so as to locate in the concern with intentionality, temporality, and concrete life a counterweight to the privileging of "theoretism" and of intuition as the grasping of presence. Levinas thus paves the way for Merleau-Ponty and Ricoeur, who see Husserl's late work as anticipating existential phenomenology. Levinas never really dissociates himself from Husserl; instead, having recuperated him by conflating him with Heidegger, he later takes him apart metonymically by turning away from Heidegger. *Speech and Phenomena* is thus the deconstruction of Husserl that Levinas might have written and should be read with "Violence and Metaphysics: An Essay on the Thought of Emmanuel Levinas." In this essay Derrida zigzags across Levinas's corpus to create a space for his own text as a radicalization of Levinas's work on Husserl. It is modeled not on this work but on the later demystification of Heidegger in *Time and the Other* and *Existence and Existents* as well as on Hyppolite's reading of Hegel in *Genesis and Structure*.

Though Derrida is not uncritical of Levinas, the nature of these criticisms is worth noting. Derrida draws back from Levinas's absolute refusal of "hypostasis" and "materiality," his pursuit of a trace that "signifies *outside* all intentionality . . . and *outside* of any project in which it would be sighted." He describes this "purely heterological thought" of "*pure* difference" as a "*dream*" and an extreme form of "empiricism." In "its most elevated nonviolent urgency" Levinas's thought proposes "a language without phrase" that is simply the reversed mirror image of Husserl's "science" (WD: 151–52, 147).

Insofar as there is "no phrase" that "does not pass through the violence of the concept" (147), Derrida is reluctant to denounce phenomenology, with which he prefers to reengage Levinas's thought from the outside. As important, he sees Levinas as deeply phenomenological and not only because breaks are always "fatally, reinscribed" in what they overturn (P: 24). The relation between Levinas and phenomenology is analogous to the one Merleau-Ponty sees between existential and transcendental phenomenology. Levinas is doubly indebted to the generative aporias of phenomenology: to Husserl for "demonstrating the irreducibility of intentional incompleteness, and therefore of alterity" and to Heidegger because "no ethics—in Levinas' sense—can be opened" without the thought of Being, which "let[s] be the existent" and thus avoids enclosing "transcendence within identification and empirical economy" (WD: 120, 137, 142).

In other words, Derrida in the early sixties sees phenomenology as facilitating Levinas's work, whereas in the period of "The Ends of Man" he sees any link to phenomenology as an obstacle produced by thought's tendency to relapse into the error it deconstructs (M: 135). Moreover, although Derrida does not stress this, Sartre is also part of Levinas's inheritance. Despite their difference on the nature of the Other, Levinas could not have made ethics into a first philosophy if Heidegger's "thought of Being" had not been read in France through Sartre's responsibility to ethics as well as ontology. As important, Levinas's complaint that Heideggerian "nothingness still has a sort of activity and being" (TO: 49) echoes Sartre's criticism that Heidegger's negatives hide a positivity. Like Blanchot, Levinas reconfigures Heideggerian philosophy within the nonspace of night rather than day. But this deconstruction, as already argued, operates through a chiasm in which Heidegger is used to contest Sartre's nostalgia for the cogito, while the thought of Being is in turn exposed to its own radical nothingness.

By emphasizing Levinas's debts, Derrida locates his thought within the community of phenomenology as the most radical outcome of that process by which phenomenology is "work[ed] ceaselessly" by the "themes of nonpresence" that it both introduces and resists (WD: 121). From this perspective "Violence and Metaphysics" is also an autoreflection on the way Derrida's own deconstruction emerges inside a phenomenology always already open to the thought of its outside. In the jewish essays Ricoeur's distinction between transcendental and existential phenomenology is intensified as the difference between greek and jew. Judaism in Jabès and Levinas takes the existential *topoi* of experience, temporality, and alterity and decouples them from their recontainment in the Hellenism of Heidegger. Thus the jew becomes the limit case of the existential, of an irremissible thrownness, and of an experience no longer linked positivistically to presence but rather to "that which is most irreducible within experience: the passage and departure toward the other" (WD: 152, 83).

Derrida's reading of Levinas frames his new work on Husserl in two ways. First there is Levinas's belief that "any consideration of method" goes beyond "a purely formal logic and deep into . . . [a] conception of being."[40] Levinas reads Husserl's intuitionism not as a neutral preface to thought but existentially as a way of being that Derrida will link to the metaphysics of presence. Second, in deconstructing Husserl, Derrida develops his own way of thinking *between* the existential and the transcendental. This analytic is not Heideggerian even if Derrida uses Heidegger to question Levinas's position on the end of man as a form of "nonhistory; nonoccurrence" (WD: 147).[41] Heidegger, as we shall see, conflates existence and transcendence, using the former as an alibi for the latter. Although he *theorizes* transcendental thinking in terms of ek-stasis and difference rather than logic, in practice he reencloses it in identification, in the interiority of Being instead of the subject. But Derrida's existential analytic emerges in the *difference* between transcendence and existence, in the "tearing" (75) or chiasm between Heidegger and his French successors produced through the occupation of interiority by alterity. This tearing, whose trauma is occasionally and strategically echoed by Derrida, is felt not just conceptually but in the distinctly un-Heideggerian *tone* of French philosophy It is felt in the violent images that occupy Sartre's wartime philosophy and in their *après coup* in Blanchot and Levinas.

In *Speech and Phenomena* Derrida explores the "existential constitution" of Husserl's distinction between expression and indication. Briefly, while "an expression is a purely linguistic sign," an indication mixes phenomenality with materiality (SP: 18). In expression, meaning therefore attains an absolute "self-relationship" whereas in indication the mind "*pass[es]* by thought from something to something else" through an "external detour" that is "the world" as a site of alterity (28, 78). For this reason, Husserl struggles to bracket indication, which threatens the very project of transcendence by reimplicating language in "everything that falls subject to the 'reductions'"

(30). Pure expression, however, is a contradiction in terms because it can occur only in "the solitary mental life" of "a language without communication" (42). Expression everywhere depends on and is "contaminated" by indication (20). The difference between the two thus contains a buried narrative about body and spirit in which language becomes the alienation of meaning in the "body of the signifier" (77), while its figuration as "expression" is the (im)possibility of Incarnation, of the recuperation of "*Körper* as *Leib*" through the agency of *Geist* or spirit (35).

That this deconstruction is itself a phenomenology is obvious. Expression and indication are not just signs but differing forms of consciousness and ways of being in the world. Reading Husserl for what he indicates as well as expresses, Derrida (psycho)analyzes the ontology (24) and ontotheology of transcendental phenomenology by using the vocabularies of existential phenomenology. To begin with he evokes Heidegger, as befits his continuation of the task Levinas had begun. He comments on Husserl's sheltering of the transcendental from the "psychic" through the choice of the technical terms "*Sein, bestehen,* and *Bestand*" instead of the ontological terms "*Dasein, existieren,* and *Realität*" (28–30). Earlier, by translating *Leib* as *chair* he had invoked Merleau-Ponty's notion of the flesh as chiasm to problematize Husserl's figuring of expression as incarnation (OG: 75).[42] Indeed, *Speech and Phenomena* contains a sustained, if unthematized, opening of transcendental phrases to their existential reinscriptions.

But this interweaving of the transcendental with the existential does not simply register the logic by which one leads to the other. And it is here that the trace of "Sartre" is significant because Sartre performs the aporia between the two, the foundering of the transcendental within the existential. As he had done with geometry, Derrida uses the *pour-soi/en-soi* distinction to frame Husserl's theory of language. Whereas in expression the intending consciousness achieves being in-itself, indication has a "structure of substitution or reference," of "deferred presence" (69, 23, 138). Insofar as it "is a sign for something" that it is not, indication brings with it an entire thematic of being and nothingness in which the sign produces the cogito as a being that is not what it is and is what it is not. Nor is Derrida analyzing a binary in which expression resolves the problems of indication. For Husserl leaves the temporal status and thus the reality of the *en-soi* in relation to the *pour-soi* radically unclear. At times expression seems entirely in-itself and has no need of indication; its meaning is "*present to the self* in the life of a present that has not yet gone forth from itself into the world, space, or nature" (40). At other times expression is the simulacrum of an inside projected outside without having to leave the inside (32). At once for-itself and in-itself, it is a "going-forth-beyond-itself" of a sense that miraculously "remain[s] in itself" (33). Given these supplementary definitions, language becomes the site at which the transcendental desire for expression is constantly "caught up" (20) and doubled by its dependence on the empirical realm it dismisses. In Nancy's terms, expression is constantly exposed through the very process of its "ex-position."

Derrida also narrativizes Husserl in terms of a Sartrean anxiety about lack, alterity, and the threat of visibility. Indication *lacks* the "inwardness of life with-itself" because it depends on an other who is also not present except as "mediately indicated" through his outside (78, 39). Because the other is a form of "nonpresence," the "relation with the other" implicit in the very structure of the sign registers the vulnerability of consciousness to (its own) exteriority (40). For Sartre too this vulnerability had been inscribed in language as the self's (de)construction by the Other. Language here is homologous to "visibility," which for Sartre is not a making present but a loss of self. Derrida echoes Sartre's sense of the threat posed by the Look when he writes that "visibility and spatiality . . . destroy the self-presence of will and spiritual animation. . . . *They are literally the death of that self-presence*" (35).

Visibility is phenomenology's trope for a pure showing, and Sartre's deconstruction of this trope places phenomenality and the associated themes of light and intuition in "a state of encounter and surface" (72). To become visible, to be seen, is to step outside "the sphere of 'my own'" into the body as other. Visibility is a form of exposure or ex-position. For the body is a skin separating inside from outside, a "surface" through which the inside is "displayed" and "exposed in the world" (79). The "body" of the signifier must likewise be a site of exposure, which accounts for Derrida's repeated linking of the sign to "death" (10, 35, 132). Thus Derrida describes indication as "the process of death at work in signs" (40). He also writes that the "relationship with *my death* . . . lurks in [the] determination of being as presence" and that the "possibility of the sign is this relationship with death" (54).

This "rhetoric of threat and loss"[43] (with its metaphors of body, surface, and death) is not Husserl's or Heidegger's. It is specific to French thinking and to the French "darkening" of Enlightenment noted by Lyotard. Derrida's metaphors cathect a trauma that happens twice over: first through Sartre's darkening of Heidegger in the replacement of being with nothingness and then through its *après-coup* in Levinas's and Blanchot's postexistential rethinking of death and of writing as a site of death. To analyze French philosophy in terms of the double blow that Lyotard sees in the structure of trauma is to confront the (philosophical) trauma concealed in postwar French phenomenology. For Heidegger death is still *Dasein*'s "utmost possibility"; for Sartre possibility is aporetically bound to nothingness. But Levinas insists that death is not "a present"; it is "absolutely unknowable" and "foreign to all light" (TO: 70). As Lyotard explains, the second blow is at once a repetition, an analysis, and a covering over of the first.[44] Sartre's lurid figures register a violence that he cannot economize and that we can explain as the traumatic effect of his still being attached to the cogito he deconstructs. Levinas takes nothingness beyond such attachment into the space of nonpossibility. He defines a "nonnegativity" (WD: 119): a negativity that avoids violence because it knows no difference between nothingness and an "irremissible being, without exit" (TO: 50). By the same token Levinas creates a space (to use Blanchot's term) in which no project can be sighted, a space without visibility and thus vulnerability. In short, he resolves Sartre's trauma only by eliding Sartre's insight into the violence of death; he has the instinctive sense that nonviolence is the cessation of consciousness in a relation of in-difference between the *pour-soi* and the *en-soi*. But this insight returns in Derrida's work in the stress during this period on violence as embedded in the very fact of writing (OGr: 101–40).[45]

Speech and Phenomena does not mention Sartre, Levinas, or Blanchot, thus incorporating the history that connects them only through metaphors that miss their representation.[46] Derrida's debt to Levinas's and Blanchot's discussions of death is clear, as is the space they open beyond Sartre. On the other hand, one notes that the relationship to death is "the possibility of the sign" (54) and that the sign is therefore constituted not only by its nonpresence but also by man's relation as for-itself to this nonpresence. The notion of a "relationship" with death accords with Foucault's insistence that man cannot "posit himself in the . . . transparency of a *cogito*" but also cannot "inhabit" the "inertia" of a being without consciousness (OT: 322). Indeed,

Derrida finally turns to Hegel, rather than Heidegger or Levinas, to argue that the "appearing of the Ideal as an infinite *differance* can only be produced within a relationship with death in general" (SP: 101–2). Derrida's evocation of (a French) Hegel to deconstruct Husserl also doubles as a reference to Sartre, the most Hegelian of the French phenomenologists. For although death allows Levinas and Blanchot to refigure the Heideggerian unthought in terms "foreign to all light," for Derrida this radical alterity signifies only in relation to man: "Only a relation to my-death could make the infinite differing of presence appear" (102).

What these echoes suggest is that Derridean deconstruction participates in the radicalizing of Sartrean anthropology we will also see in the early work of Foucault and Baudrillard. Or, put differently, the displacement of history by language is not necessarily a break from Derrida's earlier epistemic project, which he describes as an interrogation of "science, history and the history of science" from the perspective of the problems of consciousness, presence, and origin (P: 5). Indeed, in its context, the linguistic turn may involve something very different from what we now assume. It involves, to be sure, a certain asceticism and reflexiveness but also a reinvestment of the thought from the outside in a philosophical "economy": a "circulation between the inside and outside of philosophy" through a reengagement of nonviolence with "the necessity of the phrase" (P: 6; WD: 147).

Derrida's work so far is consistent with the rethinking of phenomenology in the fifties in terms of a "reciprocal envelopment" of philosophy and the social. This idea, outlined by Merleau-Ponty in 1951, is more fully developed in Lyotard's *Phenomenology*, which is divided into two sections entitled "Husserl" and "Phenomenology and the Human Sciences"—though arguably this envelopment goes back to Husserl's contemporary Georg Simmel and before that to Hegel. In its most complete form this general project thinks the aftermath of post-Kantian idealism by interrogating the very foundations of the relationship between the spheres of pure and practical reason. The division of Lyotard's book suggests two tasks combined differently by different theorists. The first involves a reconsideration of the human sciences within a philosophical framework and, specifically, a phenomenological rethinking of the relation between the social (or scientific) as lived experience and its structure as object. But the second task (more emphasized by Derrida) ceaselessly exposes transcendental and existential thinking to each other so as to question philosophy itself and "the limit on the basis of which philosophy became possible, [and] defined itself as the *episteme*" (P: 6). *Of Grammatology* is Derrida's most complete version of this historiography in the form of an antiscience and differs from the more "nomadic" character" of a subsequent French thought that Lyotard still describes as "existential-ontological"[47] in that its *bricolage* is still encyclopedic. Indeed, the intersections between Derrida and Foucault during this period are considerable. Derrida describes his work in 1971 as a "genealogy" or as a reading of "philosophemes . . . as kinds of symptoms." He also imagines extending this work to other "fields" including "mathematical and logical formalization, linguistics, ethnology, psychoanalysis, political economy, [and] biology" (P: 7). In *Of Grammatology* he begins this extension into the fields of political economy and anthropology.

Speech and Phenomena plays a prefatory role in this project, which is why Derrida describes it as a "long note" to his two other books of 1967, placing it before *Of Grammatology* in "a classical philosophical architecture" (P: 4–5). Thematically it continues the analysis of "epistimemes" (6) with reference to language theory. But where Foucault ranges across a vast canvas, Derrida's signature is a concentration on exegesis as a mode of rigor and care. More important, then, is the text's methodological contribution as Derrida's most intensive development of the analytic of finitude promised in *Genesis*. This analytic could not have occurred without the second phase of phenomenology, for, to adapt Thao, it reveals classical philosophy as reproducing on the "symbolic level of ideas" the existential (rather than material) operations by which man appropriates his world.[48] As such, it raises questions profoundly alien to philosophy as "rigorous science" by making knowledge answerable to the experience of alterity, the encounter with nothingness, and the problem of how one thinks in the absence of foundation. But the existential has all too often been determined by a metaphysics that makes experience "an encountering of an irreducible presence" and thus "the perception of a phenomenality" (WD: 152). That these questions are (un)concealed within a reading of Husserl is thus part of the "double gesture" (P: 6) by which Derrida denies to existential analysis its fragile privileges of interiority and presence.

Interlude: Derrida's Poststructuralist Turn

Speech and Phenomena can be read in two ways: retrospectively through the texts of the sixties or prospectively as foretelling Derrida's growing concern with method as it emerges through a reflection on language. The two readings correspond to two Derridas. On the one hand, Derrida is now often seen as post-Heideggerian. According to Tim Clark, Derrida's work has little to do with Yale deconstruction, which simply inverts "positivist assumptions about language" and is concerned with "epistemological" problems such as the status of representation or the unavoidability of aporias. By contrast, Derrida's thought is "ontological" and involves "a mode of 'literary' or heteronomic philosophical writing" that engages "otherness in a way inaccessible to theoretical texts." On the other hand, Clark also concedes that Derrida's work on philosophers is very different from his writing on Mallarmé and Blanchot and constitutes a form of post-Hegelian dialectics that "refuses to subsume the work of negativity in the universal."[49] This second Derrida is the one assumed by Norris, who sees both Derrida and de Man as practitioners of (Kantian) "critique."[50] Norris's reading crosses paths with the one offered here, though I have used the word *analytic* rather than *critique* to mark Derrida's more philosophical emphasis and his distance from any involvement in practical reason.

As discussed here, the Derridean analytic in the sixties has much in common with the approach I trace in the early Foucault, namely, an onto-epistemic analysis of the human sciences in relation to an unconscious disclosed by literature or language. Indeed, Derrida situates his work in relation to the rise of "the so-called *human* sciences" (M: 117). In other words, his early work is consistent with a philosophical anthropology deriving from the crossing of Sartre and Heidegger, yet very different from the work of Heidegger he later privileges. Foucault responds to Lyotard's call for a transposition of phenomenology into the human sciences. In so doing he does not simply put phenomenology to practical use, as Bourdieu does in adapting the notion of *habitus* from Husserl and Merleau-Ponty. Rather he analyzes social forms phenomenologically in terms of the structures of forgetting that constitute them. We have traced this same kind of analysis in Derrida's deconstruction of the "ideal objectivities" of geometry and philosophy. In this

process writing, rather than being a site for "something analogous to the an-
nunication or 'arrival' of being," is a form of what David Carroll calls
"paraesthetics," functioning as an "aesthetics turned against itself or pushed
beyond" itself towards the "*extra*-aesthetic . . . issues raised by the question
of form" after Kant.[51] By analogy, we could describe Derrida's deconstruction at this stage as para-ontological.

The late sixties, however, mark a shift in Derrida's work, in which
Husserl, Hegel, structuralism, and Heidegger are tropologically condensed.
As we have seen, Derrida revalorizes transcendental phenomenology under
the sign of "the end of man." He now praises Husserl for his description of
"transcendental structures" that are without genetic links to "society, culture,
language, or . . . 'psyche'" (M: 118). That Derrida credits Hegel with the
same enlightenment is doubly symptomatic when we consider *how* he constructs Hegel in "The Ends of Man." In attributing to Hegel a "science of
the structures of the phenomenality of the spirit itself relating to itself"
(117), Derrida invokes the very Hegel linked to Husserl in *Genesis* by an imperialism of the transcendental. Moreover, he polemically simplifies his own
more complex understanding of a Hegel whom Ricoeur opposes to Husserl
as an origin for existential phenomenology. For whereas Derrida had once
seen Hegel as sensitive to the relation between writing and death (OGr: 25),
he now praises him for inaugurating a "science of the experience of consciousness," a "science" of the "structures" of spirit (M: 117). Even as Derrida
alludes in the term *experience* to the phenomenological Hegel privileged in
France, he reads the *Phenomenology* through the *Logic* as a "science" of
experience.

This return to Hegel and Husserl as names for rigor and science is overdetermined by Husserl's affinities with structuralism, noted by Derrida in 1959.
As I suggest in Chapter 7, Derrida's work in the late sixties is marked by an
increasingly poststructural rhetoric. "Husserl" thus functions as a paleonym
facilitating the reconfiguration of deconstruction as poststructuralism by concealing it within the continuity of a critique of phenomenology. This continuity, however, contains a curious exchange of positions. Whereas he had
once used the second phase of phenomenology to deconstruct the first, Derrida now transposes a phenomenology contemporaneous with "the first
structuralist projects" (WD: 159) to the "end" of philosophy. In the process

Derrida reduces Husserl as well as Hegel. He forgets that beneath "the serene use of [transcendental] concepts" is a recurring "incompleteness" in which the "*structuralist* demand" for a form "organized according to [its own] internal legality" is "unbalanced" by the search for the genesis of structures. He also forgets his own statement on the "transition from the structural to the genetic" as opening philosophical autonomy to its own contingency (WD: 156–57, 164).

But the condensing of Hegel and Husserl is merely a tool for the disciplining of phenomenology as poststructuralism, which is predicated on the degradation of existential phenomenology. Yet how to read this turn is far from evident. For "Derrida" in his later work is much harder to identify as a voice or subject than are the other theorists discussed here. Moreover, if a certain voice makes itself heard in "The Ends of Man," this voice is not uniformly sustained through Derrida's other work from 1968 to 1971, nor is it consistently replaced by another (post-Heideggerian) voice in the seventies and thereafter. Butler's comments on the performative subject are particularly appropriate to Derrida inasmuch as we discern a sharp turn away from existential phenomenology in "The Ends of Man" but have no clear sense of what lies behind it. While there is therefore no subject who makes the turn, a subject is produced in this turn; the turn thus "function[s] as a tropological inauguration of the subject" on a basis whose "ontological status" is uncertain and transpositional.[52] In "The Ends of Man" Derrida emerges as a poststructural subject, but the performative nature of this subject means—more so than in other cases analyzed in this book—that the essay is less important as a key to Derrida than as the source of certain effects produced by "his" poststructuralism. This performativity—that creates space both for keeping things open and also for evasion and disavowal—also defines to some extent Derrida's post-Heideggerianism. For here too it is easier to characterize post-Heideggerianism than to attribute it definitively to Derrida. But even though we may not be able to attribute it to Derrida, we can still affirm its performative existence as a series of effects authorized by their association with Derrida.

These effects, in the case of poststructuralism, are given a political location in "The Ends of Man" but one that is constituted around a gap. On the one hand, the essay models itself on Heidegger's "Letter on Humanism," which begins by privileging thinking over action.[53] On the other hand, this turn against the political is revoked by the invocation of May 1968, although the date provides only the most oblique gesture of political engagement. The date tells us that theory is always inscribed in a politics even though the essay tells us that it should not lead to one. The rejection of anthropology, experience, and existence clearly has to do with the politics of Sartre and Merleau-Ponty (an association Derrida rightly resists in the case of de Man). A similar caution presumably attaches to the French students' attempt to "change terrain, in a discontinuous and irruptive fashion . . . by affirming an absolute break," even though Derrida is sympathetic to the American students opposed to the Vietnam war (M: 135, 113). As if to sublate all such ambiguities and contradictions, Derrida for much of the essay proclaims his stubborn attachment to a formalism of method and logic uncomplicated by the details of historical experience. And yet what is the politics of this transcendentalism of method that authorizes poststructuralism, given that its key figures, Husserl and Hegel, converted their method back into a practice in *The Crisis of European Sciences and Transcendental Phenomenology* and *The Philosophy of History*? It is a question that the curious framing of Derrida's essay perhaps deliberately invites us to ask.

It would be wrong to answer this question by treating poststructuralism as a form of neoconservatism or disillusioned radicalism;[54] poststructuralism is not a political position. Rather its turn away from phenomenology can be described (rather than explained) as a movement from empathy to abstraction, in the terms used by Husserl's contemporary, the art historian Wilhelm Worringer. For Worringer abstraction and the "regularity" it posits seek a "tranquillity" absent from the "temporality and unclarity" of the organic world. Poststructuralism, as a form of abstraction, also manifests this "self-alienative" impulse in which experience is rejected for a transcendentalism of form that does not entirely renounce a material referent.[55] Indeed, the linguistic turn is more a figure for abstraction than an actual redeployment of the mathematical models of linguistics. For as Thomas Pavel argues, poststructuralism's recourse to linguistics as part of a project of scientific "modernization" and "methodological unification" is based on a casual use of linguistics that appropriates it for the philosophical purpose of a "new transcendence."[56] Indeed, "The Ends of Man" makes the fundamentally philosophical stakes of poststructuralism quite clear in that its authorizing precursor is not even linguistics (as in de Man's work or elsewhere in Derrida's corpus) but transcendental phenomenology.

But Derrida's essay is interesting because it institutes poststructuralism at the end of an intellectual history, thus implicating itself in this history. Existential phenomenology generated certain problems that require a return to transcendental thinking, which brings back other problems. As Derrida says, this "incompleteness . . . leaves every major stage of phenomenology unbalanced" and makes "new reductions and explications indefinitely necessary" (WD: 157). By placing poststructuralism at the end of a history that seems endlessly drawn back to its middle (even in the concluding celebration of Nietzsche), Derrida allows us to see that it too might be less an advance than what Jameson calls a symbolic or imaginary resolution. For while the interviews in *Positions* are retrospective, "The Ends of Man" is very consciously presented in medias res. And indeed in the metaphorics of Derrida's career, poststructuralism is no more than a transitory phase, with terms such as *science* and *structure* largely disappearing after the early seventies.

The Return to Heidegger: A New Transcendentalism?

More important is "Heidegger," who has become increasingly prominent in Derrida's own work, but even more so in readings of it. The turn to Heidegger is already evident in "The Ends of Man," less in the argument (which is critical of him) than in the way Derrida subtextually inscribes his own very different thinking within a repetition of the "Letter on Humanism." It is conceptually as well as structurally evident in "Différance" (1968). Derrida's affinity with Heidegger is paradoxically facilitated by language, the very term that allies him with a Saussurean modernity but that can also be reconfigured within the nostalgia of the "Heideggerian meditation" (SP: 153). According to Tim Clark, Derrida "valorizes language, not as a play of diacritical marks, but as the site of something totally *other*, by which is meant something analogous to the annunciation or 'arrival' of being itself."[57] If this is not uniformly true of Derrida's work, it is true of texts such as *Aporias, The Gift of Death*, and *On the Name*, all of which cultivate a nonviolence very different from the essays on Jabès and Artaud. These later texts, as Bourdieu says of Heidegger, make thought a "gift of the self to

Being, an opening up . . . an assimilation of *Denken* to *Danken*,"[58] rather than an exposure to Bataille's "inner experience." They are ontological rather than para-ontological.

Indeed, at a certain point commentary on Derrida begins to read him not through structuralism but through Heidegger, whether critically (in the case of Renaut and Ferry and Rockmore) or appreciatively (in the case of Rapaport and Tim Clark). Derrida is also now read with the later Levinas and Blanchot and with Nancy and Jean-Luc Marion. He is placed within a field that can be loosely called post-Heideggerian, even if this means ignoring certain aspects of the work of theorists whose names are used to constitute the field.[59] The rise of post-Heideggerianism in the translation industry—aided by the dominance of Heidegger in American continental philosophy programs—has coincided curiously with the decline of de Man in literary studies. But that "Derrida" has eluded de Man's fate through an alliance with Heidegger is paradoxical and in some ways problematic for the fate of deconstruction. For inasmuch as post-Heideggerianism has replaced post-structuralism as a "metaphor for a new transcendence," the reconfiguration of deconstruction as post-Heideggerian is at once a preservation and a disavowal. This is all the more so because deconstruction has been preserved at the cost of being transferred from literature to philosophy, now that the study of literature is being reconfigured as cultural studies.[60] What is forgotten in this reconfinement of deconstruction within philosophy via Heidegger is the original interdisciplinarity of deconstruction as an opening of philosophy to the wider cultural field. While post-Heideggerian thought on one level continues this opening through its concern with such areas as community and historical disaster, on another level its religiosity continues the forgetting of Sartre and antihumanism which these very concerns remember. Post-Heideggerian thought, in other words, is constituted around a hiatus that it only intermittently recognizes.

Heidegger is not a new figure on the Derridean landscape, but in the sixties Derrida had used him diacritically rather than positively. In "Violence and Metaphysics" Heidegger is simply a way of deferring the radically antieconomic thought of Levinas. In *Of Grammatology*, where he is associated with the thought of *différance* and the trace, Derrida places Heidegger in a philosophical network that includes Hegel (18–26) and unfolds his own discussion of difference within a historiography that Heidegger would have found profoundly alien. But whereas Derrida in the sixties never ceases to rethink Heidegger through his Others (Blanchot, Sartre, and Levinas), thereafter he increasingly turns towards themes of proximity, towards the vocative,[61] and towards the circling (and self-containing) deferrals of Heidegger's style. The later Derrida eludes any secure positioning in relation to Heidegger or in relation to a single mode of thinking. For one thing a deconstructive, post-Kantian Derrida persists in such places as "Eating Well" or "The Rhetoric of Drugs," while another series of texts brings to the foreground an interest in psychoanalysis that was arguably occluded in Derrida's earlier work. Moreover, Derrida is often highly critical of Heidegger on the level of content—*Of Spirit* being the most obvious example. Still, as Renaut and Ferry argue, Derrida's "dissidence" from Heidegger is often "apparent or tactical" and is suspended within a structural or *formal* fidelity to Heidegger; here, Derrida criticizes him only on his own terms.[62] Or, to put it differently, Derrida in such texts as *Aporias* and *The Gift of Death* might still claim to work "not within but on the horizon of the Heideggerian paths" (OGr: 23). But whereas he had earlier written *on* Heidegger, he now incorporates Heidegger at a more physical, semiotic, and rhythmic level. By voicing his criticisms in Heidegger's own language, Derrida reterritorializes within the domain of philosophy his understanding of Heideggerian philosophy as deterritorialized from within by its concern with language and temporality. His relationship to Heidegger is encompassed within his own notion of *différance* in that he defers but does not break with Heidegger. Or, to adapt Kristeva's complaint, the negativity of his critique "holds itself back and appears as a delaying" that reinstitutes Heideggerian thought "through retention."[63]

At a certain stage in French thought, Heidegger became syncretized with structuralism and Marxism because of their common abandonment of the subject.[64] But Derrida's attachment to Heidegger exceeds this initial inscription in "The Ends of Man." Derrida's later work is beyond the scope of this study. One can nevertheless envision a genealogy of his relationship to phenomenology that would study not only the displacement of his critique from transcendental to existential phenomenology after 1968 but also two other tropes in his genesis. To begin with there is the persistent bonding with phenomenology evident in the privilege given to Husserl at the beginning of Derrida's career and to Heidegger at the end. This bonding suggests that the displacement of Husserl by Heidegger may conceal a displacement of Husserl *as* Heidegger. Thus, second, there is the question of the relation between Husserl and Heidegger and the role of the latter as facilitating a certain kind of metaphorical work in Derrida's corpus.

As already suggested, Heidegger's appeal stems from the way he condenses difference and identity or preserves a space for nostalgia under the cover of philosophic radicalism. Thus while promoting the thought of *différance*, Heidegger, as Bourdieu says, "introduces into philosophy a secularized form of the religious" first noted by Sartre (BN: 128) and a continued emphasis on the purity of philosophy, specifically the purity of *his* philosophy as unavailable to exoteric readings. Husserl always signified a certain idealism, a resistance of transcendence to existence and of philosophy to psychoanalysis, which Derrida appropriately criticized. Derrida cannot therefore return to him except on the general terrain of rigor. Yet the later Derrida is also at times a transcendental thinker and not just in the Kantian sense of thinking structurally rather than empirically. As Tim Clark concedes, although *écriture* may be "a negativity that cannot be mastered, or reconverted to a positivity," it also doubles as "a strange mode of the transcendental."[65] When this happens—which is not always—*écriture* becomes like *Dasein*, which, by conflating existence and transcendence, uses existence to legitimize transcendence. *Dasein* allows Heidegger to have it both ways: to be in existence yet without suffering its violence. In a sense *Dasein* repeats more convincingly Husserl's use of "transcendental genesis" as an alibi by which Being is given a genesis without having to be "borne or produced by a 'real' empirical history" (G: 250).

To see Heidegger's thought as transcendental is not unusual. Indeed, the second stage of Heidegger studies is often viewed as a corrective that restores his "transcendental side at the price of a calculated retreat from philosophical anthropology." But the point about Heidegger is that unlike Husserl he is transcendental without seeming to be so, and unlike the structuralists he seems antihumanist without actually being so. In the history of French thought "Heidegger" has been endowed with a strange ability to hold positions without seeming to hold them. As Bourdieu comments, "it is perhaps because he never realised what he was saying that Heidegger was able to say what he did say without really having to say it."[66] Heidegger can thus reintroduce a secular religiosity while seeming to verge on a postmodern thought of *différance*. He can bring back "proximity" to Being because he seems to get rid of "man."[67] But this "subtlety and equivocality" (M: 127) does not so much belong to Heidegger as to the sign "Heidegger" constructed in France and inscribed with the sedimented history of its deployment in French thought over five decades. To give but one example, it was "Heidegger" who first enabled Levinas to critique Husserl for eliding a "historicity" and "personality" that were of no real interest to Heidegger.[68] This in turn is because, as Binswanger astutely implies, Heidegger seems to take account of existence—yet not "actual human existence" but rather "Being understood as existence."[69]

"Heidegger" thus includes, within the turn to the transcendental, the existential phenomenology within which he was first configured and whose conscience he still hears even as he rejects consciousness and conscience. He includes the deconstructive analytic generated by reading *différance* and nihilation against the grain, even as he provides a secret exit from this reading that does not really represent him. As Rapaport argues persuasively, Derrida's later turn to Heidegger can be explained through the fact that he reread Heidegger through Blanchot, thus returning to a more complex Heidegger than he had earlier critiqued.[70] But Rapaport does not add that, before the current return to Heidegger, Blanchot and Levinas had separated themselves from Heidegger. Moreover, the Blanchot who facilitates Derrida's return to Heidegger is not the Sartrean Blanchot discussed in the previous chapter but a more transcendental thinker strongly influenced by the later Derrida himself.[71] "Blanchot" thus performs his own figural work in the corpus of theory as a paleonym condensing negativity and transcendentalism. Or, to put it differently, if Blanchot becomes a metonym for Heidegger, then Heidegger can seem to anticipate and encompass his own deconstruction, but without having to be what that deconstruction would make him. In short, Heidegger's currency in the theoretical economy has much to do with the figural work he performs, again as a paleonym that condenses radicality and nostalgia. More specifically his value for Derrida lies in the complex intellectual history he telescopes into the thought of transcendence, thus allowing the later Derrida (or perhaps those attached to him) to take account of the existential, but without really doing so.

The Thought From Outside: Phenomenology and Structuralism in Foucault's *The Birth of the Clinic*

Preliminaries: Deconstruction between Phenomenologies

To describe Foucault's work prior to *The Archaeology of Knowledge* as a sub-version of phenomenology may seem surprising. In the foreword to the English edition of *The Order of Things*, published four years after the book itself, Foucault claims that if there is one approach he rejects "it is . . . broadly speaking, the phenomenological approach" (xiv). A decade later he places himself as part of a generation that was trying to break free from Marxism and phenomenology (DL: 174), from forms of thinking that stress freedom over contingency or that assign "absolute priority to the observing subject." They fail, he observed, because they do not address the problem of language.[1] Historians of theory have accepted Foucault's description of his "earliest books" as an "imperfect sketch" of the enterprise that emerges more coherently in *The Archaeology of Knowledge* (AK: 14–15). Thus Alan Megill, while emphasizing the phenomenological character of Foucault's work up to *Madness and Civilization*, sees *The Order of Things* as a structuralist study that, despite residual images of depth, turns away from his earlier concern with an experience more fundamental than discourse. Dreyfus and Rabinow locate this turn even earlier in *The Birth of the Clinic*, which they see as profoundly antihermeneutic. Describing its hyperstructuralist method as an "overreaction" against the earlier work, they nevertheless see the ontological residues more generally present in the early work as an encumbrance that Foucault could well have done without.[2]

Dreyfus and Rabinow typify the received reading not only of Foucault's career but also of the path taken by contemporary theory as a dialectic of enlightenment in which phenomenology is at best an antithetical stimulus. In their influential reading, Foucault's corpus is organized along an evolutionary spiral in which the later work is the resolution of a problem unsuccessfully tackled in the early texts. While assessments of de Man view his career in terms of a shift of interest from consciousness to language, Dreyfus and Rabinow see Foucault's absorption of archaeology into genealogy as signaling a move from linguistic to social practices and thus give (post)structuralism a merely intermediate status in his career.[3] But as important as the content of these histories is their functioning as genetic narratives that reduce Foucault's early texts to shadowy types of their later counterparts. Foucault himself encourages such narratives in putting forward *The Archaeology of Knowledge* as a "resumption" and "correction" of *The Order of Things* (subtitled *An Archaeology of the Human Sciences*) and in rewriting *The Birth of the Clinic* as *Discipline and Punish: The Birth of the Prison*.[4] Marking the continuity of his enterprise, he also attributes to his work of the mid-sixties "an absence of methodological signposting" that resulted in the archaeological project being outlined "in a rather disordered way" (AK: 16, 14). He thus marginalizes the differences between his earlier and later work so as to reduce not only the autonomous contribution of the former but also the anxieties and evasions that inhabit the latter.

That Foucault's relation to phenomenology is more complex has, however, been sometimes recognized.[5] To begin with, his hostility to phenomenology prior to *The Archaeology of Knowledge* is largely directed against Husserl and the notion of a "transcendental consciousness" (OT: xiv). As Dreyfus, writing separately from Rabinow, suggests, there is more continuity than one might think between the arche/genealogical enterprise that begins with *The Birth of the Clinic* and Foucault's first book, *Mental Illness and Psychology*, whose relation to existential psychoanalysis and phenomenology is generally accepted. Moreover, *The Order of Things* is also profoundly influenced by Heidegger and Merleau-Ponty, but only as negated and displaced through Nietzsche and Blanchot. On the other hand, as Gerard Lebrun points out *archaeology* is itself a term drawn from Husserl that bears a strong resemblance to the phenomenological reduction in its emphasis on neutrality and detachment, as well as in its digging beneath historical phenomena to the structural system that is their condition of possibility.[6] Foucault seems to use one kind of phenomenology to defer the other, only to then turn round and affiliate himself with what he has critiqued.

Foucault's vacillation is clear from his introduction to Georges Canguilhem's *The Normal and the Pathological* (1943) in 1978. Canguilhem, to whom I return later, was a historian of science who served as Foucault's dissertation advisor.[7] His work provides an early model for an intellectual history that proceeds not on "the epistemological level of knowledge (or scientific consciousness)" but on the "archeological level" of what makes knowledge possible (OT: xiii, 31). Not only is his archaeology of medicine in *On the Normal and the Pathological* a seminal pre-text for *The Birth of the Clinic*; Canguilhem is also Foucault's Apollinian mask, a counterpart to the Dionysian alter ego developed through Raymond Roussel in Foucault's book on the early twentieth-century novelist. Issued on the same day in 1963, *The Birth of the Clinic* and *Raymond Roussel*[8] inscribe Foucault's work in an interdisciplinary space in which literature is the Dionysian inside of science; they serve as a way of standing outside the rationality of the arche/genealogical project that Foucault theorizes on the basis of Canguilhem's practice. Canguilhem and Roussel are figures through whom the early Foucault plays out the hiatus between structuralism and phenomenology so as to think through the task of a philosophy alternately conceived on the models of science and of literature. Foucault's own work in the mid-sixties emerges on a threshold between phenomenology and structuralism, as part of a dialogue between the two that is carried on both within and between *The Birth of the Clinic* and *Raymond Roussel*. Writing in the heyday of phenomenology, Canguilhem provided an alternative to it that is functionally similar to the one later furnished by the genetic structuralism of the early Barthes and Lucien Goldmann. Foucault turns to him, as he repeatedly indicates, to accentuate his difference from his intellectual context—from Sartre and also from the humanism of the antipsychiatry movement with which his own work on psychology had much in common.

How Foucault situates Canguilhem is thus an indication of his own relation to a phenomenology that had informed his own work in the fifties. Significantly, while he opposes Canguilhem's history of "rationalities" to phenomenology conceived as a "philosophy of meaning, subject and the experienced thing," he also locates Canguilhem's work *within* phenomenology.

This contradiction is partly explained by the positing of two schools of phenomenology equivalent to the transcendental and the existential: the Kantian school of Husserl and Canguilhem concerned with method and concepts and the personalist school of Sartre and Merleau-Ponty.[9] In his introduction to Canguilhem's study, Foucault allies himself decisively with the former. But he also cannot maintain the opposition between them, and what draws him to Canguilhem rather than Husserl is precisely the underground connection of his work to existential phenomenology.[10] Indeed, the championing of Husserl is surprising given Foucault's earlier reservations about him and is itself an indication that his differences from and use of other methodologies are "transpositions" rather than positions.[11] Husserl's usefulness is therefore tactical; he gives Foucault a way to defer certain aspects of existential phenomenology that must nevertheless be used to critique Husserl himself.

Thus Foucault argues in his introduction that (existential) phenomenology remains focused on the cogito—an indulgence one can discipline by returning to Husserl's emphasis on method. But this phenomenology also introduces "the body, sexuality, death, the perceived world into the field of analysis."[12] In short, existential phenomenology lays the groundwork for Canguilhem's use of method and concept, not to reinforce, but to question the rationality left intact by Husserl's reinscription of the cogito as the transcendental ego. Indeed, Foucault concedes as much when he describes "phenomenology" as having initiated the critique of medical "positivism" and sees the former as emphasizing finitude and the body, as analyzing the relation between language and perception, and as recognizing "the secretly linguistic structure of the datum" (BC: 199).

I shall suggest that the double inadequacy of the existential and transcendental positions makes phenomenology a particularly fruitful site for "rethink[ing] the question of the subject" through the hiatus always already inscribed in this tradition by its multiple origins. Foucault himself divides this genesis between Kant's *Critiques* and Hegel's *Phenomenology*.[13] Like Derrida, he uses transcendental and existential phenomenology against each other in such a way that his own work is mobilized not by his rejection of phenomenology but by the latter's supplementary structure as a field of differences. That Foucault nevertheless felt compelled to distinguish himself from phenomenology by simplifying it, while Lacan emphasized his continuity with it by reading it against the grain, has much to do with the time Foucault was writing: when phenomenology had become institutionalized and its radicalism had become hard to see. But even as he distinguishes two "profoundly heterogeneous" directions in French philosophy and dismisses the "interactions" and "rapprochements" between them,[14] Foucault's work in the mid-sixties is an instance of precisely such an interaction. His own position is figured in Canguilhem, whom he is compelled to place both inside and outside phenomenology.

In this and the next chapter I argue that Foucault's work of this period rethinks what he calls "the modern *cogito*" (OT: 324) through the differences between various phenomenologies. His project cannot be identified with Sartre's because he is profoundly critical of the latter's nostalgia for the cogito; Sartre's attempt (as Foucault sees it) to "end man's alienation" by "reflecting the contents of the *In-itself* in the form of the *For-itself* " (327). But neither can it be identified with the turn differently exemplified by Heidegger and Robbe-Grillet towards some form of being-in-itself removed from the human. For Foucault, while rejecting the attempt of the for-itself to found itself, also insists that man "cannot inhabit the objective inertia of something that, by rights, does not and never can lead to self-consciousness" (322). Foucault's difference from Heidegger is apparent in the way he moves between a philosophy open only to the aesthetic and a history of social and intellectual practices that Heidegger would see as anthropological. At the same time his difference from Canguilhem is evident in the way he develops archaeology into a form of ontology, thus making explicit philosophical concerns that remain unthematized by Canguilhem.

The Birth of the Clinic is Foucault's first attempt at the approach he works out on a more encyclopedic scale in *The Order of Things*. That it functions as a microcosm of the later text is signaled in the preface to *The Order of Things*, where Foucault sees disease as a synecdoche for "disorder" and therefore situates his "archaeology of the medical point of view" as a prelude to his more general study of order (xxiv). Thus *The Order of Things* provides in retrospect the methodological signposting for what Foucault begins to do in the earlier text. Here "the confused, under-structured, and ill-structured domain of the history of ideas" (BC: 195) emerges as a site from which he can revision what are essentially the questions posed by phenomenology. For in (de)constructing the history of "rationalities" (OT: xxii) or *Geisteswissenschaften* from the

Renaissance onward, Foucault is still involved in thinking about how we think. *The Order of Things*, in other words, continues the process of radicalization begun by existential phenomenology when it replaced the transcendental category of Spirit with that of consciousness. For consciousness Foucault substitutes a third term that has no label but which he describes as "the constantly renewed interrogation as to how thought can reside elsewhere than here, . . . how it can *be* in the forms of non-thinking" (324).

Neglecting the way deconstruction emerged in the spaces between other methods, critical commentary has filtered Foucault's early work through *The Archaeology of Knowledge*. Foucault's career has thus been read with a teleological positivism that valorizes an archaeology not necessarily identical with his use of the term earlier on. Despite their overt structuralism, however, the texts of the early sixties differ in profound ways from the work commonly identified with Foucault. Though concerned with institutions and discourses, they relate these concerns back to questions of being. Thus while the later Foucault sees men as determined by the structure of discourse, the earlier Foucault articulates the end of man in terms of his radical contingency in relation to the being of language. The discourses of social and intellectual history and those of ontology supplement each other such that neither stands as complete in itself.

With *The Archaeology of Knowledge* Foucault does indeed turn sharply away from phenomenology. This turn is evident in his revaluation of the term *discourse* as well as in the disappearance from his work of any interest in literature as the hiding place of a language more profound than discourse. It is evident also in the replacement of terms such as *being* with the more ascetically tabular discourse of regularities and discursive formations. Accepting the general view that the later work is antiphenomenological, I argue for a way of reading the relationship between the two Foucaults that is not a linear evolution. For as Dominick LaCapra suggests, we can also approach the parts of an author's corpus "in terms of a supplementary interplay . . . not entirely accounted for by a notion of dialectical totalization."[15] In what follows I assume three stages in Foucault's career: from the texts that culminate in *Madness and Civilization*, through the three studies published in the mid-sixties on which I focus, to the more familiar ground of *The Archaeology of Knowledge* and *Discipline and Punish*. But I also treat these stages as to some extent copresent so as to frame Foucault's poststructuralism in an earlier space that remains its other, its philosophical unconscious. This (psycho)analysis of Foucault's corpus is built into the texts of the mid-sixties, elided from the later work, but then reinsinuated by Foucault in the 1984 interview that accompanies the republication of *Raymond Roussel*. We encounter it in the interplay between the twin texts of 1963, where Foucault uses Roussel to (de)construct the mask of an Apollinian structuralism. We encounter it also in the commentary on *Las Meninas*, which focuses on a complexly self-reflexive painting so as to figure the way that Foucault's own text must be apprehended not simply as a "picture," a representation with a content, but also as a "mirror" that deflects our attempts to frame it from any theoretical perspective (OT: 7). Finally, we find this self-reflection in the sequence of *The Order of Things*, which is not just an archaeology of discourses but also a metacritical tool for analyzing the discourses of theory. For this text undertakes a phenomenology of discourses that allows us to situate Foucault's own subsequent archaeology as a form of what he here calls classicism. From this perspective, as I suggest in the next chapter, the early work functions as the analytic scene of the later work, a scene in which archaeology and genealogy emerge as discourses that are themselves caught in the dialectic between the visible and the invisible articulated in *The Order of Things*.

Beginnings, False Starts: Foucault in 1954

It is well known that Foucault's earliest work took a phenomenological direction. *Mental Illness and Personality*, published in 1954 and revised as *Mental Illness and Psychology* after the completion of *Madness and Civilization*, has affinities with existential psychoanalysis and the antipsychiatry movement of David Cooper, R. D. Laing, and Thomas Szasz.[16] In 1954 Foucault also published *Dream, Imagination, and Existence*, an introduction to Binswanger's attempt to develop a Heideggerian psychoanalysis. Although neither study is without problems, they are worth considering because the discrepancies between them create the space in which Foucault works out the sub-version of phenomenology that emerges in *The Birth of the Clinic* and *The Order of Things*.

That *Mental Illness and Psychology* can be connected to the later work has been pointed out by Dreyfus. In this study, which James Miller describes as an inchoate blend of Marxism and Heidegger, Foucault undertakes a critique of medical models of psychoanalysis that protect the rational Cartesian subject by abjecting madness as a form of illness. However, he is not concerned simply with the social construction of mental illness but also with the need for what he calls, in Husserlian terms, a "noetic" and "noematic" analysis of pathological behavior.[17] Drawing on Merleau-Ponty's view that such behavior must be revalued as a way of being in the world, but that its rigidity consists in generalizing this way of being to all situations, Foucault sees the psychologist as opening the patient to an awareness that his mode of apprehension is not inevitable by attempting a genealogy of how she or he came to it. Psychology has as its goal the restoration of what Heidegger calls the clearing, both for the patient and for the culture whose norms produce pathological behavior as a form of alienated resistance. This "inflection of phenomenology towards anthropology"[18] is not without precedents in phenomenology. Ortega y Gasset, for example, analyzes how academic disciplines cover over that faculty of meticulous perception that Heidegger terms *cura* by interpellating us into a Symbolic order that obscures the clearing.[19] On one level, then, individual psychology furnishes Foucault with a pre-text for his later attempt to mark the limits of epistemic visibility through a genealogy that begins as an extension of phenomenology. And conversely, as Dreyfus argues, genealogy can be seen as a form of "historical therapy," whose underground connections to care, though effaced from Foucault's own work, are still evident in some of the cultural analysis inspired by him.[20]

Foucault describes his work at the time he wrote *Madness and Civilization* as "divided between existential psychoanalysis and phenomenology" (DL: 174), two orientations that may not seem very different. These two terms, however, point to certain tensions between the study of mental illness and the commentary on Binswanger despite their shared origins in the work of Heidegger. While the notion of the clearing is important for Foucault's first attempt at reconceiving the relation between the normal and the pathological, at least as important in *Mental Illness and Psychology* is the sense that the philosophical opening achieved at the site of psychoanalysis must be utilized as part of a larger cultural project. Existential psychoanalysis, in other words, appropriates the insights of Heidegger and of Sartre's work on emotions for an activism largely characteristic of the postwar Sartre. This strain is particularly evident in the second part of the 1954 version of *Mental Illness and Psychology*, which makes a simplistically Marxist argument for pathological behavior as a consequence of social alienation. On the other hand, such concerns are largely absent from the introduction to Binswanger, except for a brief discussion of Freud's Dora as a case of "rejective behavior" whose challenge to the institutions of psychoanalysis and patriarchy Freud failed to see. Instead *Dream, Imagination, and Existence* is more strictly phenomenological in its concern with thinking and being. Indeed, Foucault draws attention to the paradox of his trying to understand *Existenz* by turning in dream to the mode in which human existence seems "least engaged in the world."[21] Rather than using philosophy to rethink therapy, in this essay he uses the phenomena of psychoanalysis to rethink the nature of being.

More specifically, Foucault uses dream as Merleau-Ponty had used perception: to question the logical categories imposed by the cogito through a return to something like what the latter calls the sensible. Foucault deals specifically with the way dream breaks open a linear temporality and with the dream image as a phenomenon whose "syntax" and "morphology" indicate an opening onto existence or, as Lyotard puts it, a "burst[ing] outward" that makes consciousness a "relation to the world."[22] Foucault's purpose, then, is to investigate dream as a proto-intending of the world that does not so much uncover an archaic stage of personality as cast light on how consciousness might be in the world other than as a cogito.[23] As Kristeva will do in theorizing the semiotic, Foucault draws on Husserl—not on the Husserl who is a philosopher of method and concept but on the Husserl recovered for existential phenomenology by Ricoeur and Merleau-Ponty. In particular he focuses on the distinction picked up by Derrida several years later: between signification and indication as a way of thinking beyond the visible to the invisible. Accordingly Foucault suggests that "the quasi-presence" of meaning in a dream is precisely its elusiveness; the dream indicates rather than expresses meaning, "offering it only while ephemeralizing it."[24] Focusing not on the content but on the *form* of the (dream) image as a resistance to a purely semantic meaning, Foucault argues that even the image—recently analyzed by Kristeva as a hinge between Sartre and psychoanalysis—is limiting. The image is a visual hypostasis or "a ruse of consciousness in order to cease imagining." By expanding the image through dream Foucault thus tries to open a Sartrean cogito into a Heideggerian *Dasein*. Through dream one "transcends consciousness in the direction of the world" as "existence." One gains access to a "radical subjectivity" not confined to the (un)conscious of the dreamer but in which the subject is "the whole dream in the entirety of its dream content."[25]

Not only are the arguments of the two 1954 studies interesting, but so is the way they point to the differing concerns that inform Foucault's work, and indeed deconstruction, in the early sixties. In *Dream, Imagination, Existence*, we already see Foucault's attempt to rethink the cogito by leading thought towards what he will later term the "unthought" (OT: 326) but which he here describes more positively as "imagining" or "transcendence" towards the world. For it is already the case that in dream the "'I think' [is] embedded in a density throughout which it is quasi-present, such that the 'I think' no longer leads "to the evident truth of the 'I am'" (324). In this text, then, Foucault explores the chiasm of phenomenology and psychoanalysis shortly to be articulated by Merleau-Ponty and also crucial to Derrida. Foucault will later inscribe phenomenology, via Bataille's inner experience, in an unstated psychoanalysis. Here, however, he is concerned to lead what psychoanalysis makes visible towards the invisible space of phenomenology. Thus Freud does not really disclose the unthought of indication but remains within a semantics of expression; his "symbolic translations" are a "logic of discourse . . . woven on the same psychological warp as the forms of waking consciousness."[26]

If *Dream, Imagination, Existence* begins to cross phenomenology and psychoanalysis, it also defines——in theory if not in practice——the space of Foucault's project in the early sixties. Foucault begins by promising a subsequent work that will situate "existential analysis within the development of contemporary reflection on man." *The Order of Things* is in a sense this work and resumes more negatively Foucault's first Heideggerian attempt to think, through dream, a way of being in the world in which consciousness would not be the work of understanding but would happen to us. Also consistent with his subsequent work is Foucault's insistence that one can combine anthropology, "which analyzes man as man within his human world," with an "ontological reflection which concerns the mode of being of an existence as presence to the world." Just as "anthropology resists any attempt to divide it into philosophy and psychology," so Binswanger's work allows one to avoid

"any *a priori* distinction between anthropology and ontology" while remaining aware of their mutually critical supplementarity.[27]

Foucault does not achieve "the inflection of phenomenology towards anthropology" of which he speaks here; *Dream* is too purely Heideggerian in
its abstraction from the social.[28] It is this need to reinvest ontology in practice that motivates his critique of psychiatry in *Mental Illness and Psychology*,
though at the cost of reinscribing aspects of anthropology that later lead him
to reject the term. For not only does the Foucault of the fifties want to reform society but by focusing on psychiatry he also psychologizes otherness
rather than structuralizing it as he will in *The Birth of the Clinic*. As a result
his shift of emphasis, both here and in *Madness and Civilization*, from the
individual patient to the (social) history of mental illness still assumes a cultural if not a personal subject. The introduction to Binswanger is the earliest indication of Foucault's desire for Heidegger's thinking that "abandons
subjectivity."[29] To achieve such thinking, but as part of a process that leads
to "self-consciousness," is the task of *The Order of Things* (322).

The Unhappy Consciousness of Medicine

With *The Birth of the Clinic* we encounter a more familiar Foucault. Concerned with medicine rather than psychiatry, this book differs from *Madness
and Civilization* in the replacement of a mimetic narrative with a more discontinuous account of shifts between systems of order and in a new emphasis on representation as the anxious site at which these systems maintain
themselves through a largely figural activity. *The Birth of the Clinic* is Foucault's first attempt at archaeology and genealogy. Moreover, instead of
positing madness as an alternative to classical rationalism, it allows this otherness to be felt only negatively as a dis-ease unnamed within the discourses
that regulate it. Yet the book's project is radically different from that of *Discipline and Punish*, the later text it most closely resembles. At the heart of
that difference, paradoxically, is the interest in linguistic elements such as
sign and symptom. This concern may seem to mark *The Birth of the Clinic*
as a "structural study" (BC: xix), but read alongside the distinction between
language and discourse that Foucault was soon to make in *The Order of*

Things, it is better seen as inscribing sociology as the visible mask or outside of ontology.

The Birth of the Clinic focuses on a brief timespan following a major epistemic break after the Renaissance: the years 1750–1820. It is first of all a genealogy of medical institutions as they develop during this period. It is also an archaeology of the conceptual categories (in a Kantian sense) that organize and seek to legitimate themselves through those institutions. Foucault thus maps a series of intersecting and discrepant shifts that occur between the Enlightenment and the nineteenth century—from a confidence that disease can be placed within a structural system to a fear of it as epidemic; from the treatment of disease as an interruption of health to its construction as a deviation from normality; from the hospital as a place where an individual who has certain illnesses is treated, to the clinic as a place interested in a particular genre of disease. But Foucault is just as interested in an archaeology of the conceptual forms that accompany such mutations as he is in a genealogy of their content, and it is in this archeological element that we find a radicalization of his earlier interest in phenomenology. On this level *The Birth of the Clinic* fills in a limited area of the canvas more extensively sketched in *The Order of Things* by approaching medicine as an "isomorphic" form of a classical episteme committed to total visibility and spatialization.[30] Medicine tries to create a "visible body" and a "set of phenomena without secrets" (BC: 159). It seeks to make disease perceivable on a "flat surface of perpetual simultaneity"—temporally, by placing the event or symptom in a logical series; spatially, by drawing up a "map" in which a symptom is "situated within a disease, a disease in a specific *ensemble*, and this *ensemble* in a general plan of the pathological world" (6, 29).

Foucault will later speak of episteme rather than consciousness so as to reduce the latter from origin to effect. Yet what is at issue here is something like an unhappy consciousness that achieves no more than a temporary identity with itself through the social structures upon which it is articulated. Significantly at the end of chapter 6 the classical "gaze" is described as "for a time, a happy gaze" (106). I shall return to the genealogy of the term *gaze*, but suffice it to note the reference to an aspect of Hegel emphasized by Hyppolite and the claim that the gaze is happy "only for a time." The psychoanalysis of the gaze occurs at two sites: through history and through language. As Foucault argues in *The Order of Things*, history is not just an account of how man "speaks, works, and lives" but the retroversion of this positivity into man's own "historicity" in a movement that "perpetually refer[s]" man's products "to the finitude that caused those same positivities to appear" (OT: 369–71).

This countermemory animates the history traced in *The Birth of the Clinic*. For the institution of medicine follows the same path outlined in *The Order of Things* from classical space to nineteenth-century time—a path wherein the productivity of time both extends and threatens the positivism of space. Thus, on the one hand, there is a continuity between the Enlightenment's medicine of species and the medicine of tissues and pathological anatomy that replaces it, as classification gives way to the "time of the disease" culminating in death and autopsy (BC: 144). The former locates diseases through three forms of spatialization: by placing them in relation to each other, within the human body, and within a social space where they are "circumscribed, . . . distributed throughout cure centres" and "arranged in the most favorable ways" (116). The medicine of tissues likewise involves a discursive regulation of existence. It opens up corpses to compare cases and to produce a "set of phenomena without secrets . . . entirely legible for the clinicians' gaze" (134, 141, 159). In this sense the medicine of tissues also makes the invisible visible by isolating the "*tissue*—a functional, two-dimensional area—in contrast with the functioning mass of the organ." For as "the paradox of an 'internal surface'" (xviii), the tissue simulates an inside that is no longer inside but has achieved what Husserl calls pure self-evidence: a phenomenality without materiality.

On the other hand, beneath this continuity the movement from tabular surface to morbid depth gradually unravels the medical project of an absolute "correlation [of] the visible and the expressible" (196). For the shift from classificatory medicine to pathological anatomy takes the gaze "from the manifest to the hidden" (135), reconfiguring its relation to itself through the mediation of social practices. Turning from treatment to autopsy and from the protection of life to the rationalization of death as the "summit" at which the disease has run its course and become fully visible, the gaze enters a phase of growing denial and draws closer to "the great dark threat in which [the doctor's] knowledge and skill" are "abolished" (146).

The Ex-position of the Gaze

Intersecting this genealogy of the return of death, counternature, and night at the very moment when they seem to have been "enclosed" in the "accessible space of the human body" (195) are a series of encounters with this otherness at the more archeological level of its language. The gaze is above all involved in an activity of reading, of neutralizing disease through a decipherment of its signs and symptoms. But this logic is constantly exposed by the very instability of its terms to the existence it tries to keep at bay. For the relation of sign and symptom to phenomenality and materiality is constantly shifting. This discursive slippage is already evident in eighteenth-century medicine as it attempts to decipher the sick body by finding a signifier in whose "intelligible syntax" the "signified—the heart of the disease" becomes "entirely transparent" (91). Sign and symptom alike elude this phenomenality of language in which the invisible achieves pure expression or self-evidence. Both seem to be involved in indication, pointing to something for which they cannot account and thus constituting the knowable on the trace of what exceeds it.

While neither sign nor symptom achieves pure expression, at different points in Foucault's argument it is either one or the other that seems closer to this ideal in which the signifier is "entirely transparent for the signified" (91). Thus, to begin with, signs are more resistant to reading while symptoms are a "truth wholly given to the gaze" (91). Signs (anamnestic, diagnostic, and prognostic) are traces of what has happened, is happening, or will happen (90). They "indicate" that which is "further away, below, later," but without offering "anything to knowledge" and providing no more than a frail basis for a "recognition that gradually gropes its way into the dimensions of the hidden" (90–91). Symptoms, by contrast, "restore [the truth] to their transparency as phenomena" (91), especially when read structurally as part of an *ensemble*. This would seem to be because of the synecdochic quality of the symptom; the "sign *says* the same thing that *is* precisely the symptom" (93). Even if symptoms such as "cough, fever . . . and difficulty in breathing are not pleurisy itself," they are part of the disease, thus allowing its "invariable form . . . to *show through*" (90).

But if the symptom is here (unconvincingly) privileged over the sign, a few pages later the alignment of the two terms with the phenomenal and the material seems reversed. The symptom becomes an opaque signifier that must be read as a sign if "pathological manifestations" are to "speak a clear, ordered language" (94–95). Clearly the value assigned to the sign as that which "announces" versus the symptom as that which "manifest[s]" has now changed (96). As symptoms become contaminated by signs, signs are displaced into the recuperative position once occupied by symptoms. By the nineteenth century this tenuous interconvertibility of signs and symptoms, in which each strives for expression but slips back into indication, has collapsed entirely. The sign is recognized by Foucault as a "detour: it is not an expressive symptom, but one which is substituted for the fundamental absence of expression in the symptom" (160).

Enough has been said to suggest that *The Birth of the Clinic* is still a phenomenology—an unusual mixture of social history and ontology concerned with the consciousness unstably produced and displaced in the social forms it analyzes. Foucault would, of course, want to make consciousness an epistemic reflex of medical structures instead of treating it in the manner of Hegel as the origin of the social forms in which it produces itself. Correspondingly he does not even use the term *consciousness*; instead he speaks of the gaze. Yet the word *gaze* derives from Sartre's *regard*, which is perhaps why Foucault later repudiated it (AK: 54n). And indeed the medical gaze is described in the language of phenomenology rather than the language of power used in *Discipline and Punish*. The gaze "records and totalizes" (BC: 121). It seeks a phenomenality without material remainder, a "reversibility, without residue, of the visible in the expressible" (115). It thus continues the project of the cogito in craving the "euphoria" of self-presence or "immediate transparence" (121, 117). Foucault's term is of course intended to deconstruct the cogito as "the great myth of a pure Gaze that would be pure language" (114). But this deconstruction had been set in motion by Sartre who, in presenting the cogito as subject to the gaze, had made it an unhappy consciousness constituted in the field of the other and thus of its own unconscious. Foucault takes this deconstruction one step further by locating consciousness neither in the cogito nor in its other but in the more anonymous space of the gaze as a reflex between them, of which the subject is no more than an effect.[31]

As seemingly radical a break with phenomenology is Foucault's emphasis on structure. For it is structure rather than the Other that produces consciousness as a being that is not its own foundation. Moreover, Foucault describes *The Birth of the Clinic* as "a structural study" (xix) and approaches his material from the outside, in a turn against phenomenology's habit of speaking from the inside, in the first person. But Foucault has often expressed uneasiness with the label of structuralism. Thus it is worth recalling two things about the tactical place of structuralism in this phase of deconstruction. First, writers such as Robbe-Grillet use structuralism to rethink the relation between consciousness and being; and, second, Foucault himself in *The Order of Things* and his essay on Blanchot locates exteriority as part of a post-Heideggerian project aimed at emphasizing man's finitude. Significantly Foucault's own genealogy of French intellectual history represents structuralism as taking the place of a phenomenology insufficiently estranged from itself in language.[32] Using structuralism as a tool for thinking from the outside, Foucault participates in a theory type that is very different from that of Lévi-Strauss or Greimas—one that we have already come across in Derrida's studies of Husserl and that is also exemplified by the work of Canguilhem. Foucault does with medicine what Derrida had done in approaching geometry as the epitome of a science that brackets history and language in the constitution of an "ideal object . . . at the permanent disposition of a pure gaze" (OG: 78). He attempts not just a description of structures but also a psychoanalysis and a political economy of this gaze at the uneasy site of its language.

As important, if *The Birth of the Clinic* is the first example in Foucault's career of the linguistic turn we associate with structuralism, the linguistic by the same token is reembedded in existential concerns with "counter-nature, death, in short, the whole dark underside of disease" (BC: 195). Indeed, *The Birth of the Clinic* affiliates itself less with Saussure and Lévi-Strauss than with the (highly phenomenological) Nietzsche of *The Birth of Tragedy*, whose attempt to expose the bright surface of Apollonian rationalism to Dionysian knowledge is evoked in the description of how medical positivism causes "the abyss beneath illness . . . [to emerge] into the light of language" (195).

Foucault's focus on structure, then, is not structuralism but an ex-position, and perhaps a deliberate denegation, of (Heideggerian) phenomenology. It is a way of thinking that prevents us from dwelling in thought. Structuralism allows Foucault to do what Heidegger's purely philosophical style shelters him from doing: to create a clearing for a thinking that "abandons subjectivity" through a disciplinary graft that "articulates [man] from the very outset upon something other than himself" (OT: 331). It is in this sense that Foucault can attribute to the analysis of medicine an importance "that is not only methodological but ontological" (BC: 197). Medicine, like the confinement of madness, is an attempt to make " man's being [an] object of positive knowledge" (197) through various forms of spatialization. It is not, however, the disciplinary power of these forms that concerns Foucault, but man's relation, through their failure, to a nonbeing mediated and disclosed by structure. In *The Order of Things* Foucault significantly describes his work not as structuralism but as transcendental reflection:

> This is why transcendental reflection in its modern form does not, as in Kant, find its fundamental necessity in the existence of a science of nature (opposed by the perpetual conflicts and uncertainties of philosophers), but in the existence—mute, yet ready to speak, and secretly impregnated with a potential discourse—of that *not-known* from which man is perpetually summoned towards self-knowledge. (OT: 323)

Phenomenology as Psychoanalysis: Foucault, Lacan, Merleau-Ponty

"Transcendental" clearly does not refer to Husserl any more than to Kant; indeed, the term is strangely linked to "existence." This chiasm through which man is "summoned towards self-knowledge" is a further indication that Foucault's concerns are phenomenological rather than structural. In *Discipline and Punish*, which is influenced by the post-1968 Althusser, the analysis of structures is part of a pessimistic positivism that records our interpellation by ideological and repressive state apparatuses. In *The Birth of the Clinic*, however, structure has the double role played by access to the Lacanian Symbolic within the negativity of the analytic session. The structures of the Symbolic, in other words, both articulate meaning and displace the subject from any personal identification with its positions. Foucault speaks at this time of his fascination with Lacan's recognition that "it is the structures, the very system of language, that speak through the patient's discourse and the symptoms of his neurosis."[33] Analysis, however, does not show how the structures of the Symbolic constitute the subject. Instead, by making us experience how we are not the foundation of our own being, it creates a self-estrangement that causes us to think beyond both subjectivity and structure. That *The Birth of the Clinic* extends Lacanian psychoanalysis into the field of institutions (in ways quite different from a positivist syncresis of Lacan and Foucault)[34] is something that Lacan himself may have recognized. Lacan devoted one of his seminars to *The Birth of the Clinic* and in 1966 participated in a roundtable at the Medical College of the Hôpital Salpêtrière on the place of psychoanalysis in medicine, considered as a practice " caught, like all others, in a discourse of the unconscious."[35]

More intriguingly, Lacan himself delivered a series of seminars on the gaze in 1964, with the centerpiece being an analysis of Holbein's *The Ambassadors* as a "trap for the gaze."[36] In 1966 he invited Foucault to a seminar on the splitting of the subject between *savoir* and *vérité* to discuss his analysis of *Las Meninas*, which provided Lacan with an occasion to reintroduce his own discussion of the Holbein painting.[37] We do not know whether Lacan had read *The Birth of the Clinic* at the time, though he had read it by the time of *Écrits*. But his development of the gaze is a more accurate gloss on Foucault's concept than the figure of the panopticon with which the term is now associated. For Lacan not only situates the gaze in the gap between the Symbolic and the Real, *savoir* and *vérité*. His concern is also to decenter the gaze from the control of a cogito, an eye/I that constitutes itself by delimiting a field of visibility. Thus the gaze is not a power located in a subject, nor is it even synonymous with surveillance as the anonymous power exercised by structures. Rather "it is quite clear that I see *outside*, that perception is not in me, that it is on the objects that it apprehends." For Lacan, then, the gaze deconstructs any illusion of a subject presumed to know or to know by seeing. It is the optical correlative of intentionality, which also breaches the bounded ego by articulating man on that which is outside him.[38]

This deconstruction is one that Lacan repeatedly credits to Merleau-Ponty, who "forc[ed] the limits" of a post-Kantian phenomenology concerned with "the regulation of form" and who "in setting out from painting . . . was particularly led to overthrow the relation, which has always been made by thought, between the eye and the mind." Crucial to painting for Merleau-Ponty is its enactment of a "showing" that exceeds what is framed by sight. His recasting of visibility in terms of an "it shows" rather than an "I see" is extended by Lacan into a deconstruction of a subject centered in expression and its replacement by one that emerges in the "lacunae" of its speech. Merleau-Ponty's analysis of perception thus becomes a pre-text for Lacan's analysis of the unconscious, which reinscribes Heidegger's notion of a "showing" more darkly as that which resists appearing.[39] The gaze in this sense is a conceptual trope for the psychoanalysis of phenomenology, which is also the repetition of phenomenology as psychoanalysis. For it is clear from the seminars of 1963–64 that the phenomenological analysis of perception is as much part of the genealogy of Lacanian thinking as is structuralism's recognition that the subject is spoken by the system of language.

Recovering this genealogy, which is acknowledged by Lacan but effaced by Foucault, is not just a matter of scholarly attribution. It is a matter of understanding what Foucault is doing in *The Birth of the Clinic* in replacing consciousness by the gaze. In *The Order of Things* the deployment of this latter concept in the disparate registers of structuralism, phenomenology, and psychoanalysis is condensed into the analysis of *Las Meninas*, which is a performative representation of the specular self-consciousness that Foucault calls the gaze. In this analysis Foucault uses structuralism's focus on the signifier to represent Velazquez's painting as a "showing" of what is excluded by the orders of visibility and expression. Conventionally, from Hegel to Worringer Dutch painting is associated with bourgeois realism or with "empathy" rather than the enigma of abstraction—with the positivity of a world in which man "works and lives" (OT: 369). Or it may exemplify, as for Schopenhauer, a pure representation emancipated from the will,[40] "supposing no remainder . . . but only the fact of its . . . appearance" (BC: xvii). But *Las Meninas* is a strange version of Dutch realism, not a still life but a silent family romance; it functions more like an analytic session than a Heideggerian (dis)closure. It traps vision within what Lacan calls the "inside-out structure of the gaze" as a site of transference by inviting us to look at a canvas in which people seem to be looking at us. We might recall Lacan's comment that seventeenth-century discourses on optics are the locus of a fundamental anxiety within "the very period when the Cartesian meditation inaugurated in all its purity the function of the subject."[41] Summoning up that function by inviting the reader to position himself as eye/I in relation to the painting, Foucault's analysis decenters the gaze from any subject presumed to know, whether inside or outside the social scene being depicted.

But it is also significant that this deconstruction is performed through a painting, albeit one that is mediated to us by words. For in turning to the form privileged by Merleau-Ponty to complicate the relation between eye and mind, Foucault intimates that he is still concerned with a kind of tacit cogito, though not one that is constitutive of subjectivity. Indeed, he uses the Hegelian term *self-consciousness* in a section of *The Order of Things* that should be balanced against the text's apocalyptic *finale*. Here Foucault does not so much announce the end of man as redefine man in a way that continues phenomenology's descent into its own substratum:

> man cannot posit himself in the immediate and sovereign transparency of a *cogito*; nor, on the other hand, can he inhabit the objective inertia of something that, by rights, does not and never can lead to self-consciousness. Man is a mode of being which accommodates that dimension—always open, never finally delimited, yet constantly traversed—which extends from a part of himself not reflected in a *cogito* to the act of thought by which he apprehends that part. (OT: 322)

The Mask of Method: Foucault/Canguilhem

While Foucault elsewhere distances himself from Sartre's desire to constitute the subject as being for-itself (OT: 327), in the passage just cited he conspicuously avoids any counterprivileging of Being. Providing in *The Birth of the Clinic* what he later describes as "a historical analysis of the forms of rationality,"[42] Foucault tries to grasp that part of man which is not reflected in the cogito of clinical medicine through an act of *thought* that articulates the cogito upon its unthought. He effects a chiasm: a phenomenological structuralism that prepares the way for the hiatus that is more systematically explored in *The Order of Things*. The phenomenological subtext of *The Birth of the Clinic* is evident in the curious anthropomorphism of a structure involved in the gaze, in speaking, and in hearing. Thus the terms Foucault had used in *Mental Illness and Psychology* are still appropriate here: *The Birth of the Clinic* is a "noetic analysis" of the consciousness medicine has of itself and a "noematic analysis" of the "pathological world"[43]—the institutions—intergenerated with and by that consciousness. At the same time, in moving from private to cultural consciousness by way of structuralism Foucault has changed the basis of his earlier work. He has created a theory type different both from the more purely philosophical or literary phenomenologies of Heidegger and Blanchot and from the more positivist phenomenological sociology of someone like Simmel earlier in the century.[44]

Of particular value in contextualizing *The Birth of the Clinic* is the work of Canguilhem. Canguilhem is far from being the proto-structuralist Foucault represents him as being, and in this regard he resembles no one more than Foucault himself. In 1967, at the height of structuralism, Canguilhem questions the mathematical attitude that seeks in the mechanism a model for the organism. He, like Foucault in texts from *Madness and Civilization* to *Herculine Barbin, Being the Recently Discovered Memoirs of a Nineteenth-Century French Hermaphrodite* (1978), insists that only an anthropology can value the abnormal and anomalous. Indeed, Canguilhem's *La Connaissance de la vie* is a sustained argument for the equal claims of "life" and "knowledge" or existence and method. Intelligence, he writes, "cannot apply itself to life except in recognizing the originality of life."[45] Medicine conspicuously fails in this application, being a paradigm of "intellectualism," indeed, of the "theoretical" standpoint itself as a discourse that substitutes the "calculation of identities" for "the concrete appreciation of differences."[46]

Canguilhem's importance for Foucault is multiple and has to do with the areas he opens up, his method of enquiry, but also the chiasm enfolded in this apparently objective method. On the most obvious level, Canguilhem is a historian of science who, in Foucault's words, questions rationality "not only as to its nature, its foundation, its powers and its rights, but also as to its history and its geography."[47] Continuing the concern of Kant and Husserl with method and the categories of thought, he turns epistemology towards history: he displaces the philosophy of science from mathematics and the pure sciences to the life sciences, thus bringing it "down from the heights" to "the middle regions where knowledge is . . . more dependent on external processes (economic stimulations or institutional supports)."[48] In *The Normal and the Pathological* Canguilhem focuses on medicine as an exemplary instance of rationality. Medicine is analyzed for its positivism and its apparatus of normalization. Thus the germ theory of medicine is the reflex of an optimism that makes the sources of infection fully visible.[49] The very notion that the pathological is no more than a "quantitative variation of the normal" emerges from "the conviction of rationalist optimism that evil has no reality" and that the body (politic) has an "essential and permanent structure" undisturbed by its momentary disfigurations. For Canguilhem, because culture thinks the pathological only through the normal, medicine has become an institution that protects a positivism in which "there are no negative values."[50]

While this may suggest that Canguilhem is a cultural historian, for Foucault in 1978 his importance is methodological. Canguilhem's insistence that we return to "the sick man's experience" to understand what is covered over by the "physician's knowledge" has much in common with the critique by the antipsychiatry movement of the subject-object division between doctor and patient:

> If today the physician's knowledge of disease can anticipate the sick man's experience of it, it is because at one time this experience gave rise to, summoned up, that knowledge. Hence medicine always exists . . . because there are men who feel sick, not because there are doctors to tell men of their illnesses. . . . It seems quite important to us that a doctor recognize in pain a phenomenon of total reaction which makes sense . . . only at the level of concrete human individuality.[51]

But Canguilhem is distinguished from Laing and Cooper by a refusal to enter this "experience," and it is this reticence that Foucault values. While using the term *experience*, Canguilhem does not claim that the sick have access to their experience; what they express "is not directly their experience but their interpretation of an experience for which they have been deprived of adequate concepts." Indeed, experience is introduced only as a kind of outside to a medical technology that masks its origins "in the living being's spontaneous effort to dominate the environment and organize it according to his values."[52] We will recognize here something like Foucault's re-vision of phenomenology as archaeology; experience is not an origin, a foundation for knowledge, but simply a point of resistance (as Foucault sees it) to the positivity of knowledge.

In this retreat from experience and truth to the problem of knowledge, the "formation of concepts," and the "discontinuity" and "error" characteristic of epistemology, Foucault locates Canguilhem's seminality for work by Althusser, Bourdieu, and Lacan, which all emerged around 1968.[53] In other words, Foucault in 1978 connects Canguilhem to poststructuralism and to the asceticism that came about in response to the "crisis" of the sixties: "a crisis concerning not only the University but also the status and role of knowledge."[54] In the narrative Foucault constructs, this asceticism is traced back to Husserl as a representative of "formalism" and "the theory of science" and marks a break with the "philosophy of the subject" and the "experienced thing" allegedly represented by Sartre and Merleau-Ponty.[55] Yet Canguilhem's work can be more accurately linked to the chiasm of the transcendental and the existential that we have seen in deconstruction and specifically in works such as Derrida's *Edmund Husserl's Origin of Geometry*, also notable for its methodological "auster[ity]."[56] Canguilhem, in other words, inscribes Foucault in a "history" with which his work "maintains . . . a relation that is strange . . . ineffaceable, and more fundamental than any relation of adjacency in a common space would be" (OT: 367).

Canguilhem, after all, does not write about arithmetic but about the "science of life . . . and the living being," which he cannot do without taking up "disease, death, monstrosity."[57] His concern with the forms of knowledge is thus *informed* by the content that he gives those forms. Apart from his very use of terms such as *experience*, it is worth noting two aspects of his thought that link it to existential phenomenology. First there is his sense that illness must be studied as a phenomenon and not as a fact: "by a phenomenon," Sartre says, "we are to understand 'that which announces itself,'" and "assumes its own being in an existential mode of understanding."[58] Thus the doctor must "recognize in pain a phenomenon of total reaction which makes sense . . . only at the level of concrete human individuality."[59] Second, this phenomenon cannot be isolated from a larger existential context:

> In the final analysis, would it not be appropriate to say that the pathological can be distinguished as such, that is, as an alteration of the normal state, only at the level of organic totality. . . . To be sick really means that a man lives another life, even in the biological sense of the word. To return once more to diabetes, it is not a kidney disease because of glycosuria. . . . It is the disease of an organism all of whose functions are changed. . . . It seems

very artificial to break up disease into symptoms or to consider its complications in the abstract. What is a symptom without context or background? What is a complication separated from what it complicates?[60]

Interestingly, Merleau-Ponty makes the same point a year earlier. In *The Structure of Behaviour* (1942), he also speaks of the normal and the pathological and argues that "specific disorder[s] should always be put back into the context of the total behaviour." And he too says that "pathological functioning [is not] homogeneous with normal functioning" and that sickness is therefore "a new *signification* of behaviour."[61]

Indeed, given Foucault's positioning of him as a proto-structuralist, Canguilhem's work exhibits a surprising organicism and romanticism. Not only must the pathological phenomenon be understood in its absolute singularity; this singularity itself can only be grasped within a larger system, an organic "totality" characterized by a poetics of "auto-construction, auto-conservation [and] auto-reparation" that makes organisms hospitable to the anomalies that arise in "life," in a way that mechanical systems (such as structuralism) never will be.[62] This organicism is the basis for Canguilhem's phenomenology, which in turn is the condition for his critique of discourse. As a "totality" with its own integrity, the sick organism manifests a new kind of being: "disease is a positive, innovative experience in the living being. . . . [It] is not a variation on the dimension of health; it is a new dimension of life" that calls into question our conceptions of the "norm" by dissolving the "hierarchical functions" to which we are used.[63] Canguilhem, in other words, sees disease as a form of *existence*. To "exist," as Sartre says (summarizing Heidegger) is to "*assume*" one's being as one's "own possibility," to be "responsible for it instead of receiving it from outside."[64] Disease is a form of possibility, a strange freedom of the forms of life although not invested with any personal agency; and it is this *Dasein* that is the condition for Canguilhem's critique of the forms of knowledge.

If Foucault in 1978 sees Canguilhem's contribution as epistemological, what of 1963 when he wrote *The Birth of the Clinic*? In 1978 Foucault praises Canguilhem on the grounds of method and opposes his philosophy of the "concept" to one of "experience, of sense and of subject."[65] He has apparently forgotten that Merleau-Ponty actually spoke of the "structure" of behavior, of the priority of "structure" and "system" over content, and, in almost archaeological terms, of "types and levels of organization."[66] Foucault thus positions Canguilhem as a philosopher of what Derrida calls the "science" of experience as it returns after the end of man (M: 117). Yet even in 1978 Foucault is drawn to Canguilhem for profoundly phenomenological reasons. Canguilhem is concerned through biology and medicine with "life and death," with knowledge as a way of "knowing life" through "the 'living being' himself," and with "forming concepts" as a "way of living, not of killing life." Thus it is significant that Foucault also links Canguilhem to Nietzsche.[67] Nietzsche, hardly similar to "Husserl," is the inside of Canguilhem's analysis of medicine as a form of Apollinian rationality. Moreover, in 1963 this Nietzsche would have included the more phenomenological Nietzsche of *The Birth of of Tragedy*, whose title is echoed by *The Birth of the Clinic*.

Foucault later described Canguilhem's work as "a historical analysis of the forms of rationality and knowledge in a phenomenological perspective."[68] In the mid-sixties he conjugated from this work a unique theory type that he called archaeology, which situates the forms of knowledge in the space between the cogito and its unthought. Archaeology at this point is not what it later becomes; rather it explores the hiatus between social history and ontology, structuralism and phenomenology. In *The Order of Things*, Foucault provides the theoretical foundations for this approach, traces of which can also be found in the "genetic structuralism" of the early Barthes and Goldmann and the early work of Derrida. But *The Birth of the Clinic* is Foucault's first practical attempt at this approach—a phenomenological structuralism that confronts "the positivity of the sciences" and of rationality in general with the "radicality of philosophy" after Husserl.[69] As such, it marks a crucial advance beyond *Madness and Civilization* in Foucault's attempt to extend the concerns of *Mental Illness and Psychology* into a psychoanalysis of culture that will summon the reader back to a thinking beyond subjectivity first outlined in the preface to Binswanger.

This advance can be described in two ways: as a replacement of existential by Lacanian models of cultural analysis that no longer have the pragmatic goal of therapy; and as a shift in disciplinary affiliation that confers on Foucault's work a greater exteriority. Foucault's model for this shift was Canguilhem, whom he read only after writing *Madness and Civilization*. Canguilhem's work represents a crossing of philosophy with science that generates Foucault's work as a crossing of philosophy and (social) science.

Foucault's early work did not achieve this self-discipline of science; rather, it converted madness into a transcendental signified romanticized by its association with artists such as Van Gogh and Artaud. Canguilhem's "decisive" importance for Foucault lies in a relocation of the pathological from the interiority of mental illness to the exteriority of medicine,[70] which by analogy facilitates Foucault's transference of cultural analysis from the realm of experience to that of structure.

But Canguilhem's unique status in Foucault's intellectual family romance has to do with the way he facilitates a transition that contains a return. For as we have seen, Canguilhem is not that far from Merleau-Ponty, who engaged with the details of contemporary science as Heidegger never did. *The Structure of Behavior* is an ex-position of phenomenology through highly empirical work on physiology, biology, and *Gestalt* psychology. If Merleau-Ponty thinks phenomenology from the outside by ex-posing it to the discourses of biology and physiology, Canguilhem thinks science as existence by allowing it to (dis)close what Bataille, also in 1943, calls "inner experience." Canguilhem is no more a scientist than Foucault is a social scientist; he is a philosopher who expects from medicine "an introduction to concrete human problems."[71] But he seeks it through a discipline that forces him to stand outside the security of the human only so that he can also expose science to the finitude of being human. This exposure is after all what phenomenology theorizes through the concepts of Dasein and the flesh. In this sense we can argue that Foucault, even in 1978, is drawn to Canguilhem by a form of countermemory in which the latter serves precisely as a rem(a)inder of phenomenology.

The Phenomenological Allegory: Foucault from *Raymond Roussel* to *The Order of Things*

The Closet, the Fold: Foucault/Roussel

In 1963 Foucault published not only *The Birth of the Clinic* but also a book on the early twentieth-century novelist Raymond Roussel that was not translated until 1986 as *Death and the Labyrinth: The World of Raymond Roussel.*[1] Reflecting on Roussel in 1983, Foucault says: "No one has paid much attention to this book, and I'm glad; it's my secret affair. You know, he was my love for several summers" (DL: 185). In the same interview, he links Roussel's texts explicitly to the structuralist novels of his disciple Robbe-Grillet. Thus he inscribes Roussel's modernist experiments within the postmodern turn away from phenomenology towards a new objectivism focused on things, their structures, and humans themselves as things. But in the first chapter of *Raymond Roussel* Roussel's life takes the place occupied in Foucault's theoretical landscape by Blanchot, whose work on the death of the author in the process of writing emerges, not from the linguistic turn, but from a negative and post-Heideggerian phenomenology. Or perhaps one should say that in Blanchot's theoretical texts, phenomenology and the decentering of the subject enfold one another—an enigma repeated by Foucault's enfolding of Roussel's life with his textual machines, so as to make consciousness both the inside and outside of structure.

Interestingly, Roussel, appropriated for structuralism by Robbe-Grillet, had sought treatment from the Heideggerian analyst Binswanger on whom Foucault wrote his first monograph. Foreshadowing Foucault's later sense that the syncresis of phenomenology and psychoanalysis was a missed encounter, Binswanger had not known what to make of Roussel. Roussel's (dis)appearance on the scene of phenomenological psychoanalysis and his recovery decades later as a protostructuralist frame Foucault's own career within a (self)analysis in which "Roussel" is a paleonym that unfolds the covering over of phenomenology by (post)structuralism. It is unclear whether Foucault, always fascinated by death, had premonitions of his own death in the interview with Ruas.[2] But the book, which begins with Roussel's enigmatic suicide behind a door "locked from the inside" (DL: 4), had already made him into Foucault's uncanny intellectual double. Together the interview and the book invite us to read Foucault's corpus in terms of what he himself, reading Roussel, figures as a hermeneutics of the closet. They confess and perform a certain nonidentity in this corpus. In the interview this nonidentity takes shape as a gap between the public Althusserian Foucault, with his interest in institutions and discourses, and another Foucault, interested in literature, to whom nobody has paid "much attention." But more generally the hiatus opened up by the reissuing of this apparently eccentric book invites a double reading of Foucault's work in terms of public and private, outside and inside, present and past.

Foucault sees Roussel's texts as calling for this double reading in terms of an inverse closet that signifies only that there is a secret but "without showing what it hides" (5). Because the inside always remains outside, we can also evoke another figure: the fold. As a form of involution and complication, turning and returning, the fold gathers differences into a continuum. It is a conceptual figure that allows the inside to become, at any moment, the outside. Deleuze, who is most famous for using this "matheme," sometimes treats it as unfolding dormant possibilities, while Mario Perniola links it to the enigma.[3] The fold is also a spatial figure for the temporal loop that is one aspect of the hiatus in which we read Foucault with Roussel and Foucault with his own theoretical past. In this chapter I suggest that Foucault's work in the early sixties is not yet divided along two slopes but (dis)joined by a fold. The texts published from 1963 to 1966 enfold phenomenology within the very turn to archaeology and structure that seems to repudiate it. In allowing these binaries to unfold each other, Foucault creates a uniquely self-reflexive form of writing. *The Order of Things* is the theoretical *summa* of this phase of his work. It provides a history of epistemes that is also an allegory of the return and retreat of phenomenology. However, I approach this text in the first instance through *Raymond Roussel*—a book that already approaches Roussel's corpus as a baroque structure "constructed on multilevels of secrecy" (7). Roussel is Foucault's figure for reading his own work as multiply folded. Indeed, the book on Roussel also functions as an allegory of *The Birth of the Clinic*. In this doubling the life folded up inside Roussel's textual machines figures the "inner experience" that is disavowed both by the institutional structures of medicine and by the shelter that Foucault himself seeks in (post)structuralism.

As deployed here, allegory is not a totalizing structure. It is "constructed on multilevels of secrecy, one ordering the other, but without any of them . . . being absolutely revelatory" (7). Or, as Jameson puts it, it is a "system of figures" that opens up the text "to multiple meanings, to successive rewritings and overwritings which are generated as so many levels and . . . supplementary interpretations."[4] As the very structure of a hiatus or ir-resolution between these levels, allegory keeps its secrets, which is why Foucault introduces the figure of the closet only to complicate its epistemology of inside and outside. For, as we have seen, inner experience in Bataille's sense is characterized by its absolute exteriority. Foucault intimates this exteriority in the use he makes of the mirror in analyzing *Las Meninas*, where he turns the interiority of reflection towards the "tain" of the mirror: "just as we are about to apprehend ourselves . . . as though in a mirror, we find that we can in fact apprehend nothing of that mirror but its lustreless back. The other side of a psyche" (OT: 6).[5] The "other side," however, suggests something other than the surface. After *The Archaeology of Knowledge* Foucault will abandon a writing structured by the fold and the double to seek what is indeed "an enunciative domain identical with its own surface" (AK: 119). And yet in reissuing *Raymond Roussel* at the end of his life, Foucault reopens his work to precisely this double reading that joins and separates inside and outside, past and present, and more obliquely phenomenology and (post)structuralism.

A Door Locked from the Inside

Foucault approaches Roussel by way of Roussel's self-commentary that seems to unlock his corpus: *How I Wrote Certain of My Books*. This fittingly posthumous text is itself made up of multiple levels whose relationship is unreadable (DL: 7). Using the key that Roussel provides in this last book, "a key which is itself locked up, a cipher which deciphers and yet is encoded" (5), Foucault reads him on "levels" that are related laterally, not as surface and depth. On the one hand, he is concerned with the texts as intricate "machines" and "game[s]" (14) whose technical experimentation foreshadows the *nouveau roman* with its turn away from phenomenology to a focus on language as its own object (175). These machines defamiliarize words and disclose "a chasm in the identity of language" (17). Referring to the discussions in eighteenth-century grammar of how a single word is used to represent more than one thing, Foucault describes Roussel's fascination with "tropological shifts," with rhetorical figures such as "catachresis, metonymy, metalepsis . . . and many other hieroglyphs drawn by the rotation of words into the voluminous mass of language" (16). At work here is an interest shared by de Man in Saussure's discussion of hypograms in a literature "structured by the coded dispersal (or dissemination) of an underlying word or proper name," a literature that "substitutes a process of formal elaboration for a referential reading" (RT: 36).

On the other hand, as if to challenge this senseless self-containment of language, Foucault in the first and last chapters returns Roussel's language games to the puzzle of his life as a form of being towards death. But this is not Heidegger's death as mastery; it is rather death as Blanchot and Levinas describe it, as "ungraspable. . . . not linked to *me* by any relation of any sort," not graspable by author or reader.[6] In June 1933 Roussel settled in Palermo, "where he spent every day drugged and in an intense state of euphoria." On the morning he was to leave for a drug cure he was found dead, behind a door "which had been open at all times" but was now "locked from the inside" (DL: 4). In approaching the texts by way of this death, Foucault does not use it as a key to their bizarre experimentation. Instead, death marks the incomplete and supplementary status of life and text, indicating "that one must look further and in greater depth" (7). By locating in the texts the structures of a pathological world (un)available for noematic analysis (159–60) and thus tantalizing us with the phenomenological reading he cannot provide, Foucault makes us aware of the desire underlying the transcendence Roussel sought to grasp through the exteriority of language. Thus Roussel's death is both a moment of disclosure and foreclosure, the locked door being a displacement of the Heideggerian clearing: "The death, the lock, and this closed door formed, at that moment, and for all time, an enigmatic triangle where Roussel's work is both offered to and withdrawn from us" (4).

Foucault links Roussel to a concern with language in-itself that he finds in writers as diverse as Blanchot, Mallarmé, and the *nouveaux romanciers*. De Man later discusses this same concern in connection with Benjamin's concept of *reine Sprache*, as "language completely devoid of any kind of meaning function, language which would be pure signifier, . . . a purely technical linguistic language . . . limited to its own linguistic characteristics." *Reine Sprache* as de Man represents it is "inhuman," a site of "linguistic events" that are independent "of any intent . . . or any desire we might have" (RT: 96–97). But seen through the locked door of Roussel's death this language, and the poststructuralist project that his texts figure, conceals a concern with the enigma of Being, though displaced from the phenomenality of a philosophical discourse that would claim to grasp Being as meaning. This in fact is Foucault's point: that even a concern with language in-itself is part of the project of a for-itself, a project that is (un)readable because the door is locked from the inside.

Whether Roussel was aware of the ontological desires encrypted in his formalism is unclear. But Foucault's interest in Roussel's hypotext is phenomenological as well as formal. Thus the chasm in the identity of language becomes "a thin blade that slits the identity of things, showing them as hopelessly double and self-divided" (DL: 23). Similarly the process by which Roussel's "language, in its reversal of style, surreptitiously tries to say two things with the same words" (16) becomes the means by which Foucault says two things about Roussel. Each of these modes of reading is, in a Lacanian sense, the unconscious of the other. Gesturing towards a phenomenological psychoanalysis of Roussel's textual world, Foucault recognizes his formalism as one of those "ideal objectivities" critiqued by Derrida (OG: 26): a reversed mirror image of the pure conceptuality we find in Husserl. Roussel, as Lacan might say, uses tropes as "algebraic formulas 'formed of small letters'" to keep the Real at bay.[7] But if Foucault's reading thus interrupts logic with existence, he also will not let us shelter in the interiority of a psychobiographical approach. Hence the frequent formalism of his own analysis, which uses form as materiality rather than transcendence. Foucault, in other words, defamiliarizes "inner experience" by grasping it through the uncanny formal properties of texts that interrupt cognition with what de Man will call "the uncontrollable power of the letter as inscription" (RT: 37).

Foucault tells us that he "developed an affection for [Roussel's] work, which remained secret, since I didn't discuss it." Making the acquaintance of Robbe-Grillet at about the same time, Foucault "never spoke of Roussel with him" because of a "mental lapse that can't have been entirely innocent" (DL: 172). Perhaps he sensed that Robbe-Grillet would find his chiasmatic reading of Roussel queer and unfashionable. Phenomenology is Foucault's secret, to which he could not confess in a structuralist environment. Indeed, it may be this subtext in Foucault's reading of Roussel that put off Robbe-Grillet, who wrote what seems a similar essay on "Enigmas and Transparency in Raymond Roussel" (1963) but who did not like Foucault's book. Noting Roussel's fascination with mysteries and concealed exits, Robbe-Grillet sees their purpose as "purely formal" and attributes to Roussel an "opacity" that is an "excessive transparency" in which there are "only surfaces, no inside, no secret." Roussel thus enacts Robbe-Grillet's own project of creating a "flat and discontinuous universe where each thing refers only to itself," a literature that is *choiste* rather than *humaniste*.[8]

Robbe-Grillet's structuralist representation of Roussel allows us to see why Foucault's reading remains phenomenological, though in a way that opens up a hiatus within phenomenology itself. Whereas Robbe-Grillet uses the figure of a locked drawer that proves to be empty, Foucault speaks of a door that opens and closes and of words that are "filled and emptied by the possibility of there being yet another meaning" (4, 11). The images of doors and exits and the notion of a "void" (11) that is also a space evoke the Heideggerian and Merleau-Pontian notions of (dis)closure and opening, as do the recurrent accounts of Roussel's texts in terms of the visible and the invisible (58, 66). Foucault's book is, moreover, traversed by figures of light and darkness that recall not only Nietzsche but also what Derrida identifies as "the *phenomenological* metaphor" par excellence, elaborated through "all the varieties of *phainesthai*, of shining, lighting, . . . etc." (M: 132).

Roussel's texts, however, open onto an absence: a death through which he "defines the empty shell where his *existence* will be evident to others" (DL: 156; emphasis mine). Reading his texts, one does not know "whether there is a secret or none," and, paradoxically, to affirm that a secret exists would be to close the door, "dr[ying] up Roussel's work at its source, preventing it from coming to life out of this void which it animates" (10–11). The texts provide no illumination. For the figure Foucault uses is of a "solar void" that is also "its own mirror and nocturnal opposite" (164). This figure provides the title of the last chapter "The Enclosed Sun" and recalls the black light ("noire lumière") of Levinas's essay on Blanchot, which Foucault would have read before writing his essay on Blanchot in 1966. Using figures of night and absence, Blanchot deconstructs the Heideggerian notion of a *Lichtung*. Blanchot, as Levinas indicates, is Heidegger turned in a negative direction.[9] "Black light" (echoing Nerval and picked up in Kristeva's "black sun") figures that turning and intimates the phenomenological unconscious that underwrites the first phase of deconstruction.

Blanchot's work reinscribes Heidegger so as to shift his concern with the being of language from the phenomenality of philosophical discourse to the materiality of a literature that functions as the tain of philosophy's mirror. Foucault further unsettles this phenomenality by approaching Roussel's texts through a psychoanalysis of the ways in which his language encrypts the Real. He provides what he had sketched in *Mental Illness and Psychology*: a "noematic analysis" of the spatiotemporal structures that constitute Roussel's pathological world, but in the form of a "phenomenological analysis [that] rejects an a priori distinction between normal and pathological."[10] The last chapter is shadowed by the figure of Pierre Janet, Roussel's alienist or psychologist. It places Foucault's reading of the Rousselian hypotext on a path that leads to de Man's essay on the hypogram. Perhaps even more so, it leads to a psychoanalysis of the anagram that de Man never quite engages. Thus Foucault anticipates Abraham and Torok's notion of cryptonomy[11] and Kristeva's analysis of experimental literature as a form that cannot finally be reduced to a linguistic paradigm. In *Revolution in Poetic Language* Kristeva describes the fetishism of the signifier that organizes experimental literature as a withdrawing of language from its "symbolic" or phenomenal function. She thus opens it out as a "semiotic [or material] articulation." Fetishism is "a compromise with the thetic" that uses things as signs because it is still stuck in abjection. The fetishizing of signs themselves as things is a phenomenon that Kristeva discusses at greater length in "Within the Microcosm of the Talking Cure." Here she speaks of "borderline patients" attachment to the signifier: "The analyst notices a tendency to play with signifiers: puns, port-

manteau words, the condensation of signifiers. . . . Yet this manipulation of
the signifier leaves the analyst, as well as the patient, at special moments—
that is, moments of suffering—with a feeling of void."[12]

In analyzing Roussel's language, then, Foucault does two things. He
makes it the site for a reflection on nonbeing, thus disclosing an ontological
subtext in deconstruction marked more reticently in Derrida's suggestion
that language "is the process of death at work in signs" (SP: 40). But beyond
that he provides a psychoanalysis of the poststructuralist flattening of the
Real into the signifier. For despite Roussel's simulation of a "language which
only speaks about itself" (DL: 167), his obsession with masks, doublings,
and tropological shifts discloses death as the unconscious of "the play of duplication and repetition" which covers up "the proliferating emptiness of
language" (160, 165).

Foucault, in short, was drawn to Roussel for two reasons: because of his
complex textual mechanisms that redirected attention from the signified to
the signifier and because those mechanisms concealed the ontological questions that he did not ask except in death. Inscribing Roussel's life as the inside of his texts, Foucault uses that inside to make the reader rethink the
technology of poststructuralism from outside its own protective exteriority.
Roussel thus figures the relationship that exists in Foucault's own work between poststructuralism and phenomenology or between the history of social practices attempted in *The Birth of the Clinic* (and later in *Discipline and
Punish*) and the ontological questions that the very positivism of history
risks deferring. The relationship between Roussel's texts and his life is reen-
acted in the relationship between *The Birth of the Clinic*, as the kind of text
by which Foucault was later represented (and wished to be represented),[13]
and the "secret" life he led through writers such as Roussel and Blanchot.
Thus the publication of the two books—*The Birth of the Clinic* and *Raymond Roussel*—on the same day inscribes the very project of archaeology/ge-
nealogy within an autocritique absent from Foucault's later work. For the
book on Roussel is the unconscious of its public counterpart, linked to it by
"underground passages" (AK: 17) that are particularly evident in the preface
and conclusion to *The Birth of the Clinic*. Reentering the latter by way of
these (Nietzschean) passages, we become aware that Foucault is performing
what Canguilhem merely asserts, namely, a self-analysis in which the ra-

tionality of theory is called to account for life. Theory itself, then, becomes what it describes—a fold, a form of thinking between the *cogito* and its doubles.

The Return and Retreat of Language

Roussel's fascination with labyrinths, his concealment of his life behind the locked door of his texts, and his opening and closing of that door in the moment of death provide us with a way of understanding Foucault's own more deliberate reticence. As Michel de Certeau notes (although with some frustration at the resulting "obscurity") *The Order of Things* enacts "the opposition it so often underlines between 'surface effects' and the hidden 'ground' they ceaselessly signify and conceal." This opposition can be described, as de Certeau describes it, with reference to Foucault's subject matter: as one between "the 'positivism' of science or the 'objectivity of things,'" and the "nocturnal underside" onto which these positivities open as we discover that "the fabric of words and things" contains the "secret of its own ungraspable negation."[14] Or it can be described with reference to Foucault's method: as an opposition between social history and ontology or between the "structural analysis of discourses" (BC: xvii) and the rethinking of the subject that this analysis conceals. However we describe it, it is important that we experience *The Order of Things* as overdetermined by its multiple levels. In this sense the text must be "read as an open site" (OT: xii); by overlapping phenomenology with structuralism, it avoids choosing between them or "avoids the distinction without eliminating it or rendering it impossible."[15]

Foucault's turn to something like structuralism with its attendant "formalization" of analysis is signaled by the term *archaeology*, which he uses to defamiliarize mimetic or "living history."[16] But *The Order of Things* is also profoundly phenomenological in its structuring by figures of depth and *telos* that are absent from the nonnarrative format of *The Archaeology of Knowledge*. In synchronic terms its argument is shaped by a distinction between the invisible and the visible, a distinction aligned with the difference between language (*langage*) and the concept of discourse that will later be Foucault's exclusive concern. In diachronic terms this difference is worked out in terms of a counter-Hegelian (or Nietzschean) phenomenology involving (a) the replacement of language by discourse in the transition from the Renaissance to the classical period and (b) the return of language in the more opaque and dispersed medium of literature as a form of *Dasein* that marks the end of man. Structuralist in its attention to "the system" or "network of simultaneities"[17] that organizes each episteme, *The Order of Things* is also persistently dialectical (in the manner of Nietzsche's *Birth of Tragedy*) in its own organization as a history of rationalities whose goal is to disclose the ontological unconscious of rationality. Indeed, insofar as he allies himself with structuralism at this stage, Foucault describes it as a historical symptom, as "the awakened and troubled *consciousness* of modern thought" (OT: 208; emphasis mine). Thus he seems to reach beyond structuralism, to "a perhaps inaccessible discourse—which would at the same time be an ontology and a semantics" (208).

Crucial to Foucault's endeavor is the difference between language and discourse,[18] which anticipates Kristeva's distinction between the semiotic and the symbolic. This distinction makes archaeology in *The Order of Things* not simply into a historical taxonomy but also into a metacritical and self-reflexive scheme of evaluation for Theory itself. Briefly, "language," which first appears in the Renaissance, involves a ternary rather than binary organization of the sign. It presupposes not simply a relation between signifier and signified but also a third term: a *resemblance* between the two that "ma[kes] it possible to see in the first the mark of the second" (64). This configuration is one in which "language and things [are] endlessly interwoven" so that language is a form of existence rather than a mere "function" (54, 79). It would be easy to stabilize the third term by interpreting it as Derrida's transcendental signified. But, as the metaphors of play and weaving indicate, "resemblance" is rather a (dis)similarity between words and things that keeps their relationship open. Resemblance "oscillat[es] endlessly between one and three terms" (42): between the unification of signifier with signified in a transcendental signified, and their difference in that words only resemble things.

Language, in short, circulates meaning between words and things so as to constitute what Foucault calls "the prose of the world" (17). The very phrase "prose of the world" intimates a constant re-vision of the linguistic and the material by each other. For it is not clear what resembles what: whether words are like things or whether things are further words in "the vast syntax of the world" (18). Resemblance makes words and things interchangeable so that these elements can play either "the role of content or of sign, that of secret or of indicator" (34). If things are words, then the meaning of things cannot be fixed: "by duplicating itself in a mirror the world abolishes the distance proper to it; in this way it overcomes the place allotted to each thing" (19).

In the classical period this "more complex organization" of the sense of the world is "fixed in a binary form" that renders words "stable" by laying out their relationships on a flat surface (64, 42). "Resemblance" (a quality of things) is replaced by "comparison" (a function of order). "Resemblance" is now denounced "as a confused mixture" that must be subjected to a structural analysis "in terms of identity and difference" (52, 54). The "facts of discourse" are located paradigmatically and syntagmatically

> not as autonomous nuclei of multiple significations, but as events and functional segments gradually coming together to form a system. The meaning of a statement [is] defined not by the treasure of intentions that it might contain, revealing and concealing it at the same time, but by the difference that articulates it upon other real or possible statements, which are contemporary to it or to which it is opposed in the linear series of time. (BC: xvii)

The result, as Foucault says, is "an immense reorganization of culture" (OT: 43) through a restructuring of the ways we know and perceive. Whereas resemblance had located knowledge in the shifting relationship between words and things, "order" locates it purely within "representation" or the system of signs: "Once the existence of language has been eliminated, all that remains is its function in representation: its nature and its virtues as *discourse*" (81). Because the two parts of the sign are no longer required to pass through the detour of the world for signification to occur, signifier and signified now enjoy a "pure and simple connection" (67) in the tabular space of an order that needs no further commentary. But this is by no means a merely technical mutation. Discourse does not *indicate* anything that remains un*expressed* within the sign; it assumes "no remainder" and no discrepancy between the visible and the invisible. Supposing "nothing in excess of what has been said, but only the fact of its historical appearance" (BC: xvii), discourse posits a self-sufficient rationality profoundly resistant to ontology (OT: 381).

As these remarks suggest, the distinction between language and discourse is not existentially neutral. Classicism, as an epistemological rearrangement that associates knowledge with order rather than being, is itself an ontology: "an ontology defined negatively as an absence of nothingness, a general representability of being, and being as expressed in the presence of representation" (206). With classicism, which curiously anticipates structuralism, we witness the disappearance of the "massive and intriguing existence of language" as a form of *Dasein* (79) and its replacement by method, epistemology, clarity.

The Three Epistemes: Dialectic, Hiatus

But this is not to say that Foucault constructs language as the binary opposite of discourse. For the Renaissance, where language first emerges, occupies a profoundly ambiguous position in *The Order of Things*, as is signaled by the lyricism of this section, which marks this epoch as at once naive and originary. One cannot say that classicism is an impoverishment of the Renaissance or that it is a necessary demystification. Foucault's ambivalence towards the passing of the Renaissance is nowhere more evident than in his attitude to its preeminent epistemological form, commentary. On the one hand, he is a good structuralist who eschews commentary; he yearns for an analysis of the statement limited to "the fact of its historical appearance," and not one defined phenomenologically "by the treasure of intentions that it might contain, revealing and concealing it at the same time" (BC: xvii). But, on the other hand, this rejection of "interpretation"[19] in favor of "formalization" sits oddly with everything else he says (OT: 40–41), including what remains as late as 1969 a critique of "formalization" and "mathematization."[20] For Foucault himself speaks constantly of language as an excess or lack that reverberates behind or beneath itself. Thus he tacitly privileges commentary as the analytic reflex of a language in which "the signified is revealed only in the visible, heavy world of a signifer that is itself burdened with a meaning that it cannot control" (BC: xvi–xvii).

Foucault's ambivalence towards commentary is connected with his reservations about language, which, as we shall see, is a phenomenological category. The error of the Renaissance is to theologize excess by encoding interpretation as exegesis, thus grounding commentary in the illusion of "an original Text" (OT: 41). Correspondingly, Renaissance semiotics also practices an Apollinian sublimation of *différance*, apparent in Foucault's description of it as inconsistently a "unitary and triple system" (64), more logocentric and yet more complex than classical binarism. Because language oscillates "between one and three terms" (42), the complicated systems of correspondence that constitute Renaissance epistemology both cohere into a totality and disseminate infinitely. These systems of linkage—*convenientia*, *aemulatio*, analogy, and sympathy—seem to be synchronized so as to create the order that used to be called the Elizabethan world picture. Yet they also overlap, rewrite, and supplement each other so that the "system is not closed" like the tabular order of classicism but finally "escap[es] from itself" (25). In this sense the Renaissance is a moment of potential. But its grammatology is *un livre à venir*. For the unworking of the order of things at the heart of Renaissance semiotics is finally recontained in the mirage of a totality compromised by its very complexity.

Because of this ambivalence of the Renaissance towards the *différance* it dis-closes, Foucault's own order of things leaves it in the past. In the end, then, the rationality of discourse is contested not by language but by the literature that emerges on the far side of the dissociation of sensibility brought about by classicism (43). Literature is not a collection of texts but a philosophical category, denoting a particular view of language after the nineteenth century: as "folded back upon the enigma of its own origin and existing wholly in reference to the pure act of writing" (300). Literature is the ascetic negative of Renaissance language, its return as a *being* "separated" from things (49) after the reinscription of excess as lack.

But what this also means is that the history that leads from language, through discourse, to literature is driven by remainders within each episteme that generate—despite Foucault's insistence on rupture—a kind of dialectic. This dialectic is structured by hiatus; it becomes a retreat and return of the origin, a progression towards the future unworked by a perpetually missed encounter with the past. In each stage of Foucault's history something is accomplished and something missed, the very return of what is disavowed being a further disavowal. Thus language in the Renaissance had been possessed of a certain materiality "both because things themselves hide and manifest their own enigma like a language and because words offer themselves to men as things to be deciphered" (35). This materiality involved at once a proximity to being, a tremendous complication of being through language, and yet a naiveté about origins. Under the guise of a demystification, classical discourse instituted a nominalism (296) that entailed a different kind of idealism. As pure representation it established itself in a phenomenality that allowed for nothing outside representation. In this sense classicism, though antianthropological in its emphasis on the sign,[21] is also allied with the cogito in attributing to "discourse" the power subsequently given to man to "represent the order of things" (OT: 312).[22] Its enlightenment is, moreover, a simplification that forgets the complicated relationship of structure to being contained in the Renaissance's poetic rather than taxonomical systems of order.

This same doubleness marks the relationship of classicism to the nineteenth century or "modernity" (304); there is a hiatus between the two within which literature emerges as a further incomplete supplement. On the one hand, the nineteenth century forgets structurality by investing structure in man. Order is not just a nominal but an empirical truth by which man controls history. On the other hand, man, though a positivist category, also generates an analytic of finitude. For man is the point at which space enters time and structure becomes life, most obviously in the privilege given to biology and history. It is through these new "empiricities" (250), as we have seen in *The Birth of the Clinic*, that the atemporal, transcendental ego of classical medicine is exposed to the time of the disease culminating in death and autopsy. For this reason Foucault describes modernity in terms of depths and interiors, density and enigma, as harboring an "inner side" to its "visibility" (237, 251, 310). Man "by a sort of internal torsion and overlapping," is that "strange . . . being whose nature . . . is to know nature, and itself, in consequence, as a natural being" (310).

Not surprisingly, then, the nineteenth century is marked by a second retreat from totality—this time not towards infinity but towards finitude. The nineteenth century sees a return of commentary (OT: 298) combined with a renewed sense of the being of language as that which exceeds both man and order. But whereas language in the Renaissance was "ontologically interwoven" with the world (296), the being of language is now encrypted in "literature" as "the manifestation of language in its thickness."[23] It can no longer be deciphered because it possesses "neither sound nor interlocutor" and has "nothing to say but itself" (OT: 300). Nor can it any longer be made to "do" anything, preferring to "enclose itself within a radical intransitivity" (300) that makes it the nocturnal mirror of production, enlightenment, and capital.

As my references to structuralism and phenomenology suggest, Foucault's text is not just a table of epistemes and their associated disciplines. It also doubles as a phenomenology of theoretical styles reminiscent of the tripartite metasemiotics of culture in Hegel's *Aesthetics*—where classicism is again an unsatisfactory middle and where the triadic dialectic also ends in ir-resolution. Hegel's phenomenology is a dialectic not of progress but of supplementation. Turning this phenomenology in a reflexive direction by opening with a painting that implicates its spectators as well as its painter, Foucault makes *The Order of Things* into his own phenomenology of mind, inscribing himself in his own text as Hyppolite had done with Hegel. He attempts the difficult task of a phenomenology that is at once post-Hegelian and post-Heideggerian: cultural, ontological, and autobiographical. In this narrative Foucault's ambivalent structuralism—including his distaste for commentary—confesses itself as a belated form of classicism. And Foucault, instead of placing his classicism in "the movement of the concept," unworks its logic by exposing it to existence. As he says of Hyppolite, he transforms theory into "an endless task, against the background of an infinite horizon" (AK: 236).

Allegories of Theory: Foucault, Merleau-Ponty, Sartre

As a structural study that conceals a more profound ontological project, *The Order of Things* also allegorizes Foucault's own relationship to contemporary philosophy. For embedded in its history of epistemes is his attempt to rethink phenomenology through a dialectical encounter with a structuralism figured as classicism. Foucault himself makes the connection between Enlightenment "rationalism" (54) and Saussurean linguistics as a "rediscover[y]" of the classical view that there is "no meaning exterior or anterior to the sign," no "genesis interior to consciousness" (66–67). The allusions to phenomenology are even more striking. Foucault's early work is full of references to "the visible and the invisible" (BC: xii)—the title of the book on which Merleau-Ponty was working when he died in 1961. Moreover, Foucault at one time considered entitling his archaeology of the human sciences *The Prose of the World*, the title of a collection by Merleau-Ponty published posthumously.[24] Choosing instead to use this title for the section on the Renaissance, Foucault inscribes the thought of his precursor within a past that is both naive and originary: a past that cannot represent *The Order of Things* as a whole but from which its entire project unfolds. In short, Foucault's three-part history of epistemes narrates his own return to and retreat from his phenomenological origins. In this autobiography of theory, Foucault remembers a certain phenomenology, which he submits to the discipline of the linguistic paradigm so as to work towards his own version of deconstruction. As I shall suggest, this unfolding of phenomenology into deconstruction is thematically anchored in the "return of language as literature" that occurs in the movement from the Renaissance to modernity through the "chasm in the identity of things" created by classicism.

The position of Merleau-Ponty's thought as a hinge that opens onto deconstruction is in keeping with the way Foucault situates phenomenology itself, not in the later "Foreword to the English edition" (1970), but in the text itself:

> If phenomenology has any allegiance it is to the discovery of life, work and language; and also to the new figure which, under the old name of man, first appeared less than two centuries ago; it is to the interrogation concerning man's mode of being and his relation to the unthought. This is why phenomenology— . . . in so far as . . . it revived the problem of the *a priori* and the transcendental motif, has never been able to exorcize its insidious kinship, its simultaneously promising and threatening proximity, to empirical analyses of man; it is also why, though it was inaugurated by a reduction to the *cogito*, it has always been led to questions, to *the* question of ontology. The phenomenological project continually resolves itself, before our eyes, into a description—empirical despite itself—of actual experience, and into an ontology of the unthought that automatically short-circuits the primacy of the 'I think.' (OT: 325–26)

The mixed hermeneutic signals sent by this passage are undoubtedly responsible for a misunderstanding of the entire subsection in which it occurs. Because of its association with humanism and the cogito, we assume that Foucault must be condemning phenomenology. And yet scattered through this passage are terms that Foucault clearly valorizes, such as the "unthought" and, more surprisingly, "language," which he will later condemn phenomenology for ignoring. While "life, work and language" also constitute the trinity that underwrites the nineteenth-century episteme (250), phenomenology's alliance with the material and the empirical pulls in different directions and creates the aporia that Foucault rethinks as a hiatus. Empiricism on the one hand leads to a mimetic investment in history and experience and thus to what Foucault dismisses as "anthropology." It is for this reason that phenomenology revives the "transcendental motif" as a way of resisting "psychologism" (325) by insisting on what Sartre calls the "transcendence of the ego"—its existence as a function that is not immanent within man. On the other hand, empiricism is also a way of complicating the abstraction of Husserl's transcendentalism through a return to what Merleau-Ponty calls perception as the site of differences bracketed by the phenomenological reduction. Moving between empiricism and transcendentalism as ways of protecting the cogito, phenomenology also finds itself using them to question the very primacy of the "I think." As a result its legacy lies in the questions it raises, in its profoundly un-Cartesian willingness to think from and within its own gaps.

Seen from this perspective *The Order of Things* is Foucault's attempt to think from the questions left unanswered in *The Visible and the Invisible* or, more accurately, to think in the obscure clearing that Merleau-Ponty opens up between himself and Sartre. Thus while *The Order of Things* is a history of the disappearance of language and its return as literature, this narrative also allegorizes Foucault's own relationship to a phenomenology projected back into the Renaissance and reinscribed more negatively as deconstruction, after the break between words and things effected by structuralism. Foucault's terms are often closer to Merleau-Ponty's than one might think. His references to the "raw, historical" being of language (OT: 35) manifestly recall the latter's use of the "sensible" to "restore to us the brute being of the unreflected."[25] That Foucault often locates in language what Merleau-Ponty associates with perception is a sign of his participation in that "vast shift . . . from a form more dense in living models to another more saturated with models borrowed from language" (OT: 360). But Foucault also refers to the "density of perception" and to a "region where 'things' and 'words' have not yet been separated" so that "seeing and saying are still one" in an intermingling of the semiotic and the Symbolic (BC: xiii, xi; cf. OT: 43). Through "language," moreover, he seems to be straining towards something nondiscursive—whether idealized in the Renaissance, where language possesses the "ancient solidity of . . . a thing inscribed in the fabric of the world"; or de-idealized at the turn of the century, where it returns as a literature "rejected as discourse and re-apprehended in the plastic violence of the shock, [where it] is referred back to . . . the tortured body, to the materiality of thought, to the flesh" (OT: 43, 383).

Merleau-Ponty's perception, in other words, is an important pre-text for Foucault's return to language particularly when taken in conjunction with the former's emphasis on the flesh and the chiasm, as well as with his concept of inscription. It is important to remember that perception is not the act of a subject; rather, it is "a confused totality where all things, the bodies and minds, are together" in a world of "non-language significations" or "indications" that are "*differences*" and not "positive" terms.[26] Using perception to figure Heidegger's thinking beyond subjectivity, Merleau-Ponty therefore privileges "the sensible" over the concept. The sensible, as a "medium in which there can be *being* without it having to be posited,"[27] is one version of what Foucault is seeking when he speaks of a way in which thought "can *be* in the forms of non-thinking" (OT: 324). But it would be wrong to equate Merleau-Ponty with what develops from him, for he idealizes deconstruction as phenomenology, eliding the destructive violence associated with the flesh in Artaud and Bataille.[28] Through the Renaissance Foucault bids farewell to his own nostalgia for what his predecessor had sought, namely, a *différance* without dualism or a world that precedes the choice between identity and *différance*. Instead, he inscribes phenomenology within two narratives: a Nietzschean eschatology that tells of the occultation and return of the Dionysian; and a Hegelian dialectic in which the sensible must be reapprehended at a more profound point on a negative spiral as the materiality of writing. Structuralism is the midpoint of both these narratives. As an Apollinian veil that seeks in discourse a phenomenality without material remainder, it is also a necessary stage in the deconstruction of that unself-consciousness which (re)covers *différance* in a form of (dia)logocentrism.

That Foucault is closer to Merleau-Ponty than to Heidegger has much to do with Merleau-Ponty's last book. *The Visible and the Invisible* is a sustained disagreement with the Sartre of *Being and Nothingness*, whose presence in the text seems excessive. Excessive, but only if we neglect the way Merleau-

Ponty's critique of Sartre enfolds an uneasy attempt to do justice to his former friend. "Sartre" figures a gap in Merleau-Ponty's work that he verges on recognizing. His relationship with Sartre is not unlike the one Foucault acknowledges with Hegel in his tribute to Hyppolite; even as he struggles to "escape" Sartre, Merleau-Ponty is "brought back to him . . . from a different angle" only "to leave him behind, once more" (AK: 235). The richness of Merleau-Ponty's work consists in the way that he, like Hyppolite, viewed phenomenology as "accessible only through a phenomenological method."[29] In other words he did not see philosophy as exposing itself to its others only to reschematize this difference conceptually within a "totality" "dispers[ed] and regroup[ed] . . . in the movement of the concept" (AK: 236). He saw it as the unfinished work of a community where one "risk[s]" one's thought through its very ex-position (236). Because Merleau-Ponty's reading of Sartre remained overdetermined by a break that had never quite healed, *The Visible and the Invisible* is a missed encounter with this hiatus. But it is his sense of an unexplored potential in Merleau-Ponty's thought that leads Foucault to preserve his terminology, yet as if superimposing it "upon itself in a secret verticality" so as to open within it "an infinite space where doubles reverberate."[30]

Crucial to Merleau-Ponty's "difference" from Sartre is his attempt to rethink the latter's concept of the prereflective cogito; this project recurs in Kristeva's concept of the semiotic. For in critiquing Sartrean negativity, Merleau-Ponty also finds in the prereflective cogito the possibility of what he calls a "tacit cogito." Briefly, he criticizes Sartre for an inverse Cartesianism that divides existence, not between extended and thinking matter, but between being and nothingness. Reducing man to a "negativity" excluded by the "world as positivity," this dualism protects the desire for a bounded ego while also precluding an openness upon being that allows for "interaction" between thought and things.[31] However, Merleau-Ponty finds in Sartre's prereflective cogito a trace of that pre-thetic world he himself terms "perception," as if Sartre recognizes for a moment "the denseness of an unreflected being" admitted in the for-itself.[32] Developing that trace, Merleau-Ponty senses in Sartre the promise of "a broader sense of being, which contains Being and nothingness" and of which the very end of *Being and Nothingness* is the abjected remainder.[33]

Merleau-Ponty thus recasts *Being and Nothingness* within his own attempt to establish a relationship between thought and the unthought or between

the for-itself—as what Foucault calls "thought-conscious-of-itself"—and
the in-itself—as a form of "non-thought" (OT: 324) inaccessible to reflection
and yet present as a density at the very heart of the cogito. By 1960, moreover, this attempt has passed through the detour of a post-Heideggerian
thought complicated by its contact with Sartre; while resisting Sartre, Blanchot and Levinas also resist Heidegger's idealization of the unthought. Merleau-Ponty thus echoes Levinas in his "working notes," where he distinguishes a tacit from a "language cogito" and where he also distinguishes the
speaking and thinking subjects that are "the subject of a praxis" from a per-
ceiving subject that is "a tacit, silent *Being-at (Etre-à)*" possessed of no more
than an anonymous selfhood.[34] The tacit cogito is remarkably close to what
Foucault describes as "the modern *cogito*." For Foucault does not so much
reject the cogito as distinguish the modern from the Cartesian cogito. In a
passage that signals a certain continuity with the terms of previous philosophy, he writes:

> the modern *cogito* is as different from Descartes' as our notion of transcen-
> dence is remote from Kantian analysis. . . . In the modern *cogito* . . . we are
> concerned to grant the highest value, the greatest dimension, to the distance
> that both separates thought-conscious of itself and whatever, within
> thought, is rooted in non-thought. The modern *cogito* (and this is why it is
> not so much the discovery of an evident truth as a ceaseless task constantly
> to be undertaken afresh) must traverse, duplicate, and reactivate in an ex-
> plicit form the articulation of thought on everything within it, around it,
> and beneath it which is not thought but which is nevertheless not foreign to
> thought. . . . In this form the *cogito* will not therefore be the sudden and il-
> luminating discovery that all thought is thought, but the constantly renewed
> interrogation as to how thought can reside elsewhere than here, and yet so
> very close to itself; how it can *be* in the forms of non-thinking. (OT: 324)

Whereas Descartes sought to insulate *res cogitans* from *res extensa*, what
Foucault defines here is a phenomenological cogito, intentionally articulated
upon its outside or unthought. Foucault's understanding of this cogito develops in important ways in the space between Merleau-Ponty and Sartre. For
one thing, Merleau-Ponty was dissatisfied with the tacit cogito, feeling that
he should not even use the term *cogito* for what he was trying to articulate.[35]
Foucault shared this dissatisfaction with a philosophy of consciousness signaled by the qualifier *tacit*. But *cogito* remains an appropriate term for

Foucault, who is closer to Sartre than to Heidegger in defining man as a "dimension . . . which extends from a part of himself not reflected in a *cogito* to *the act of thought by which he apprehends that part*" (OT: 322; emphasis mine).

Second, and more important, Merleau-Ponty can still be accused of idealizing the unthought in ways with which he was himself uneasy and that contribute to giving this book the unconcluded quality noted by its editor, Claude Lefort.[36] This uneasiness comes out in the working notes, which are often more radical than the text itself, as for instance in the striking statement that "perception opens the world to me as the surgeon opens a body, catching sight, through the window he has contrived, of the organs in full functioning."[37] But it also emerges in the very choice of "Sartre" as a figure through whom to pursue the Heideggerian project of finding a place for the unthought. For in contrast to Heidegger, who can see Sartre's differences from him only as mistakes, Merleau-Ponty tries to see where Sartre might have gone. Seeking the common ground between himself and his contemporary, he also allows us to glimpse the mutually supplementary relationship between himself and Sartre.

Merleau-Ponty's deployment of Sartre as a hinge is clear enough. Even as Sartre projects the density of an unreflected being away from the self, abjecting it in *Nausea* as being "de trop," he also recognizes it as something within the cogito and allows for a more fruitful relationship between being and nothingness. As interesting is Merleau-Ponty's investing of this relationship and of his own notion of the chiasm in "Sartre"—a figure dismissed by Heidegger with defensive condescension. What we sense in this move is something that never quite happens in the text: a rearticulation of the tacit cogito in the *différance* between Sartrean and Heideggerian being, which nevertheless differs from the rearticulations attempted by Blanchot and Levinas. Conceding the enormous importance of Sartrean negativity to French philosophy, Merleau-Ponty in effect recognizes that the phenomenality of the clearing must be inscribed within a radical materiality (mis)recognized by Sartre as the *en-soi*: "One cannot account for this double 'chiasm' by the cut of the For Itself and the cut of the In Itself. A relation to Being is needed that would form itself *within Being*—This at bottom is what Sartre was looking for."[38]

If Merleau-Ponty's work generally is a point of beginning for *The Order of Things*, his last book is a starting-point for the important section on "The '*Cogito*' and the Unthought." It is Merleau-Ponty who recognized the importance of locating Being within the cogito as something by which thought is outside itself "yet so very close to itself" (OT: 324). This articulation of thought with the unthought is crucial to Foucault both because he does not want to identify the cogito with nothingness (as in the inverse Cartesianism of which Sartre is sometimes accused) and because he does not want to abandon self-consciousness in favor of the "inertia" of the material (OT: 322), as in Robbe-Grillet's anti-Sartrean *chosisme*. But Foucault also responds to the space left by Merleau-Ponty, to his need to deal with a negativity that for him is (mis)represented by Sartre. Deconstructing the unthought as Merleau-Ponty never quite did, Foucault turns not so much to Sartre as to Bataille and Blanchot, who are seldom named in *The Order of Things* but who preoccupied his attention between 1963 and 1966.

Both these writers allow Foucault to deconstruct phenomenology—in the sense of forming an intellectual community with it: one that continues phenomenology's attempt to think the nature of being negatively and yet without tying this negativity to the failure of the cogito. Thus Foucault's 1963 essay on Bataille picks up on the latter's use of phenomenological phrases such as "inner experience" and "the sovereign Subject" in a strange and empty way, as if this terminology is inhabited by "another language that also speaks and that [the philosopher] is unable to dominate."[39] Lacking a clear subject or context, Foucault's essay performs rather than defines Bataille's "inner experience" as a transgression that transgresses nothing, an inside that is not an inside because there is no outside to define it against. Bataille rewrites phenomenology by hollowing it out from within. He allows Foucault to think "excess" in a more tragic way than Merleau-Ponty or Heidegger, as a nonproductive negativity or "radical intransitivity" (OT: 300) irrecuperable into any kind of clearing or even *Destruktion*.

Where Bataille locates this negativity in a Sadeian transgression—in the "violence" of a "language . . . rejected as discourse" (OT: 383)—Blanchot finds it in a literature conceived in terms of "death, the mirror and the double."[40] That Blanchot is Heidegger with a minus sign is suggested not only by Levinas but also by Foucault's description of him in terms that echo

Heidegger's essay on "Language," which stands behind the opposition of language to man at the very end of *The Order of Things*.[41] In his monograph on Blanchot, also written in 1966, Foucault speaks of "the being of language" that "appears for itself with the disappearance of the subject"; and he speaks of the "irremediable incompatibility between the appearing of language in its being and consciousness of the self in its identity." Defining "literature" as the exteriority of language to itself, he echoes and displaces Heidegger: "And if, in this setting 'outside of itself,' [language] unveils its own being, the sudden clarity reveals not a folding back but a gap, not a turning back of signs upon themselves but a dispersion."[42]

As a deconstruction of "Heidegger," "Blanchot" figures the survival of ontology after the trauma and separation of discourse as an ascesis imposed on perception. This same refiguration of the phenomenological project can be seen in the relationship of Blanchot to Merleau-Ponty or of literature to language. For Foucault's work is traversed by the strange association of language with "murmuring": a figure used to signify "that language is speaking of itself, that the letter is not the letter, but the language which doubles it within the same system of reality."[43] Used by both Merleau-Ponty and Blanchot, and by Levinas and then Foucault with reference to Blanchot, the figures of murmuring and of a language that repeats itself "to infinity" are also used with reference to language and its return as literature.[44] They inscribe *The Order of Things* in Foucault's reading of Blanchot as the hidden story of how phenomenology became deconstruction. In this allegory of epistemic history as a dialectic of theoretical consciousness, it is significant that Foucault does not stay with the structuralism that he often simulates. This structuralism, as classicism, is no more than an unsatisfying middle: an (un)fortunate fall leading to a further ir-resolution.

The University in Ruins: The Human Sciences and Literature

Chapter 3 discussed how Blanchot facilitates the transition from phenomenology to deconstruction by transferring Sartre's analysis of nothingness from the cogito to writing. This transference helps to clarify what Foucault is doing in de-positing being in language rather than perception as early as the section on the Renaissance. It underwrites even more clearly his use of literature to unwork language. For Blanchot, as Foucault says, literature is "what constitutes the outside of every work, what ploughs up every written language and leaves on every text an empty claw mark."[45] Literature is the outside of language as deconstruction is the outside of phenomenology. But as important as *what* Foucault derives from Blanchot and Bataille is their *style* of thinking: a style unlike anything in Merleau-Ponty or even Sartre. As Foucault himself points out, it "is extremely difficult to find a language faithful to this thought. Any purely reflexive discourse runs the risk of leading the experience of the outside back to the dimension of interiority." Foucault comes closest to capturing the "undialectical negation" underlying this thought[46] in "A Preface to Transgression." This essay is closed in on itself and profoundly resistant to discursive assimilation; it does not discuss texts by Bataille or concepts in his work. Rather it performs Bataille's deconstruction (or "transgression") as an unassignable negation, "a visibility devoid of shape." In effect it constructs a style of "the outside" that cannot be taken back "to the interiority of our philosophical reflection and the positivity of our knowledge."[47]

But in general this is not the style of *The Order of Things*, which we can more easily "repatriate to the side of consciousness."[48] Thus it is important to distinguish Foucault's work from Blanchot's or Levinas's transposition of Sartrean nothingness into a Heideggerian reflection on being, at least at the near end of the text (OT: 303–82). This section moves restlessly between an analytic of finitude that takes us towards the "interiority" of a being without transcendental guarantees and "the exteriority of knowledge" (354)—a dimension absent from Blanchot's work. De-idealizing Merleau-Ponty's focus on a being that exceeds the cogito by locating this being in language rather than the sensible, Foucault also differs from both Merleau-Ponty and Blanchot in replacing the "density of perception" (BC: xiii) with "the density of the historic."[49] History as archaeology is a counterscience that maintains with the human sciences "a relation that is strange, undefined, ineffaceable" (OT: 367). But, on the other hand, history, even when submitted to its own "historicity" (370), cannot yield a purely negative experience: it is concerned, as Hegel says, with the forms by which man "produces" himself in the world through his work and not with what Blanchot calls "worklessness" (*désoeuvrement*).

Foucault's terms *interiority* and *exteriority* are worth pondering. Interiority does not connote identity but rather the disappearance of the visible with its attendant qualities of space, face, and solidity—in short, everything that facilitates "property" and (self)-possession in Levinas's sense. Interiority, like Bataille's inner experience, thus folds into Blanchot's thought from the outside so as to inscribe this thought as a radical, intransitive existentialism. Knowledge, from this perspective, is condemned as the evasion of inner experience. But Foucault, like Derrida in his essay on Levinas, cannot rest with the "pure difference" of interiority as a "language without phrase," an existence without activity that "signifies outside all intentionality" (WD: 151, 152). Thus he also deploys the word *exteriority* in a Hegelian sense, seeking a dialogue between inner experience and what Derrida, using a Sartrean term, refers to as some "*project* in which it would be sighted" (147; emphasis mine).

Following Derrida's view that there is "no phrase which does not pass through the . . . concept" (147), the domain of Foucault's research in *The Order of Things* is not literature as nothingness but the ambiguous positivity of the *Geisteswissenschaften*: the human sciences and related disciplines. Indeed, Hegel is as important to Foucault as is Nietzsche; *The Order of Things* is not only antiscience but also an encyclopedia of the forms of (non)philosophy for the university of the sixties. To recapitulate: synchronically Foucault's text is anchored in the distinction between language and discourse. But diachronically it develops as a Nietzschean counterphenomenology of mind in which a language interwoven with the world in the Renaissance is replaced by a discourse entirely committed to science and then returns as literature in the nineteenth century. Each of the three epistemes arranges fields of knowledge and has its own conception of order: poetic and analogical in the Renaissance, taxonomical in the classical period. This genealogy then culminates in a survey of the present "order," which in effect involves two epistemologies. First there is the order of the human sciences constituted by the modern university in emulation of the technological project of science; this is an order committed to a pragmatic anthropology that inscribes man as a historical and productive being. Then there is Foucault's own "order," which is as much an ontology and an ethics as an epistemology. This arrangement consists of triadic series that organize knowledge within the three orders of the sciences, the human sciences, and the countersciences.

But it gravitates around the "counter-sciences," which form a "perpetual principle of dissatisfaction" with the principle of knowledge as "science" (OT: 379, 373).

This order is more systematic than it seems. Foucault, as he explains later, starts from a division of the sciences themselves into the theoretical and empirical.[50] He then outlines three empirical sciences, each of which has a contiguous human science and a corresponding counterscience. The sciences dealing with "life, labour and language" are biology, economics, and linguistics or philology (366); the human sciences that exist in their vicinity include psychology, sociology, and "the study of literature and myths" conceived as a pedagogically transmissible science (351–55). Each human science has a corresponding counterscience. Thus psychology's counterpart is psychoanalysis: "whereas all the human sciences advance towards the unconscious only with their back toward it," psychoanalysis "points directly towards it" (374). The same relation would obtain between literary criticism (as the human cousin of linguistics) and analyses based on the philosophical category called literature, such as those attempted by Yale deconstruction or by Foucault in his own study of Roussel. Underwriting this arrangement are literature and philosophy; they are not so much countersciences (which would still contain an element of science) as ways of thinking. Literature, as Foucault defines it after Blanchot, is a form that "curve[s] back in a perpetual return upon itself" as if seeking out "the movement that brought it into being" (300). Philosophy is nowhere explicitly mentioned in *The Order of Things*. But throughout the text Foucault analyzes man's doubled and duplicitous relation to knowledge in terms of a quadrilateral of concepts drawn from phenomenology: the analytic of finitude, the empirical and the transcendental, the cogito and the unthought, and the return and retreat of the origin.

Foucault thus starts with the empirical sciences of life, labor, and language as the foundation of modernity in order to focus on the *human* sciences as a (de)construction of the projections involved in the transcendentalism of science. The shift from theoretical to empirical sciences is already significant- because it implicates even the sciences in the problems of genesis and historicity also traced by Derrida's studies of mathematics and linguistics. But even more important is the related ambiguity of the human introduced by the next supplementary series. The human sciences occupy a strange space between positivity and reflexiveness. Resisting structuralism's attempt to claim for them the self-certainty of the sciences, Foucault sees their pretentions in that direction as making them "dangerous intermediaries in the space of knowledge" (348). But he also sees their emergence as "correlated to a sort of 'de-mathematicization'" by which they "surreptitiously" lead the sciences back to the analytic of finitude (349, 354). As medicine in Foucault's earlier study had been unraveled by its own history, so the transcendentalism of science is further opened up to existence by the aporia of sciences that are human. The human sciences, in other words, are a *pharmakon* that is dangerous *to* the sciences.

The deterritorializing effect of the human sciences in the cartography of knowledge is entirely unintentional on their part. It comes from their being "meta-epistemological" practices that "extend" from "what man is in his positivity (living, speaking, laboring being) to what enables" him "to know (or seek to know) what life is" (355, 353). The human sciences thus repeat the structure of the modern cogito, which "extends from a part of [man] not reflected in a *cogito* to the act of thought by which he apprehends that part" (322). This structure is evident in the "duplication" that defines their very existence. Not only do they "repeat" themselves in a reflection on what they do; they also uneasily duplicate the sciences (354). Foucault describes their relation to the sciences as one of "vicinity" (366) or metonymy. But we can also see the desire that drives the human sciences as de Man in "The Intentional Structure" sees the relation of words and things, namely, as an attempt of the *pour soi* to achieve a being-in-itself whereby its existence would coincide at all times with its essence (RR: 1–4). As words cannot be things, so the human sciences cannot achieve the transcendence that Husserl sought through geometry. Arising after the sciences, they can never be their own foundation; instead, they mimic the sciences, thus marking both themselves and the sciences with the negativity of being what they are not and not being what they are. This doubling marks the human sciences with a certain inessentiality but also makes them the unconscious of the sciences: "they exist only in so far as they dwell side by side with those sciences—or rather beneath them, in the space of their projections" (OT: 366).

Duplication and reflection are terms Foucault had used of language, which he describes with reference to Blanchot as a "doubled writing" that "mirrors" itself behind "its visible and permanent signs" so as to disclose it-self as "already existing behind itself, active beyond itself, to infinity."[51] In-deed, the vocabulary of duplication and repetition is most extensively worked out in the book on Roussel, whose texts are inhabited by a "subsur-face language" that "speak[s] of something other than what is said" (DL: 66). Thus it should be clear that in *The Order of Things* Foucault transfers to knowledge and its history those structural features of language that he had insisted must also "be read as ontological indications."[52] They are ontologi-cal in the sense that structural doubling covers over a "profound void un-derlying objects and words," in which the repetition of the signified in the signifier is tied up with "the duplication of life in death" and thus with "the moment when death erupts in life" (DL: 28, 68). This void also underlies the very project of rationality, which is the duplication of the sciences in the human sciences, and before that of the "theoretical" in the "empirical" sciences.

Mirroring, doubling, and infinitization also characterize the Renaissance (OT: 21, 25, 30–31, 41). But there the mirror seems to produce self-confir-mation (20), as in the traditional dialectic of reflection described by Gasché, wherein reflection constitutes subjectivity. As Gasché explains, self-reflection or self-consciousness, as a "self-illumination" that "sees itself by mirroring objects," forms part of the "metaphysics of light.[53] In the Renaissance, the world, "by duplicating itself in a mirror" (19) seems to be taken up into this light, which is Levinas's figure for a naive phenomenology—except that for Foucault this "untroubled mirror" is "in reality, filled with the murmur of words" (27). Literature is a return to these words that unworked the self-complicating structures of Renaissance epistemology and a disclosure of its deconstructive process. We remember that Foucault also sees literature as a "recent" phenomenon isolated "from the discourse of ideas" (300), unlike language in the Renaissance, which was part of the domain of knowledge. But at the near end of his text, he tries to bring literature back into an epis-temological project that would reform the university of the sixties. Indeed, though he runs together the entire period from Marx to his own time, this last section of *The Order of Things* clearly has a context in the disciplinary crisis of the sixties. It is about the university in ruins. Foucault wants to re-order the university, not around the critical human sciences espoused by the

Sorbonne students (which would still be caught up in positivism), but around the countersciences that remain uneasily on the fringes of the modern university.

Foucault's identification of *several* countersciences reflects his desire to work literature as first philosophy back into the fabric of culture. The exact provenance of the human sciences varies; at one point they consist of "psychology, sociology, and the history of culture, ideas and science" (354); elsewhere the last category is replaced by "the analysis of literature" or "language analysis" (367, 360). The human sciences are always forms of pragmatic anthropology that put knowledge into practice. But what is important is that just as each empirical science has its "false" double in a human science (366), so too each human science is brought back to its finitude by a counterscience. Together the three series form a grid that takes in the various fields of study at the university and redistributes them within an interdisciplinary curriculum that returns the cogito to its unconscious. This curriculum asks us to work in the hiatus between ontology and anthropology (as the term is used in philosophy). For it is still concerned with knowledge, a term Levinas and Blanchot eschew. The countersciences, Foucault insists against Blanchot, Nietzsche, and others who disengaged themselves from the university, are not "less 'rational' or 'objective'" than the others. But they "flow in the opposite direction," "ceaselessly 'unmak[ing]' that very man who is creating and recreating his positivity in the human sciences" (379). In so doing, they nevertheless reinvest finitude in knowledge; they do not so much turn away from the human sciences as "make visible, in a discursive mode, the frontier-forms of the human sciences" (381). The work of Nancy and others, which rethinks the positivist concept of society through the finitude of community, is a continuation of precisely this epistemic imperative outlined by the early Foucault.

It is not clear that Foucault saw this reconfiguration of knowledge as viable in the university of his times. Indeed, it is striking that he omits all reference to the university, given that both *The Order of Things* and *The Archaeology of Knowledge* are concerned with the curriculum of knowledge. Foucault's discussion of ethnology is his one topical allusion to the sixties, notable because he shows no interest in it elsewhere. But he also has doubts about countersciences still caught up in science, even though he insists on (and will later pursue) objectivity and method. He accuses Freud, for instance, of the "erasure of the division between positive and negative" through the enlightenment of the unconscious (361). And throughout his career he reserves a special place for madness as a limit that exposes the potential positivism of psychoanalysis. Both psychoanalysis and ethnology risk falling back into positivity, unless submitted to a further vigilance that makes the countersciences mutually supplementary. Thus in *The Order of Things* Foucault insists that psychoanalysis and ethnology must each function as the unthought of the other in a "double articulation of the history of individuals upon the unconscious of culture, and of the historicity of those cultures upon the unconscious of individuals" (379). In his extensive discussion of this doubling (373–81), Foucault is careful to avoid a positive synthesis of the two fields in "cultural psychology," seeking instead for an "intersecti[on of] two lines differently oriented" (380).

It is therefore appropriate that despite the Hegelianism of its architecture, Foucault is imprecise about the contents of his triads. At various points the triad of the human sciences includes psychology, sociology, positivist forms of history or cultural history, and forms of literary analysis that have as their goal either science or practice. The identity of the countersciences is equally unsettled. After 1966 Foucault was to give up on psychoanalysis as well as on ethnology in the form it took as the social science of anthropology. Nor is it always clear where a discipline belongs; history as one of the new "empiricities" produced by the nineteenth century is nothing if not a human science, but as archaeology or genealogy Foucault struggles to make it a counterscience. On the other hand, philosophy—in its analytic version—could easily be a human science, but in the form practiced by Foucault it is the condition for a radical rethinking of knowledge. Disciplines migrate between triads, as is befitting given that Foucault's "order" is not a division by departments but a movement between fields of knowledge that exposes them to each other. Foucault's interdisciplinarity involves exposure not synthesis; it frames knowledge within an ongoing vigilance about disciplinary identifications.

Foucault's interdisciplinary, sometimes antidisciplinary order did not find a practical embodiment in the university of the sixties. Nor has it found one now when interdisciplinarity is often used to create new forms of pragmatic anthropology and communicative rationalization. As Bourdieu points out, the philosophers of deconstruction occupied a marginal place in the French system even when, like Foucault, they were part of the university.[54] The university is a form of civil society, whereas the work Foucault imagines can happen only within what Nancy calls an "inoperative community." Nevertheless, the "curriculum" for which Foucault's *Order* serves as a *summa*, and which frames his study of the institutions of medicine in *The Birth of the Clinic*, works across the two slopes that divide the humanities today: prose and poetry, cultural studies and (continental) philosophy. Among other things, deconstruction thus offers different models for cultural studies than the ones based in social constructionism currently dominant.[55] Inasmuch as the academic crisis from which deconstruction emerged is the one in which we still find ourselves today, to see deconstruction simply as a form of literary analysis constituted "after the New Criticism" is to forget one of its most important lessons.

The Turn to Poststructuralism: Archaeology, Art, and Discipline in the Later Foucault

A Door Closed on the Past

It is appropriate at this point to ask why the early Foucault writes in a double register, signifying and effacing his phenomenological commitments. For Foucault never mentions Sartre, Heidegger, or Merleau-Ponty even though his writing in the early sixties is dense with allusions to their work. Continuing the task of phenomenology in a hostile climate was doubtless difficult, and the texts between 1963 and 1966 are structured by a subtle (self)censorship. But Foucault's silence is also strategic. In her analysis of *The History of Sexuality*, Eve Sedgwick has described an analogous silence that extends beyond her immediate concern with Foucault to the effects of reticence generally. Writing on Foucault's refusal to be explicit about (his) homosexuality, she suggests that he "forces" onto the reader the "articulation or denial" of what he will not say. The text thus "interpellates" the reader "as 'the other who knows . . . the knowledge [the text] holds unbeknown to itself.'"[1] Reticence is a way that Foucault, like Derrida in *The Origin of Geometry*, has of holding the text open to its unconscious. Moreover, it is a way of inscribing the reader as well in this scene of reading. For to articulate or deny Foucault's links with phenomenology or his identity as a structuralist are all positings that uneasily fail to sum up what is (not) said.

Foucault's way of working between expression and indication serves a partly enabling function. It allows him to develop a form of "transcendental reflection" (OT: 323) without being drawn into the idealism of Heidegger or

Merleau-Ponty. It also allows him to keep working on the precise nature of this reflection. But the text's reticence also (un)covers an undecidedness in Foucault's relationship to phenomenology and to the multiple, contradictory forms in which it returns. We have already intimated this ir-resolution in the hiatus between the discussion of *The Order of Things* in Chapter 6 and that in Chapter 3. On the one hand, Foucault works between different phenomenologies so as to construct, at the near end of his text, a new table of relations between disciplines that produces a new form of understanding. He unworks various orders so as to open up what Derrida calls other "possibilities of arrangement."[2] On the other hand the actual end of the text—if ends are ever final—is less compatible with this affirmative deconstruction. Here Foucault speculates about the end of man, who will be "erased, like a face drawn in sand at the edge of the sea" (387). That this is not just the closure of a set of disciplinary formations but a negation of all order is evident from the apocalyptic question: "Since man was constituted at a time when language was doomed to dispersion, will he not be dispersed when language regains its unity?" (386). The question echoes nothing so much as Sartre's account of Mallarmé's poetics of suicide, also (partially) published in 1966. Sartre, moreover, brings out the vicarious transcendence of the unhappy consciousness that is the subtext of this end of man, which he associates with Heidegger: "Through Man's very disappearance. . . . Being [is] restored in all its purity. . . . If Being is dispersion, man, in losing his being, achieves an incorruptible unity."[3]

Foucault is powerfully attracted by this temptation to permanence, which de Man also associates with Heidegger. For the writers he connects to literature all exemplify some form of absolute negation—a hypostasis of nothingness as negation—in which death or madness becomes a return to (non)being. These writers include Artaud, Hölderlin, and Nietzsche; Roussel, Mallarmé, and Kafka—the writers whose relation to death Blanchot also probes.[4] To be sure, death is a kind of de(con)struction; as Baudrillard says, the death drive "dissolves assemblages, unbinds energy and undoes Eros's organic discourse by returning things to an inorganic, *ungebunden* state" (SED: 148). Yet the literature discussed by Foucault walks a tenuous line between the death drive and the death wish in the suicide of Roussel and the near suicide of Mallarmé. Moreover, literature is cathected with a certain kind of phenomenology. As that which "buri[es] itself within its own density as an object," it is a form of "being" constituted by the absolute separation of ontology from anthropology (OT: 300).

This schism also characterizes madness, to which Foucault is similarly drawn. Whereas psychoanalysis works between "the knowledge of man" and "the finitude that gives it its foundation" (381), madness cannot be repatriated to the side of consciousness. Much of Foucault's early work is motivated by the "affirmative exigency" of rethinking psychology: first through Binswanger's *Daseinanalyse*, then through existential psychoanalysis in *Mental Illness and Psychology*, and finally through psychoanalysis as discussed in *The Order of Things*.[5] But his uncertainty about this project and, thus, about any kind of philosophical anthropology is apparent in his return to the absolute opacity of madness in *I, Pierre Rivière* (1973), a documentary account of the nineteenth-century parricide that includes Rivière's own memoir. As a further item in the series of Foucault's texts on psychology, this text gives up the deconstructive project of rethinking psychology in relation "to the positivities in which [the human sciences] are framed" (OT: 381). But, simulating as it does a documentary objectivity, it also confronts Foucault's new genealogical project with a door locked from the inside.

Unlike Derrida's allusions to death or Blanchot's references to writing as an "*insane game*" (GO: 154), death and madness for Foucault are curiously literalized. This literalization—and indeed his personification of literature itself through writers whose *lives* cut into the abstraction of epistemology (OT: 383)—is of course a figure. It is a figure for the ultimate risk one takes through literature, the risk that Roussel and Artaud take, which ends literally in death or madness. At the same time these writers intimate the literal threat posed to the social by death or madness as figures for the extremity of (non)philosophy. They represent the absolute separation of being and knowledge that Foucault wants to avoid, which is why he does not speak of a certain kind of phenomenology even as he seeks through phenomenology a way of healing this schism that may compromise precisely what he values in phenomenology.

At issue here is the delicate balance between ontology and epistemology that informs the early writing. For the partitioning of Foucault's work into the book on Roussel and the book on the clinic repeats in a darker vein the difference between *Dream, Imagination, and Existence* and *Mental Illness and Psychology*. This repetition, moreover, discloses in transcendental reflection a will-to-death that makes it a dangerous intermediary in the space of knowledge. Foucault's reticence about phenomenology is a self-protection against death and madness even as it allows him to think in the space opened up by phenomenology between a Nietzschean destruction and a more affirmative deconstruction. His work is full of the murmuring of other voices and folds round the enigma of its origins so as to keep a door to the past open. But beginning with *The Archaeology of Knowledge* Foucault aims for a different style, "supposing no remainder, nothing in excess of what has been said" (BC: xvii). While he may not immediately attain this zero degree of theory, it is clear that his work has undergone its own archaeological mutation.

New Terms of Reference: Archaeology, Discourse

The turn away from phenomenology is nowhere more evident than in Foucault's rewriting of archaeology. Although Foucault says he initially used the term "somewhat blindly," this is not so; it instinctively brings together usages by Husserl and Merleau-Ponty.[6] One of its earlier occurrences is in *Madness and Civilization*, where it designates what has been excluded from history. Speaking of the "stammered, imperfect words" that preceded the division of reason from madness by the language of psychiatry, Foucault claims "I have not tried to write the history of that language, but rather the archaeology of that silence."[7] By 1966 this binarism has been abandoned, and archaeology is closer to its subsequent function as a term defining the mode rather than the materials of analysis. It signals a turn away from anthropology to method and the forms of thought (OT: 200). But it is important to emphasize that though archaeology is distinguished from history in *The Order of Things*, it is not opposed to it (xi); it is not associated with atemporal structures but is a way of writing history so as to defamiliarize it.

Foucault, moreover, sees the archaeological method as mobilized by psychoanalysis and ethnology, considered not in their more positivist manifestations but in their potential for "unmaking" the human sciences through the "double articulation" described in the previous chapter (379). Using ethnology to decenter psychoanalysis from its Freudian connection to a subject, archaeology also avoids turning the study of cultural systems into a form of positivist "historicism" by returning structural study to the unconscious of individuals and their *Dasein* (377). Foucault continues to emphasize the relation of archaeology to psychoanalysis in 1968 when he describes his work as an attempt to discover "the unconscious of knowledge."[8] Just as the unconscious is less a separate region than a relation of knowledge to itself, so archaeology is a relation of history to itself that avoids the positivity of empirical narrative. We must therefore read its association with surfaces and exteriorities not as a form of structuralism but as a transference to history of models drawn from Lacanian psychoanalysis. Archaeology is said to study mutations "distributed across the . . . visible surface of knowledge." Its operation at the surface does not indicate a rejection of depth. Rather it is a perceptual function of the fact that the "law" organizing these mutations, like the Real, can be known only through the "signs, shocks, and effects" that are the traces of this "radical event" (OT: 217). "Lacan," in other words, allows Foucault to mediate between his own attraction to "formalization" and "interpretation"[9] by bringing together Husserl's association of archaeology with method and Merleau-Ponty's connection of it to psychoanalysis.

In 1966 Foucault was still positioning his analysis between the Symbolic and the Real by addressing himself to "surface effects" of "archaeological events" (OT: 232). Archaeology was still "the general space that defines [a] *common ground*" between structuralism and phenomenology (299). By 1969, however, he denies that the term ever carried connotations of depth and insists that he is concerned only with "phenomena" and surfaces, not with "psychology."[10] No longer locating archaeology in the space between event and effect and, indeed, locating the event itself purely within discourse, Foucault now slants archaeology towards formalization pure and simple. Thus the "general" as opposed to "total" history that it subtends is concerned not with the reference of events to a political unconscious but with the relations that organize these events: with "series, divisions, limits, differences of level, . . . particular forms of rehandling, possible types of relation" (AK: 10). Not only does *The Archeology of Knowledge* repeat the classical bracketing of reference in favor of order; it seems concerned only with its own order. It is as if Foucault, like Roussel, is seeking "a language which only speaks about itself, a language absolutely simple in its duplicated being" (DL: 167).

Foucault's rewriting of archaeology accompanies two other mutations that mark the distance between *The Archeology of Knowledge* and *The Order of Things*. Discourse is now decoupled from its normative link to language and thus from a psychoanalysis of knowledge in which the Symbolic is made accountable to the semiotic (in Kristeva's sense) as the visible to the invisible. Henceforth Foucault does "not seek below what is manifest the half silent murmur of another discourse"; rather he follows Althusser in reconfirming the power of structure by "show[ing] why it could not be other than it was" and in what respect a discursive formation "is exclusive of any other" (AK: 28). Correspondingly literature all but disappears from Foucault's corpus, an absence he himself notes. Asking whether literature resists an analysis in terms of "discursive formations and systems of positivities" (and therefore marks archaeology itself as a discursive formation constituted on principles of limitation and exclusion), Foucault concludes that an archaeological analysis of literature is still feasible (178, 183). Yet he does not provide such an analysis, whose positivity would emerge in uneasy tension with the negativity and duplication he had earlier seen as constituting literature. The effective exclusion of literature has important consequences for a reading of the new Foucault. For the frequent discussions of literature in the early sixties had encouraged us to approach his theory *as* literature. Dismissing literature to assume "the historian's mask," Foucault, as Hollier notes, "break[s] away from the problematic of self-referential mirrors, be they those of death or . . . writing."[11] This same dismissal, in other words, also allows him to disavow—though not entirely—both the ontological concerns he now projects onto literature and the (psycho)analysis of his own theory embedded in such concerns.

This new positivism is evident in a vocabulary organized around "rules," "regularities," and "discursive formations"; Geoffrey Harpham notes its resemblance to structuralism in its "mortification" of all notions of consciousness.[12] That *The Archaeology of Knowledge* has affinities with structuralism is often noted, as is the uneasiness that haunts this affinity. Manfred Frank points to the structuralist origins of *discourse*, a term borrowed from Benveniste's linguistics and functioning midway between *langue* and *parole* or "structure and event." Discourse transposes the analysis of *langue* from a level that has phonemes and syntagms as its smallest constitutive units to one organized by larger units such as sentences.[13] Frank's analysis needs to be qualified in the sense that the unit of analysis for Foucault is not the sentence but the statement, a nebulous concept that he introduces to avoid sounding structuralist. But while the statement signals a concern with "functions" rather than "units" and thus with "events" or "element[s] in a field of coexistence" rather than "structures" (86–87, 109), its deployment is further evidence of what Frank describes as Foucault's "neostructuralism." For the statement, as the smallest constitutive unit of discourse, is the condition of possibility for propositions and sentences, yet it is itself completely "non-significant" (90). At the same time *discourse* has historically been used to bring back some element of reference into semiotics, as we see in Ricoeur's appropriation of Benveniste's term as a way of distinguishing his hermeneutics from a structuralism inspired by Saussure.[14] Thus Foucault's coupling of discourse with the statement rather than the sentence seeks to close off the possibility of reference opened up by his use of Benveniste's concept, by bracketing meaning[15] and thus the "polysemia" that infects the sentence and necessitates a recourse to the dreaded phenomenon of "commentary" (110). In contrast to Ricoeur's use of the term, Foucault's use of *discourse* marks his stubborn attachment to the style if not the terminology of structuralism.

Analyzed in this way Foucault's neostructuralism exemplifies the psychic complex that de Man calls "resistance" (RT: 3–20). Not only is its repudiation of structuralism as an essentialism resisted by its own complicity with the latter's positivism, but this very structuralism is also complicated by its reimposition through a terminology elsewhere used to critique structuralism. Repeating and indeed imitating structuralism as neostructuralism, Foucault constructs a method "absolutely simple in its duplicated being" (DL: 167), which bears the same uneasy relationship to structuralism as the human sciences do to the sciences. The human sciences do not deconstruct the sciences in the way Foucault himself had used structuralism and phenomenology to unwork each other. Rather they are "dangerous intermediaries" in the space of knowledge because they *imitate* the sciences (OT: 348), thus disavowing their implication in the analytic of finitude.

It is important to draw out what is implied in using the term *imitation* to describe this uneasy difference of archaeology from structuralism. *The Archaeology* is not a "parody" of structuralism, as Megill suggests.[16] As an imitation it is, in the terms of the early de Man, intentional; it seeks the ontological stability of science even as it knows this to be an impossible goal whose deferral—or folding—we must mark through the prefixes *neo-* or *post-*. Moreover imitation, as Harpham suggests, can also be thought of in pseudoreligious terms. Thus Foucault pursues "an ascetic imitation, a humbling and depersonalizing submission to the Rule of Discourse," whose discipline carries "a cenobitic emphasis: routine, anonymous, nontranscendent, 'external.'"[17] As Bataille notes, ascesis reinstates the very cathexes it questions. On the one hand, it aims at a destruction; it "*is a sure means of separating oneself from objects*" by "*kill[ing] the desire which binds one to objects.*" On the other hand it converts this very destruction into a "*positive object*" through which it asks for "*salvation. . . . a beatitude, a deliverance.*"[18] Through asceticism Foucault destroys the naiveté of phenomenology so as then to claim an identity in the Symbolic Order of theory. And yet, as we shall see, this identity is precarious, its very tenuousness being evident in the way Foucault can only posit archaeology apophatically in terms of what it is not (cf. AK: 28, 119).

Stubborn Attachments: The Archaeology of Knowledge as *(Post)structuralism*

The Archaeology of Knowledge, however, can also be described as (post)structuralist, bearing in mind our previous definition of the term as a variety of "superstructuralism."[19] For poststructuralism reconverts deconstruction to what William Spanos calls "spatial form,"[20] by recasting it in a relation of (dis)continuity with structuralism rather than phenomenology. Or following Henri Lefebvre we might say that poststructuralism reeconomizes deconstruction and "crushes time by reducing differences to repetitions, to circularities."[21] Thus, on the one hand, Foucault clearly draws on deconstruction and therefore makes some kind of *différance* central to his project. He speaks of "deploy[ing] the space of a dispersion," of analyzing "the discontinuity of the planes from which [the subject] speaks," and of locating "contradictions" through which "the dispersion of the subject and his discontinuity with himself may be determined" (AK: 10, 54, 151, 55). He speaks of archaeology as a "decentring" activity (205). As important, Foucault's turn away from what he now discards as phenomenology is made through a terminology based on force rather than form. The statement is not something we can grasp, even as form let alone as content. The distinction of the statement from the proposition and the sentence is correlated to other distinctions that likewise connote movement and relation rather than structure, a microphysics rather than a geometry. Thus "discursive formations" are distinguished from "disciplines," which constitute bodies of knowledge and organize them for institutional transmission (178–79). *Savoir* is differentiated from *connaissance*, which is a form of knowledge in which "the subject may take up a position and speak of the objects with which he deals in his discourse" (182) and which constructs "domains" where archaeology constructs "territories" (183). These terms, as Deleuze says of the *dispositif*, "do not outline or surround systems which are each homogeneous in their own right, . . . but follow directions, [and] trace balances that are always off balance."[22] They suggest a practice that is nomadic rather than taxonomic. Indeed, Deleuze and Guattari will soon develop the figure of territories, which they describe as having "no points, paths, or land" and as characterized by "rhizomatic vegetation that is temporary and shifts location" according to the circumstances.[23]

On the other hand, Foucault's concern with "gaps" and "interplays of differences, distances, substitutions, transformations" is not deconstructive in the manner of his earlier work; he is instead interested in "*systems of dispersion*" (37) and the "regularity" (38) of difference. Troping *différance* as dispersion, Foucault now sees it as operating in terms of a horizontal diffusion of depthless signifiers instead of a nonidentity linked to a secret verticality. The shift from the vertical to the horizontal spatializes *différance*, thus eliding both its temporality and its materiality. Indeed, Foucault often uses the figure of space, writing of "the space on which various objects emerge and are continuously transformed" (32). Consequently, "gaps" and "exclusions" are no longer linked to the unthought so that Foucault in spite of his emphasis on dispersion is able to construct a "space that is entirely deployed and involves no reduplication" (119).

The structuralizing of deconstruction through the assumption that *différance* can be approached in terms of regularity and system appears at the same time in the work of Derrida (P: 26–29). But it is in Foucault's text that its paradoxical consequences are most apparent. Noting that the lacunae in a discourse may mark it as ideological, he suggests that an analysis of discourse must nevertheless proceed not in terms of silences (as in the Marxist work of Pierre Macherey) but only at "the level of the positivity" (AK: 186).

Indeed, Foucault's refusal to "give voice to the silence that surrounds" discourses (119) seems specifically aimed against his own definition of archaeology in *Madness and Civilization*. We should not be surprised to read that the "enunciative domain is identical with its own surface" and that archaeology now "define[s] a limited system of presences" (119). For the term *presence* is simply one example of what Foucault himself defines as his unconventional "positivis[m]" (125). It is unconventional because it uses the language of gaps and dispersions to avoid any kind of essentialism, but it is positivist because it makes *différance* an effect of the surface so that gaps are fully visible and without hidden potential. Kristeva describes the conservatism of this reduction of difference within the movement of the signifier in her comments on grammatology. She admits that the positivism of grammatology is unconventional: "its chronologically distended and topographically uneven strategy cannot be reduced to a homogeneous system." But she also suggests that because the trace works through "retention" instead of the "'dichotomies,' and 'oppositions' that Hegelian negativity concatenates," grammatology "holds itself back" and "becomes merely positive and affirmative." In the process negativity becomes "positivized and drained of its potential for producing breaks."[24]

This positivism limits any resemblance to Deleuze, who also keeps *différance* at the surface. Deleuze claims an affinity with Foucault, whom he reads in terms of "multiplicities" that make up an "archaeology-poem." For Deleuze, as Paul Bové points out, Foucault is a visionary and utopian thinker.[25] But while Foucault anticipates Deleuze in speaking of "archaeological territories," these spaces are not then "deterritorialized." Instead, archaeology is a defamiliarizing but at the same time a "reterritorializing" because it is "nothing more than a rewriting," a submission to the Symbolic "in the preserved form of exteriority, [as] a regulated transformation of what has already been written" (AK: 140). Foucault's superimposition of a geometrical diction (of planes, surfaces, and levels) on the vocabulary of *différance* may well be a symptomatic site of this reterritorialization. This diction creates the effect of an "Apollonian formalism."[26] As important, it converts what Bataille calls "general economy" into restricted economy by recontaining excess and transgression within the concept of "regulated transformation": an oxymoron that names the absorption of difference into order.

But in this respect Foucault is typical of poststructuralism. It radicalizes Saussure's recognition that there are no positive terms in language and renders negativity spatial by making language what Derrida calls a "system" of differences (P: 28). Poststructuralism's stubborn attachment to structuralism is evident in Derrida's surprising statement that *différance* "is not astructural: it produces systematic and regulated transformations which . . . leave room for a structural science" (28). In the essay of that name he defines *différance* as "the structured and differing origin of differences" (SP: 141). That Derrida's position is more than methodological becomes evident when Foucault picks up the concept of "regulated transformation" or "linked and hierarchized transformations" (AK: 37) to describe an archaeology that applies grammatology to intellectual history. Characterizing *différance* as "the regulated transformation of what has already been written" (140), Foucault makes it vulnerable to Kristeva's charge that it actually "inscribes and institutes through retention." Indeed, he provides us with a way of defining poststructuralism itself, which is not so much an overturning as a "regulated transformation" of structuralism, "in the preserved form of exteriority" (140). Poststructuralism remains "attached" to structuralism as a self-mortification that renounces deconstruction, even though this attachment negates its goal of *différance*. Judith Butler refers to such attachments as "stubborn" because they are deeply, doubly resistant. Stubborn attachments typify the unhappy consciousness as a "prefiguration of neurosis" in that they paradoxically involve a "repression of the libido" that is "itself a libidinally invested repression." Moreover, they are doubly "self-negating" in that they work against their own interests as well as against the very work of self-sacrifice they perform.[27]

Foucault concedes the complicity of archaeology with order when he comments that "the most fruitful region" for archaeology is "the 'Classical' age, which . . . saw the epistemologization of so many positivities" (195). But even more interesting is a phenomenon noted by both Deleuze and Shumway, namely, the curious resemblance of *The Archaeology of Knowledge* to the linguistic "machines" Foucault had earlier attributed to Roussel.[28] Indeed, Foucault himself describes his new terminology as a "strange arsenal," an "apparatus" with "somewhat bizarre machinery" (AK: 135). The parallel invites us to read Foucault's theory as he himself reads Roussel—through a noetic and noematic analysis of its psychic (and cultural) structures. As early as the preface to *The Birth of the Clinic* (1963), Foucault had sought for "a structural analysis of the signified that would escape the fatality of commentary by leaving the signified and the signifier in their original equivalence."[29] At the time this desire for a method fully present to itself in the vicarious medium of the signs it analyzed was framed within a larger interrogation of rationality from the perspective of the death it excluded. But in *The Archaeology of Knowledge* Foucault returns more positivistically to "the project of a *pure description of discursive events* as the horizon for the search for the unities that form within it" (AK: 27). Rewriting his original preface to *The Birth of the Clinic* in 1972 after *The Archaeology of Knowledge*, he invests this presence in what he now calls "discourse" rather than the "signified." He once again claims for a method that itself operates as *discourse* rather than *language* a self-identity liberated from the lack and absence that generate "commentary:" "Is it not possible to make an analysis of discourses that would escape the fatality of commentary by supposing no remainder, no excess in what has been said, but only the fact of its historical appearance?"[30]

The Search for Purity: Blanchot on Foucault

Foucault's concern with *purity* and his association of it with a "discourse entirely surface and shimmering" has been described by Blanchot. In *The Archaeology of Knowledge*

> Foucault . . . pretended to unveil discursive practices that were virtually pure, in the sense of referring only to themselves, to the rules of their formation, to their point of insertion (be it without origin), to their emergence (be it without author), to decipherings that would reveal nothing at all that was hidden. They are witnesses that don't confess, because they have nothing to say other than what has been said, writings refractory toward all commentary (ah, Foucault's hatred for commentary), domains that are autonomous, but neither truly independent nor immutable.[31]

As Blanchot hints in returning Foucault's impersonality to the subject in whom it originates, Foucault's emphasis on discourse tries to achieve a consciousness that in Sartrean terms is entirely *in-itself,* freed from the anxiety of being *for-itself.* Crucial to the self-identity of this consciousness is a neostructuralism focused on events and surfaces, which allows the theoretical gaze to operate in a space that is fully deployed. On one level, then, neostructuralism is a disciplined and disciplining renunciation of phenomenology. This renunciation is marked throughout *The Archaeology of Knowledge* in language that corrects *The Order of Things* by promising to substitute "for the enigmatic treasure of 'things' anterior to discourse, the regular formation of objects that emerge only in discourse" (AK: 47). But paradoxically it is (existential) phenomenology, with its emphasis on the subject, that had "confessed" the implication of the theoretical project within its own intentionality and contingency. Thus on another level Foucault's search for a method "purged of all anthropologism" (16) actually reinscribes transcendental consciousness through a discourse that is "anonymous" and "impersonal" (63). That the project of a "pure" or transcendental description remains intentional (and thus open to a phenomenological critique of its Cartesianism) is marked by the intellectual "apparatus" used to enforce it (135). Awkwardly self-conscious about this apparatus and the "rigour" for which it stands (79), Foucault seems to confess in his questionings and interruptions of his own text the figurality of that zero degree of theory that is alternately represented for him by Husserl and by structuralism.

The intentionality of the archaeological project is also marked by the fact that neostructuralism takes the specific form of poststructuralism. For if the first term names the mimetic desire that impels archaeology to emulate structuralism, the second intimates the difference of the epistemic territory explored by archaeology from the one organized by structuralism. A noetic analysis of the archaeological consciousness therefore needs to be augmented by a noematic analysis of the world at which this consciousness is intentionally "directed," which "it constitutes" and through which it reciprocally constitutes itself.[32] This world is one of "dispersions" and "gaps" in which one can nevertheless discern a "regularity . . . an order . . . correlations . . . assignable positions in a common space."[33] Seeking to structure this domain, archaeology constructs it as a world of "systematically fabricated chance" like the one created by Roussel's machines (OT: 383) They compensate for a certain randomness at the level of what is signified by positing a nonreferential organization at the level of the signifier. In other words, archaeology simulates the impossible: it reduces deconstruction to order, thus claiming to be, in Derrida's term, a "science" of differences (P: 28).

Once again it is Blanchot who provides a genealogy of this science. For the notion of a systematically fabricated chance goes back to Mallarmé, whom Blanchot had represented as early as *The Space of Literature* as trying to create through "pure language" a "structure calculated to exclude chance" and thus one that "escapes all determination and every form of *existence*."[34] Whereas literature for Blanchot himself is nothingness, Mallarmé misrecognizes it as the phantasm of what Lacoue-Labarthe and Nancy call the "literary absolute"; he effects a hypostasis in which chance becomes the form rather than the content of the work. Contingency is thus contained by being displaced from experience to structure. Blanchot returns to the linguistic sublimation of contingency in "The Absence of the Book," an essay published in the same year as *The Archaeology of Knowledge*. This time he analyzes more explicitly the complicity between "Hegel" and "Mallarmé" as names for the "Book" and the "Work." Mallarmé on the one hand seems to anticipate deconstruction by constructing the "Work" as "the absence of the work as it *produces itself* through the work and throughout the work" (GO: 147). Describing the work as a "center that is always off center" and even more significantly as "writing," "exteriority," a "ruse," and as an "insane game" (154, 156, 147), Blanchot approaches Mallarmé through a Derridean vocabulary developed by the transposition of Blanchot's own negative phenomenology into deconstruction. Furthermore he suggests that the difference between Hegel and Mallarmé is evident "in their different ways of being anonymous in the naming and signing of their works"—Hegel through the objectivity of a transcendental "System" and Mallarmé through the "more uncertain" anonymity of a writing that functions "without someone writing it" (153). But, on the other hand, Mallarmé's Work is also oddly complicit with the Hegelian Book that it deconstructs when it replaces "completion" with "disaster" (154):

> The absolute of the book, then, is the isolation of a possibility that claims not to have originated in any other anteriority. An absolute that will later tend to assert itself in the Romantics (Novalis), then more rigoruously in Hegel, then more radically—though in a different way—in Mallarmé, as the totality of relations (absolute knowledge or the Work), in which would be achieved either consciousness, which knows itself and returns to itself after having been exteriorized in all its dialectically linked figures, or language, *closed around its own statement and already dispersed*. (146; emphasis mine)

Blanchot's recognition that Mallarmé finds his "transcendental 'parallel'" in Hegel[35] helps to isolate certain ways in which poststructuralism is the disseminative mirror image of logocentrism. For it is hard not to suspect that Blanchot's distinction between Book and Work is meant to echo and unsettle Barthes's distinction between work and text. In turning Barthes's text into Blanchot's Work, and in thus collapsing the opposition by which poststructuralist textuality valorizes itself, Blanchot allows his own discussion of Hegel and Mallarmé to double as an allegory of the complicities between transcendentalism and the theoretical episteme that was achieving dominance in the late sixties. Mallarmé, in other words, can be read as a figure for the way poststructuralism both radicalizes the problem of language and yet curtails its own negativity by constructing a theory "closed around its own statement and already dispersed." That this closure conceals the survival of the cogito is something to which Blanchot points when he speaks of an "anonymity" that "takes the *name* of Mallarmé" (153; emphasis mine). Mallarmé makes no claim to (author)ity, but he does construct himself as the "capacity—never a unique or a unifiable capacity—to read the nonpresent Work, that is, the capacity to respond, by his absence, to the work that continues to be absent" (153). The same absent cogito mobilizes *The Archaeology of Knowledge*, where Foucault's self-effacement returns, in a pathetic fallacy, as the "anonymous dispersion" of regularities that reflect back to him his own desire for a "blank, indifferent space, lacking in both interiority and promise" (AK: 63, 39).

This cathexis between author and text implicit in Foucault's attribution of anonymity both to himself and to discourse is important to understanding the interpellatory role of poststructuralism in the late sixties. With *The Archaeology of Knowledge* Foucault refashions himself in a new theoretical style. He renounces the lyricism and imagery that had characterized *The Order of Things* and cultivates a style ascetic in its abstraction. Foucault's purging of the poetic from his style is a renunciation of that phenomenology he had earlier sought to continue in "the preserved form of exteriority" and for which lyricism had provided a kind of closet. For images, as he notes, have the "dangerous" character of "showing while concealing" (BC: xvii). Avoiding the image, Foucault places his method in an "enunciative domain . . . identical with its own surface" (AK: 119). That the turn away from phenomenology may conceal another agenda is, however, suggested by his own comments on Roussel some years earlier. "Lyricism," he writes, "is carefully excluded" from Roussel's *How I Wrote Certain of My Books*; instead Roussel's text is profoundly "reserved" while also being conspicuously "verbose in types of deciphering, rites of threshold and lock" (DL: 2, 8). But the very "rigor of this exclusion," evident also in the formalism of the novels, is itself symptomatically reinscribed in the interiority it would evade. Providing "information . . . but no confidences," Roussel's impersonality does in the end confide "something . . . through this strange form of the secret that death would preserve and make known"(2).

Foucault's choice of a method "purged of all anthropologism" (AK: 16) confides what may be the other side of this secret, namely the search for an autonomy in which the theoretical subject can be entirely *in-itself*. Such a subject would be identical with its own surface and would originate like the discourse it analyzes, "supposing no remainder . . . but only the fact of its historical appearance" (BC: xvii). Renouncing phenomenology for a blank space that is "lacking" in interiority and promise (AK: 39), Foucault claims as the reward for this "methodological rigour" (22, 79) what de Man had earlier called the "possibility for consciousness to exist entirely by and for itself, . . . without being moved by an intent aimed at a part of this world" (RR: 16). Moreover, Foucault attempts to reproduce this self-sufficiency, this being in-itself of theory, not only in his style but also in the method he sets out to describe. For discourse in *The Archaeology of Knowledge* seems almost like Roussel's machines, which "originate within themselves" (DL: 64). As Dreyfus and Rabinow point out, while discursive practices are "determined, and controlled," they are controlled by "discourses" that "are assumed to be autonomous." The result is the "strange notion of regularities which regulate themselves"[36] or effects contained within a circularity that allows them to double as their own causes.

The psychic investments that mobilize Foucault's turn to poststructuralism are not his alone. Traces of a similar claim to autonomy can be found around 1968 in the work of Derrida, for whom *différance* is both a series of effects and the cause of these effects: the "primordial constituting causality, . . . whose differings and differences would be the constituted products or effects" (SP: 137). More importantly, Foucault's concern with space and surfaces is part of the same episteme that produces Barthes's and Robbe-Grillet's search for a zero degree of writing. This writing freed from figure supposedly demystifies the anthropologism of Sartre through a geometrical and formal focus on objects that conveys a "textual being-there (not to be confused with the being-there of things themselves)." But the reimplication of this "chosisme" in the "humanism" it evades is suggested by Bruce Morrissette, whose book on *The Novels of Robbe-Grillet*, with an introduction by Barthes, appeared in the same year as Foucault's study of Roussel. Morrissette's extensive psychological commentary on the novels refutes the claim of *chosisme* (promoted in particular by Barthes)[37] to say "nothing in excess of what has been said" (BC: xvii). By extension it also allows us to stand back from the new theoretical realism inspired by the *nouveau roman*—a realism that (to adapt Derrida's critique of Husserl) tries to be "absolutely objective" and thus identical with itself in a discourse that is "only what it appears to be" (OG: 27)

This new realism legitimates itself through a rhetoric of purity and abstraction as Wilhelm Worringer uses abstraction. As a sub-version of structuralism the theory that gained prominence in the late sixties continues the essentialism and search for noetic autonomy that structuralism inherits from both literary and pictorial formalism. But it does so in a way that is specifically inflected by late capitalism and the overdetermined, unreadable aftermath of 1968. For poststructuralism does not claim transcendence. Indeed, it does the precise opposite by arguing that there is nothing outside textuality and discourse, which are in turn conceived as system, law, or rule.

The appeal of poststructuralism is thus very different from that of other essentialisms. *Différance*, de Man's "positional power of language," and Lacan's Symbolic are forms of absolute contingency, but as forms of *absolute* contingency they possess a regularity, which is why Derrida can speak of a "system of *différance*" (P: 28). Put differently, they are transcendental (though not transcendent) categories, and as such they are the basis for a science—a term earlier repudiated by deconstruction. As systems or "structure[s]," in Derrida's words (27), these terms name regularities that regulate themselves, thus internalizing contingency as autonomy. In a curious way, moreover, absolute contingency is *in-itself* because it leaves no space for the *pour-soi* as the difference between contingency and the possibility of something outside it. Subjecting themselves to the rule of this contingency, writers such as Foucault accept the cultural logic of reification in which man is a product of his products. In return they claim a certain disciplinary authority, which allows them to form (self)critical subjects who recover through theoretical sophistication and analytic power the material agency they renounce as naive. But this claim is in turn based on an *internalizing* of reification, which has been the source of poststructuralism's curious interpellatory power. In other words, just as the subject in the régime of reification is the product of its objects, so too the poststructural subject is the product of language. Yet this reification has by the same token been internalized, sublated, by virtue of being located in language that is, to adapt Derrida, a kind of "spirit . . . rigourously distinguished from anthropology," a "consciousness without man" (M: 117–18).

Apathetic Formalism or the Zero Degree of Theory

Still, it would be wrong to read the power claimed by poststructuralism wholly in terms of the Bourdieuvian analysis of professionalization that Guillory provides in *Cultural Capital*. Analyzing de Man's appeal as a "master-theorist," Guillory attributes it to a form of technobureaucracy: "the sheer 'technicality'" of rhetorical reading, "its iterability, which can then take on the properties of routinized [bureaucratic] labour." As I argue in the next chapter Baudrillard, following Lefebvre, sees in structuralism precisely such a "technocratic position." This adaptability of rhetorical reading to "rational administration"[38] explains why certain work by de Man and Foucault became so marketable. It does not explain the work itself, the product of an essential solitude, of authors who are uneasy with public identities and seek to disappear into the "blank, indifferent space" of a work that is not their own (AK: 39). More revealing of the private face of poststructuralism is Gasché's account of de Man's "apathetic formalism," a term he takes from de Man himself. Unlike Guillory, Gasché sees de Man's work as absolutely "singular," resistant to being used by philosophy or literary theory. Apathetic criticism is addressed to no one. It is not for anyone, "not even for its author;" it is "a type of discourse so objective that it is utterly idiosyncratic."[39]

De Man's singular vision crystallizes around the "materiality of the letter" and the "positional power of language"—notions developed in "Shelley Disfigured," *Aesthetic Ideology*, and the *Resistance to Theory*. For de Man, this materiality means that nothing "ever happens in relation . . . to anything

[else] but only as a random event whose power, like the power of death, is due to the randomness of its occurrence" (RR: 122). As Gasché argues, rhetorical reading unconceals this randomness by "explod[ing] the text into [its] linguistic atoms," each of which is so singular as to be unrelated to anything else. Gasché's analysis has resonances for *The Archaeology of Knowledge*, a text that, unlike the genealogical studies, has proved difficult to assimilate into the cultural work of the American academy. Foucault's "statements" are like de Man's linguistic atoms; they are nonphenomenal, nonsymbolic, and resist any "dialectics of universality." Despite Foucault's self-questioned fondness for the term "unities" (AK: 71), the statement resists structures of unification. It is not a proposition, formulation, or speech act; nor is it a sentence or structure (106–9). As an "ultimate, undecomposable element" it "exists outside any possibility of reappearing," and although "it cannot be hidden, it is not visible either" (89, 110). As such, statements, while associated with order rather than randomness, are like de Man's "linguistic corpuscles" cut loose from the production of meaning: "the possibility of being possible elements of possible worlds."[40]

Apathetic formalism is both a noematic and a noetic term. It describes, first of all, a world made up of nonsignificant particles. This underlying stratum is analogous to the *langue* of the structuralists; but whereas for them the order underlying individual discourses is legible, for Foucault it is unreadable, not hidden but not visible either. This is not to deny that Foucault differs from de Man, at least in his genealogical phase. As Gasché explains, ancient atomistic theories conceived of the "atoms as *apathe*, [or] impassive;" for de Man this means that they do not change, nor do they "have any emotional value effect attached to them." Foucault's genealogical work will bring him closer to the early materialists; his apathetic atoms do become "*capable* not only of forming worlds" or discourses "through their combinations but affects (*pathe*) as well."[41] However, this unfolding of apathetic structure as ideological practice is arguably a truth-effect produced by the reprojection of archaeological space as genealogical time. If we take the former as the *langue* underlying the latter, what *The Archaeology of Knowledge* insists upon is that the order formed by the atoms is random, and the shifts between orders are thus illegible. Deleuze points to this randomness when he says that for Foucault,

> the relations between forces . . . concern not only men but the elements,
> the letters of the alphabet, which group either at random or according to

certain laws of attraction and frequency dictated by a particular language. Chance works only in the first case; while the second case perhaps operates under conditions that are partially determined by the first, as in a Markov chain, where we have a succession of partial relinkings . . . a line that . . . link[s] up random events in a mixture of chance and dependency.[42]

For Deleuze the random is the realm of possibility. But the random determinism described above rather suggests a process without a subject, a history that is nonhuman. This in turn accounts for a second noetic resonance of the term *apathy*. For apathetic formalism also names the response of consciousness to this profound indifference at the core of time and language. By focusing on form one avoids being hurt by the absence of meaning. As Gasché hints, apathetic criticism thus forecloses the possibility of a for-itself, insofar as it is "for no one, not even for its author himself." In this anonymity it achieves, through a strange transference, the status of its own object; "such a rhetoric, cut off from . . . all communication, all mediation," "reenacts" the very position of language and becomes what it beholds.[43]

This Is Not a Pipe: *The Simulacrum of Difference*

The diminished role of art in Foucault's work after 1968 parallels the reduction of language to discourse and depth to surface. We can trace this mutation through the shifting use of the terms *similitude* and *resemblance*. In *The Order of Things* these terms are interchangeable, becoming tacitly distinguished only after the Renaissance. In *This Is Not a Pipe*, published in 1968 and then expanded in 1972, they have been reconfigured within a binary opposition that reduces and simplifies resemblance to a form of mimesis so as to valorize similitude as "a play of transferences that run, proliferate, propagate." Resemblance now presupposes a model that allows a vertical reference from signifier to signified, where similitude develops laterally "in series that have neither beginning nor end, that can be followed in one direction as easily as in another, that obey no hierarchy, but propagate themselves from small differences among small differences."[44] Resemblance, in other words, is identified with closure, where similitude is linked to openness and *différance*. In the process resemblance has also been shifted from the Renaissance to the classical period and has thus assumed a different actantial function in Foucault's narrative. For in *The Order of Things* resemblance had been at the positive end of a decline that came into effect in the classical period, whereas in *This Is Not a Pipe* it is resemblance that is associated with cognitive oppression, and similitude is linked to *différance*.

To elaborate on this point, in Foucault's account of the sixteenth century resemblances are linked to signs in a dialogue between words and things that precedes the opposition between "identitites and differences" (OT: 50). Resemblance in the Renaissance is not mimetic; rather, it "becomes double as soon as one attempts to unravel it" (18), and as "aemulatio" it renders undecidable the priority between original and copy (19). Resemblance thus partakes of what Foucault will later confine to similitude, namely, "an indefinite and reversible relation of the similar to the similar."[45] At the same time resemblance is not just the deferral of a self-identical meaning; it is the site of a mingling between words and things that gives it a cognitive and ontological function such that *différance* is still aletheological. For the term *resemblance* indicates some "affinity" between words and things (OT: 58); indeed, within the "triple system" characteristic of the Renaissance it is resemblance that "ma[kes] it possible to see in the first [the signified] the mark of the second [the signifier]" (64). But at the same time the presence of similitude as a component of resemblance prevents this link from becoming an identity as in madness, maintaining a fluid relationship between images and realities (50). The classical period in *The Order of Things* marks the "close" of this "age of resemblance" and its replacement by forms such as simile and allegory, which reduce the aesthetic to games and chimeras. Now "similitude is no longer the form of knowledge but rather the occasion of error" (51); it has become pure illusion, renouncing the earlier claim of resemblance to reconstitute the world through metaphor.

This conceptual economy is radically redistributed in *This Is Not a Pipe*. For similitude is now divided from resemblance so as to make the latter a trope of identity, while the interplay now removed from resemblance returns in similitude as a surface without ontological depth. Correspondingly, the history that underwrites Foucault's narrative has been refigured; the Renaissance has disappeared, and a story of decline has been replaced by one of enlightenment. Ostensibly the classical period (now associated with resemblance) still occupies a negative position in this story. However, its correction occurs through a concept of art that resumes or sublates in the postmodern certain characteristics of the classical in *The Order of Things*. For similitude is associated with surfaces; it "circulates the simulacrum as an indefinite and reversible relation of the similar to the similar" and "ranges across the surface" in a simulation of pluralism that dissimulates the efface-ment of the Real.[46] It is of course true that Magritte's postmodern surfaces generate free play, where the tables and regularities of classical discourse re-inforce order. But the two are not so much opposed as related. In the same way, again, poststructuralism is related to the structuralism of which it is a sub-version and which Foucault recognizes as a form of classicism (OT: 67). For structuralism resembles classicism in instituting a "binary organization" of the sign that resituates signification, not between words and things, but exclusively within the system of discourse (64). Within this organization, which returns in inverted and dispersed form in poststructuralism, signs are "set free from that teeming world in which the Renaissance had distributed them. They are lodged henceforth within the confines of representation . . . in that narrow space in which they interact with themselves in a perpetual state of decomposition and recomposition" (67).

Foucault, in short, breaks up the category of resemblance by reducing the affinity it maintains between words and things to identity while, at the same time, displacing its disseminative potential onto a similitude that operates purely at the level of the signifier. He likewise shifts the historical axis on which his argument turns. Instead of being focalized through the Renais-sance and its more negative return in the literature of the period 1880–1930 (OT: 49), his theoretical narrative now finds its center in modern art from Kandinsky to Magritte, which is read through such recent essays as Barthes's "From Work to Text" (1969) and Derrida's "Structure, Sign, and Play in the Human Sciences" (1967). Replacing literature with painting, Foucault artic-ulates dissemination upon a medium associated with pure visibility; it is a medium without secrets, like discourse itself, which differs from language in being pure expression without any trace of indication.

These historical and terminological displacements signal a profound shift in Foucault's philosophical investments. Resemblance in *The Order of*

Things is a phenomenological category that lies midway between what Foucault later calls similitude and representation. In resemblance things become signs, not in the way characteristic of poststructuralism, but in an intermingling of language and reality that Foucault designates by Merleau-Ponty's phrase "the prose of the world." Echoing both Merleau-Ponty and Blanchot, Foucault had previously spoken of classicism's effacement of the "murmuring resemblance of things, that unreacting similitude that lies beneath thought" and that, like Kristeva's semiotic, furnishes the "raw material" for the "divisions and distributions" (OT: 58) that occur in the Symbolic order of discourse. The reduction of resemblance to mimesis, and its transference from the semiotic to the Symbolic order, parallel Foucault's reduction of phenomenology itself to a philosophy of identity. But this simplification, necessary to Foucault's interpellation as a poststructuralist subject, is resisted by the very genealogy of the term *resemblance*, which inscribes the turn he makes after 1968 within the traces of his own theoretical past.

This Is Not a Pipe confirms Foucault's transition to poststructuralism in more than one way. In *The Order of Things* the "rationalism" of the classical period is characterized by the way it refigures constitutive as regulative categories (54) so as to replace "transcendental reflection" with a nominalism that makes understanding an operation that occurs purely within discourse. Thus resemblance, which had previously provided "both the form and the content of what we know" by "revealing how the world is ordered," survives as "comparison," which is no more than a "function of order," a form of arrangement that allows us to organize what we already know (54). The transition from the Renaissance to classicism more or less describes what happens as Foucault's deconstruction develops into poststructuralism. For in *The Order of Things* Foucault had operated under the sign of resemblance, a process evident in the text's evocative and metaphoric style. By blurring the distinction between terms such as *similitude* and *resemblance*, which resembled each other and yet differed from/deferred one another, he had kept the process of thinking about the relations between signs and things open. Resemblance, in other words, had been both the form and the content of Foucault's own work. But the author of *This Is Not a Pipe* is classical in distinguishing resemblance and similitude within a binary analysis that excludes any third, and more indeterminate, term. He thus closes off the possibility of a deconstruction consistent with phenomenology: a similitude that may also be resemblance because there exists a "previous discourse that must be reconstituted in order to reveal the autochthonous meaning of things" (OT: 66).

Second, the essay on Magritte also provides an interesting example of the attenuated role played by the aesthetic within a new episteme that is by no means limited to Foucault. For *poststructuralism* as I have used the term, to suggest an emphasis on the linguistic purged of affect and depth, is replaced here by *poststructuralism*, as the term is used by Christopher Norris, to indicate a free play dissociated from effect and responsibility.[47] But the two poststructuralisms are faces of a single coin, which is why it is appropriate to consider *This Is Not a Pipe* alongside *The Archaeology of Knowledge*. By accepting the laws of discourse, Foucault consciously refashions himself in accord with a reality principle enunciated by Althusser in his definition of human beings as "subject to the law." In the essay on Magritte he allows himself a moment of resistance to this discourse, but only apparently. For whereas resemblance in *The Order of Things* had functioned in terms of a phenomenological openness, similitude challenges the rigidities of discourse through a play that flattens subversion and aestheticizes freeedom as free play. Resemblance, in other words, protects the affinity between *différance* and what Merleau-Ponty had described in less linguistic terms as an openness (*ouverture*) upon being or upon the world. But similitude recontains this openness within the simulacrum—a term soon to be picked up by Baudrillard. It economizes openness as a merely lateral, a hyperreal freedom.

The earlier connection of the aesthetic (or of literature) with depth has not disappeared entirely; it survives in a 1973 note on a series of paintings by Paul Rebeyrolle entitled *Prisoners*. Here, in terms reminiscent of Blanchot, Foucault describes the liberation that occurs when the "within, despite itself, begins to open onto the birth of a space. The wall cracks from top to bottom. . . . The vertical . . . now opens up a liberty."[48] But Foucault chooses to keep this piece secret. Instead it is the essay on Magritte that he expands into a book, though a book whose very slenderness figures the marginality of the aesthetic in the economy of poststructuralism and indeed figures affirmative poststructuralism as the (an)aesthetic. Nor is Magritte approached through the surrealism that engaged Bataille and Lacan by inscribing the

Real within the unconscious. Rather he is an artist of surfaces, of the post-modern and the hyperreal.

Corporal Punishment

If the aesthetic, carefully put aside in a piece of whimsical marginalia, is one place of resistance to discourse, power is often thought to signal Foucault's turn away from classical poststructuralism. Thus despite his own view that genealogy and archaeology are complementary,[49] Dreyfus and Rabinow typically see them as successive, with genealogy said to mark the completion of Foucault's project through a reorientation from linguistic to material practices provoked by 1968. This teleological valorization of genealogy has created, at least in Anglo-American criticism, a binary system in which "Foucault" is opposed to "de Man"; and this value-system, first set in place by Lentricchia's *After the New Criticism*,[50] remains evident in current cultural criticism's use of the later Foucault in the service of a progressive politics that has fought back the hegemony of Yale deconstruction. A discussion of Foucault's entire corpus is beyond the scope of this study. Suffice it to say that genealogy has been politically corrected by its appropriation in literary and cultural criticism, domesticated, and rendered affirmative. In the process we miss its recalcitrant singularity by converting it to a form of contingent pragmatism. While not as idiosyncratic as de Man in Gasché's reading, the Foucault of the period following *The Archaeology of Knowledge* (and particularly of "Nietzsche, Genealogy, History" [1971], which is a poststructural archaeology of genealogy) needs to be read not for his use-value but for the strangeness of his vision of the world and for the encrypted pathos of this strangeness.

Briefly, genealogy in *Discipline and Punish* repeats the same pattern we have noted in archaeology, where a vocabulary of destabilization that has its origins in what Bataille calls "general economy" is reeconomized within the circuitry of structure and law, in an ascetic submission to the law wherein subjectification is subjection. Power only seems to locate an element of *différance* within structure. Rather it describes the survival of discourse through the mutation of individual discourses or the performance of difference as that which contains differences. Foucault's more leftist followers have looked for the spaces left open by power. His more conservative followers—such as the New Historicists—have derived from their ability to analyze how power recontains resistance a noetic authority that takes the place of the material power lost by the academy. But Foucault's own relation to power is more anonymous, apathetically formalist, more like what Baudrillard will call "objective irony."

Thus I would suggest that genealogy in the seventies does not so much improve or complete archaeology as transfer it with all its resistances from the level of *langue* to *parole*. Nor is this recursive overlapping of the two methods at odds with the fact that genealogy replaces theory with practice. Indeed, we can argue that by shifting the study of regularities from a linguistic to a sociological plane, Foucault moves that much closer to his desired positivism: to defining "a limited system of presences" (AK: 119) that deals only with the event as we *see* it. A pure positivism is impossible because, as we shall see, a certain folding—or doubling—is in the nature of "post"structuralism. Nevertheless, Foucault's positivist desire is evident in the way *Discipline and Punish* is constituted upon certain rigorous exclusions. For the new work avoids those meditations on method that, even when Husserlian in style as in *The Archaeology of Knowledge*, had resulted in an uneasy duplication of description as self-reflection. As significantly, it also avoids the troublesome interdisciplinarity of its most obvious precursor, *The Birth of the Clinic*.

In the latter the study of institutions had been articulated upon a background that included psychoanalysis and literature, thus provoking us to ask what kind of transference or cathexis might operate in an analysis of discourses that supposes nothing but the fact of their "historical appearance" (BC: xvii). But in *Discipline and Punish* Foucault more definitively assumes the mask of the historian, focusing on "the facts of discourse" (BC: xvii) as what Derrida calls "object[s] for a pure consciousness" (OG: 27). Moreover there is nothing in the new book like the introduction and conclusion to *The Archaeology of Knowledge*, where Foucault momentarily discloses the social scientist as a writer. This elision of writing is also apparent in genealogy's redeployment of the linguistic terminology characteristic of theory so as to enforce rather than unsettle social constructions. As in *The Birth of the Clinic* institutions are analyzed as discursive phenomena. Thus the tortured body is "inscribed" in a legal ceremony, making the sentence "legible" and instituting a "poetics" of jurisprudence.[51] But *écriture* has now crossed over to the side of the state apparatus, writing the docile body through a language no longer suspended between sign and symptom but fully expressive.

The fate of writing is connected to an aestheticization of suffering that runs through Foucault's account of the transition from torture to less public and more "humane" forms of punishment. Carroll has discussed the way the spectacle of the scaffold is staged in terms of a theatre of cruelty used to critique our own theatre of surveillance without positing itself as an alternative. He thus focuses on the undecidable play between the performative and constative aspects of Foucault's text so as to recuperate the theatricalization of torture as part of a "transgressive aesthetics" that links *Discipline and Punish* to an earlier "poetics of self-reflexivity." But it is significant that the aesthetic returns only in accounts of torture, as when Foucault describes how the transition to the interiority of the prison marks the loss of a symbolic exchange inscribed in public torture as "the social play of the signs of punishment and the prolix festival that circulated them."[52] Valorizing torture as carnivalesque but thereby placing the aesthetic inside the law, Foucault offers us in torture a metonymy for the sadomasochistic ascesis of power itself; it is a concept that submerges transgression and discipline in the same space. In effect, power functions in terms of what Hertz, with reference to de Man, calls a "pathos of uncertain agency."[53] One is never sure whether its analyst is a victim or collaborator, whether the dis-figuration of the body is a source of pain or aesthetic pleasure, or even whether that choice has any meaning. Or, to put it differently, the body as pathos is not the site of a materiality beyond discourse as in Elaine Scarry's humanist adaptation of Foucault in *The Body in Pain*.[54] Rather it is displayed in an autobiography of defacement in which the author pays the price of power, as "the inscribed surface of events . . . a body totally imprinted by history and the process of history's destruction of the body."[55] To be sure there is a resistance at work here, which allows us to unravel the conflation of discipline and trangression in the way Hertz does with de Man. But it is closer to the psychoanalytic resistance that de Man himself calls "the resistance to theory": it is a resistance of theory to our humanism that in turn enfolds a resistance of "Foucault" to his own theory.

Perhaps the most intriguing argument for power as a form of alterity that preserves genealogy as a "thought of the outside" has been made by Dreyfus, who suggests that it takes the place of Foucault's earlier Heideggerian concern with being and the unthought.[56] That there are resonances between the early and late work finds support in the curious way that "the capillary functioning of power"[57] is already anticipated in the description of disease as something that cannot be grasped because it "travel[s] from one point of localization to another, reach[ing] other bodily surfaces, while remaining identical in nature" (BC: 10). Disease anticipates two characteristics of power: a difference that contributes to its elusiveness and a homogeneity that allows it to differ from itself "while remaining identical in nature." This indifference of power and disease as forms of being in-itself is what makes them so resistant to comprehension by the *pour-soi*. But the parallels also mark a difference. Disease manifests an otherness that remains fundamentally beyond medicine's attempts to grasp it phenomenally. In this sense it is the catalyst for human being's recognition of itself as *Dasein*. Power seems in no way linked to ontological issues. For in rewriting disease as power, Foucault re(covers) it as an *economic* principle that circulates within the social apparatus it perpetuates.[58]

The notion of power is thus susceptible to Kristeva's complaint that in grammatology "negativity has become positivized and drained of its potential for producing breaks." As I argue elsewhere, Kristeva criticizes grammatology for flattening the semiotic into the Symbolic instead of allowing it to operate from the outside.[59] Both in its aestheticized form as free play and in its socialized form as power, poststructuralism is just such a restriction of *différance*. Yet Kristeva's critique could be seen as naive—a continuation of a deconstructive project of which poststructuralism spells the end. Perhaps the most chilling example of the autoconsumption of *différance* is the work of Baudrillard. As I suggest in the final chapter, Baudrillard's late work is at once a submission to, a commentary on, and a hysterical mimicry of the turning of deconstruction into poststructuralism. In this turn he seemingly renounces all possibility of the symbolic exchange he had earlier opposed to simulation by effacing the difference between general and restricted economies. In Baudrillard's world the potlatch associated by Bataille with a radical questioning of use and production, and thus with an opening of structures to their outside, is digested by capitalism as the conspicuous consumption that is both its motor and its uncontrollable effect. Baudrillard pushes to an extreme what is implicit in Foucault's conflation of difference with structure in the period of *The Archaeology of Knowledge*; he describes a "circularization of power"[60] in which excess is always already foreclosed and enclosed in an "indeterminate mutation . . . governed . . . by the code" (SED: 60).

It is thus wrong to see the shift from being to power as simply enabling. Following his earlier reading of the unthought in *Mental Illness and Psychology* in terms of an affirmative deconstruction, Dreyfus views power as producing an epistemic clearing.[61] Deleuze similarly idealizes power; indeed, this may explain his current popularity in the American academy. Interestingly, Deleuze's affirmative poststructuralism, as well as his recuperation of Foucault, rely on a sleight-of-hand with phenomenology. Connecting Foucault's interest in the fold to Heidegger and Merleau-Ponty, Deleuze also decisively separates Foucault from phenomenology. For phenomenology "the fold of being surpasses intentionality only to found the latter in a new dimension. . . . Light opens up a speaking no less than a seeing, as if signification haunted the visible which in turn murmured meaning. This cannot be so in Foucault, for whom the light-Being refers only to visibilities, and language-Being to statements."[62] Deleuze subtracts phenomenology from Foucault's work and then adds it back so as to romanticize power as a postmodern form of spirit. That he is able to do so has much to do with his debts to another phenomenology: that of Bergson.[63] Thus on the one hand Foucault deals only with surfaces—visibilities and statements—and avoids any phenomenological illusions of depth or (non)being. On the other hand a phenomenological affect is projected back onto Foucault's work through the figure of a "light-Being," as if Foucault can be postmodern without the consequences. Correspondingly, Deleuze treats visibilities with a curious innocence, separating productive from juridical power. Visibilities "are not defined by sight but are complexes of actions and passions . . . which emerge into the light of day."[64] Visibility is thus the phenomenality of social production without the material rema(i)nders of power or without the knowledge that the lighted space is the space of surveillance.

As against this view I suggest that the affinity of power with being, or of the "epistemology" of visibility with the "ontology" of the fold,[65] or of the statement with the facelessness of the "there is" (AK: 111) are rem(a)inders that both mark a self-disciplining and encrypt something lost.[66] Butler is among the few to focus on this structure of "constitutive loss" when she notes that the body "is not a site on which a construction takes place" but "a destruction on the occasion of which a subject is formed." The body is a destruction because positing, in Sartre's terms, is nihilation; the body is the ground nihilated by the figure of identity. But the body is itself the contained site of a prior destruction in that it is the encryption of the psyche in "the preserved form of exteriority" (AK: 140). In fact the body is, in de Man's terms, an anthropomorphism or catachresis. For as Butler strikingly comments, "the body has come to substitute for the psyche in Foucault."[67] At issue here is not just the body but the corpus, which is to say that the loss is philosophic as well as psychic and personal, if these losses can even be separated. Thus Foucault must refuse what Deleuze calls light-Being, as de Man must also do in his own defacement of the phenomenological "shape all light" in "Shelley Disfigured." The body of Foucault's work in the seventies emerges through a reiterated erasure of his previous work, including such terms as *being*, *language*, *murmuring*, and *doubling*. The mark of this loss is precisely the body—the examination of power at the site of a body that is really a psyche disciplined and dis-affected as visibility. The body that is Foucault's empirical object doubles, in this sense, as an auto-graph: an encryption of the subject within and as the object.

If power is the subjugation of difference by structure, de Man's version of this structuralization is his discussion of the hypogram as "coded dispersal" in his essay on Riffaterre's response to Saussure's work on anagrams (RT: 36). De Man's work is also constituted by losses that leave their "bodily remainders" anagrammatically dispersed through his various later texts. Drawing on the same material as Kristeva in *Revolution in Poetic Language* and Baudrillard in *Symbolic Exchange and Death*, but a decade later (51n), de Man refuses to make the anagram—as a form of antimatter within matter—into the utopian figure for a revolutionary semiotics or an "ex-termination" of codes. On the contrary, his deployment of the anagram—with its focus on "the suffix *gram* (letter) rather than *phone* (sound)"—remembers and systematically dismembers grammatology as the possibility of an affirmative deconstruction. As the breaking up of the word or "proper name" into nonsignificant "parts and groups," the anagram is the "undoing of cognition and its replacement by the uncontrollable power of the letter as inscription" (37). In de Man's essay, *différance*, once associated with a dialogue of the cogito and its unthought, thus becomes mechanically structural. As with power, this "dissemination" of difference as structure is all the more traumatic because it is politically illegible (36). For de Man is not saying anything so simple as that transgression is recontained by the system—a position that is still intelligible as a form of neoconservatism. On the contrary, the materiality of the letter as antimatter is "uncontrollable," randomly transgressive, and punitive of transgression.

De Man's turn to rhetoric in the seventies has indeed been seen as neoconservative, especially in the light of the "revelations" about his past. However, the delayed effect of these revelations has been to disclose a fold in the late work between the ascetic, technical essays of *Allegories of Reading* and the more speculative essays that follow them after 1976. As we have seen, these essays increasingly confess the "pathos" of the "bodily mutilation"—also the political and historical mutilation—that inhabits the rigorous submission to "textual models" (RR: 289). In other words, the self-discipline of rhetoric emerges as a covering over of a punishing vision that is the inner face of poststructuralism. This vision, focused on the nothingness that underlies the positional power of language, crystallizes in the account of the zero in de Man's essay on Pascal. De Man's essay stands as a powerful defacement of the affirmative antihumanism of Barthes's *Writing Degree Zero*, whose asceticism reconverts the renunciation of the subject into what Bataille calls a "beatitude." For de Man, as being is constituted on the trace of nothingness, so too the sign as position is dependent on a "different notion in which language functions as rudderless signification." Since we cannot grasp the zero, the zero "always appears in the guise of a *one*, of a (some)thing"; it is always "*called* a one" though it is "actually nameless, 'innommable.'" "The name," de Man says, "is the trope of the zero." But as a nihilation, the something shares in the nothingness effaced by "the violence of position" (RR: 118). For that reason, language always "transforms what it denominates into the linguistic equivalent of the arithmetical zero."[68]

To read Foucault with de Man is to glimpse in Foucault's work a similar encounter with the zero, through the folding back of the genealogies onto *The Archaeology of Knowledge*, itself a work that folds back onto a "blank space" (AK: 17). To be sure, Foucault seems very different from de Man in focusing on power as productive, as positive, as position. He is not concerned with how figures are annihilated by their absent ground, but with their "emergence" (41). Even *The Archaeology of Knowledge*, in its elusive abstraction, speaks of the rules of formation of concepts, enunciative modalities, and objects; it therefore deals with those "synecdochal totalizations" that reconvert the zero "into a name."[69] As for the genealogies, it is hard not to see them in the very terms Foucault eschews, namely, as providing a history of the referent that replaces method with content. In the genealogies and the interviews in *Power/Knowledge*, Foucault constructs himself as a disciplined and (un)committed public intellectual. As suggested in Chapter 3, he repeats the very turn made by Sartre when he chooses prose, or the instrumental use of thought and language, over a poetry that continues—and abjects—the reflexivity of *Being and Nothingness*. In this turn, Foucault manages to work with power, unlike Baudrillard and de Man. He even finds a certain pleasure in it. It is a pleasure that is as ideologically indecipherable as it is aesthetic and technical—a pleasure in the fact that forms emerge and in their functioning.

We can ask, however, why power? Genealogy as an analysis of practices names power as something. But why should what it names be named power—or the positional power of language—rather than the unthought, or "the rich uncertainty of disorder" (AK: 76)? Although power is Foucault's empirical subject, it is also part of a figural structure of what Butler calls stubborn attachments. Despite Foucault's attempt to normalize it by generalizing it across history, power is not a timeless figure, as he concedes when he refers to "this power which has surged into view in all its violence, aggression and absurdity in the course of the last forty years." Moreover, despite his linkage of power to Stalinism and Fascism,[70] the term enters Foucault's vocabulary only in the mid-seventies, just as it is only late in his career that de Man speaks of the positional power of language. Whereas de Man had earlier seen language as consciousness's lack in relation to itself, in associating language with power he conceives of it as radically outside consciousness and randomly violent, as though cathecting onto it something else altogether. Power threatens us with a particularly contemporary form of nothingness that may be what Blanchot calls "disaster." Genealogy, by tracing its discursive forms and practices, tropes power as something, and in the process it tropes itself as something. Genealogy, even if it is not able to do something about power, can at least describe it. Moreover, to do something with power it must produce itself through power as a form of auto-affection—hence Foucault's stubborn attachment to power.

Because genealogy deals with the real world rather than discourse, it allows Foucault to produce himself as a public intellectual. But to go back from the mimetic mode of genealogy to the autodiegesis of *The Archaeology of Knowledge* is to witness the emergence of this voice as position, as a nothing writing itself as something. *The Archaeology of Knowledge* is beset by a certain *désouevrement*. It is a strangely abstract text, not apparently about anything, backing away from the naiveté of reference. In this sense, though it avoids talking of literature, it finds itself constantly in the space of literature—not just parergonally in disclaimers about its "strange arsenal" and "bizarre machinery" (135), but fundamentally. Foucault says of literature that it "curve[s] back in a perpetual return upon itself," existing only "in reference to the pure act of writing." *The Archaeology of Knowledge* is likewise a form that often seems to have "no content other than its own form" (OT: 300); Foucault writes that "to analyse the rules for the formation of objects, one must neither . . . embody them in things, *nor relate them to the domain of words*" (AK: 63; emphasis mine). If we take this statement seriously, genealogy is *prima facie* impossible in the terms of archaeology except as a figural imposition. Indeed, discursive formations are described precisely as "figures" (135).

But perhaps Foucault simply means that *The Archaeology of Knowledge* is the methodological preamble to the genealogies, providing the rules for the formation of objects and concepts traced by the latter. *The Archaeology of Knowledge* would then have a content, namely rules of formation, and genealogy would be linked to archaeology by a process of logical development. Yet *The Archaeology of Knowledge*'s avoidance of the something goes beyond a mere neo-Kantian focus on method. For we must ask what rules it gives us and whether they emerge at all except by a catachresis. Foucault has great difficulty articulating his rules except as something that is not there: a "dispersion." He wants to see in discursive formations "unities" that are simply "less visible, more abstract" than the conventional ones—regularities that could then be the basis of Kantian synthetic judgments. But he wonders whether the "re-division" he proposes is really "capable of individualizing wholes" (71).

The visibilities of which Deleuze speaks—"practices, or positivities"[71]—emerge after *The Archaeology of Knowledge* "at the crest of [an] immense reserve" (AK: 76), as this text itself is made possible by a similar reticence. Of that which we cannot speak we must remain silent, as Wittgenstein says, if we are to speak at all. In order to write *The Archaeology of Knowledge* Foucault must leave behind the ontophenomenological issues of his previous work (76). His "achievement" according to Deleuze is this "conversion"—or displacement—of "phenomenology into epistemology."[72] But it is questionable whether anything becomes visible as a result of this reconfiguration; a further reserve is thus necessary with regard to the epistemological aporias uncovered by *The Archaeology of Knowledge*, which threaten to stall the genealogical project altogether. In the genealogies visibilities are indeed set in place, but not through any process of logical development from *The Archaeology of Knowledge* and only through a setting aside of that text, which is the condition of possibility for its refiguration as the prelude to future work. In this way the blank space of archaeology is able to appear as something: namely, genealogy.

Genealogy is thus grounded upon a series of multiple reserves or, one could say, forgettings. We can follow Foucault through the doors he closes behind him, leaving archaeology and genealogy in themselves, not speaking of their production by a for-itself. Or we can enfold them in what Derrida calls their genesis. In the end it is Foucault himself, in republishing the book on Roussel, who allows for such an overlapping of past and present through a return and retreat from his own origins. Moreover, in the conversation with Ruas, and in the very giving of this interview, Foucault allows that "the work is more than the work: the subject who is writing is part of the work." He lets us approach theory auto(bio)graphically, not in the sense that the work "translates" the life, but in the sense that it "includes" the life in a process wherein concepts double as figural displacements and synecdochal encryptions of that life (DL: 184).

CHAPTER EIGHT

Jean Baudrillard: From the Human Sciences to the Society of Communication

The reading of Baudrillard with phenomenology may seem the most unusual part of this study. Baudrillard is usually taken as a theorist of the object-form or the mode of information and thus as a sociologist, not a philosopher. Baudrillard, however, reads many of the same writers as the theorists studied here, including Nietzsche, Bataille, and Sartre. Moreover, philosophy in this period is not classically stable; it participates in a larger dialogue in which it is reconfigured by and interrogates other disciplines. As François Dosse argues, the university of the fifties and sixties saw the decline of conventional philosophy and the rise of the social sciences with a consequent attempt to renew philosophy as theory and more specifically deconstruction.[1] Deconstruction is neither an analysis of literature nor is it "continental" philosophy—a term that makes sense only within a debate internal to the single discipline of philosophy. Rather it is the form in which philosophy makes itself responsible for an *inter*disciplinary rethinking of rationality. As Gasché emphasizes, deconstruction is part of rationality in that it tries to "bring reason—especially in its modern, technoscientific form—before the tribunal of reason itself." Terms such as *rationality* and *science* are frequent in Baudrillard's early work,[2] which, I argue, can therefore be read in the same broadly philosophical framework as Derrida's and Foucault's.

As already suggested the analysis of rationality emerges in part within phenomenology as a network of questions and differences. To recapitulate: Husserl's work already brings phenomenology into relation with other disciplines, though on the ground of philosophy itself as a rigorous science. However, subsequent writers such as Lyotard and Merleau-Ponty envision a more genuine complementarity between philosophy and its others, specifically the human or social sciences. In Lyotard's case phenomenology is positivized as having specific attributes it can bring to a synthesis with the social sciences.[3] Foucault draws on a more negative phenomenology, developing an analysis of disciplines as enframing, but without Heidegger's reconsolidation of philosophy as the sole refuge of thinking. For Foucault, then, a philosophical deconstruction must question the very identity of the terms *human* and *science* through an opening of discourses to their unthought.

To this negative turn of phenomenology and its dialogue with the social sciences, Baudrillard adds a new element in his focus on what Gianni Vattimo calls the society of "generalized communications" and the mass media. Indeed, Vattimo is worth citing because he illuminates the profound continuity in the disciplinary stakes that mobilize two apparently different stages of Baudrillard's work. For Vattimo the relation between the "human sciences" and a society characterized by an "intensification in the exchange of information" is closer than commonly realized, as both develop from "changes in individual and collective life . . . shaped directly by forms of modern communication" and by a "modernity" that begins well before our century. These discourse networks suppose and create a certain "transparency," indeed, a "utopia of absolute *self-transparency*."[4] As Niklas Luhmann explains (writing on the later seventeenth century and on the apparently unsocial topic of the passions): "generalized symbolic media of communication" allow even "improbable communications . . . to be made successfully." Through codes and systems "the number of communicable topics grows"[5] as the marginal and the problematic is taken in and thus positivized by the social. Everything is exchangeable, communicable through the code as a "universal system" of recognition (SO: 271; 193) and thus transparent—though, according to Baudrillard, this can be only a "false transparency" and "legibility" (274; 196).[6]

By virtue of this transparency, as Vattimo writes, the human sciences can be traced back to the subjects "that make up what Kant called pragmatic anthropology. . . . These give a 'positive,' as opposed to a transcendental-philosophical, description of humanity, taking as their basis not what humanity is by nature, but rather what it has made of itself, that is to say, its institutions, culture and symbolic forms." The human sciences, then, are the second instance of a post-Enlightenment rhetoric of emancipation whose first instance is the (pragmatic) anthropology spurned by Foucault. The most recent instance would be television and the internet. As such, they are expressions of technology "in the broadest and most 'ontological' sense implied by Heidegger's notion of the *Ge-stell*."[7]

Baudrillard would agree with Vattimo on the positivism transferred from the human sciences of communication to the media. But he would not agree that this (post)modern episteme leaves a place for opacity, nor would he agree with the reassurance implied by a folding back of the media into the human sciences.[8] On the contrary, Baudrillard, while analyzing both as technical cultures that repress ontological questions, would make a sharper difference between the modern and the postmodern foreclosure of negativity. In these chapters, then, I trace his career through the successive stages of his engagement with the society of communication. In his work up to *Symbolic Exchange and Death* Baudrillard, like the early Foucault, is engaged in an analysis of the hegemony of the social sciences (specifically economics and sociology) from the perspective of an antiscience invested, at different points, in anthropology, poetics, psychoanalysis, and philosophy. In terms of the struggle between philosophy and the social sciences that continues today, Baudrillard is still very much on the philosophical side of the divide. He is, to be sure, even less of a conventional philosopher than Derrida or Foucault. Still, if Derrida is concerned to rethink philosophy itself, the early Baudrillard is engaged in an affirmative deconstruction that creates a space for a philosophically grounded antisociology. But, beginning in the mid-seventies, Baudrillard turns from commodification to simulation, escalating his critique from the social sciences to their hyperconsummation in the media. This escalation responds to the evolution of technoculture beyond even the late capitalism analyzed by the Frankfurt school theorists. Baudrillard's later work thus assumes the failure of deconstruction and the end of philosophy. Even so, I suggest, what he offers is a phenomenology of media culture—a psychoanalysis of the mode of consciousness of technology in a time when the very category of consciousness is passé.

Baudrillard sees himself as a theorist of the sign form and not just the commodity or object form. Sign and symbol, metaphor and metonymy are recurrent topics of his texts. There is thus a further dimension to his work. Derrida, Foucault, and de Man make language the basis of all further analysis; in the process they also deconstruct specific, historical figurations of language such as expression, discourse, or symbol. But Baudrillard is unique in considering the language used to analyze language, the discourse of theory itself. At Nanterre, he studied with Henri Lefebvre who saw structuralism as responsible for the implantation of a technocratic society—a society of space without time and history. Lefebvre's work was conventionally Marxist, but Baudrillard more systematically develops it into an antiscience of the sign form. His own work is thus a "political economy of the sign," but it is as importantly a "phenomenology of structuralism"[9] and, more silently, (poststructuralism as reification.)Recognizing structuralism and poststructuralism as themselves modes of consciousness, it is concerned with the sign system as a form of social organization and also with the psychological and ethical effects of this system. Baudrillard thus allows us a unique vantage on the linguistic paradigm that became for poststructuralism an end as well as a means, and in that sense he provides an appropriate culmination for this study.

The System of Objects: Baudrillard's Missed Encounter with Phenomenology

This semiocritical project can already be seen in *The System of Objects*, but it is recaptured by a positivism that Baudrillard subsequently avoids. As others have observed, Baudrillard's first study, despite its title, is only superficially structuralist.[10] Analyzing consumption as maintained by a self-reproducing logic in which signification occurs not with reference to the real but through the differential values of terms in a code, Baudrillard is nevertheless interested in how these differences are "lived (*vécus*)" (SO: 9; 4), although not as a ground of authenticity or "ownness." Indeed his axial distinction is between a "structural technology" and a "psycho-sociology" of objects (12, 31; 7, 22). Baudrillard describes the former, which is the ground of "science" and epistemic "rationality" (10, 12; 5, 7), as "essential" but by the same token "essentialist" (9, 12; 5, 7).[11] Hence he does not deal with objects as "defined by their function or by the classes into which they might be subdivided" (9; 4). Rather he deals with the "inessential," with "the processes by which people relate" to objects and with their "lived psychological and sociological reality" (9, 13; 4, 8). He seeks to capture objects in their flight "from technical structurality" towards their "diffusion" in "secondary meanings" (14, 17; 8, 10). Bourdieu describes *The System of Objects* as a "phenomenologico-semi-ological analysis,"[12] and Baudrillard himself describes his work of this period as a "phenomenology of consumption" (CS: 29). Indeed, except for the repeated postulate of a system, the language of semiology is conspicuously absent from this text.

Yet Baudrillard describes his early work as a "critical structuralism" in keeping with "the spirit of the times." And for the most part the *The System of Objects* is a form of "phenomeno-structuralism,"[13] a genetic structuralism inflected by phenomenology in ways whose more profound ramifications Baudrillard does not yet explore. At issue here is the question of whether phenomenology is simply a supplement to structuralism—and not yet a dangerous one—or the thought of its outside. For Baudrillard's first book is traversed by an unexamined ambiguity as to whether the psychosocial sphere, apologetically described as "inessential" (SO: 15; 9), is in excess of the technological or is itself a "cultural system" that, as system, recontains its gaps in "internally consistent" ways (12, 14; 6, 8). Thus, on the one hand, phenomenology seems to challenge sociology, as "mental structures" are said to "disturb" the "coherence of the technological system" with which they are "interwoven," even calling in question the "objective status of the object" as a ground of science (9, 13–14; 4, 8). On the other hand, "needs" emerge inside the system as its raison d'etre. And in that case the "system of needs" is already "the product of the system of production" (CS: 74) as consumption takes the structural place of labor in the ideological apparatus of late capitalism (50).

This pervasive tension in Baudrillard's first work indicates a missed encounter with phenomenology rather than its subsumption into structuralism. Yet the *The System of Objects*, with its focus on lived experience but at a purely collective level, easily slips into a phenomenology of interpellation—an account of *habitus* as embodied social structure. Its phenomenology thus becomes an alibi for structure; it becomes a way of "operationalizing" (and confirming) structure by translating it into "the subjective domain" of the lived body.[14] Only occasionally are there hints of the more ontological analysis characteristic of Baudrillard's next work. One example is the (psycho)analysis of collecting as a deferral of death; collecting is the "repetition or substitution of oneself" along an "infinite chain of signifiers" in the series of collected objects. Recognizing the object as "our own death," which we try to "transcend (symbolically)" by possessing the object (SO: 136–38; 96–97), Baudrillard momentarily discloses the larger "system of objects" as similarly constructed by a substitution of being for nothingness that forgets consciousness in things. But if the text at such points opens itself to man in his "negativity," its catalogues of successfully mediated objects also reinforce the "codified, classified . . . system of products in all their positivity" (263; 187–8). Put differently, critical reflection in this first book still occurs in the mirror of production as an accumulation and collection of examples. It is in this sense that the text practises "critical structuralism," a critique "subtly haunted by the very form(s) it negates"[15]: classification, accumulation, and consumption—the consumption, we could say, of critique itself.

It is not surprising, then, that the reflection on language in this early text is also underdeveloped. At the end Baudrillard hints at what will become a radical deconstruction not just of consumption but of the linguistics that makes it possible. He suggests that the *langue* instituted by a structuralization that makes needs a mere epiphenomenon of technological rationality is not really a language (*langage*), even if its "simplification(s)" and "technemes" can be personalized to facilitate the expression of "recurrent modalities of 'speech' (*parole*)" (SO: 264; 188–89). Through this third term outside the *langue/parole* distinction, Baudrillard seeks to bring back a "lived relation" or "lived existence." His claim that technology is not a language because it lacks a "living syntax" (262, 270; 187, 193) can thus be read with his later assault on a similar loss of totality through the digital order of "segments" and "cells." In this order "each fragment of a hologram can become a matrix of the complete hologram; all the information being contained in each of the scattered fragments . . . (such that) the whole loses its meaning" (S: 170). In *Seduction* Baudrillard is explicit about the phenomenological consequences of a *langue* that reduces the individual to an abstract "formula . . . destined to serial multiplication." Digitalization as the interconvertibility of signs in the code becomes the interchangeability of cells in cloning and marks the "end . . . of this singular being we call the body." The technology of the code thus "makes possible the generation of identical *beings*, without any possibility of a return to an original *being*" (S: 170–71; emphasis mine). *The System of Objects* edges towards such an analysis, particularly at the end. But Baudrillard also remains fascinated by the code as the fulfilment of the Enlightenment project of universal language; the code "constitutes for the first time in history a *universal* system of signs and interpretation" (SO: 272; 195).[16] And, significantly, he still seeks a linguistic solution— as is perhaps even more evident in the neostructuralist "Sign, Function, and Class Logic" (1969). For the way out of the langue/parole impasse is not the body but "syntax"—an alternative to "order" (SO: 266; 190) that replaces structural with communicative rationality.[17]

Baudrillard's work at this point occupies the transitional space of Barthes's "Rhetoric of the Image" (1964) that inconclusively questions his "critical structuralism" in "The Photographic Message" (1961). In the earlier essay Barthes synchronizes the technological and cultural or, in the terms Baudrillard borrows from him, denotation and connotation, objects and subjectivity (SO: 16; 9). In "Rhetoric of the Image" he recognizes the fluidity of connotation as a " 'floating chain' of signifieds, " the reader able to "choose some and ignore others." In other words he moves towards a partly phenomenological, partly semiological analysis, concerned (in Kristevan terms) with the semiotic as well as the symbolic. But Barthes still focuses on the methods of "anchorage" used to "counter the terror of uncertain signs."[18] Moreover semiotic fluidity, rechanneled through signs and kept at their surface, is at best an aestheticized source of "terror." Barthes's interest in the writerly and textual in the late sixties is thus a form of mere pleasure, a subversion of the code that allies theory with capital in a consumerism of signs.

Barthes's decentering of the subject thus retains a humanism that blocks a deeper encounter with phenomenology. Indeed his emphasis on choice makes his brand of affirmative poststructuralism a curious alibi for the voluntarism that Baudrillard later labels the "anthropology of needs." In light of his later critique of *Tel Quel* for the complicity it betrays between "unlimited textual productivity" and capitalism,[19] Baudrillard's first account of this anthropology at the end of *The System of Objects* doubles unintentionally as a (self)criticism of Barthes. Baudrillard complains that the "choices" mobilized by connotation stimulate desire only "to generalize it in the vaguest terms." Far from "liberat[ing] drives," advertizing "mobilizes phantasms which block these drives." It thus performs an insidious "censorship" that operates not through discipline but through "free behaviours [and] spontaneous investment" (SO: 269–70; 192–93). As we shall see, Baudrillard will later develop much more extensively this critique of (even poststructuralist) excess as a forgetting of fundamental negativity.

Baudrillard's critique of advertising is a curious *mise-en-abîme* of his own flirtation with Barthes's soft semiology, which uses rhetoric to personalize structure without giving up the linguistic paradigm. This paradigm and Barthes's methods are the phantasms that block the theoretical drives mobilized by Baudrillard's critique of consumption. Rhetoric "rechannel[s] conflict" from depth to surface and permits a "guiltless" analysis (SO: 270; 192).[20] Because a code is not a language, because it "designates" but does not "structure the personality" (270; 193), codes are without deep consequences. Thus Barthes can recognize that the "*only goal*" of the fashion system is to "*disappoint the meaning it luxuriantly elaborates*"; this system ceaselessly "disseminate[s] meaning through a structure of signification . . . but this meaning is finally nothing more than the signifier itself."[21] Yet Barthes does not probe the ontological consequences of this structure of lack and deferral, which he describes only in its linguistic functioning. Baudrillard, as we have seen, does sometimes probe these consequences. But he follows the touristic, episodic mode of Barthes's examples of cultural practice in *Mythologies* and *The Fashion System*, which keeps his insights at an anecdotal level. Barthes's examples—and even his theorizing—are offered in short, separate sections of a modular text organized in sound bites. They reflect what Poster calls the new "mode of information" in which "contextualized linear analysis" is replaced by "a montage of isolated data."[22] In this sense the example functions like the Baudrillardean object: "the goal is to permit the drives hitherto blocked . . . to crystallize on objects, concrete instances where the explosive force of desire abolishes itself and the ritual repressive function of social organization is materialized" (SO: 261; 186).

The Question Concerning Technostructuralism: From *Consumer Society to* The Political Economy of the Sign

While *La Société de consommation* (or *Consumer Society* [1970]) deals with the same terrain as its predecessor, it does so differently. For one thing, it is not haunted by the project of "classification" evoked in the *The System of*

Objects, which gives up the construction of a "table" of objects as unmanageable only to explore a cultural system parasitical on this same project (SO: 7; 3). Whereas *The System of Objects* burgeons with "the vegetation of objects" (7;3), its successor is more theoretical, using examples only within a contextualized linear analysis. As important, *Consumer Society* more fully explores the negativity and lack that haunt the system in terms of a psychoanalysis that marks Baudrillard's first break with Barthes's claim for linguistics as the future "science of every imagined universe."[23]

Negativity is the first signal of Baudrillard's links to a tradition very different from Barthes's semiology—namely, that of Bataille and Nietzsche (CS: 44)—and of a phenomenology that, after Hegel, focuses on an unproductive rather than recuperable negativity. In his previous work Baudrillard had contrasted man's negativity with the positivity of a system of products "entirely coherent with itself, entirely unified" (SO: 12; 8). He had thus placed negativity outside the system as an other that was not theorized. In this second study he recapitulates, in the examples of the drugstore and washing machine, a semiological analysis of the "ensemble" as an *en-soi* founded on a coded logic of differences which subsumes differences into the same (CS: 27–30). But his real interest is in how such systems, as *"the product of a human activity"* (26) or *pour-soi*, internalize in their very structure the negativity they mask. The immense positivity of affluence has as its byproduct "nuisances" such as pollution, which are results of technological progress, indeed of the very economy of "consummation" (39–40).[24] More important, in "'this rapid growth . . . a non-negligible fraction of the population is not able to keep up with the pace'" (40). To deal with the unemployed and the unproductive the system devises "compensatory expenditures" in social welfare. Paradoxically these "expenditures . . . intended to cope with dysfunctions rather than increase positive satisfaction" are accounted on the plus side of the ledger as enhancements of living standards. Thus "the positive and the negative" are "added together indiscriminately as society puts "nuisances and palliatives to them" on the same plane as "the production of objectively useful goods" (40–42). Baudrillard allows that these moral and fiscal deficits may be, paradoxically, the motor of the economy (42). But he tends rather to see them as the system's autoconsumption (*autodévoration*): "we are everywhere reaching a point where the dynamic of growth and abundance becomes circular and turns on itself" (40; trans.

mine). In this self-reflection or "autopsy" on "homo oeconomicus" (69), Bataille's term *dépense*, meaning both expense and waste, is the point of insertion of the consumer economy into a more "general" anthropological and psychic economy.

Baudrillard's use of the philosophical term *negativity* reinflects what would otherwise be a sociological analysis in a more phenomenological direction.[25] Thus he considers social facts not just in themselves but also for what they disclose about man's relation to his existence. Baudrillard's destruct(urat)ion of sociology and economics is thus broadly consistent with Heidegger's project of restoring the sciences to their essential ground. Heidegger had associated a science's "level of development" with "the extent to which it is *capable* of a crisis in its basic concepts." Emphasizing that sciences are not sources of information but forms of *Dasein* or "ways in which human beings behave," he had distinguished *Dasein* "by the fact that in its being this being is concerned *about* its very being." *Dasein* is "being held out into the nothing," about which science "wants to know nothing,"[26] just as for Baudrillard economics recognizes only the "measurable" and ignores "the negative sign" (CS: 41; trans. mine). For Heidegger fundamental ontology, in analyzing the primary structures of human existence, provides a necessary foundation for the (human) sciences. Heidegger's comments on science respond to an earlier crisis: Husserl's last desperate attempts in *The Crisis of European Sciences and Transcendental Phenomenology* to preserve philosophy in the mode of "the mathematical projection"—a mode whose positivism, according to Heidegger, sets modern science radically at odds with philosophy. But the 1960s see a return to a generalized crisis, not just of philosophy, but of the cross-disciplinary identifications, the theoretical imaginary, of the entire human sciences. In this crisis, which produced, on the one hand, the Marxist structuralism of Barthes and Goldmann and, on the other hand, the analyses of Derrida, Foucault, and Baudrillard the mathematical is replaced by the linguistic projection as a means of scientific legitimation and self-sufficiency.[27] Whereas Baudrillard had earlier protected this sufficiency by showing how technology *functioned* as a "practical system" fertilized by its "incoheren(ce)" (SO: 17; 10), he now emphasizes how it does not function. Through this failure, similar to Heidegger's equipmental breakdown, he turns economics back on itself, situating it as "a mode of historical," late capitalist *"Dasein."*[28]

At the same time Baudrillard's use of the Hegelian term *negativity* (rather than *nothing*) marks his radical difference from Heidegger. In other words his work, though inflected by "the new 'impulses' which anthropology has gained from ontological problems,"[29] focuses on man rather than being. Like Foucault, Baudrillard brackets the specular realm of "empirical" needs and objects (CS: 74) that had distracted him in *The System of Objects* to "re-duce" consumption (in a phenomenological sense) to the existentials or pri-mary structures that inform it. But unlike *The Order of Things, Consumer Society* is concerned with the psychological rather than ontological aspects of these existentials. Baudrillard describes the primal scene of human being as "lack and difference" (78). In so doing, he invokes, not Heidegger, but Lacan and Sartre.[30]

This genealogy also suggests why "Bataille" (at this point) is an anachro-nism in Baudrillard's text. Bataille's Blakean program images expenditure as part of a "life-force" that seems curiously outmoded in the world of late cap-italism.[31] As Baudrillard sees it, Bataille's primitive excess has been rational-ized in the profusion of drugstores and malls that brings back the "*gift*" and the "inexhaustible and spectacular prodigality" of the "*feast*," but in the "metonymic, repetitive discourse of consumable matter" (CS: 26). Expendi-ture—including Bataille's notion of it—thus veils a fundamental absence. For Baudrillard draws on Lacan's distinction between need and desire to "re-duce" consumption to the primary structure of a nothingness that lacks be-ing. Describing it as metonymically displaced through "successive objects" (77), he inscribes *homo oeconomicus* within the general economy of an end-lessly deferred search for the being that Lacan parodies and dis-figures as the phallus. While consumption is associated with needs, needs misrecognize desire by associating it with a "*particular* object," the attainment of which gives satisfaction. Needs, however, are not signs but "symptoms," signifiers at two removes pointing to "another language" through which "something other" speaks. In this sense the "flight from one signifier to another is merely the superficial reality of a *desire*" whose insatiability "is based on lack" (77). The whole process of consumptive excess can be read through this *lack*: "the 'symbolic' transfer of a lack" through a "chain of signifiers/objects succes-sively invested as part objects" (184).

We shall return to Baudrillard's complex view of Lacan, whom the text does not name. Suffice it to say that in evoking him, Baudrillard reads Lacan's desire against the grain of the latter's structuralism. In other words, Baudrillard unforgets Lacan's sublimation of the psychological in the linguistic so as to remember the linguistic as the psychosomatic. He suggests that consumption's logic of "slippage, transference, limitless and apparently arbitrary convertibility" is a language whose structure designates another language of "*generalized hysteria*" (77). This hysteria unconceals the lived body first mentioned in *The System of Objects*, but it does so through the detour of psychoanalysis as the discourse of what Drew Leder calls the "absent body." The body returns and is repressed within a catachresis that figures its (dis)appearance. Just as, in hysterical or psychosomatic "conversion" "all the body's organs and functions become a gigantic paradigm for the symptom to work its way through, in consumption objects become a vast paradigm for another language to work through, for something other to speak" (77).

Here, the body, like the Lacanian "real," is (un)representable—both the referent of the symptom in the first clause and, when transferred by a syntactic parallelism into the world of objects, the signifier that refers to another symptom. If the body is thus doubly deferred, we nevertheless feel its insistence in the catachresis by which the system of objects becomes the very body it represses. In fact at the end of *Consumer Society* Baudrillard sums up his future project as an analysis of consumption's body set against the body's "status as object within the system of modernity." The body is an "epitome" of the "ambivalent processes" simplified by culture (184). Baudrillard hints at these processes in his exploration of a new "mal du siècle" evident in "the profound anomalies" and "'dysfunctions' of prosperity" (181). These anomalies include not only "objectless" violence (as in the Polanski murders) but also fatigue, exhaustion (174–84), or the loneliness of the long-distance runner who deliberately fails to win. Dealing with this "counter-economy" of social waste,[32] Baudrillard sees in fatigue "an *activity* . . . a concealed form of protest, which turns round against oneself and 'grows into' one's own body"(183). He sees in violence an irruption of a "lost symbolic function" quickly reabsorbed by the media into the "*phantasmic organization*" of consumption in which "desire is fulfilled and lack resolved."[33] Baudrillard, in short, attempts a psychoanalysis of the body politic aimed at reading within its language a further language through which something other speaks.

That Baudrillard is often critical of psychoanalysis should not obscure its importance to his earlier work. For one thing his concerns pertain to Freud more than Lacan, Lacan being praised as the "destroyer" of psychoanalysis.[34] Arguing for the importance of symptomatic reading and of Freud's discovery of the death drive, Baudrillard also criticizes Freud's "scientific positivity" and commitment to "rationality."[35] He attacks psychoanalysis for two reasons: its bourgeois individualism and its conformity. Psychoanalysis creates the unconscious as a way of abjecting what cannot "be exchanged socially or symbolically" (SED: 134). It then privatizes this unconscious to foreclose a social analysis that would engage man with his doubles. Thinking the drives only within the oedipal structures of the family, psychoanalysis reinscribes rather than threatens the Law of the Father (136–37). Even as it analyzes repression, we must ask what repression (and what society) produces psychoanalysis.[36]

This said, Baudrillard does not reject psychoanalysis. As with Marxism, which he is often seen as dismissing, he seeks rather to open its restricted economy to more general human concerns. Baudrillard draws on psychoanalysis for a self-reflection not concerned with "self" in the narrow sense but with the social as a responsibility to the unthought. He thus uses terms such as *desire* and *death*, but to pose existential questions that exceed and question psychoanalytic rationality. Indeed, as Derrida suggests with regard to Foucault's similar ambivalence on the subject, psychoanalysis is a "hinge" that is evoked for the doors it opens even as it is revoked for those it closes.[37]

Baudrillard's psychoanalytic phenomenology of consumption now also takes shape as a de(con)struction of "the linguistic imaginary" (SED: 213). For the first time he questions—rather than uses—structuralism. Asking about its value for the analysis of consumer society, he points to the circular relationship of the two; structural analysis *will* seem the most persuasive description of consumption given that consumption is itself organized by a form of structural linguistics. Structuralism is a managerial mode with its own "order of values and classification" in which "the ordering of signs" is "the integration of the group" (CS: 78–79). In this order even "difference," as the negativity that Saussure glimpses in the play of signs, is repositivized as the same. Differences, far from dividing, bring people together; it is the regulated play of differences within the code that unites a group, which, sharing this code, is different as a whole from other groups (92–93). Thus uncovering the work of technology within the very structure of signs, Baudrillard points to the hegemony of the sign form in late capitalism as what binds man into the technological system. He suggests that the sign is an agent of reification, its reorganization of primary processes being "one of the specific modes, and perhaps *the* specific mode, of transition from nature to culture in our era" (79). Or, as he later puts it, the "free play and circulation of signifiers," in a system that is nothing more than the signifier itself, mirrors "the logic of the exchange value system." (Post)structuralism is thus a pathology complicit with the general abstraction of signification from use and of language from the lived body.[38]

Baudrillard's critique of the political economy of the sign is familiar from his essay of that name, which ends with the clarion call: "Even signs must burn."[39] But what is important here is the presence of phenomenology in *Consumer Society* as the basis for a *de(con)struction* as well as a political economy of the sign. Signs become a "denegation of the real" (CS: 34; trans. mine) as they veil "the true sphere of signification— . . . lack and difference" (78). The political economy of the sign is thus intergenerated with an (un)concealing of this true sphere that signs mask, yet also "signify" in their "substitution" and deferral (78). In other words, Baudrillard does not stop at a post-Marxist critique of the society of the sign. He attempts a self-reflection that, in Foucault's words, extends from what "man is in his positivity to a part of himself not reflected," as critique must be, in a cogito (OT: 322, 353). This reflection or duplication is the theme of the two stories at the end of *Consumer Society*: Chamisso's *Peter Schlemihl* and *The Student of Prague*, a silent film from the 1930s. In both stories a man sells his image to the devil for wealth, thus dis-integrating himself from (his) reflection. In both cases this loss of self-consciousness or interior duplication takes its own vengeance. In the case of the Prague student it happens through a catachresis: a monstrous literalization of reflection as an external double (CS: 188–90).

As we have seen, Baudrillard's questioning of "signifier-fetishism"[40] seeks to disclose, beneath language, a "fluid" realm of desire and difference (45). But this "unconscious" is readable only as and through language (SED: 236) and only as genotext (in Kristeva's term). That Baudrillard thus works in the space between phenomenology and linguistics we have called deconstruction is evident in his focus on the term *difference*, which he uses ambivalently in both a structural and Derridean sense. Indeed, his critique of structural difference from a Derridean perspective that he never names[41] also doubles as a reading of Derrida that shows grammatology tacitly doing the work of phenomenology. Suggesting how each of us seeks the "profound idiosyncracy, the difference" that makes us "ourselves" (CS: 84; trans. mine), Baudrillard traces the absorption of difference by structure. He shows how the production of "marginal" differences, through the interpellation of subjects into different slots on a combinatory grid, is "*industrial*" rather than "*personal*" (88).

"Structural logic" thus participates in a monopolism that abolishes "*real differences*" in favor of "*differentiation*" (92, 89). It "eliminates the specific content, the (necessarily *different*) specificity of each human being, and substitutes the *differential* form" (93). As against this logic Baudrillard discloses another "difference"—not the positivist difference that makes us "ourselves" but the difference within the self that makes us "*contradictory* beings" (88). He begins from Barthes's perception that consumption "disappoints" meaning by disseminating it "through a structure of signification that is only the signifier itself." But he hears in this structure "another language" through which "something other" speaks (77). In thus opening the structural to the existential, Baudrillard evokes Derrida's accounts of deferral and difference. But he does so silently, perhaps because of Derrida's own forgetting, after *Speech and Phenomena*, of an inside that is outside structure—a "something other" figured as "the process of death at work in signs" (SP: 40).

Baudrillard's work up to 1976 is best described in his own ambivalent terms as a critique of the political economy of the sign. As political economy it develops (late) Marxism's analysis of the commodity into an analysis of the sign form, thereby replacing the notion of alienation associated with "the subject of consciousness," with reification, in which the subject is already commodified by the code. On this level Baudrillard's early work is post-Marxist in its analysis of the social effects of the sign.[42] Yet he also describes his goal as a critique of the political economy of the sign; he critiques not only the economy administered by the sign but also the political economy that analyzes the sign or the very modes of political economy and critique. For Marxism, according to Baudrillard, remains a domination of nature by man committed to "science, technique, progress, history."[43] Marx, despite his radicalism, is concerned with "the production of useful ends" in the context of "human finality" or with what Kant calls "pragmatic anthropology." Analyzing this "Western rationalism" in terms similar to those of Levinas, Derrida, and Foucault, Baudrillard's own work tries to avoid being drawn

into the "linear temporality of accumulation and unveiling" that he describes as "the phantasm of science."[44] The sign's technological organization
thus becomes the site for a reflection on human being as what Derrida calls
a "relationship with death" (SP: 54). For Baudrillard the sign excludes "all
symbolic ambivalence on behalf of a fixed and equational structure" whose
"internal contingency" semiology has progressively "banish[ed]." Signs offer
themselves as "full value: positive, rational, exchangeable." Against this "rationality," Baudrillard seeks a "beyond of semiology," which will make us responsible to "what is other than the sign," of which *we can say nothing . . .*
except that it is ambivalent."[45]

After 1970 Baudrillard's object shifts from consumption (and the disciplines of economics and sociology) to "the super-ideology of the sign . . .
[and] the new master disciplines of structural linguistics, semiology, information theory and cybernetics." The later essays in *For a Critique of the Political Economy of the Sign* (1972) are concerned with linguistics, while *The
Mirror of Production* (1973) is a polemical introduction to a "revolutionary"
as opposed to pragmatic "anthropology."[46] Concrete social analysis plays a
lesser role than in Baudrillard's first two studies. But this does not mean that
he elides the social as the possibility of praxis; rather, he makes it answerable
to the analytic of finitude. Baudrillard's revolutionary anthropology is both
transformational and reflexive, Bataillean and post-Heideggerian. To grasp
its full dimensions it is important that we read the texts written from 1970 to
1976 not separately but as a body of work that brings together semiology,
psychoanalysis, aesthetics, and anthropology with economics and sociology.
Baudrillard *practices* a version of Foucault's new curriculum described in
Chapter 6. The earlier and more concrete analyses of the sign's social functioning are thus assumed in *For a Critique of the Political Economy of the
Sign's* more abstract discussion of the sign's structure. Moreover these analyses—of consumption and its "counter-economy"—were not simply sociological, but submitted objects (and the object-form) to an existential analysis. This analysis still inflects Baudrillard's work even as he develops, through
symbolic exchange, a more "excessive" and Bataillean (SED: 158) thought of
the outside. At the same time negativity, in Kristeva's words, is not "drained
of its potential for producing breaks"[47] by being confined within the aesthetic, ontological, or linguistic spheres. Instead, Baudrillard also traces its
eruption into the social as a rootless, inexplicable violence, a "death drive"

which is "the emergence, in action, of the negativity of *desire* . . . occulted, censored by the total positivity of *need*" (CS: 177). Significantly it is Lacan whom Baudrillard here echoes in distinguishing desire from need.

As a single body of work, Baudrillard's writings in the early seventies thus create a "*total* social practice" through the (dis)integration of the disciplines. At the beginning of *The Accursed Share*, Bataille extends his economic principles to the epistemic field, arguing for a general economy of the human sciences—an antithesis to idealist anthropology's segregation of the faculties in Kant's *Conflict of the Faculties*. In his own version of this argument at the end of *The Mirror of Production*, Baudrillard attacks "the parcellization of . . . fields of knowledge" as the means that ideology uses to "closet" more profound "contradictions within the economic realm." What Bourdieu calls the "autonomization" of fields as "partial totalities . . . closed off from everything else by a perfect and fragmented knowledge"—an idea Baudrillard evokes—thus forecloses larger concerns, such as the relation of human beings to the body and death. Baudrillard's focus in *The Mirror of Production* is the institution of the economic as a "detached field that then becomes the vector of a total reorganization of social life." For our purposes, however, his contribution also lies in his analysis of the autonomization of the signifier. Baudrillard, in other words, makes explicit the desire more mutedly present in the early work of Foucault and Derrida: to rethink knowledge outside discourse, and against science's bracketing of existence, through a language inscribed with "the totality of life and social relations."[48]

Revolutionary Anthropology: One Way of Reading Symbolic Exchange and Death

Symbolic Exchange and Death (1976) is a threshold in Baudrillard's corpus. Hereafter he will indeed insist on the "end" of production, history, and all referential models of analysis. In one sense, then, *Symbolic Exchange and Death* can be read with the later texts as the first in a line of "fatal strategies" that move between revolutionary desperation and total cynicism. These strategies, from death and the anagram to irony and seduction, should not be taken literally. They are "imaginary solutions . . . science fiction[s] of the system's reversal against itself at the extreme limit of simulation" (SED: 4–5).

Anticipating the next turn in his work, Baudrillard admits the obsoleteness not only of Marx and Frankfurt school critical theory but also of his own previous work (55, 7), which he sees as an analysis of third-order simulacra still emotionally in the second (57).[49] This analysis of the sign-form had been postmodern in its object but not its method. Still assuming a "Reason of the sign and a Reason of production" (57), it had sought a reasoned deconstruction of rationality quite different from the later Baudrillard's "unreasonable," performative, and digital style. On the other hand, as Baudrillard also says, classical and political economy are not dead but lead a phantom existence (8). In this sense *Symbolic Exchange and Death* is a culmination of the earlier work, elaborating, in the guise of renunciation, a previous methodology and hope. Briefly put, this pivotal text has yet to replace argument and analysis by tactics and "strategies," and consecutive reasoning by the "cool" modular style of later texts. Even as he asks whether it is any longer a matter of "political economy" (7), Baudrillard seems to construct a "general" disciplinary economy that opens the economic to the social, the aesthetic, and now also the anthropological. Or, put differently, one could still see the text in terms of the radical self-reflexive analysis that Baudrillard calls "revolutionary [rather than pragmatic] anthropology."

Symbolic Exchange and Death consists of an array of chapters on the economic, the body, anthropology, and the aesthetic. These chapters are premised on the end of the social. Yet by unfolding as histories from which simulation emerges as a recent development or forgetting of earlier social modes, they also question the inevitability of this premise. History can be read forward into sameness so that the past is only the beginning of the end, but it can also be reversed into the possibility of the difference that was. We see the first tendency in chapter 2, which traces the simulacrum back to the Renaissance counterfeit as a self-fashioning still committed to "caste" and "distinction" rather than to a leveling play of signifiers (50, 55). In this chapter, which also deals with Jesuit "technocracy" and "universal semiotics" (52–53), the past is already the future—the scene of "first-order" simulacra. But we see the second tendency in the fifth chapter's de(con)struction of political economy by death. Indeed, the text changes direction halfway through, escalating from renunciation to denunciation, but also unconcealing what is before, beneath, or other than the positivity of Western man (125–26).

The beginning of this turn occurs in the chapter on fashion. Fashion is not simply one sphere of investigation but the metacode of the commodity. Moreover, as the commodity is ubiquitous, so too is fashion as the law of its functioning; fashion "*haunts* the model disciplines of "politics, morals, economics, science," all of which have their fashions (91, 87). To "radicalise the analysis of fashion" (90) would thus be to rethink the very form of the commodity and of the commodity as the form of knowledge. As metacode, fashion seems to transgress the code of structure because there is no longer "any determinacy" to its signs, which are "free to commute and permutate without limit" (87). Whereas under the commodity "time is accumulated like money," in fashion it is "exhausted and discontinued" in "festival[s]" of senseless "squandering" (88, 90). Fashion is "the incessant abolition of forms," an "immorality" that reminds us of Mandeville's claim that a society is "revolutionized through its vices" (88, 98). In the end Baudrillard accepts the hegemony of the economic, as he compares fashion's "flotation of signs" to the last stage of capital—that of pure speculation in currencies—and concludes that its seduction is after all "the enchantment of the commodity" (92, 95). In the end, then, "the desire for death is itself recycled" as fashion into the simulacrum of transgression (88). But even as he makes this renunciation, Baudrillard also experiments with radicalizing fashion through a general economy of the disciplines. Working against Barthes's autonomization of the linguistic, he opens up fashion by thinking about it through anthropology and aesthetics (90), not just semiology and economics.

This general economy is at the center of chapter 5's interrogation of political economy through "death," as this term functions in poetics, anthropology, psychoanalysis, and (implicitly) philosophy. By political economy, Baudrillard means the entire ideological apparatus of a culture focused on "the Idea of Man" and of "life as positivity" (125, 147). Death for its part defines a field of investigation, namely, the forms through which we abject what we cannot economize. As in *Consumer Society*, Baudrillard thus develops a phenomenology of social malaise through an existential analysis of social practices. These include concepts such as immortality; institutions such as funerals, cemeteries, and hospitals; and ways of treating the sick and old. In these practices, because life has been drained of its ambivalence, life and death are no longer symbolically exchanged. All these practices are subtended by the opposition between "life as accumulation" and "death as due payment" (147), thus instituting the primal separation of life and death as the general structure underlying more specific forms of "alienation" and "abstraction" (130). The hospital provides one example, contrasted with the exchanging of disease in primitive societies where disease is "a mark of election . . . [a] social value" (193n): "As regards recognising the madness of disease as difference, as meaning, a wealth of meaning, as material *from which to restructure an exchange*, without trying in any way to 'return the sick to their normal lives', this presupposes the total elimination of medicine and the hospital, the entire system of enclosing the body in its 'functional' truth" (184)

As the echoes of Canguilhem and Foucault suggest, *Symbolic Exchange and Death* is also a critique of rationality and science—both terms it uses frequently. In other words its analysis of specific practices is accompanied by a questioning of separate disciplinary spheres, each with its specialized discourse. If the model for the first project is *Madness and Civilisation*, which used the example of madness to reflect on "modernity" (SED: 126), the model for the second is Foucault's metatheory of the disciplines in *The Order of Things*. Baudrillard, however, is more utopian than his precursor. He does not simply question discourse from the perspective of a language described as symbolic exchange. He suggests that the abstraction of the disciplines into "sovereign science[s]" is what protects the "hegemony of the code" (153). In this sense his analytic of rationality is an organicism that tries to re-vision human being beyond the dissociation of faculties and to construct a phenomenological cultural studies outside pragmatic anthropology.

To his criticisms of economics and linguistics (which he takes up again in chapter 6), Baudrillard now adds psychoanalysis. But one can argue that he rejects psychoanalysis on very specific grounds, namely, that it autonomizes the "psychic" and protects, by default, the ego and law (153, 158). Psychoanalysis has become a closed discipline recirculating its own jargon. Once there was a "*work* of the unconscious" determined by "its object"; now the unconscious is determined by "*psychoanalysis itself*" (91). Psychoanalysis is now a code, a part of political economy. It reconfirms the law as the "triad of the family . . . crowned by the fourth purely 'symbolic' term, the phallus," so that the (Lacanian) symbolic is now the only access to "desire" (136). Since Lacan too is now on the same side of the bar as Freud, Baudrillard's rejection of the term *desire* is consistent with his promotion of it in *Consumer Society*.

For *desire* no longer has its previous meaning but is wholly within discourse. It is no longer a phenomenological category, but simply a "negative phantasm of the rational order," codified by "the reigning prohibition" (137).

Yet, despite these criticisms, Baudrillard's analysis of the foreclosure of death by the contemporary *habitus* is profoundly "psychological." Each of the forms by which man constructs himself in his positivity is "haunted" by its "other" as "*by its own death*" (133). Death in this sense is the unconscious. But Baudrillard will not use the term *unconscious* because of its association with the "individual . . . domain" (158). Instead he chooses *death* because it connotes, after Blanchot and Lévinas, something ungraspable by the cogito as "experience" or "knowledge" and thus something unthought within rationality.[50] Up to a point, then, we can see the last hundred pages of *Symbolic Exchange* as a deconstruction of political economy accompanied by a reconfiguration of psychoanalysis and linguistics. A deconstruction in Derrida's sense has to do with systems, with "the closure and opening of the system," not to "bring (it) down" but to disclose "other possibilities of arrangement."[51] Baudrillard, we could say, wants to rethink psychoanalysis within a larger economy so as to make it once again a thought of the outside.

At the center of this project is psychoanalysis's "strangest offspring," the death drive. Death cannot be caught "in the mirror of psychoanalysis" (SED: 154); it cannot be reflected in a cogito. Recovering its radicality by reading death beyond Freud's "scientific positivity," Baudrillard tries to think psychoanalysis outside "western reason" and economics (152–53) by opening it to philosophy and anthropology. This rethinking, if sustained, would effect the crossing of psychoanalysis and ethnology sketched by Foucault in *The Order of Things*. Arguably Baudrillard dismisses psychoanalysis as it now exists only because it has been rationalized into an economic rather than symbolic process (134–35). But at the same time psychological reflection is his own means of access to this lost process. Nor is it just that such reflection is his way of exchanging intellectually with death; psychoanalysis itself is the last vestige of symbolic process. Thus even as Baudrillard criticizes modern society's hospitals and cemeteries for removing the dead from symbolic circulation, he grants a certain value to the unconscious as the abjected site of the "inevitable exchange" with death (126, 134). As we get rid of the dead physically we pay with an "*equivalent death*," which is the concept of death (127). Insofar as we still "exchange with the dead" through "our anxiety about death" and through the unconscious (134), we are still symbolic beings. And, insofar as he discloses this anxiety, Baudrillard, we could argue, simply seeks to restore to psychoanalysis a more social, yet also existential, dimension. Indeed, as Derrida says of Foucault, Baudrillard speaks "of" a psychoanalysis that he rejects. But psychoanalysis, in a more fundamental sense, is also "that out of which he speaks."[52]

Savage Thought or the Cannibalizing of Psychoanalysis and Death

But this is not the whole story. For if *Symbolic Exchange and Death* increasingly transgresses its cynicism in a return to revolutionary anthropology, this anthropology is also changing in ways produced by the new cynicism. Baudrillard's hostility to psychoanalysis is often excessive, crossing over from deconstruction to denial. Symptomatic of this shift is the fact that he begins to privilege the restricted discipline of anthropology, but without submitting it to deconstruction. His idealization of cruelty (in a Lévi-Straussian and Artaudian sense), of the "'oral drive,'" and of "a society that eats its dead" (137–38), manifests—to evoke Derrida—a disturbingly "carnivorous virility." This negation of psychology by anthropology reflects a turn to the outside, an abjection of interiority that mourns self-consciousness. The turn follows a trend already noted as the aftermath of 1968—a toughening of theory through the search for the hard edge, the unsentimental surface.

The "virile figure," as Derrida calls it, is always linked to the violence of a sacrificial structure.[53] But here, as in *Seduction*, Baudrillard's phallogocentrism is also complicated by what Hertz calls a "pathos of uncertain agency." Discussing de Man, Hertz describes the resurfacing of "a drama of subjectivity" within a discourse that questions "its privilege as an interpretive category." He focuses on scenes of violence that harbor a certain pathos, wherein the theorist is undecidably victim and perpetrator of this violence. Violence—often figured as terrorism or misogyny—has been a part of theory's uncertain relationship to antihumanism from Blanchot and Sartre onward. Baudrillard likewise pays his dues to antihumanism when he sacrifices psychoanalysis to the "reigning prohibition" against conscience and consciousness. But as with the theoretical murders that disfigure de Man's corpus, we can ask whether Baudrillard is the "killer, [or] perhaps only the discoverer of the corpse."[54] Similarly we can ask whether his toughening of theory is not also a self-sacrifice, the first step in a painful extermination of his own past escalated after 1976 through the replacement of critical by fatal theory.

We can trace Baudrillard's self-hardening in the linked areas of his title: symbolic exchange and death. Symbolic exchange has a strange function in his corpus; it serves as an exit from political economy not always consistently elaborated. Always present as a principle of hope, it becomes a paleonym that contains and elides shifts in Baudrillard's thinking. The first full development of the concept is in "The Ideological Genesis of Needs" (1969), which uses the example of the ring. While rings can be interchangeable commodities within the sign system, they can also be recontextualized as symbols. Thus the wedding ring is a gift, a unique object, whose value is "inseparable from the concrete relation in which it is exchanged." As symbol, it cannot be dissociated "from the subjects" using it and disappears as signifier "in the relation" it establishes."[55]

At this early point symbolic exchange is a multidiscursive concept. Though evoking Mauss, Baudrillard's social semiotics also draws on aesthetic theories that associate sign or allegory with rationalization and symbol with full presence. If his theory of the symbol is Benjaminian (and romantic),[56] his concept of exchange is phenomenological—based on a lived relation with an object founded on cathexis and psychic investment. Indeed, Baudrillard's concept recalls Merleau-Ponty's "The Experience of Others" (1951–52), which also uses Mauss to rethink the relation between language and experience in ways that stress the Eurocentrism of the linguistic paradigm. Merleau-Ponty writes: "For societies rich in myth, the relationship between the experienced and the signified is so close that they are nearly identical." These societies are not primitive or natural in the sense of being outside language—a point Baudrillard also makes in using the term *symbolic*. They are fully within language, but not the code. What Baudrillard describes as symbolic exchange, Merleau-Ponty describes as ritual: "The ritual is not a signal-language, which lies outside what it signifies, but rather an emblematic language in which signifier and signified cannot be isolated from each other."[57] Baudrillard similarly writes: "As distinct from language, whose material can be disassociated from the subjects speaking it, the material of symbolic exchange, the objects given, are not autonomous, hence not codifiable as signs."[58]

Symbolic exchange fleetingly resurfaces in *Consumer Society* in those acts of wasted violence that assume "a lost symbolic function" before being made over into consumable signs by the media (CS: 178). Acts are initially not a language that can be dissociated from its performance. Rather, as with Merleau-Ponty's concept of dramatic expression, they originate in the body and not as "signs whose signification is given apart from them."[59] In this version, symbolic exchange is a darker but still multidiscursive concept. Acts possess a phenomenological immediacy that, however, indicates the *absent*—not the lived—body. For the term *symbolic* has now passed through Lacan, marking the body's distance from its narrativization in the political unconscious. Acts of violence are vestiges of the antieconomy of ritual, but (dis)figured by the pathology of the social that requires psychoanalysis as a supplement to anthropology.

In *Consumer Society* acts of violence are still part of a negative phenomenology concerned with a self-reflection on the social and what it excludes. The "exchange" is not *in* the acts themselves, which would then become "autonomous,"[60] but in our engagement with them, which is at once passionate and hermeneutic. In *Symbolic Exchange and Death*, however, Baudrillard theorizes symbolic exchange from two symptomatically discrepant directions. In the chapter on poetics it is approached in the abstract through a chaos theory of the anagram as the antiscience of Saussurean linguistics. The anagram has fascinated theorists from Foucault to de Man. As explained by de Man, it is the disruption of the signified through the "coded dispersal (or dissemination) of an underlying word or proper name throughout the [text]" (RT: 36).[61] For de Man this "dismemberment" is "the uncontrollable power of the letter as inscription," a certain randomness of language as the inhuman (37). But for Baudrillard the encounter between "the vowel and its counter-vowel" or between any signifier and its "anagrammatic double" is the release of the "fabulous energy" of symbolic exchange (SED: 236). The poetic as expenditure is thus fundamentally opposed to the linguistic as economic. Baudrillard evokes Foucault when he critiques linguistics for wanting to get rid of the "utopia of language and to bring it back to the topic of discourse" (205). But his real allies are Bataille and Kristeva.

Linguistics is committed to "science as a process of accumulation," whereas the true "analytic operation eliminates its object" in a radical "deconstruction" (204, 195). Baudrillard calls this process "extermination:" the "dispersion" of the name that becomes "the *extermination of the term*" (199–200).

As developed in Baudrillard's sixth chapter, symbolic exchange is an affirmative destruction that remains safely symbolic by being limited to a revolution in poetic language. On the other hand, in chapter 5 Baudrillard offers several instances of symbolic exchange drawn not from poetics but from anthropology. These include primitive initiation rites and the circulation of women, all relentlessly biologized as acts of eating (131–34). If eating well is the dominant figure in this series, the examples climax catachrestically in a discussion of actual cannibalism. Cannibalism, we are told, is profoundly social. The eating of the dead is neither due to hunger nor contempt but "to pay homage to them. . . . This devouring is a social act, a *symbolic* act, that aims to maintain a tissue of bonds with the dead man or the enemy they devour" (138).

Baudrillard's literalization of eating bears a strange relation to the "symbolic"—a term he purportedly uses against a "naturalism" that allows "desire" to "roam freely" outside language (137). Through the symbolic Baudrillard maintains his responsibility to Lacan, but he engages in a duel, not dialogue, with him. As duellist, Baudrillard does not attend to what Lacan is saying but rather fights him for the signifier, the word *symbolic*. Digesting his master by making this word his own, Baudrillard also lays claim to the rigor of the linguistic turn. Yet his neoprimitivism essentializes, even if it does not naturalize, the symbolic. For one thing, symbolic exchange is not negatively *indicated* through a violence that (dis)figures it; it is given full *expression* through eating. As important, these acts of eating are "autonomous" and thus positive; they are signs, not symbols in the sense earlier defined in *For a Critique of the Political Economy of the Sign*.[62] They are autonomous because they contain a fully codifiable meaning that Baudrillard decodes for us. But they are also autonomous because exchange occurs within the act itself and not beyond it—as the exchange between eater and eaten and not as the exchange between the act and us. Eating well is the self-sufficing activity of an anthropology not exposed to its finitude; it has swallowed up its own death. Put differently, the incorporation and biologization of exchange seals it off from any questioning exchange or self-reflection. For how can we exchange with cannibalisman otherness figured so flagrantly other and so entirely in-itself?

This same repositivizing of the other as an exteriority sealed against interiority can be traced in Baudrillard's duel with the term *death*. As we have seen death is both the subject of the fifth chapter and its modus operandi. In the first sense death is the unthought. It cannot be caught and economized in social forms so as then to be theorized and reflected in a disciplinary mirror. In the second sense death is what deconstructs rationality and economy; the death drive is "the system's double, its doubling into a radical counter-finality."[63] Nevertheless, Baudrillard does try to capture death through a duel between psychoanalysis and anthropology. In this process death is de-ontologized; it is primitivized and drained of its ambivalence. Death, rather than being the cogito's ungraspable double, figures Baudrillard's own mastery over his epistemic others. This mastery, in turn, has two sources. First, Baudrillard objectifies death as "that of which he speaks" rather than that "out of which" he speaks, to evoke Derrida on Foucault.[64] Second, he encloses death within anthropology—a discipline newly masculinized and virilized by being associated not with the gift but with sacrifice and sovereignty.

We can trace Baudrillard's reinvention of death through the figure he once used to connect it to a certain reflexivity, namely, the double. In his first analysis of *The Student of Prague* the linked figures of death, the mirror, and the double inscribed psychoanalysis as the space out of which Baudrillard spoke in summoning consumer society to self-reflection. Indeed, the connection is explicit in his reference to Freudian "repression" (CS: 190). In *Symbolic Exchange and Death*, however, Baudrillard brings back the Prague student to transfer the double from psychoanalysis to anthropology. He repudiates his earlier analysis point by point. Baudrillard evokes Foucault to castigate the inside-outside structure of the psychological double. The internalization of the shadow as conscience and consciousness (*conscience*) and its subsequent exteriorization as the "haunting" or "avenging" double that appears when "the moral and psychological principle" is ignored are, he insists, part of the subject's confinement by modernity. They resemble "the confinement of the mad at the end of the seventeenth century" (SED: 141–42). This internalization under the sign of "psychology," accompanied by a vocabulary of "alienation" and "consciousness" (141), is itself the product of alienation.

As against the psychological and "separated" double of the unhappy consciousness (142), Baudrillard celebrates the external double of anthropology. Thus primitive man has a "non-alienated duel-relation with his double" that, as "tutelary or hostile shadow," is a *"partner"* with whom he "converse[s]" (141). In promoting the external double, Baudrillard cleverly reverses terms so as to counterfeit as a deconstruction of modernity what is really a profound neoprimitivism. He condemns "consciousness" (despite the split between self and double) for being a principle of "unification," and he praises the external double in the name of a certain dissemination: a "proliferating exchange with spirits and doubles" (141). Yet it is clear that his own anthropology figures a nostalgia for a unified, nonalienated, organic world. Similarly, he repudiates psychology on the basis of the body as materiality: "By a final ruse of spirituality, this internalisation also *psychologises* doubles" (142). He confuses consciousness and spirit, thus refiguring a principle of dividedness as one of unification so as to promote his own neoprimitivist idealism as what Bataille calls "base materialism."

Baudrillard's duel with death puts an end to any kind of inwardness; he places death either outside the self as primitive double or inside as material digested. Inwardness as self-difference, as a reflection that raises the "ontological question," is de Man's post-Sartrean term for an interiority that is not self-identity.[65] As suggested, Baudrillard's resistance to inwardness follows the path of a turn away from psychoanalysis. It is worth recalling here Derrida's "'To Do Justice to Freud'" (1991), which revisits his own silence about psychoanalysis in "Cogito and the History of Madness" (1963). Drawing Foucault into the loop of this silence, Derrida asks whether Foucault's work could have happened "without psychoanalysis." He locates Foucault's secret affinity with psychoanalysis in its link to death as "the power of the negative." The "tragic Freud" who breaks with evolutionist psychology is, Derrida says, one who "deserves hospitality" in the line of Nietzsche "because he is foreign to the space of the hospital."[66] It is on this basis that Foucault in *The Order of Things* recognizes psychoanalysis as a "counter-science" that points to what exceeds "consciousness and representation," thus opening the human sciences to "originary finitude." Indeed, Derrida's characterization of psychoanalysis "as an analytic of finitude"[67] returns to the opening glimpsed by Merleau-Ponty when he spoke of the missed encounter between psychoanalysis and phenomenology, in effect recognizing phenomenology as a hinge between philosophy and psychoanalysis.

Such psychoanalysis breaks with positivism to become a form of "transcendental philosophy," as Foucault uses this term (OT: 323). Speaking of Lacan, Slavoj Žižek further defines "transcendental philosophy" as a deconstruction that "demonstrate(s) that the 'condition of impossibility' of a philosophical system" is actually its "condition of possibility."[68] In other words, transcendental philosophy (to recall Derrida's discussion of Levinas) deconstructs the *en-soi* not to end in a "purely heterological thought" of "*pure* difference" (WD: 151) but to re-turn death into "the possibility of the sign" (SP: 54). As the most radical exploration of death, psychoanalysis had been for Baudrillard the hinge of this negativity. But after *Symbolic Exchange and Death* he finds a negativity linked to inwardness too naive or too painful. Instead he pursues his own thought of the outside by submerging consciousness in the absolute exteriority of the object. "Fatal" theory, as Baudrillard describes his later work, assumes that the "object is more cunning, cynical, talented than the subject" (FS: 181). Whereas the subject lacks being, the object is "always already a *fait accompli*. . . . without finitude and without desire" (EC: 88). As Robbe-Grillet had also recognized, the object is "the emergence of a necessity other than the human" (EC: 89). The fatal subject must therefore mimic the object by becoming inhuman, whether through seduction, terrorism, or eating the dead.[69] These strategies bypass language for "something faster . . . challenge, the duel:" "Communication is too slow . . . working through contact and speech. Looking is much faster, it is the medium of the media" (FS: 8) Or one can short-circuit the system by going slower, not faster, into a "silence insoluble by dialogue" (8)—as in the entropic inertia of the silent majorities. Either way, fatal theory denies what Derrida calls the necessity of "speech" and "concept" as well as "glance" (WD: 147, 151). In this respect, it is the reversed counterpart of an earlier heterology, except that for Levinas's pure nonviolence[70] Baudrillard substitutes pure violence, "theoretical violence . . . speculation to death" (SED: 5).

CHAPTER NINE

The Double Spiral: Baudrillard's (Re)Turns

Baudrillard's Kehre

Baudrillard's abjection of psychoanalysis continues in both *Fatal Strategies* (137–44) and *Seduction* (57–59) and is part of a turn found in the careers of other theorists. A career is, however, different from a life, and it is the inwardness of the life as much as the *persona* of the career that concerns us here. From this perspective the dejection of psychoanalysis is part of a self-sacrificial structure. For after *Symbolic Exchange and Death*, Baudrillard forgets everything that he values; he forgets Foucault, he rejects desire for seduction, and he denies death. His books ritualistically perform the end, whether of history, man, or theory. Indeed, they enter the field as performances, not as theory with a content. For as Poster argues, the new "mode of information" is not meant for reading. And it is to this "nonrepresentational . . . communications mode"[1] that Baudrillard responds when he insists that to enter "into a relation of critical negativity with the real" is no longer "theory's end." Theory itself is at an end; instead of "acting as a mode of production" it must act "as a mode of disappearance" (EC: 97). It cannot simply "analyse" but must be "an event in the universe it describes." It must (dis)appear in the "enigma" of its own discourse (99) to achieve a subversion "more aleatory than the system itself" (SED: 4).

I shall come back to the psychotropology of this disappearing theory and its overdetermined relations to Baudrillard's past. But for the present let us consider his own figure for his turn. In *L'Autre par lui-meme*, the overview written for his *habilitation* at the Sorbonne (1987), Baudrillard describes his work as a "double spiral" involving two "antagonistic" paradigms: "On the one hand: political economy, production, the code, the system, simulation. On the other hand: potlatch, expenditure, sacrifice, death . . . seduction" (EC: 79).The double spiral condenses a self-returning with radical change. On the one hand, Baudrillard—against those who like Norris or Kellner see him abandoning Marxism for postmodernism[2]—insists that a single thematic underwrites all his works. This is the dialectic of matter and antimatter, code and symbol, between which he seeks a symbolic, catalytic exchange; indeed, the spiral is a well-known figure for dialectic. On the other hand, the persistence of this thematic now marks the impossibility of a project whose return can only be ended by the end, or self-destruction, of theory. For the two paradigms have "undergone considerable inflection:"

> The simulacra have passed from the second to the third, from the dialectic of alienation to the giddiness of transparency. At the same time, after *L'Échange Symbolique* and with *De la Séduction* the dream of a transgression . . . and the nostalgia for a symbolic order of any kind, born out of the deep of primitive societies, or of our historical alienation, have been lost. With *Séduction* there is . . . no more recovered object, no more original desire. (EC: 79–80)

With this escalation into the hyperreal, the spiral has been involuted into a system that is "Moebian and circular," a "möbius-spiraling negativity," the spiral as the vertigo of distinct poles. There is no exit from this system, no duel/dual or dialectical resolution, only "*exacerbation*" and "catastrophic resolution."[3]

A Phenomenology of Poststructuralism

We can trace Baudrillard's turn on two levels, social and semiotic, through his original project of providing a phenomenology of the contemporary involving linked analyses of the object- and sign-forms. Baudrillard himself foregrounds the first level when he notes the shift in late capitalism from "alienation" to "reification": "It is no longer the desire of the subject, but the destiny of the object, which is at the centre of the world" (EC: 80). This shift is reflected in his own move from a second-order analysis of the economy to a third-order focus on mediatization. But more explicitly than that of other theorists discussed here, Baudrillard's work has also been a political economy and a phenomenology of *theory*. And in theory, too, he raises the stakes by effecting yet another turn.

As we have seen, Baudrillard's analysis of the régime of objects evolves into a critique of structuralism and the linguistic turn. By the late seventies structuralism is passé. That Baudrillard does not discuss poststructuralism can be explained by his growing sense of the inefficacy of analysis. Nevertheless, poststructuralism generates the double spiral in the allegory of theory that shadows his account of the escalation of commodification into simulation. Insofar as the sign was still associated with "Reason" (SED: 57), structuralism in *Consumer Society* was a form of rationality that allowed for the counterscience of deconstruction. But poststructuralism is the hegemony of the sign in a field *"unhinged by simulation,"* a madness of codes in which deconstruction is absorbed by an *ir*rationalism of signs. Madness, in short, no longer stands outside reason, even as capital is no longer a form of rationality. Rather, capital is itself a "delirium," a "totally generalized exchange" that is the "fantastic spectacle of its decomposition."[4]

As a way of being in the world that turns the spiral into a vortex, poststructuralism has a cryptic presence in the later texts. Picking up on chapter 2 of *Symbolic Exchange and Death*, "The Precession of Simulacra" in *Simulacra and Simulation* (1981) is a sustained analysis of simulation as a vast general economy in which expenditure—Bataille's *dépense*—is itself a system. As before, Baudrillard analyzes the code as the transition "from signs which dissimulate something" to ones that "dissimulate that there is nothing." But a subtle change inflects his descriptions of the code. Whereas structuralism was the simulacrum of an order, the system—now the media, not the economy—has become disordered, viral. Thus Baudrillard speaks of a general reversibility in which there is no center—no "active or passive," a "floating causality where positivity and negativity engender and overlap with" each other. This decentering is "the impossibility of a determined discursive position." The system and its alternative have become "two sides of a curved mirror . . . circularized, reversibilized from the right to the left" in a spiraling of "surfaces" that exchanges "the positions of the dominator and the dominated . . . in an endless reversion."[5] Elsewhere Baudrillard speaks of a "decentering" and "dissemination" at the heart of simulation, of digital culture as a world of "differences," and of "a viral loss of determinacy."[6] While Baudrillard does initially describe structuralism in terms of "indeterminacy" and the "commutability of dialectically opposed terms" (SED: 8), this merely reflects the earlier French tendency to conflate poststructuralism with structuralism. But Baudrillard will later recognize that structuralism was dual not digital. Indeed, he will define the generalized difference that is the in-difference of opposites as the end of structuralism and of the "dual, polar structures" around which it constructed language.[7]

This end of structure in a "*generalized hysteria*" of signs (CS: 77) is, Baudrillard suggests, the unseen consequence of the theories of Deleuze and Lyotard. As for Foucault, he must be forgotten because the panopticon still presumes an objective space and an absolute gaze. Yet Foucault's description of power is itself the end of this rationality, for when Baudrillard speaks of a "circularization of power" that makes it "unlocatable" it is Foucault he evokes.[8] On the one hand, then, Foucault differs from Deleuze in being guilty of nostalgia rather than complicity; though he "pulverize[s]" power he does not question its "*reality principle*" and is committed, against the facts, to "a possible coherence of politics and discourse." On the other hand, there is little difference between the two theorists, both of whom reveal "a strange complicity with cybernetics," a strange submission in which power for Foucault and desire for Deleuze are alike "molecular version(s) of the law." Interestingly for our purposes, Baudrillard locates Foucault's betrayal in the turning that occurs between *Madness and Civilization* and *Discipline and Punish*.[9] At this point madness is replaced by power, which is itself madness and thus a cooptation by the system of what had once been madness's absolute exteriority.

If Foucault thus neutralizes the Bataillean force of "madness," he and Deleuze form an odd couple whose very pairing marks the reversibility of left and right in theory as much as politics. It might seem that Foucaultian power is based on "interdiction" and Deleuzian desire on the "positive dissemination of flows and intensities." But "*in Foucault power takes the place of desire*" and has the same structure—a *metamorphic* structure quite distinct from the *metaphoric* structure of Lacan's desire. This new structure is Foucault's desire to which he is stubbornly attached. He is fascinated, indeed constituted, as a "fractal" subject through identification with a dissemination that metastatizes as power. "Dissemination" in turn is pure "immanence," pure "positivity," "purged of all negativity . . . a rhizome, a contiguity diffracted ad infinitum."[10]

But lest we see in Baudrillard's analysis of poststructuralism his own hysterical (if not stubborn) attachment, it is worth noting that this analysis is still anchored in "negativity" as a way of questioning the linked terms *transparency, positivity,* and *immanence.* This triad characterizes poststructuralism's containment of *différance* in metamorphosis, as distinct from a metaphor linked to transcendence and negativity. Metaphor, Baudrillard suggests, is the "possibility of language, of communicating meaning."[11] This language, in turn, is traversed by negativity in that the sign as metaphor points to a "real" that is elsewhere or "transcendent" (in the Sartrean rather than Husserlian sense of this term). To put it differently, metaphor is "still a figure of exile: the soul's presence in relation to the body, desire in relation to its object, meaning in relation to language." Metamorphosis, however, "abolishes" metaphor as the separation that founds language (EC: 50).[12] Metamorphosis is "a process without any subject, any death . . . in which only the rules of the game of forms are involved." Because there is nothing outside this process—no difference of subject and discourse, or meaning and language—there is no separation or "transcendence" (51). Man is wholly "*immanent in [his] signs,*" which is to say that there is "no longer any contradiction within being" or any "ontological" problematic. There is no reflection (CS: 191) that would make language the activity of a *pour-soi* different from itself. Instead, there is the game of forms, self-sufficient and self-satisfied—"meaning does not slip from one form to the other, it is the forms which slip directly from one to the other" (EC: 46).

Because of this absence of reference, Baudrillard can also describe metamorphosis as pure positivity, without distance or negativity. Metamorphosis is a strange positivity in that its structure is immensely complex and endlessly self-deferring. But its "difference" is purely formal and without inwardness; in metamorphosis the "forms play with one another, exchanging one another without passing through the psychological imaginary of a subject" (48). While metamorphosis is proliferation and multiplication, it is therefore also narcissistically closed—a "body . . . given over to the pure promiscuity of its relationship to itself—the same promiscuity that characterizes networks and integrated circuits." This cyborg body now only "*plays at difference*"[13] through a "ludic ramification of the person into . . . shifting differences" that never form an image and never impose on us the necessity of reflection (CS: 193). Indeed, metamorphic difference is a form of identity, an "internal, infinite, differentiating of the same." For this reason it effects a complete transparency and visibility of depth as surface. Metamorphic structures such as the rhizome only simulate complexity. In fact they neutralize difference in a ramified surface extension that is fully visible—"the same immanence, the same positivity, and the same machinery going every which way."[14]

More recently Baudrillard has linked the "maleficent ecology" of this "metonymic eternity" to the "technical immortality" of a society that will never end because it has never "passed through death."[15] In elaborating this endlessness of the technological, "dissemination," and the "interactive" as forms of "self-identity," he also harks back to an earlier concept of *différance* as negativity: "the mass of floating signifier is what prevents language from calling on all its resources, which in turn preserves human beings from expressing everything. . . . Yet this is precisely the aim today with computer technology . . . mobilizing all the neurons, all possible senses, and simultaneously reducing all margins, all the interstitial spaces."[16]

Baudrillard's analysis of metamorphosis continues his critique of structuralism into a psychoanalysis of poststructuralism and its viral forms of textuality, dissemination, power, and the rhizome. In this context it is worth mentioning his earlier exploration of the differing sub-versions of structuralism. In *Symbolic Exchange and Death* Baudrillard discusses the *Tel Quel* group and in effect distinguishes poststructuralism from deconstruction. Focusing on Kristeva, he delineates two tendencies in her work. On the one hand, she recontains "ambivalence" within a "theory of intertextuality" as the "plurality of codes." In this sense she does no more than generalize and expand structuralism, which is where she and Barthes began. Hence, alluding to Foucault's distinction of "language" from "discourse," Baudrillard complains that for Kristeva the "poetic" is indistinguishable "from discourse save by 'the infinite nature of its code'" and that "semanalysis" is simply an alibi for "the hegemony of linguistics" (SED: 220–21).

On the other hand, Kristeva also opens up a "radical negativity" (219) through the *semiotic* as "signification without representation."[17] The semiotic maintains reference, but "no longer to the concept" through the medium of *langue* or syntax; rather, reference occurs genotextually through the very movement of signifiers and phonemes. Through this movement language *indicates* "the unconscious," not by "express[ing] it, but because it is of the same structure" (SED: 213, 236). This account aptly describes Baudrillard's own method of reading when he analyzes the genotext of consumer society as a "hysterical" body (CS: 77); and it also describes deconstruction as a process oriented not to the positivity of language but to the negativity of its movement.

Baudrillard returns to deconstruction when he differentiates a fascination with the "pure movement" of forms from a concern with form as trace or with how "meaning . . . slip[s] from one form to the other" (EC: 46). This difference of *meaning* from language, analogous to "the separation" of discourse from the subject," is what facilitates the position of "analyst,"[18] and it is what Baudrillard calls by the philosophical term *transcendence*. It is also what he indicates through the psychoanalytic term *separation* in assailing the disappearance of the "psychological body" (EC: 46) into the obesity of the postmodern. The obese have not gone through "the mirror stage, which allows the child, by distinguishing limits, to open himself to . . . imagination and representation." The obese, to adapt Sartre's figure, are stuck to themselves in a pure immanence; they are "pregnant . . . with all the objects from which they have been unable to separate. Their bodies are convex or concave mirrors; they have not succeeded in producing the flat mirror that could reflect them" (FS: 30).

The concept of the obese entails the disappearance of all boundaries in the transpolitical and the transnational (FS: 25), the disappearance of any difference between the "visible and invisible" (EC: 32–33). It is likewise the in-difference of inside and outside: the "forced extraversion of all interiority . . . [and] introjection of all exteriority" that results from mediatization (FS: 26). But, as we have seen, poststructuralism plays a key role in this "transversal and universal process" by valorizing deterritorialization and depthless surfaces. Moreover, poststructuralism is isomorphically linked to late capitalism. Capitalism "was the first" to undo binary oppositions and "referential[s]" by practicing "deterritorialisation."[19] Poststructuralism's viral forms are the equivalent of the networks and circuits privileged by capital's self-fascination with structure as it mutates from a controlled system into the "immense polymorphous machine" that is "the organless body of capital-

ism" (SED: 35). Poststructuralism, in its ex-orbitant (if not apathetic) formalism, thus becomes the last twist in the spiral of reification:

> Every aspect of human beings . . . now floats free in the shape of mechani-
> cal or computer-aided replacement parts. McLuhan . . . conceives of all this
> as a positive expansion. . . . [But] the functions of man's body, so far from
> gravitating around him in *concentric* order, have become satellites ordered
> *excentrically* with respect to him. They have gone into orbit on their own
> account; consequently it is man himself . . . who is now in a position of ex-
> orbitation and ex-centricity.[20]

Baudrillard's anger at the postmodern is evident in such figures as obesity,
saturation, virality, and cancer. But he is unique among these theorists in
that this anger also silently implicates poststructuralism. While his targets
are Deleuze and the later Foucault, other shadows also haunt his texts. For
instance his assault on the displacement of metaphor by metonymy may
bear the traces of de Man's use of metonymy to "dis-illusion" metaphor.[21]
For Baudrillard poststructuralism is linked to what Poster calls "the mode of
information"; it is a way of being that is the end of death, the subject, and
history, and therefore the end of any responsible mode of human being.

Baudrillard's later work is thus intermittently a phenomenology and a political economy of poststructuralism as total positivity and in-difference. The
"indivisible" or "full body" of the informational mode is the end of the "psychological [and] sexual body" (FS: 30; EC: 47–48). As an "uninterrupted
production of positivity," it is also the end of a "critique" that requires difference and "negativity." Indeed Baudrillard's concealed bitterness towards
poststructuralism has to do with its ingestion of difference, such that difference is no longer heterological. Bataille's waste is no longer revolutionary
but is inside the system as its infinite self-proliferation.[22] There is no longer
any thought of the outside because there is no difference between inside and
outside. Instead, resistance is turned in the same direction as the system as a
self-subversion self-contained by the system.

The End of Philosophy?

Baudrillard describes himself as a philosopher more than a sociologist,[23] and
this places him (unlike Bourdieu) on the side of deconstruction. His analysis

of a postmodern "positivity" begins when he criticizes the reconstitution of the "individual not as alienated substance but as shifting difference" (CS: 193). It continues when in *Fatal Strategies* he assails the "undivided multiplication of bodies without images" (30). Indeed Baudrillard sometimes calls even his late texts "metaphysical"[24]—a description borne out by his continued references to transcendence and negativity. Thus in 1992 he still speaks of capitalism as having "cannibalized all negativity." And in 1997 he still speaks of his work as concerned with a "society losing its transcendence."[25] He likewise shelters the modern from the postmodern when he distinguishes the photographic and cinematic image from the video image; the former "still pass through the negative" whereas the "digital and synthetic" images of video are "without a negative," These images "are *virtual*, and the virtual is what puts an end to all negativity, and to all reference to the real or to events." Television, he says, shields us from "an unbearable responsibility."[26] On one level, then, Baudrillard is still on the side of the modern, still writing a phenomenology of technoculture:

> The uninterrupted production of positivity has a terrifying consequence. Whereas negativity engenders crisis and critique, hyperbolic positivity . . . engenders catastrophe, for it is incapable of distilling crisis and criticism in homeopathic doses. Any structure that hunts down, expels or exorcizes its negative elements risks a catastrophe caused by a thoroughgoing backlash, just as any organism that hunts down and eliminates its germs . . . risks metastasis and cancer . . . [and] is threatened by a voracious positivity of its own cells . . . its own—now unemployed—antibodies.[27]

This attack on positivity recalls Kristeva's critique of grammatology for a microstructuralism that "neutralizes productive negativity" by reducing the "terms" and "oppositions" that produce "breaks." Her response had been a revolution through poetic language that Baudrillard briefly took up two years later in his analysis of the Saussurian anagram (SED: 195–213). But Baudrillard is also too much of a sociologist not to feel that the mediatization of society now makes such aesthetic revolutions nostalgic. His relationship to deconstruction in his later work is thus more tortured, more oblique than that of Kristeva, which I analyze elsewhere.[28] On one level Baudrillard follows the same turn away from deconstruction as de Man and Foucault, but with an added pathos; his new postmodern style is at once mastery, mimicry, and mourning. On another level, as we shall see, Baudrillard maintains a cryptic link to deconstruction, but in a performative rather than constative way. In other words, deconstruction and phenomenology are no longer tenable positions but return as phantasms or (dis)simulations.

In a 1984 interview Baudrillard discusses the outmodedness of conventional analyses, including the rational critique instituted by Cartesian doubt, the negative dialectics of the Frankfurt school, and, we might add, the more radical analytic of "originary finitude." Insofar as all "critical" (rather than fatal) theory assumes a "separation of discourse from the subject,"[29] such theory assumes a negation—what Sartre calls a "nihilation" wherein the *pour-soi* (un)grounds itself as not being in-itself. This negation underwrites the structure of both language and philosophy as against the "realism" of sociology:[30]

> As we all know, philosophy is based on the negation of the real. There is at the heart of philosophy a primordial act regarding the negation of reality; and without that negation there is no philosophy. . . . Throughout a certain period this negation was the privilege of philosophers. But today . . . the negation of the real has penetrated inside things themselves, so much so that it is no longer the privilege of just philosophers. . . . What has happened is that the negation of reality has now been incorporated into "reality" itself. In short what we have now is a principle of non-reality based on "reality"—a principle of "hyperreality." . . . The mutation is interesting, since it implies nothing other than the end of philosophy.[31]

In the new order of things negation is itself banal. More important, it is no longer the source of philosophy because it is no longer the prerogative of the *pour-soi*. Instead, it has been sucked into things; it has become the unreality of everyday reality itself.

This is why Baudrillard, in a bitter reaction, rejects as "banal" all analyses based on a separation of discourse and subject that make the subject seem "more cunning than the object" (FS: 181). Yet the end of philosophy is not necessarily its closure, to reverse Derrida's famous distinction. For Derrida the book has not literally ended but its "historical closure" has been "outlined" (OGr: 4). For Baudrillard there is no sense of closure—hence the repetitiveness of his writing, which cannot end. Baudrillard's texts rehearse the end over and over; they repeat themselves and his past. This compulsive repetition resists ending even as it carries out a systematic extermination of earlier terms. It is at the same time an act of mourning—a return to and of what is denied. Like Foucault in *The Archaeology of Knowledge*, Baudrillard forgets the past only by remembering it again. His *Kehre*, or turning, is thus also a return that evokes the (im)possibility of history, the body, death, and the Real. Indeed, Baudrillard still draws on *topoi* he denounces as passé. To give but one example, in *The Illusion of the End* he recalls *Consumer Society*'s parable of the loss of the shadow and the capacity for reflection—this despite his repudiation of the story in *Symbolic Exchange and Death*.[32] Baudrillard also consistently employs binaries such as the fatal and the banal, subject and object, production and seduction. It seems that caught as he is in what Deleuze and Guattari call the "smooth" space of technoculture, he still craves a "striated" space structured by "biunivocal relations."[33]

Not surprisingly, then, negation does not disappear from Baudrillard's work, nor does philosophy. Significantly, what he describes in the passage on the end of philosophy is the banality of the negative, but also its *persistence* in the banal. In other words, the system, having "absorbed all negativities,"[34] now harbors an invisible negation that Baudrillard hopes might be the principle of its unworking. Baudrillard labels this negation objective irony—the irony that "arises from within things themselves," from a system "functioning against itself." Fatal theory tries to access this negativity through "provocation." It plays (along) with the system by accelerating its logic so as to "precipitate" it towards its end:

> One goes therefore in the same direction as the text—but one accelerates, one goes much faster towards the end of the text. And one plays on the logic itself to be able . . . to reach a point beyond it, so as to make the system reveal itself more clearly. . . . One produces . . . meaning *as if* it arises from the system (even if in fact the system lacks meaning) in order precisely to play that meaning against the system itself.

This process whereby "one" makes the system "work against itself"[35] recalls Derrida's account of deconstruction as using "the instruments or stones available in the house" against "the edifice" itself (M: 135). Moreover, the very focus on systems is deconstructive; Derrida (following Heidegger) insists that a deconstruction always has to do with systems and their destruction so as to disclose "other possibilities of arrangement."[36] If fatal theory is a kind of deconstruction, it is also at times an abjected psychoanalysis. For all his bitter rants against psychoanalysis, Baudrillard's excoriation of the obese for not having gone through the mirror-stage clearly draws on Lacan (FS: 30), as does his description of the object as being without an "imaginary."[37] Indeed, his "pathology of the obese" (FS: 30), of the "fetal" body as an inside that cannot be brought outside (27), is nothing if not a continuation of his much earlier project of providing a psychoanalysis of consumption and its place in the social "body" (CS: 184).

For this reason Baudrillard, denying his complicity with a postmodern apocalypticism, complains that the fatal strategy has been misread as "the catastrophic development internal to the system"; it is rather "a form of play" that thwarts "the implacable development of the system.[38] But this claim too simply restores irony to the control of a subject. Baudrillard has after all pronounced the end of philosophy. As he explains, the analytic position, based on a separation of discourse and subject, is no longer tenable as the analyst has been sucked into the vertigo he describes. The result is that one tries "to constitute the subject of discourse . . . as an object" within a theory that is event rather than statement, or provocation rather than analysis. Of course, as Baudrillard also concedes, "one always in a sense remains the subject of a discourse," which is always about the subject even when he is an object. In this sense one also cannot get rid of analysis, which remains potentially enfolded within provocation.[39] But the subject returns only within the pathos of an uncertain agency; or perhaps the subject returns not as the author but as the reader provoked to a deconstruction that cannot be consolidated as method.

In what remains, then, I shall follow Baudrillard both through his duel with the technologies that foreclose conventional forms of theory and through his attempt to seduce the postmodern into its own deconstruction. Crucial to this double movement will be the folding of the banal term *simulation* into the more fatally metaphysical term *illusion* as the trace of a phenomenology that leads back not to phenomenology but to an agonistic, performative reworking of deconstruction. As the system contains the negation it absorbs, so too fatal theory contains critical theory and deconstruction. But this is not deconstruction in any recognizable form; it is not analytic but ecstatic, pushing arguments to their limits as a provocation to thought that is always at risk.

The Obscene Object(ivity) of Fatalism

Fatal theory is Baudrillard's response to the outmodedness of philosophical analysis and at first is staged within a binary opposition of banal and fatal, past and present.[40] Its apparent rejection of deconstruction and critical theory is explained by a second image of the spiral as the "catastrophic spiral" of the Möbius strip. In the double spiral there were two opposed paradigms. But in the Möbius strip "the reversibility of surfaces" cannot be resolved; left becomes right, and the "simulation destructive of the system" folds uncontrollably into one "internal to the system."[41] "Banal" theory fails to grasp this "worsening spiral" of reification; it still assumes a subject "more cunning than the object" and still uses language and reference. But the initiative has now passed to the object, whose "metamorphoses . . . surpass the subject's understanding" (FS: 181). In a sinister reversal this object has become a quasi-subject; it "isn't a subject in the sense that, unlike the subject, it has no imaginary" but that in turn is its "power" and "sovereignty."[42]

Fatal theory thus seeks to deal with the ontological priority of the object by being-object as a way of not becoming-subject. In retrospect Baudrillard recognizes his earlier primitivism as a first way of being-object by becoming "inhuman" as either god or animal (FS: 183). But a more contemporary form of this self-reification of the *pour-soi* as *en-soi*, discussed in *In the Shadow of the Silent Majorities*, is inertia or the reabsorption of revolution into the masses: a "black hole . . . without attribute, predicate . . . [or] reference." The silent majority does not practice subversion in the banal sense. Its resistance consists in a "hyperconformist simulation of the very mechanisms of the system," which, like an unreflective mirror, "doubles" the system's logic and returns "meaning without absorbing it." As pure mass, the masses also come close to being a metaphysical principle; they are pure being, indifferent, beyond "any polarity between the one and the other." They absorb everything "without leaving a trace"; they have reached that "zero degree," in Barthes's phrase, that Baudrillard describes as "the strength of the neutral"[43] or that Sartre foresaw in the precedence of the *en-soi*. The mass is thus pure immanence without any transcendence or difference; it does not seek to go beyond itself and is wholly in-itself because it is outside any dialectic of subject and object.

This being-object, as well as its figurality, are also evident in seduction. What seduces Baudrillard in seduction is its exteriority; "it's what tears beings from the psychological sphere" to return them to the "superficial play of appearances" and "what tears you from your own desire to return you to the sovereignty of the world" (FS: 142). Seduction is less a thought from the outside than a being outside: "being doesn't give a damn about its own being" (33). But what is interesting are the contradictory metaphors used to describe this exteriority to the system of meaning—which in turn reveal the anxieties behind object(ivity) as the desire not to desire. Seduction is a fluid, aleatory form of pure metamorphosis that "breaks the referentiality of sex" (S: 21). It is a "secret circulation" that "plays by its own rules" (80–81). As a force that eludes understanding it is both threatening and captivating, which is why it is both (dis)approved as feminine and reclaimed as masculine. For seduction is also linked through the rules of its game to ritual. Ritual, in turn, is connected to "cultures of cruelty," to "defiance," to "sovereignty," and ceremony (17, 124, 81, 86, 92).

As these last figures suggest, seduction is a feminine power insensibly masculinized to contain a difference that, though subversive, has no principle. That difference has grown seductive rather than productive has to do with the way transgression has disappeared inside the system. The figure of rules grafts a "duel" order back onto this indeterminacy (155), conjuring a "soft" seduction troped as feminine into a "defiant," masculine seduction (178). Seduction's ambiguous gender and illogical figuration are thus the fault line that reveals the defensive nature of exteriority. Less important than a logic of seduction is the illogic of the desires it cathects. Rules are purely formal and thus freed from difficult thought. While the "Law" elicits interpretation and responsibility, "the Rule has no subject" and is pure form—"only [its] observance matters" (132). Rules, in short, are the formality of the law without its "responsibility" (137). They maintain order in a viral world, but without reverting to a "soft" humanism. For the rule is not the "free" play of signifiers, nor is it any kind of "freedom." Ritual signs "are *binding.* . . . Each sign is tied to others," not as in language, but as "the senseless unfolding of a ceremonial" (137), in an apathetic formalism. This "structure," in sacrificing meaning, also sheds negativity for autonomy: "The Rule is immanent to a . . . restricted system, which it describes without transcending, and within which it is immutable" (134). Interestingly, seduction is pure metamorphosis, but through its contiguity with game and ritual it confers "immutability" on the seductive subject.[44]

Sartre plays a significant role in this turn to objectivity. As Denis Hollier observes, he was the first theorist of an antihumanism embodied in such tactics as terrorism,[45] which Baudrillard also takes up. Indeed, Baudrillard invokes Sartre in theorizing seduction as a form of objectivity: "Sartre: 'In seduction I am not at all trying to expose my subjectivity to the other. To seduce is to assume entirely . . . my object-ness for the other; it is to put myself before his gaze and to be looked at by him; it is to run the risk of being seen to appropriate the other in and by my objectness. I refuse to leave the terrain of my objectness" (FS: 120; BN: 484). More than any of his contemporaries, Sartre was at once a prophet, analyst, and victim of the postmodern. For it is Sartre who first identified, and also turned away from, the fatality of objects. Likewise, it is he who placed being on the side of the *en-soi* as the inhuman, thus reconstituting the freedom of the *pour-soi* not as "critical negativity" but as radical nothingness. But Sartre also deconstructs as inhuman any attempt of the *pour-soi* to overcome its nothingness and incorporate being; his defence of inwardness is not a defense of identity because identity belongs to the object and is inhuman. Sartre's dialectic of the *en-soi* and *pour-soi* is thus his psychoanalytic of finitude—an analytic seminal for deconstruction.

Yet this analytic proves irrelevant to a world that is postmodern and posthuman, and herein lies both Sartre's pathos and his relevance to Baudrillard's trajectory. For at the end of *Being and Nothingness* the transcendence of the *pour soi* is itself swallowed by the "full and dense" being of the viscous, as a Being that is pure immanence. Indeed, in *Nausea*, when Roquentin is overwhelmed by the sheer mass of a world that is "*de trop,*" Sartre confronts this immanence of the nonhuman. This dead matter as the in-difference of the *pour-soi* and *en-soi* (BN: 773–74) is the end of philosophy, comprehensible only through the strange anti-idealism of a psychology without interiority—what Sartre calls a "psychoanalysis of *things*" (765).

Sartre's nightmare of an "ecstatic . . . metastatic" world of things is philosophy's first encounter with the reification that Baudrillard finds in the "unrestrained redundancy" of information systems (FS: 27–28). Indeed, it is his deconstruction of Spirit, his insight into what Baudrillard calls the metastasis of Being as "dead meaning in living signification (32), that makes

Sartre so much more contemporary than Heidegger. Sartre does not accept this world and instead figures as "slimy" the disappearance of boundaries that occurs when the "indifferent in-itself" sucks in "the for-itself which ought to dissolve it" (BN: 774, 776). Yet his nausea is not "humanism" as Robbe-Grillet had argued in his seminal attack on Sartre and Camus.[46] Rather, it is trauma, the trauma of phenomenology in a postmodern world.

Baudrillard's version of the viscous is the obese—also "an obscene mass" that does not "separate the body from the non-body" (FS: 32–33). The obese knows no "limits" and thus is without "transcendence" (27). Baudrillard evokes a famous phrase from *Nausea* when he says that "what makes the obese obscene is . . . that the body is superfluous, *de trop*" (32). In his early work he had used the Sartrean analytic to reflect on man's avoidance of finitude through objects. But this whole analysis was dependent on the difference of *pour-soi* and *en-soi*, whereas the obese are neither inside nor outside-because they are "pregnant with their own bodies but [cannot] be delivered of them" (27). Technological systems are forms of "secondary obesity"; in a monstrous catachresis, they too are "bloated with information they can never deliver" (28). To adapt Sartre, this obesity is "everywhere similar to itself, . . . a being . . . without memory, which eternally is changed into itself, on which one leaves no mark" (BN: 774). Baudrillard rails against this eradication of boundaries in his castigation of the "orgiastic" excess of the transaesthetic, the transsexual, the transpolitical.[47] The self-hardening of objectivity is a fatal strategy against this viscosity—one that Baudrillard himself recognizes as inhuman. But Baudrillard, as both analyst and victim, also needs this self-hardening. For it restores the duel of subject and object by reversing their positions, thus at least allowing the object to retain the autonomy of a subject, which the subject vicariously regains by becoming an object.

The Ecstasy of Deconstruction

Objectivity, however, comes at a cost. As an imaginary resolution to the failure of deconstruction, it has much in common with the dejection of phenomenology we have seen elsewhere. Like de Man's rigor, it banishes desire, the imaginary, and inwardness. Like Foucault's discourse, it regains power through a self-sacrificial asceticism. Furthermore, strategies such as terrorism are disciplines; even seduction prescribes self-rule rather than pleasure. For Baudrillard rejects "soft" poststructuralisms that play with libidinal politics and deterritorialized flows.[48] Nor does he embrace Nancy's difficult but postexistential freedom or the postphenomenological "humanism of the other" theorized by Levinas in *Humanisme de l'autre homme* (1972). Rather, his self-sacrifice resembles other fatalisms underwritten by a "logic of failed revolt"—the term Peter Starr uses for "explanations" of why 1968 failed. These logics include structural repetition and specular doubling—in which category Starr puts Baudrillard's dismissal of Marxism.[49] But I would argue that the various turns explored in this book respond to a psychocultural complex far more extensive than 1968.[50] Moreover, rhetoric, archaeology, discourse, or Lacan's structuralized unconscious are not explanations of the fatalism that resulted from 1968 but figural responses whose political unconscious one can only speculatively narrativize. Starr's analysis nevertheless allows us to see that the strategies associated with the linguistic turn are "truncated dialectics" caught in a missed encounter with their own desire. As he also argues, these logics, though antifoundationalist, are in their own way absolutist and can be criticized for an "essentializing of that margin of failure endemic to . . . revolution."[51]

Fatal theory is homologous with these psychologics, and Baudrillard has indeed been seen as fetishizing failure. But there are differences, both in style and in the persistence, within his fatalism, of some form of deconstruction and thus some principle of hope. Baudrillard's strategies all respond to a new mode of information tied to the fractal subject. For him communication is too slow to catch the system, inasmuch as we live in the age of speed theorized by Paul Virilio in his analyses of globalization and technoculture. Accordingly, Baudrillard does not follow the asceticism of the linguistic turn; his style is instead ecstatic and extreme. More desperate than de Man and Foucault, he is also less anonymously resigned. Fatal theory bypasses language through a form of "magic,"[52] which is both exacerbation *and* potential. Its hyperboles simulate the system's extremity, "accelerating" it or (in the case of inertia) slowing it down to its own extermination (FS: 8). This exaggeration conveys Baudrillard's entrapment within the infernal machine of the system. But it also gives his texts a hysterical, unpredictable, and reversible performativity that is anything but essentialist. In other words his fatalism is not a logic or set of principles, but an event aimed uncontrollably at an audience through whom anything can happen.

We can see this performativity in *Seduction*, where it is never clear what Baudrillard thinks of seduction nor how his arguments are engendered. Seduction is uncontrollable simulation, threatening the masculine logic of oppositions that Baudrillard both distrusts and clings to as a source of stability. It must be dismissed and feminized; yet it contains an irreducible remainder of difference that leads him to become feminine and assail Freud for not understanding seduction (S: 57). Insofar as seduction is a figure for difference, Baudrillard's self-feminization is undecidably hyperconformity and a desire to recapture in simulation some trace of a more authentic difference. This hysteria that speaks with two voices—one postmodern and one modern—is also evident in the ways Baudrillard deals with seduction. On the one hand he appropriates it, thus resisting nonmeaning through a game that is itself meaningless. Games, as Baudrillard says, are free of "internal negativity" (149) and thus connote mastery. On the other hand, the gendered terms are themselves autocritical, meant precisely to provoke the feminist anger they elicit. Indeed, Baudrillard's very definition of irony—as "the fulfilment of the object without regard for the subject or its alienation" (FS: 182)—is provocative in its irresponsibility. Finally, this postmodern irony is unstable, unreadable, an extermination of all terms. Is Baudrillard immoral or not, and does it matter? To further complicate matters, towards the end of *Seduction*, Baudrillard opposes seduction unironically and clearly. In a return to his critique of in-difference, he critiques the masses as a "clone-like apparatus that functions without the mediation of the other" (S: 173). He appeals to the very modern concepts he denounces, such as interiority, meaning, and the integrity of the body.

Yet analysis is outmoded, and Baudrillard knows it. Thus having deconstructed seduction, he returns to it by distinguishing a soft "minimalist" version from a "defiant," neoprimitivist ancestor (176). This latter is the seduction of magic, which confers on seduction a metaphysical status as traffic with spirit(s) (177). Even here, however, it is hard to figure out what game Baudrillard is playing. Interestingly *magic* is the term Sartre uses to describe emotion as a short-circuit in which the subject, by a form of simulation, reconstitutes a difficult world on his own terms.[53] As magic, fatal theory is bad faith, except that in a world of simulation there can be no ethics or bad faith. And yet strategies such as seduction, terrorism, and Baudrillard's denial of the Gulf War *are* completely scandalous and unethical.[54] In a desperate wager, they simulate both the disappearance of truth into "the system" and, (im)possibly, their own disappearance as provocations capable of conjuring truth by their fraud. In this sense Baudrillard's bad faith with ethics folds undecidably back into Sartre's anguished search for an ethics. For *magic* names the fraud of theory, but also its performativity. Magic signs are pure appearances without any referent, but as such they are a world "reversible in signs" (S: 177). In "magic thought" signs "evolve, they concatenate, and *produce themselves*"[55] in a "diabolical . . . and reversible" game with the audience that may well generate "some unprecedented development—some *Witz* of the events themselves."[56]

Magic thought is mobilized by two principles of hope, both equally desperate. One is reversibility—the very structure that collapses the oppositions anchoring meaning. For if left can become right, then the reverse too is possible. The other is Baudrillard's Manicheism—at once a symptom of his antagonistic and duel rather than dialectical thought[57] and an indication that magic, far from being pure simulation, is deeply metaphysical. The Manicheans saw the world as created by an "evil demon" and as "tainted from the very beginning" or "seduced by a sort of *ir*real principle."[58] It is as if a "perverse god" created "the world on a dare" (FS: 10). Our goal, then, must be "to repudiate this evil phantom"[59] through an "implosion" or "short-circuit between poles"[60] that will reverse reality and illusion by destroying both. In effect the Manicheans fall somewhere between what Baudrillard calls *dis*simulation and simulation. While "simulation threatens the difference between 'true' and 'false'," dissimulation protects a "reality principle" that "is only masked."[61] But the Manicheans know the difference between true and false, even as they do not believe there is anything but illusion and do not accept the conventional opposition of reality and illusion. The Manicheans believe in destroying an illusory world, yet not in "'realising' [another] world through any rational or materialist principle"; there is no reality that is not evil and thus no "possibility of rebuilding the world."[62]

In this context of a fatal theory that (dis)simulates metaphysics it is worth returning to the archaeology of the word *simulacrum*. Baudrillard gets the term from Bataille's contemporary, Pierre Klossowski, a heroic precursor of fatal theory and Manichean seduction.[63] Klossowski's surreal parodies of industrial society attempt to preserve the sacred amidst the profanity of commodification through a Sadeian extremity. His Nietzschean theory is a radical anticapitalist schizoanalysis that tries to get at the lost affects or "phantasms" behind simulacra. However, especially in some of his fiction, this analysis is also allegorized through a gnostic theology that links the simulacrum to the occultation of the pagan gods after Augustine. Thereafter, these gods speak through what has effaced them in a form of d(a)emonic narration. Gods are masked and (dis)simulated as demons. Insofar as we have no direct access to them, we invoke the souls of angels and demons to "seduce" the gods through imposture. Or as Jean-Pol Madou explains, "Klossowskian *mimesis* . . . [is] a simulation of the unrepresentable." It consists "in seducing an invisible model, to capture through recourse to imposture an unrepresentable power."[64] The simulacrum as icon has, as Foucault says, a complex identity: "It is a lie which leads one to take one sign for another; a sign of the presence of a deity (and the reciprocal possibility of taking this sign as its opposite); [and] the simultaneous irruption of the Same and the Other. . . . Thus is formed the wondrously rich constellation so characteristic of Klossowski: simulacrum, similitude, simultaneity, simulation, and dissimulation. "Unlike signs, which can be subjected to exegesis, the simulacrum is elusive and illusive—at once deconstructive and theological. The simulacrum is a symbol, an allegory, but of a curiously nonpositive variety. Because what it says is simulation, it always points beyond itself to something "other than that which it says," but only in the mode of simulation.[65]

Klossowski's corpus is a reflection on industrial society that attempts to (un)conceal some form of symbolic exchange within simulacra. And Baudrillard's fatal strategies clearly emulate his form of "hard" seduction (S: 177). Yet on the face of it the Baudrillardean simulacrum is more banal and apparently on the side of signs rather than symbols. As Mario Perniola defines it in a book to which Baudrillard refers, the simulacrum is the mechanically reproducible, serial product of the media in a context where the nostalgia for the real has been superseded.[66] However, Perniola's very analysis of simulacra as leaving behind the earlier conflict of iconoclasm and iconophilia suggests the limits of Baudrillard's adherence to the "secularization without residue" that legitimizes the simulacrum as the occasion for a "technology" or "practice."[67] For Baudrillard is still an iconoclast. To be sure, he is not an iconoclast as he himself uses the term because he seeks what the iconoclast fears: the "destructive, annihilating truth" that simulacra "allow to appear—that deep down God never existed . . . [and] was never anything but his own simulacrum."[68] But if he thus rejoices in simulation, it is because he discerns in the *form* of simulation, as the principle of "the radical illusoriness of the world,"[69] a destructive, deconstructive power. Our "modern media images" so fascinate us, he writes, "not because they are sites of the production of meaning . . . but because they are sites of [its] *disappearance* . . . of [a] denegation of the real and the reality principle."[70] Baudrillard, in other words, embraces, not the simulacrum, but simulation as (its own) deconstruction. He is thus an iconoclast in the sense envisioned by Perniola, who describes the persistence of the "millennial quarrel" between the "contemporary iconophiles" who are "realists and hyperrealists of the media" and the iconoclasts who are "hyperfuturists of authenticity and an alternative truth."[71]

Yet this truth, as in Manicheism, does not posit anything. It is a *destruktion* that still harbors a certain utopianism. And this is where Baudrillard parts company with the banal, materialist simulacrum of Perniola to return to Klossowski's simulacrum as antimatter, described by Baudrillard as the "diabolical" power of images. For images are evil in a "duel" sense, at once technological and theological. They seduce the real into a precession of simulacra, thereby also seducing it into "the realm of metamorphosis." Put differently, they are not simply bad but "evil" in the sense meant by Nietzsche, Sade, and Klossowski, for whom evil is a "form" more than a "value"—a form of "negation, illusion, destruction." Baudrillard himself locates this destruction in "objective" irony, as a form of antimatter within matter, arising "from within things themselves" as they "function against" themselves. But in his most recent book he also links the "antimatter of the social" to the possibility of utopia: "What I object to in sociology is . . . its realism, its taking of the social for the social and its failure to envisage that it might, at a particular moment, be an opportunity, a dream, a utopia, a contradiction."[72] Thus we might also approach the utopianism of destruction through another form of irony that Baudrillard renounces as subjective. According to Kierkegaard irony is "infinite absolute negativity." It "is negativity because it only negates; it is infinite because it negates not this or that phenomenon; and it is absolute because it negates by virtue of a higher which is not."[73]

The Illusion of Phenomenology

Insofar as negation is linked to the bringing forth of something that is not (yet), Baudrillard sometimes favors the word "illusion" over "simulation."[74] Simulation, as we have seen, is a kind of deconstruction, but the simulacrum has led to simplifications of Baudrillard's work as capitulating to a banal postmodernism of mechanical reproduction.[75] Illusion, as a playing with appearances or a (dis)appearing of the real, has a different genealogy, which is romantic and phenomenological. In *The Illusion of the End*, Baudrillard develops this genealogy, connecting his own play with evil as "an unbinding agent" to the "transvaluation of values" that is Nietzsche's form of deconstruction: "Nietzsche has written magnificently of the vital illusion . . . the illusion of appearances, of the forms of becoming, of the veil and, indeed, all the veils which, happily, protect us from the objective illusion, the illusion of truth. . . . To which we can only oppose *the illusion of the world itself*."[76]

Both Schiller and Nietzsche play on the German word *Schein* as at once "appearance" and "shining" or what Baudrillard calls the "radical illusion" that cannot be critiqued because it does not posit itself as "representation or belief."[77] In this sense illusion is not simply "non-reality: rather it is, in the literal sense of the word (*il-ludere* in Latin) a *play* upon 'reality' or a *mise-en-jeu* of the real."[78] Illusion thus plays a double game. On the one hand, because the real is a "coherent illusion" with the appearance of "rationality," to recognize the "illusoriness of the world" is to see through the ob-scene, to avoid "consent[ing]" to this reality. On the other hand this seeing through is also a "showing-through":

> We play at mastering the world through our technologies . . . but on the other hand we might, without knowing it, be partners in another game. . . . There is something like a secret reversion, a showing-through of the illusion of the world in the very techniques we use to transform it. . . . The irony of technology: its alleged reality, its palpably high-level performance, much too dazzling to be true, might be said to be the veil of a duplicity that eludes us.[79]

Baudrillard had earlier described his texts as playing on the system's logic so as to turn it "against itself."[80] In this sense they perform the system's irrationality, thus deconstructing it in a "showing-through of the illusion of the world." But "showing-through" is a significant phrase, and at this point magic thought folds into phenomenological notions of (un)concealing. For what shows through is not just unreality but possibility. Illusion in this sense is not "simulacrum or unreality" but "something which drives a breach into a world which is too known. . . . The singular, original illusion, the illusion born of the slip, the breakdown . . . the tiniest gap in things."[81]

This gap is also intimated in the antiphonal counterpart to the system's self-deconstruction by its inertia and mass, namely, its disappearance in a slowing down of light described near the opening of *Fatal Strategies*. Baudrillard begins with an illusion: the fact that the "speed of light" is what protects "the reality of things" by guaranteeing "that the images we have of them are contemporaneous." He then constructs another illusion, of a universe in slow motion: "Light like the wind, with variable speeds, even dead calms, where no image could get to us from the zones affected" (FS: 18–19). If this almost mystical postmodernism of light is an attempt to change the speed of communication (8), it also harbors a reference to phenomenology, itself a slowing down of thought, especially as practiced by Heidegger. Light is both Levinas's and Derrida's metaphor for phenomenology. According to Levinas, light makes "objects into a world" that "belong[s] to us" and is thus "a condition for phenomena, that is, for meaning." As such, light facilitates an "enveloping of the exterior by the inward, which is the very structure of the cogito" (EE: 48). But for Baudrillard, light is more complex—a figure that suggests at once the return and the retreat of phenomenology. The unmooring of light from speed deconstructs the "illuminated space" of phenomenology as the appearing of meaning (EE: 48). At the same time, this light that is irreducible to phenomenality is also a clearing in the obese immanence of information. Yet the clearing shows nothing and instead simply "points to something future."[82]

In *Paroxysm*, Baudrillard refers to this change of lighting in terms reminiscent of phenomenology. He describes it as a change in which "everything is restored to its raw self-evidence, its quality as pure event—a kind of immanence, but one which might be said to have retained the quality and energy of transcendence." We can also sense a cryptic phenomenology in the curiously Heideggerian turn now given to the death of the subject:

> If we look at it this way, it's no longer we who think the world, but the world that thinks us. It's the world which restores a metamorphosis of

forms in which thought itself is caught in a dynamic which is no longer its own. We no longer know very precisely what role it plays in this. . . . We become the objects of thought, but objects of a thought which no longer belongs to us, which is no longer the thought of the subject.[83]

Indeed we can now also hear the phenomenological resonances of Baudrillard's term *ecstasy*—a pushing of phenomena to their extreme limits such that they exceed or stand outside themselves and thus a pushing of social thought itself towards an analogous ec-stasis.

These phenomenological references do not mark a return to phenomenology; they are after all illusions. For one thing, light is here opposed to the obesity of matter, as in Ionesco's contrast of "evanescence" with the "solidity" and excessive "presence" of the redundant bourgeois world.[84] But one must also question this dissolution of the world in terms of Baudrillard's own metaphorics of transparency. Baudrillard writes that transparency occurs "in all things when they lose their image . . . their shadow, when they no longer offer any substance, distance or resistance, when they become both immanent and elusive from an excess of fluidity and luminosity." Light is thus no different from mass in being a "catastrophic development internal to the system."[85] Second, the slowing down that Baudrillard here describes resembles nothing more than Foucault's end of man, the cultural equivalent to the Heideggerian ec-stasis. Of the latter Levinas writes that it abolishes the other, because "in ecstasis the subject is absorbed in the object and recovers itself in its unity" (TO: 41). In both these ways light is no more than the (un)veiling of one illusion by another.

At the same time, Baudrillard's association of the illusion of the end with light introduces, within the catastrophe "internal to the system," a "form of play" or illusion that thwarts the system's "implacable development." In terms of his distinction between "exponential stability" and "instability," it interrupts the predictable with the "singular" catastrophe.[86] Exponential stability "defines a state in which no matter where you start out, you always end up at the same point." Thus Baudrillard's texts might be seen as a redundant series, all saying the same thing, such that "none of [their] potentialities develops." By contrast, exponential *in*stability—as in his increasingly frequent references to antiscience and chaos theory—allows these potentialities to "extrapolate demonically" and unpredictably towards the

unfolding of "new energies." Critics such as Kellner and Norris have fixed
Baudrillard's corpus as exponentially stable. My concern is also to locate
those instabilities by which Baudrillard quite deliberately "drive[s] a breach
into this world that is too known."[87]

The choice of light as an instance of "extreme phenomena" is one such
instability. Along with other rema(i)nders of phenomenology and deconstruction, which nevertheless do not gain the status of arguments, it extrap-
olates demonically beyond its function as an instance of inertia (FS: 20).
What is at issue here is not light itself but what it figures. Baudrillard speaks
of the precipitation of the text towards its end as also a movement towards
"*something lost.*"[88] One must read this movement with his own comment on
the return to "beginnings" as arising from our failure to "resolve the problem of the end."[89] In forgetting Foucault, philosophy, and history, Baudrillard signally failed to bring theory to an end. Thus his recent work, in its
circling back on itself and its past, is increasingly a return and retreat from
its origins, rather than (like *Seduction*) a bitterly performative self-rejection.
It is as if Baudrillard, travelling into the dead future, also travels back to a
missed encounter with theory's past. In this context, the dissolution of the
system into light rather than mass introduces a gap in what many expect of
him. This gap opens the possibility of catastrophe as a writing of the disaster more profound than simply a consumption of the end "as spectacle."[90] It
opens the possibility of a *destruktion* that is not simply catastrophic but allows for what Derrida calls "new possibilities of arrangement."

The beginning of *America* is the best example of this travel back to a past
that is yet to come. Indeed, in choosing travel as the text's mode, Baudrillard
chooses a form different from game or duel, "a trip without any objective
which is . . . endless" and open.[91] Much of the text is still concerned with a
society of surfaces, communications, networks. This is not, however, only a
fatal text that develops a form of "superficial reading."[92] It is also a presenta-
tion of phenomena in their "raw self-evidence."[93] Baudrillard carefully sets
the scene by beginning with the desert as "the negative of the earth's surface." Like the slowing down of light, the disappearance of the "social and
cultural America" into a landscape of "speed . . . and mineral surfaces" is an
illusion that allows the illusoriness of the world to show through. Entering
the desert's "archives," Baudrillard travels back to the civilizations that

precede white America and the "signs that predate" man himself. As important, he also travels back to an earlier form of theory: "I sought the finished
form of the future catastrophe of the social in geology, in that upturning of
depth that can be seen in the striated spaces . . . the immemorial abyss of
slowness that shows itself in erosion and geology."[94]

As in all his texts, Baudrillard works by intensification; "unbearable" heat,
intense speed, and slowness combine to make the desert an "ecstatic critique
of culture." This use of catastrophe as epistemic destruction or an "ecstatic
form of disappearance" is not new for Baudrillard. But what is different is
the way destruction makes visible an "earlier stage than that of anthropology," through a "mineralogy"[95] that recalls Foucault's earliest uses of the
term *archaeology*. For the desert is, in its own way, a place from which man
has been "erased, like a face drawn in sand" (OT: 387). In this infinite perspective, the society of generalized communication appears as but a "recent
invention" (386). Insofar as this society, so obscenely present in other works,
is "neither the oldest nor the most constant problem . . . for human knowledge" (386), its bracketing is the letting-appear of a different order of things.

What the text lets-appear is not an alternative material order but a new
way of seeing that returns to the primacy of perception. To be sure, Baudrillard goes back from the desert to "social and cultural" America and repeats some of his own earlier analyses in the process. But the desert lingers
on: "When you emerge from the desert, your eyes go on trying to create
emptiness all around."[96] The desert strips away received categories of understanding, those that inform the social but also, more importantly, those that
inform Baudrillard's own analyses of the social. In New York, on the free-
ways, in Los Angeles, Baudrillard leaves analysis not for provocation but for
phenomenological description. Flying over Los Angeles, he discovers a "lu-
minous, geometric, incandescent immensity. . . . [like] Bosch's hell." *America* is at once faster and slower than conventional analysis; it passes by people and objects too quickly for commentary, yet lingers carefully on their
singularity. "Speed creates pure objects."[97] Thus the clearing initiated by a
landscape void of people allows the elements of the urban landscape to appear in their "raw self-evidence"—unmediated and unmediatized, as if they
too were natural phenomena. Seen in this way the components of contemporary culture have an "immanence that retains the quality of transcen-

dence";[98] they are pure surface, yet have a certain strangeness and possibility. In short, what is facilitated by this beginning from phenomenology is a reperception of the ob-scene that deconstructs Baudrillard's own enframing of contemporary culture. It is of course an illusion. But it lets us play with the hope that our system, even in its normally catastrophic course, might still contain the possibility of difference.

Reference Matter

Notes

1. Dews, 110.
2. Blanchot, "Michel Foucault," 71.
3. That deconstruction is a form of philosophy and not literary criticism is a point also made by Gasché, *Tain*, 1–3. However, in part because I do not take up deconstruction solely with reference to Derrida, I see this "philosophy" as considerably more interdisciplinary than Gasché does.
4. Merleau-Ponty, "Phenomenology and Psychoanalysis: Preface to Hesnard's *L'Ouevre de Freud*," in *Merleau-Ponty and Psychology*, ed. Hoeller, 71.
5. Butler, *Psychic Life*, 92; Derrida, *Points*, 143–44.
6. Gasché, *Wild Card of Reading*, 104–12; Butler, *Psychic Life*, 6, and more generally, 31–62.
7. Butler, *Psychic Life*, 92.

1. One notes the following titles: Josué V. Harari (ed.), *Textual Strategies: Perspectives in Post-Structuralist Criticism*; John Sturrock (ed.), *Structuralism and Since: From Lévi-Strauss to Derrida*; Christopher Norris, *Deconstruction*; Edith Kurzweil, *The Age of Structuralism: Lévi-Strauss to Foucault*; Robert Young (ed.), *Untying the Text: A Post-Structuralist Reader*; Jonathan Arac, Wlad Godzich, and Wallace Martin (eds.), *The Yale Critics: Deconstruction in America*; Vincent Leitch, *Deconstructive Criticism: An Advanced Introduction*; Stephen W. Melville, *Philosophy beside Itself: On Deconstruction and Modernism*; Peter Dews, *Logics of Disintegration: Post-Structuralist Thought and the Claims of Critical Theory*; and Richard Machin and Christopher Norris (eds.), *Post-Structuralist Readings of English Poetry*. See also Frank Lentricchia, *After the New Criticism*, 156–211, 282–317. In most of these studies, *deconstruction* and *poststructuralism* are not distinguished, although each term has different yet overlapping resonances. See Lentricchia, who discusses Derridean deconstruction in a chapter entitled "History or the Abyss: Poststructuralism" (157–77); Leitch, who frequently refers to the authors he treats in

Deconstructive Criticism as poststructuralist (e.g. 102–3); and Donald Pease who uses both terms to describe Hillis Miller ("J. Hillis Miller: The Other Victorian at Yale," in *The Yale Critics*, 88). Young says that a "straightforward identification of deconstruction with poststructuralism" is simplistic, but then does not really distinguish them (15). I discuss later on Norris's distinction between the two terms— a shift from his initial identification of them in *Deconstruction*.

2. See Leitch, 73–85, 87–102, 105–15, 286.

3. See Harari who sees poststructuralism as continuing from structuralism and sees deconstruction as providing a set of tools for the former (445–46, 34–37).

4. De Man, *Allegories*, 17.

5. Habermas, *Modernity*, 185, 189, 190, 192, 199.

6. Kurzweil describes Kristeva, Derrida, Ricoeur, and Deleuze and Guattari as poststructuralists and notes that Althusser, Foucault, and Barthes all "reneged on their structuralisms" (9–10, 240–44). Dews's book on "poststructuralist thought" deals with Derrida, Lacan, Foucault, and Lyotard. Harari's collection of "poststructuralist perspectives" includes Foucault, Derrida, de Man, Deleuze, Eugenio Donato, Serres, Genette, and Barthes. Finally, Baudrillard and Lyotard are associated with poststructuralism by Pefanis (2, 50, 85, 147n13).

7. Thus Eagleton includes Derrida, Barthes, Foucault, Lacan, and Kristeva under the heading of poststructuralism, making a point of their different disciplinary orientations (134). He defines "deconstruction" as a more narrowly literary critical movement (145). Although he does not reduce Derrida to his American appropriation into literary criticism, Michael Ryan also sees deconstruction as narrower than the work it affected: the work of "such overtly politicized intellectuals as Julia Kristeva, Gilles Deleuze, and Michel Foucault" (103). Young associates deconstruction with "textual aestheticism" (19). Leitch also notes the view that deconstruction is confined to the literary sphere, using the term "poststructuralism" to refer to the "wider social and cultural contexts" taken up by Jameson, Said, and Foucault (142), although Leitch does not rigorously distinguish the two terms.

8. See Lentricchia, *After the New Criticism*, 157–77; Jonathan Culler, "Jacques Derrida," in *Structuralism*, ed. Sturrock, 55. Other deconstructive theorists are also loosely referred to as poststructuralist: for instance Hillis Miller (by Pease in *The Yale Critics*, 88) and Joseph Riddel (by Lentricchia, 159).

9. The inaugural status of this essay is evident in Lentricchia's discussion of Derrida (157–60). "Structure, Sign, and Play" was first delivered as a lecture at the international colloquium on "Critical Languages and the Sciences of Man" at Johns Hopkins in 1966, and published a year later in *L'Ecriture et la différance* (WD: 278–93). It is also the essay by which Derrida is often represented in anthologies of literary theory, which also represent de Man by "Semiology and Rhetoric" (e.g.,

Richter). Until the translation of *Of Grammatology* in 1976, Derrida's other translated work (except for "White Mythology"—1974) appeared in philosophical—specifically phenomenological—contexts: journals, collections, and the Northwestern series in Phenomenology and Existential Philosophy, which published SP (1973). In other words, in the world of "theory" Derrida until 1976 would have been known largely by "Structure, Sign, and Play" and perhaps by "The Ends of Man" (delivered as a lecture in New York in 1968). "Structure, Sign, and Play" would then have framed the reading of OGr as an overturning of structuralism that continued its focus on the sign, even though Derrida might have been known to a very small circle of philosophers as a late phenomenologist. (Indeed de Man, as we shall see, sees the importance of OGr as lying in its discussion of Rousseau rather than of Saussure).

10. For the former see Lentricchia, *After the New Criticism*, 163; for the latter see Leitch, 102–13, 198–204.

11. Frank, *What Is Neostructuralism?*; Harland, *Superstructuralism*. "Ultrastructuralism" is used by Dosse (II.17).

12. See Gasché, who polemically argues that "deconstructive criticism" has "little in common" with Derrida's thought and originates "in New Criticism; it is a continuation of this American-bred literary scholarship" (*Tain*, 3).

13. This transference to literary studies is inaugurated by de Man in "Criticism and Crisis," first published in 1967 and reprinted as the opening essay of *Blindness and Insight* (1971). De Man specifically evokes the crisis I take up later in this chapter, a crisis provoked by the rise of the social sciences and Lévi-Straussian structuralism in the French university system but going back three decades to Husserl's *Crisis*. But, importantly, he reframes the crisis of philosophy as one that is resolved by literature: not literature in a Blanchotian sense but the implementation of this philosophical category in literary *criticism* (14–19). Although de Man later reextends his focus on literature to larger epistemological, historiographical, and ontological questions—as when he invokes the division into the trivium and quadrivium in the opening chapter of *Allegories* and more extensively in *Aesthetic Ideology*—at this point he insists on his credentials as a literary critic: "My interest in criticism is subordinate to my interest in primary literary texts" (viii).

14. Derrida, *Points*, 79.

15. On the importance of literature to the early Baudrillard see Genosko, xi.

16. Dosse notes its American origins (II.17); Žižek describes it as an "Anglo-Saxon and German invention" in *Looking Awry* (142). Frank coins the related term "neostructuralism," which is equated with poststructuralism on the back cover of the translation of *What Is Neostructuralism?* which deals among others with Derrida, Foucault, Lacan, and Deleuze and Guattari. Habermas also uses the term *poststructuralism* in 1985, although only once (*Modernity*, 106).

17. Stanley Corngold, "Error in Paul de Man," in *The Yale Critics*, 92.

18. One of the earliest translations of Baudrillard is *Simulations* (1983), which begins with an essay from *Simulacra and Simulation* (1981), *followed* by the second chapter of the earlier *Symbolic Exchange and Death* (1976). The translation provides no bibliographical information, thus leading us to assume that texts arguably drawn from different stages of Baudrillard's work are part of a single text. The effect is to fold what I shall argue is the deconstructive Baudrillard into the bitterly poststructuralist Baudrillard. *Simulations*, which was preceded by English translations of *The Mirror of Production* (1973) in 1975 and *For a Critique of the Political Economy of the Sign* (1972) in 1981, was followed by translations of *In the Shadow of the Silent Majorities* (1978), also in 1983, *Forget Foucault* (1977) in 1987, *America* (1986) and *The Ecstasy of Communication* (1987) in 1988, *Seduction* (1979), and *Fatal Strategies* (1983) in 1990. It is only very recently that Baudrillard's earliest work has been made available to an English-speaking public, with the translation of *Symbolic Exchange and Death* (1976) in 1993, of *The System of Objects* (1968) in 1996, and of *The Consumer Society* (1970) in 1998.

19. Levinas, *Humanisme de l'autre homme*. My use of the phrase is suggestive because deconstruction as defined in this study is more concerned with the ontic than Levinas himself is (TO: 39)—a concern that reflects its crossing of Sartre with Heidegger.

20. I do not deal with de Man extensively in this book, partly because my focus is on French theory and partly because I have discussed his position between phenomenology and poststructuralism elsewhere (see n. 24). Nevertheless as a migrant European intellectual, de Man cannot entirely be fitted into his American identity as a literary critic, which he initially emphasized (see n. 13), but later resisted once he had attained the security of being a public intellectual figure. De Man has a borderline status as an American and European figure. Whereas Miller and Hartman are literary critics, de Man really is a philosopher—of language—which is why I discuss him at various points in this study.

21. Norris, *Deconstruction*; Waters, "Introduction: Paul de Man: Life and Works" (de Man, *Critical Writings*, lii–liii).

22. De Man, *Critical Writings*, 214–17.

23. De Man, *Blindness and Insight*, 276.

24. Rajan, "The Erasure of Narrative in Post-Structuralist Representations of Wordsworth," 350–70; "Displacing Post-Structuralism," 451–74. De Man's translation of Harold Bloom's psychological terminology into rhetorical terms as a way of making manifest what he sees as latent in Bloom's work is revealingly autobiographical in this respect (*Blindness and Insight*, 267–76).

25. De Man, *Critical Writings*, 34–39; *Blindness and Insight*, 250–55.

26. Levinas, *Theory of Intuition*, 41, 43, 39, 50–51.

27. Sartre, *Imagination*, 133–34. See also *The Psychology of Imagination*, which opens with a section entitled "The Intentional Structure of the Image" and posits an absolute division between imagination and perception, 153–56.

28. De Man, "Structure intentionelle de l'image romantique," 69 (trans. mine). Other changes that de Man makes in translating this article for inclusion in Harold Bloom's *Romanticism and Consciousness* and then *The Rhetoric of Romanticism* include the excision of the terms "existential" (71; RR: 4) and, at five places, "being" (72–3; RR: 5–6).

29. De Man, *Critical Writings*, 38–39.

30. Derrida uses almost the same language seven years later: "Imagination alone has the power of *giving birth to itself*. It creates nothing because it is imagination. But it receives nothing that is alien or anterior to it. It is not affected by the 'real'" (OGr: 186). Compare Sartre's notion of the image as doubly negative: first because it "freely" posits by negating the real, but second because it is thereby nothing and is "deprived of the category of the real" (*Psychology*, 229, 238–39).

31. De Man, *Critical Writings*, 104, 155, 34.

32. Ibid., 105, 32.

33. Ibid., 39.

34. Ibid., 39, 32–33.

35. De Man, *Blindness and Insight*, 50, 18–19, 69, 127, 207.

36. Ibid., 17, 71, 49.

37. Sartre, *Psychology*, 215. It is important to recognize that bad faith for Sartre does not imply the possibility of good faith; good faith is, if anything, even more profoundly in bad faith than bad faith itself.

38. Even if the word *poststructuralism* is not actually used by French theorists, Foucault does locate himself as not being a structuralist, as do even early French commentators on his work (e.g. Piaget, 108–15). Derrida places himself in a phenomenological context in his discussion of Rousseau, which makes considerable use of the perception/imagination distinction, but OGr also places itself after Saussure and Lévi-Strauss. And in *Allegories of Reading*, de Man positions himself against formalism and speech-act theory, not phenomenology.

39. Spanos, *Heidegger and Criticism*, 43, 87, 97–100; see also 30–33, and more generally 84–131. While sympathizing with Spanos's attempt to establish a position outside poststructuralism (which he too equates with deconstruction), I would disagree with his absolute dismissal of Derrida and de Man, and his sense—on which he wavers (6)—that Heidegger provides an adequate basis for thinking the limitations of a postmodernism and technology deeply implicated in capitalism. Moreover, Spanos's "destruction" is more transformative than the deconstruction I

analyze here; indeed this need for a transformative critique is very much a product of the American academy. Curiously, Heidegger appeals to Spanos for precisely the reasons that affirmative poststructuralisms remain popular on this side of the Atlantic: Heidegger is more amenable than Derrida to the "radical, emancipatory task of contemporary oppositional intellectuals" (82)—a point we can see if we contrast the affirmative Kojèvian tone of Heidegger's 1966 essay "The End of Philosophy and the Task of Thinking" (in *Basic Writings*) to the greater caution of "The Ends of Man" (1968). Destruction is aimed only against the past and the forgetting it has gone through and does not deconstruct its own amnesias. In this sense Heidegger's phenomenology—if it can be called that—is radically different from French phenomenology.

40. Interview with Vincent Descombes, quoted by Dosse (II.19). Dosse nevertheless presents Derrida as a poststructuralist who adopted the strategy of deconstruction (II.17–27).

41. Ricoeur, *Husserl*, 4.

42. Foucault, "Introduction" to Canguilhem, *Normal*, 8–9.

43. Ricoeur, *Husserl*, 203; Levinas, *Discovering Existence*, 39.

44. Canguilhem, *Normal*, 8–9.

45. Thus in OT, in the section on "Man and His Doubles," Foucault notes that "the analysis of actual experience is a discourse of mixed nature." On the one hand, the belief that one can grasp experience leads to a certain positivism in which "the empirical, in man, [is made to] stand for the transcendental." On the other hand, this empiricism is "simultaneously promising and threatening." For the "phenomenological project continually resolves itself, before our eyes, into a description-empirical despite itself-of actual experience," wherein empiricism as an anti-idealism doubles back on itself so as to interrupt the positivity of a naive (or undoubled) empiricism (321, 328). In *Inner Experience*, published in 1943 and then expanded in 1954, Bataille similarly tries to reconceptualize the term *experience* by thinking it in terms of a transgression of the bounded ego. Inner experience is paradoxically the same as the "absolute exteriority" or "thought from the outside" that Foucault associates with Blanchot in his 1966 monograph, in which he picks up Levinas's phrase to describe Blanchot (*Proper Names*, 133).

46. Wahl, *Philosophies of Existence*. Wahl notes considerable "diversities" and indeed "grave conflicts" among these philosophies. Heidegger and Jaspers refuse the designation "existentialist," while Sartre, Merleau-Ponty, and Marcel accept it (3–4). Heidegger, for his part, is concerned with existence only insofar as it illuminates "being" (3–4). The common denominator for all these thinkers is an "empiricism" that relates to "the element[s] of *facticity*" and affectivity, and that goes back to Schelling (7, 29), as well as "an intimate union of the existential and the

ontological" (45). Wahl includes Levinas among the group (103), while Levinas himself speaks of his debt to Wahl (*Éthique*: 47).

47. Levinas, *Theory of Intuition*, liv, 124.

48. Howells, "Sartre and Derrida: Qui perd gagne," 148. See also my roughly contemporaneous appendix on Sartre, Derrida, and de Man in *Dark Interpreter*, 267–71. Howells is virtually the only commentator to have emphasized Sartre's importance for Derrida in the face of the latter's dismissals of him; see also her "Derrida and Sartre: Hegel's Death Knell" (169–81), and her recent *Derrida* (27–8, 86–94).

49. Derrida, *Of Spirit*, 18.

50. Ricoeur, "Hegel and Husserl," 229–31.

51. Ricoeur, *Husserl*, 206; "Hegel and Husserl," 228.

52. Kojève, 6, 39, 41–44, 158–61. Thus for Kojève "the Negativity which *is* Man" is the "Action of Fighting and Work by which Man preserves himself in spatial being while *destroying it*" (5, 155).

53. Butler, *Subjects of Desire*, 92.

54. Kant, *Anthropology*, 3. Kant relegates to the realm of the physiological anything that is in excess of man's free cognition of himself: in other words, the entire realm of the "unthought" that is the object of the phenomenology discussed here and by which Kant himself remains fascinated even as he tries to keep it outside the bounded ego of pragmatic anthropology.

55. Butler, *Subjects of Desire*, 93. Hyppolite himself identifies Sartre with Kojève. But although the Kojèvian influence on Sartre is conspicuous in *The Psychology of Imagination* and returns in *Critique of Dialectical Reason*, I would argue that BN is closer to the work of Hyppolite, providing a psychoanalysis of its own troping of desire and negation into forms of mastery. It is significant that Kojève describes his work as a "phenomenological *anthropology*" (39), whereas Sartre subtitles BN *A Phenomenological Essay on Ontology*. As I argue in the next chapter, BN contains an anthropology, but inscribed as a figure within an excessive, unreadable ontology.

56. Hyppolite, *Genesis*, 52.

57. Ibid., 16, 203; see more generally 56, 62, 190–215. I have not included in this brief genealogy Wahl's *Le Malheur de la conscience dans la philosophie de Hegel*. Although Wahl foregrounds the unhappy consciousness well before Hyppolite does, his religious perspective leads him to make it the mere "darkened image of happy consciousness" and thus to positivize negativity (147–48).

58. Dews, 19–31. Dews also points to the importance of Merleau-Ponty, particularly for Lyotard (31–44). Frank, *Neostructuralism*, 87–101.

59. Descombes, 48–50. Descombes does go on to make the point I make here

(51), but in so doing locates a philosophical inconsistency in BN which I see as strategic.

60. LaCapra is one of the few commentators to note the functioning of a certain supplementarity in Sartre's thought, although typically he dismisses Sartre's writing as "the scene of relatively blind internal contestation." Nevertheless La-Capra is unusual in at least relating Sartre to contemporary French theory, albeit only as a "foil" and antithetical stimulus for it (25, 221–22, 42).

61. I obviously disagree with the common view that Sartre neglected language or spoke of it only in the most simplified and unreflexive fashion; see for example La Capra, 25–26; Lacan, *Speech and Language in Psychoanalysis*, 300–301. It is not clear whether Sartre had read Saussure or Lacan. However, his comments on the term *language* as not being restricted to the "articulated word" and extending to semiotic phenomena generally (BN: 486) and his extensive discussions of "reflection" in ways that imbue the philosophical concept with the figurality of the mirror place Sartre in the same intellectual ambience as Saussure and Lacan, perhaps in advance of the latter, who by 1943 had published only his short essay on the mirror stage.

62. Sartre's use of the terms *figure* and *ground* will be discussed in Chapter 3. While these terms, drawn from *Gestalt* psychology, could be seen as part of a phenomenological debate about "perception," as Piaget points out *Gestalt* psychology, which initially developed in the ambience of phenomenology, was subsumed into structuralism as part of its "positive" or constructionist side, as distinct from the "negative" side taken over by Foucault and others who accept the structurality of structure and the death of the subject (114–15, 46–52). Inasmuch as structuralism absorbs *Gestalt* theories of perception into its linguistic model, Sartre, one could argue, redeploys a linguistic sense of figure as constructed in order to deconstruct the hypostasis effected by perception (in Levinas's terms) in ways that contribute to de Man's notion of deconstruction as a "disfiguration." Sartre, moreover, sees perception and language as analogous and speaks of their collusion in the process of hypostasis (BN: 410).

63. Ideally, Sartre writes, reflection would be "pure reflection" or "the simple presence of the reflective for-itself to the for-itself reflected-on" (BN: 218). Reflection as "simultaneously an objectivation and an interiorization" (216) would then be a dialectic that allows self-consciousness to be self-constituting: "By reflection the for-itself, which has lost itself outside itself, attempts to put itself inside its own being" (216). However, as Sartre describes it, reflection is the permanent disintegration of such identity (217; cf. also 122, 126).

64. Sartre writes: "Language by revealing to us abstractly the principal structures of our body-for-others (even though the existed body is ineffable) impels us

to place our alleged mission wholly in the hands of the Other" (BN: 463). Later he continues: "Language is not a phenomenon added onto being-for-others; It *is* originally being-for-others" (485).

65. The terms are Lacan's, but Sartre's work is, I would argue, the switch-point that makes it possible for Lacan to develop the concept of the Real through a deconstruction of Husserl's theory of intuition. Sartre's extensive exploration (in the section on "The Body") of how the body is not directly known but is known only as it is named by the "language" and "concepts" of the other (BN: 463–65) prefigures Lacan's understanding of the Symbolic as an order constituted by the bar s/S. Sartre does nevertheless preserve a place for intuition, and also for a Real that exceeds language and is absolutely inaccessible to language, but that conveys our irreducibility to discourse. Intuition is what gives us noncognitive access to "the existed body," the body as "non-thetically existed" (465, 468). The usefulness of intuition, given the remoteness of Sartre's use of the term from its origin in Husserl, is that this body, which can only be "alienated" through language and can only be known as other, is nevertheless "present to intuition" (567), but as materiality rather than phenomenality: "the *body which is suffered* serves as a nucleus, as matter for the alienating means which surpass it" (465). This is not the place for an extensive tracing of Sartre's influence on Lacan. But if Sartre's account of intuition versus knowledge through language and concepts lays the basis for Lacan's distinction between the Real and the Symbolic, Sartre's account of the Imaginary in *The Psychology of Imagination* is arguably also important for Lacan.

66. Levinas, *Éthique*, 52, 58.

67. Only at two points does Levinas concede the radical potential of intentionality. In *God, Death* he writes: "Phenomenology seems to make possible the thinking of nothingness (*le néant*) thanks to the idea of intentionality as an access to something other than oneself, and an access that can be had in a non-theoretical manner (thus, in sentiments, actions, etc., which are irreducible to serene representation). . . . Anxiety, which has no object, has the non-object as its object: nothingness" (68–69). In *Éthique* he speaks of a "non-theoretical intentionality" and thus of a "Husserlian possibility which can be developed beyond what Husserl himself has said on the ethical problem and on the relation with the other which for him remains representational (even though Merleau-Ponty has tried to interpret it otherwise)" (22–23).

68. Levinas, *Theory of Intuition*, 39.

69. Levinas, *Discovering Existence*, 61; *Éthique*, 79, 31.

70. Levinas, *Theory of Intuition*, 154–5; *Éthique*, 29–30. Levinas's first criticisms of *Heidegger* as well as Husserl can be found in TO: 40–48. See also *Éthique* (31–33), *God, Death* (31–55), and *Proper Names* (127–39). Although Levinas rarely

speaks of Heidegger's politics, they are undoubtedly at issue in his reassessment of Heidegger, although in the subtle ways analyzed by Bourdieu, who sees politics as embedded in ontology and linguistics in *The Political Ontology of Martin Heidegger*.

71. Derrida, *Points*, 273.

72. Levinas, *God, Death*, 19; *Discovering Existence*, 33.

73. Bataille, *Inner Experience*, 3–4, 8, 24, 54–55, 178.

74. Levinas, *Éthique*, 30.

75. Levinas says of his *Theory of Intuition* that "the goal of this book prevents us from making a thorough criticism of the philosophy which we shall present" (lvi). His criticisms are reserved and are found largely in the "Introduction" and "Conclusion."

76. "Preface" to the second (1979) edition of EE, included in the third edition of *De l'existence à l'existant*, np; *Éthique*, 32.

77. Ricoeur, *Husserl*, 4. An interesting, because completely unexpected, example of the kind of heresy envisioned by Ricoeur is Deleuze and Guattari's derivation of the notion of "protogeometry" from Husserl (*Thousand Plateaus*, 367, 407–10).

78. Merleau-Ponty, *Phenomenology of Perception*, vii–viii, xxi. The notion of the fold is obviously drawn from Deleuze, who sees phenomenology as recognizing that "Being was precisely the fold that it made with being" (*Michel Foucault*, 110). I suggest, however, that phenomenology is also the fold that it makes with itself.

79. Lyotard, *Phenomenology*, 32.

80. Ibid., 32.

81. Merleau-Ponty, "Phenomenology and Psychoanalysis," 69–70. For a discussion of Merleau-Ponty's relation to Angelo Louis Hesnard, Hesnard's own attempt to bring psychoanalysis and phenomenology together, and the greater role played by psychoanalysis in French as distinct from German phenomenology, see Spiegelberg, 136–40.

82. Ibid., 71. A valuable development of this latency, linking (Heideggerian) phenomenology and psychoanalysis can be found in Lukacher's *Primal Scenes* (21–114).

83. Derrida, *Resistances*, 78.

84. Ibid., 81.

85. Ibid., 84.

86. Derrida, "'Il courait mort': salut, salut," 7–54 (translation mine). Derrida's essay in the form of a long and passionate letter to Claude Lanzmann is a gesture of amendment more than a detailed and rigorous reading of either *BN* or *Critique of Dialectical Reason*. He quotes mainly from Sartre's essays in *Les temps modernes*, thus dealing not with Sartre as a theorist but with his role as a public intellectual,

in terms of the risk or "wager" involved in "engagement," and in terms of what it means to "write for one's time." As a gesture, the essay is a promissory note, deferring but opening the way for more detailed intellectual-historical readings, such as the one Derrida provides of Freud. The one area in which Derrida does express reservations, in an imaginary interview with himself, is Sartre's view and practice of literature (except for *Nausea*) and "the experience of language *for* Sartre. . . . As if he had passed by everything that counts for me." Yet even here, like de Man (RT: 119), Derrida does note Sartre's opening up of philosophy to literature via Blanchot and Bataille ("'Il courait mort,'"44 n.6).

87. Sartre, "Il courait mort," 19, 30, 44, 34, 40.

88. Ibid., 22, 30–31, 38, 21–23, 11n4.

89. Deleuze and Guattari, *Thousand Plateaus*, 21, 86.

90. Levinas, *God, Death*, 158–59.

91. Kristeva, *La révolte intime*, 225–334.

92. Wahl, *Philosophies*, 4.

93. Lyotard, *Phenomenology*, 32.

94. The first two phases would be those of transcendental and existential phenomenology. But one must be careful about an overly linear separation between these phases because the turning of phenomenology in a third, interdisciplinary, and thus theoretical direction already occurs in the work of Merleau-Ponty and Sartre, and indeed it can already be said to occur in the work of Hegel and such post-Hegelian theorists as Georg Simmel.

95. Lyotard, *Phenomenology*, 34.

96. Husserl, "Phenomenology" (1927), *Shorter Works*, 32–33. In the "Inaugural Lecture" (1917) Husserl describes phenomenology as providing a "scientific" and transcendental foundation for all "Things in Nature, persons and personal communities, social forms and formations, poetic and plastic formations, every kind of cultural work" (ibid., 16).

97. Lyotard, *Phenomenology*, 33, 68, 34.

98. Merleau-Ponty, "Phenomenology and the Sciences of Man" (1961), *Primacy*, 94. Merleau-Ponty tries to bring phenomenology into dialogue with biology and psychology as early as 1942 in *The Structure of Behavior*, where he criticizes these disciplines for their mechanistic and reifying tendencies, 7–10. See also *Merleau-Ponty à la Sorbonne*, in particular 397–464.

99. Lyotard, *Phenomenology*, 42, 134, 127, 135, 105.

100. Nancy, *Community*, 104.

101. Lyotard, *Phenomenology*, 136, 112–32.

102. I refer to such books as Lyotard's *The Differend* and *Heidegger and 'the jews'*; Nancy's *The Inoperative Community*; Blanchot's *La communauté inavouable*

and *The Writing of the Disaster*; and Giorgio Agamben's *The Coming Community*. It is appropriate to call these texts post-Heideggerian, but not in the same way as the work of Spanos, which is a largely unproblematized transatlantic and disciplinary translation of Heidegger's thought to the field of literary criticism in North America. By contrast the work of these theorists is enabled by a radicalization but most importantly an unworking of Heidegger's work (see Nancy, *Community*, 104).

103. See Merleau-Ponty "Philosophy and Non-philosophy since Hegel," which deals with Hegel and Marx, though it credits neither thinker with bringing together philosophy and nonphilosophy.

104. See Regan, *Paul Ricoeur*, 35, 69.

105. Fisera (ed.), *Writing on the Wall. May 1968*, 247–8; Dosse, I.4, 9, 13, 39, 136–41, 146–47, 292, 326–27, 380–83. On "the end of philosophy" see also Renaut and Ferry, *French Philosophy of the Sixties*, 4–12. On the response of avant-garde to institutionalized philosophy in the face of the rising power of the social sciences, see the "Preface to the English Edition" of Bourdieu's *Homo Academicus*. Bourdieu categorizes as "philosophers" not only Derrida and Foucault but also Baudrillard (xviii–xxiv, 279n).

106. Heidegger, *Basic Writings*, 434; Vattimo, 12–14.

107. I refer to Husserl's unfinished *The Crisis of European Sciences and Transcendental Phenomenology*. In the related Vienna lecture (*Crisis*, 269–99), Husserl traces the blame for this crisis, obviously intensified by Europe's standing on the threshold of war, back to the abandonment of philosophy's disciplinary rigor by the post-Kantian idealists, who allowed philosophy to leak into and be modified by other areas (such as religion, law, history, aesthetics, and so on).

108. Heidegger, *Basic Writings*, 434–35.

109. Levinas, *Humanisme*, 103, 97. It is important to note that Levinas sees a deep complicity between the transcendentalism of the human sciences and that of Heidegger himself (99–101), which may explain why Heidegger reads the end of philosophy in emancipatory terms that we do not find in the French theorists who draw on his work.

110. Lefebvre, *Position*, 25, 109, 142–43, 43, 75, 195–97, 201–4, 212–17; Vattimo, 12–22. Baudrillard returns to Lefebvre's phenomenological theme of a forgetting of finitude twenty-five years later in the chapter on "Immortality" in *The Illusion of the End* (89–100). While I have distinguished Lefebvre and Lyotard, it is worth stressing the phenomenological side of Lefebvre's thinking, which thus picks up Tran Duc Thao's influential attempt to connect Husserlian phenomenology and Marxism, discussed in Chapter 3. Lefebvre shared the student radicals' view that structuralism was part of the Intellectual State Apparatus (see Turkle, 72). But he does not advocate a reorganization and continuation of the human sciences as

critical instead of orthopaedic and eventually returned to the philosophy department.

111. Lyotard, *Phenomenology*, 136.

112. Nancy, *Community*, 104; Lyotard, *Phenomenology*, 136, 34.

113. Nancy defines *exposition* as follows: "it is a question of understanding before all else that in 'communication' what takes place is an *exposition*: finite existence exposed to finite existence, co-appearing before it and with it" (*Community*, xl). As "ex-position" the word obviously recalls Heidegger's ec-stasis, a standing outside of one's own interiorized identity.

114. Lyotard, *Phenomenology*, 34.

115. Merleau-Ponty, "Philosophy and Non-philosophy since Hegel," 9, 61, 73. In his notes Hugh Silverman describes Merleau-Ponty's "chiasm" as "an intertwining of visible and invisible, seen and seeing, touched and touching. It is associated with an inside becoming outside, outside becoming inside, in short, a reversibility" (300).

116. The early Foucault is profoundly interested in literature and psychoanalysis but nowhere else mentions ethnology. In *OT* he feels nervously obliged to take in the newest of the disciplines, yet also to point it in a more recursive direction, which it was not to take, with the result that he makes no further reference to it.

117. De Man, *Critical Writings*, 215.

118. De Man, *Blindness and Insight*, 102–41.

119. Lyotard, *Phenomenology*, 32.

120. I offer here my own "supplementary" reading of de Man's early work on the critical tradition, which consists of essays and reviews, not books, and which is focused on the work of others and reluctant to assert its own voice, working instead by subtraction and retreat. The dialectic of blindness and insight can easily be taken for one-upmanship. But I suggest that it is a vigilance that has not quite redefined itself as a work of friendship and community, terms later coined by Derrida, Nancy, and others (as Derrida recognizes in his *Memoires*).

121. Lyotard, *Phenomenology*, 34, 132.

122. Lyotard, *Heidegger and 'the jews,'* 15.

123. Nancy, *Community*, xxxviii–xl; Wahl, *Philosophies*, 4.

124. I refer to the two key figures of Nancy's that I deploy in this book: community and exscription (see Chapter 3). Nancy draws on Bataille to think about both these figures (*Community*, 16–31; *Birth to Presence*, 319–20, 333–40).

125. See Rockmore, xvi.

126. The modernity of deconstruction has been emphasized by Norris and Dews. Although Norris now differentiates deconstruction from poststructuralism (as postmodernism), and Dews uses the term *poststructuralism*, the two agree in

privileging Kant and Habermas, while Norris makes the rejection of Nietzsche (as postmodern nihilist) a condition of deconstruction's modernity (*The Truth about Postmodernism*, 38–69). By contrast I would see Nietzsche as absolutely pivotal to the modernity of deconstruction, hence my term *radical* modernity. It is, however, a Nietzsche read through *The Birth of Tragedy* that I have in mind, rather than the Nietzsche of *Thus Spake Zarathustra* and *The Will to Power* assumed by Norris.

127. Nancy, *Community*, xxxviii. The word echoes Levinas's valorizing of infinity over totality.

128. Žižek, 141, 146.

CHAPTER 2

1. Donato, "The Two Languages of Criticism," in Macksey and Donato, ed., *The Structuralist Controversy*, 89–92; Macksey and Donato, "The Space Between— 1971," ibid., x, xii.

2. Like the early de Man, Blanchot works in a deconstructive vein in the forties—well before Derrida, whom he influences—and then reworks his earlier deconstruction in a way that registers the impact of the linguistic turn, for instance in his 1969 essay, "The Absence of the Book" (GO: 145–60). Levinas, on the other hand, seems unconcerned with structuralism, to which he refers only once (*Humanisme*, 77).

3. Pavel, 9.

4. 1968 has been the subject of several studies that place it at various points on a spectrum leading from liberation, through failed revolt, to recuperation. See Touraine; Renaut and Ferry, *French Philosophy*; Reader. Peter Starr provides one of the most trenchant psychopolitical analyses of the specific effects of 1968 on Theory in *Logics of Failed Revolt: French Theory after May '68*. Finally Bill Readings, concerned with how the student revolt speaks to the future, reads it through Nancy and Blanchot's work on the constitutive incompleteness of community, 135–49.

5. Eagleton, 142.

6. Kristeva is the one among these theorists who does talk of practice in a text that is indeed vulnerable to Eagleton's charge of vicarious revolutionism: *Revolution in Poetic Language* (193–226). This is, however, an entirely theoretical text, and when she actually turns to a practice, it is psychoanalysis—and by no means in the affirmatively destructive form taken by the antipsychiatry movement. On the other hand the Anglo-American concern with practice is evident in the popularity of Bourdieu and the later Foucault; earlier on, it can be seen in the way deconstruction was converted into a literary critical practice.

7. Dews describes this shift (110–11), though it may be partly a shift in our *re-ception* of French theory. One must also add that theorists of this "second" post-

1968 phase of poststructuralism such as Lyotard and Kristeva subsume language into desire rather than emancipating themselves from it.

8. The term is used by Todd May in *The Political Philosophy of Poststructuralist Anarchism.* May is typical of the new poststructuralism in having no interest in language but emphasizing "the end of humanism" (75–83). He draws on Foucault and Deleuze, and before them Nietzsche (53, 89–93), to propose a new kind of anarchism concerned with tactics rather than strategies (9–13), in which Nietzsche's antifoundationalism and will-to-power are assimilated to American pragmatism. "Poststructuralist political theory" assumes "the positivity or creativity of power and . . . the idea that practices or groups of practices (rather than subject or structure) are the proper unit of analysis" (87).

9. See Simpson. Simpson criticizes the academic postmodern for its "deeply conventional" attack on theory and its reinstatement of "the organic individual" and "identity politics" (14, 18, 58–9, 65). Under this rubric he includes postcolonialism, feminism, cultural studies, and an anthropology reconfigured through literature (18–27, 32, 40, 96).

10. Ulmer, 4–5, 7, 12.

11. See David Wellbery's foreword to Kittler (xiii). However, I am not grouping Kittler with Ulmer. *Discourse Networks* does not exemplify cultural studies' emphasis on practice, being rather a *history* of shifts in practice that is deeply sensitive to their psychological ramifications.

12. Mowitt, 24, and more generally 23–79.

13. Harland, 3, 9.

14. Levinas, *Humanisme,* 74

15. The word is Levinas's in the section "Atheism and Inhumanism" that begins his essay on Blanchot (*Proper Names,* 127).

16. Dews, 2. However, I do not agree with Dews (1) that Foucault's *Madness and Civilization* falls into the same category because it in no way foregrounds language or structure and is, rather, an example of Heideggerian *destruktion.*

17. On the phenomenological resonances of Lacan's earlier work, see Dews, 70; Spiegelberg, 139, 141–42; Renaut and Ferry, *French Philosophy,* 191–200. See also Kristeva, who notes the influence on Lacan of Sartre's transcendence of the ego and his focus on the Other (*La révolte intime,* 233, 237, 253).

18. Barthes, "Writing Degree Zero," in *Writing Degree Zero and Elements of Semiology,* 46, 76–78, 84–85; *Critical Essays,* 15–16, 21, 198–99, 203; Robbe-Grillet, *For a New Novel,* 53–56, 58–59, 64, 72–73.

19. See Lentricchia, *After the New Criticism,* 317; Dews, 96.

20. Lukács, 44.

21. See for instance Guillory, 198–201 (on de Man); Starr, 48–56 (on Lacan)

and 77–87 (on Althusser); Hertz, 85, 91 (on de Man); and Harpham, 220–36 and 255, 267 (on de Man).

22. Levinas, *Humanisme*, 97. Authority and mastery are most commonly attributed to de Man (see Lentricchia, 284, 299–300; Guillory, 182–95, 199–203) and debated through Lacan, who is sometimes seen as succumbing to the illusion of mastery and sometimes seen as playing with it.

23. Lacan, quoted by Starr, 52. Starr also comments that "Lacan's psychotic 'trial in rigor'" was aimed against "ego psychology . . . [and] that underlying ideology of happiness and personal liberation he associated with 'the American way of life'" (55). From this perspective his response to 1968 (discussed by Starr, 56–76), can also be seen as aimed against affirmative poststructuralism, including its French exemplars.

24. Quoted in Marini, 243.

25. Butler, *Psychic Life*, 6–10, 92, 102.

26. Levinas, *Humanisme*, 23, 118n3, 74.

27. Butler, *Psychic Life*, 92.

28. Derrida does not actually refer to Hyppolite in "Ends," but in "The Pit and the Pyramid" (also 1968) he allows that his own sense of semiology—as being at the center of Hegel's *Logic*—contains "an implicit and permanent reference" to *Logic and Existence* (M: 71). This implicit reference also underpins the revised view of Hegel in "The Ends of Man" and its dismissal of the "anthropologistic" French reading of Hegel as a "serious mistake" (M: 117). For it is difficult to believe that Derrida could so harshly dismiss the French Hegelians if he were not implicitly exempting Hyppolite, his former teacher, from his castigation of Sartre and Kojève.

29. Deleuze comments on this tension in his 1954 review (included in LE: 191–5). He notes that reintroducing "finitude . . . into the Absolute"—in other words what I see as the deconstructive aspect of the book—risks bringing back "anthropologism" (194).

30. Roustang notes that the transference onto theory is more dangerous than the transference onto an empirical, fallible subject because theory's alleged impersonality prevents one from understanding that a transference is involved (58).

31. Hyppolite, *Genesis*, 212; Butler, *Psychic Life*, 3.

32. Renaut and Ferry, *French Philosophy*, 129–31.

33. Lyotard, *Heidegger and the 'jews,'* 4–5; Derrida, *Of Spirit*, 4, 25, 60 and see also 65–72.

34. Butler, *Psychic Life*, 92, 94. Guillory provides a hostile psychoanalysis of de Man's fetishizing of scientific rigor; see especially 198, 201, 231–33. Hertz provides a sympathetic psychoanalysis of de Manian rigor as the other side of pathos (82–104).

35. *Aesthetic Ideology* and *The Resistance to Theory* were not published during de

Man's lifetime. As for *The Rhetoric of Romanticism* (1984), it was not put together at de Man's initiative, and what he describes as the "melancholy spectacle" (viii) of its heterogeneity—spanning as it does work of four decades—precludes seeing it as a book.

36. De Man, *Allegories*, 82–83; *Blindness and Insight*, xii.

37. De Man, *Allegories*, 205, 252; Guillory, 201.

38. Commentators on de Man often make de Man's last work a separate entity but do not necessarily assume a difference from his work of the seventies. See Chase, 82; David Clark, 40. I choose the date 1976 approximately to mark a shift in de Man's work that is not absolute or without overlaps. Most of *Allegories of Reading* was published from 1972 to 1976: only chapters 8 and 9 were written for the book. Chapter 12 (published in 1977) already introduces the figure of the machine, but its nightmarish potential is still contained within the notion of system. On the other hand, the following key essays that disfigure the scientific project of AR were published or given as lectures after 1976: "The Epistemology of Metaphor" (1978), "Shelley Disfigured" (1979), "Autobiography as Defacement" (1979), "Pascal's Allegory of Persuasion" (1981), "Hypogram and Inscription" (1981), "'Conclusion': Walter Benjamin's 'The Task of the Translator'" (1983), and "Aesthetic Formalization: Kleist's *Über das Marionettentheater*" (1984). These essays can be found in RT, RR, and *Aesthetic Ideology*.

39. De Man, *Allegories*, 268, 122–24.   40. Ibid., 162.

41. David Clark, 41.   42. Derrida, *Points*, 83, 212.

43. De Man, *Allegories*, 249, x.   44. De Man, *Aesthetic Ideology*, 42.

45. De Man, *Allegories*, 15.   46. Ibid., 268, 298.

47. Leclaire, 50, 57–96, 163; Lacan, quoted in Marini, 149.

48. De Man, *Allegories*, 205, 300.

49. Žižek associates deconstruction with modernism and sees Lacan as the only postmodernist. Following Lyotard, he also does not place postmodernism after modernism; Beckett is a modernist writer whereas Kafka is postmodern (*Looking Awry*, 144–50). The reference to Sartre seems implicit in Žižek's discussion of presence as "nauseous" (146). Cf. also Baudrillard's discussion of the loss of the dialectic of lack and transcendence in the transition from modern alienation to postmodern reification (CS: 187–93).

50. Kittler, 178–96. See also Orrin Wang's suggestive analysis of de Man's machine in terms of (late) capitalism, in "De Man, Marx, Rousseau, and the Machine."

51. De Man, *Allegories*, 294.

52. David Clark, 41; Canguilhem, *La connaissance de la vie*, 116.

53. De Man, *Allegories*, 300.

CHAPTER 3

1. Dosse, I.3–10; Rockmore, 95.

2. However, Corbin had also *earlier* translated "Dasein" as "existence" (see Hollier [ed.], *The College of Sociology*, 399n7).

3. Corngold, "Error in Paul de Man," in Pease, 92–97.

4. This is according to Hans-Georg Gadamer, to whom Heidegger gave away his unread copy of the text (see Wolin, 238n15).

5. Derrida, "The Time of a Thesis: Punctuations," 38.

6. Heidegger, *Basic Writings*, 231.

7. Heidegger, ibid., 250, 260. The phrase "infinite absolute negativity" is Kierkegaard's and describes the infinite regress of a negativity that is projective if not exactly productive in a Hegelian sense (278).

8. Ibid., 149.

9. Sartre does often use the two terms side by side in BN, but he is not equating them so much as deliberately moving from one to the other. In BN he is quite clear about the differences between his thinking and Heidegger's; he is aware that *Dasein* is a "pure 'being-outside-of-self'" (486), and slides between the two terms so as to insist on the inadequacy of *Dasein* for a concept of "human" being. However, Sartre did not intensively study Heidegger until 1939, and it is true that in *Sketch for a Theory of the Emotions* (published in 1939) he reads *Being and Time* existentially (23–80). But this is not to say that he identifies with the existential viewpoint, from which he tries to distance us by moving between Heidegger and empirical psychology.

10. Levinas, *Theory of Intuition*, 78.

11. Levinas further comments on the egotistical sublimity of Heideggerian being when he writes, "Light is that through which something is other than myself, but already as if it came from me" (TO: 64). The term *nonviolence* is used by Derrida to describe Levinas's own thought in "Violence and Metaphysics: An Essay on the Thought of Emmanuel Levinas" (WD: 147). Levinas's insistence on nonviolence has much to do not only with the Holocaust but also with the French Left's fascination with terror, which I discuss later.

12. In 1934 Levinas writes that Heidegger "inaugurates" a third phase of phenomenology, "that of *existential phenomenology*" (*Discovering Existence*, 39). In 1940 he still reads Heidegger as an existentialist (61, 84). Wahl, despite an early enthusiasm for Heidegger, also came to the view that he was not a philosopher of existence (*Mots, mythes, et réalité*, 183).

13. Levinas, *God, Death*, 70.

14. Nancy, *Birth*, 319, 339–40; Bataille, *Inner Experience*, 8–9, 178.

15. Similarly Sartre writes: "The image must enclose in its very structure a nihilating thesis. . . . first it is the nihilation of the world (since the world is not offering the imagined object as an actual object of perception), secondly the nihilation of the object of the image (it is posited as not actual), and finally by the same stroke it is the nihilation of itself" (BN: 62).

16. See for instance the essay "Différance," where Derrida does and does not use the words "transcendental" and "primordial," even as he insists that *différance* "is not marked by a capital letter" (SP: 130, 136, 139, 143, 153).

17. Hollier, *Absent without Leave*, 145.

18. Heidegger, *Basic Writings*, 103.

19. Žižek, *Looking Awry*, 146, 151.

20. Corngold, in Pease, 95.

21. Gasché borrows the term *hyperreflection* from Merleau-Ponty to distinguish a "dialectics without synthesis" that is proto-deconstructive from a Hegelian "reflexivity" that founds consciousness (*Inventions of Difference*, 28–35).

22. Žižek, *Looking Awry*, 144.

23. Robbe-Grillet, 60–68; Žižek, *Looking Awry*, 143–46.

24. Sartre, *Nausea*, 182–85; Levinas, *The Levinas Reader*, 30–31. Levinas refers to Sartre and distinguishes horror from nausea (31), as does his editor Seán Hand, who speaks of the "inner peace" of the Sartrean *en-soi* (29). Yet the in-itself is much closer to the Levinasian *sans-soi* than to the Heideggerian *es gibt*.

25. "Thus there appears a whole system of verbal correspondence by which we cause our body to be designated for us as it is for the Other by utilizing these designations to denote our body as it is for us. . . . Here therefore it is language which teaches me my body's structures for the Other" (BN: 464).

26. The turn is signalled by Levinas (TO: 39), although by 1946 he is also critical of Heidegger. See also Hyppolite, who rereads Hegel through Heidegger, thus diverging from Kojève to make Hegel a thinker of antihumanism (LE: 177, 188).

27. Kojève, 160. Sartre attended Kojève's lectures (given from 1933 to 1939), as did Lacan and Levinas.

28. Levinas's proximity to Sartre is mentioned by Hollier, *Absent without Leave*, 157. Levinas is highly critical of Sartre, whom he rarely names (TO: 50). Nevertheless, if he will not credit Sartre with giving nothingness its due, this is because he misreads him as identifying *le néant* and *la négation* as a negative predication, although Sartre clearly uncouples the two. Thus Levinas complains that "all nothingness is the nothing of something." He also writes that the "nothingness that comes out of negation always remains tied to the intentional gesture of negation, and thus keeps the trace of being which this gesture refuses, repels, and repudi-

ates." Although this is not untrue, the diacritical link between being and nothing-ness is not the same thing as a negative predication (*God, Death*, 124, 113).

29. Derrida, *Of Spirit*, 18.

30. Blanchot, "The Beginnings of a Novel," in *The Blanchot Reader*, 33–34.

31. Heidegger, *Basic Writings*, 101.

32. Ibid., 103.

33. Levinas, *De l'évasion*, 115–17—(trans. mine); Rolland, introduction to *De l'évasion*, 35–41; Heidegger, *Basic Writings*, 101, 103. Levinas's essay first appeared in *Recherches philosophiques* in 1935–36. Rolland points out the close proximity of Sartre's and Levinas's treatments of nausea and observes that the "*philosophical en-counter*" between the two men is all the more interesting in that Sartre, though he may subsequently have read Levinas's essay, had already written an unpublished draft of his novel in 1931. In effect Rolland attributes to Sartre the same re-vision of Heideggerian anguish as he does to Levinas (29, 79n).

34. Levinas, *De l'évasion*, 115–16.

35. Sartre writes: "So much for the exterior. What happened in me did not leave clear traces. There was something which I saw and which disgusted me, but I no longer know whether I was looking at the sea or at the pebble" (*Nausea*, 10).

36. Wahl, *Philosophies*, 7, 29–30. Wahl does not deal with Levinas, though he had read EE and links it to Sartre (103). Wahl's account of empiricism pertains rather to Schelling as a precursor of the philosophies of existence. The link be-tween Levinas and empiricism is made by Derrida, who clearly has Wahl in mind as he too links empiricism to metaphysics in the context of Schelling (WD: 151–52). Levinas himself discusses a "new sort of empiricism" in "Jean Wahl and Feeling" (*Proper Names*, 110).

37. Sartre, *Sketch*, 24–25 and more generally 14–31. Sartre writes, "phenomenol-ogy is the study of phenomena—not of the facts. And by a phenomenon we are to understand 'that which announces itself.' . . . From this point of view, Heidegger thinks that, in every human attitude . . . we can rediscover the whole of the hu-man reality . . . the human reality assuming itself and 'emotionally-directing' itself towards the world" (25).

38. Merleau-Ponty, *The Visible and the Invisible*, 270. Although Merleau-Ponty is not talking of Sartre here, but of Freud, this passage from the working notes is framed by two others that discuss Sartre and thus tacitly places Sartre at the con-junction of phenomenology and psychoanalysis sketched in "Phenomenology and Psychonalaysis." See Chapter VI for a more detailed discussion of *The Visible and the Invisible* as Merleau-Ponty's attempt, after his break with Sartre, to acknowl-edge his obligation to Sartrean thought.

39. Sartre, *The Wartime Diaries*, 153, 148–49.

40. Ibid., 148.

41. Bataille, *Visions of Excess*, 83. The piece from which this quotation is taken, "The Pineal Eye," was written around 1930 but not published until much later. However, many of Bataille's texts on bodyparts, including *Histoire de l'oeil* (1928), had appeared prior to BN.

42. Merleau-Ponty, "Phenomenology and Psychoanalysis," 71.

43. Bloom uses the term *revisionary ratio* to name various structures of influence that he reads in terms of an oedipal dynamic that I am not evoking here (*Anxiety*, 14).

44. Blanchot, *The Space of Literature*, 41.

45. Levinas, *Proper Names*, 132–33, 136–37. Sarah Lawall makes a similar point when she argues that Blanchot is a reversed mirror image of the Geneva critics, replacing presence with absence, the individual author with the impersonal creator (221).

46. Lyotard, *Heidegger and the 'jews,'* 4–5.

47. Holland, "Introduction to Part I," in *The Blanchot Reader*, 22; Blanchot, ibid., 33–34. The relationship between Sartre and Blanchot is not purely one-sided. Sartre reviewed Blanchot's novel *Aminadab* in 1943. His *Mallarmé: Or the Poet of Nothingness*, written in 1952, published posthumously in 1986, but partially published earlier, continues a subterranean dialogue with Blanchot, to whose work on Mallarmé he refers (133, 137).

48. Sartre, *What Is Literature?* 6.

49. Lycette Nelson points out in her introduction to Blanchot's *The Step Not Beyond* (1973) that in Blanchot's idea of the trace there "is nothing of Derrida's idea of the trace as constitutive of the present." The trace is rather "the idea of writing as effacement, as opposed to the traditional idea that writing preserves what would otherwise disappear" (xv).

50. Sartre, *What Is Literature?*, 6–8, 29–30.

51. Ibid., 17. In *The Psychology of Imagination* Sartre struggles to attribute a kind of positivity to the image conceived as unreal and empty: "an image is not . . . simply the *world-negated*, it is always *the world negated from a certain point of view*, namely, the one that permits the positing of the absence or the non-existence of the object presented 'as an image'" (268). But as Peter Caws says, it is difficult to see how "nothingness," as Sartre will later develop the concept, can take this "kind of initiative" (42). Indeed this aporia is at the heart of Sartre's attempt to build on his ontology a theory of praxis that must always be in bad faith.

52. TO: 42–44, 52, 54–57. Levinas in fact refers to Blanchot's novel *Aminadab* (56), though in general he seems to associate the term with the more strongly monadic solitude of romanticism (55).

53. Levinas, *Theory of Intuition*, 65–66, 74.

54. De Man, *Blindness and Insight*, 251.

55. Rockmore, 56, 97.

56. Hollier, *Absent without Leave*, 157 and 147–57 more generally; Blanchot, "How Is Literature Possible?" in *The Blanchot Reader*, 49–60.

57. Sartre claimed to have nothing in common with the Surrealists; however his relationship to them was deeply ambivalent, as William Plank argues (61–72).

58. Hollier reads Blanchot's portrait of the terrorist as an account of Sartre (*Absent without Leave*, 7–8), though there may also be a muted reference to Merleau-Ponty's *Humanism and Terror* (1947).

59. Sartre sees the political group as formed through the "free violence" of terror, in which individualities are negated in the common interests of the group. Insofar as the "fused group" is not a community or society but an artificial unity created by resistance to the enemy, the "freedom" of terror is a necessary form of internalized "counter-violence." Sartre's terrorism, as late as *Critique*, is an example of his continuing antihumanism: any naive belief in the integrity of the group has to be subjected to the critical knowledge that, first, negation always proceeds by way of a repression that makes what is posited purely figural and, second, that the collective ego projected by the group is "transcendent," and is thus an exteriority, an in-itself, something inhuman (*Critique*, 428–44)

60. Heidegger, *Basic Writings*, 231.

61. Hertz, 85–86.

62. De Man, *Blindness and Insight*, 208.

63. See for instance Norris, *Paul de Man*.

64. Sartre, *Mallarmé*, 129, 136–37. Although Sartre's full text was published posthumously in 1986, a shorter version, containing the passages cited, appeared in an introduction to an edition of Mallarmé published in 1966.

65. De Man, *Critical Writings*, 39.

66. Rockmore, 70, 179. A related point is made by Roger Frie, who notes that "the division between ontology and anthropology in fundamental ontology is not nearly as obvious as the later Heidegger makes it out to be. For example, the distinction . . . between the ontological character of existentials, such as anxiety, and their psychological dispositions is not entirely apparent" (85).

67. Levinas, *Discovering Existence*, 43; Ricoeur, "The Antinomy of Human Reality and the Problem of Philosophical Anthropology," 20–35. Raising the question of how to think the human sciences, as Foucault will do in OT, Ricoeur in a sense turns away from his own earlier work on Husserl and argues for a dialectic of "pathos" and "logos" that seems inflected by Levinas, wherein "philosophical discourse" is made responsible to the "pathos of misery," which is "the nonphilosophical origin, the poetic matrix, of philosophical anthropology" (20–21, 35).

68. Foucault, *Dream*, 31.

69. Renaut and Ferry, *Heidegger and Modernity*, 87.

70. See Spiegelberg, 136–37.

71. While the book is strongly influenced by Merleau-Ponty, its second part develops the crudely Marxist argument that mental illness is caused by social alienation and is written in the shadow of a postwar, Sartrean view that philosophical thought must be useful. Foucault suppressed this section and rewrote it when he reissued the book as *Mental Illness and Psychology* in 1962. The suppressed section reveals his links to the antipsychiatry movement of Szasz, Cooper, and Laing, which was strongly influenced by Sartre. Interestingly, while Foucault has tried to distance himself from this movement and from phenomenology generally, the English translations of *Madness and Civilization*, BC, and OT all originally appeared in two series edited by Laing: "Studies of Existentialism and Phenomenology" and "The World of Man." A certain Sartrean activism persists in *Madness and Civilization* and perhaps returns, albeit highly qualified and complicated, in the later social studies.

72. Foucault, *Mental Illness*, 50.

73. In 1942 Binswanger writes to Heidegger: "I have repeatedly emphasized the difference between your pure ontological intentions and my anthropological endeavours. I would be satisfied if you would acknowledge that I have made use of the new 'impulses' which anthropology has gained from ontological problems" (quoted by Frei, 86).

74. Binswanger, "Ellen West," 269–70.

75. Derrida, *Points*, 83, 212.

76. Miller, 137–44.

77. Foucault, "Maurice Blanchot," 16, 19.

CHAPTER 4

1. Derrida, "The Time of a Thesis," 39.

2. Translations from Derrida's *Le problème de la genèse* are mine.

3. Derrida, "The Time of a Thesis," 38.

4. Merleau-Ponty, "On the Phenomenology of Language," *Signs*, 84.

5. Merleau-Ponty, "Phenomenology and Psychoanalysis," 70; "Phenomenology and the Sciences of Man," in *Primacy*, 45. Borrowing from romantic hermeneutics the notion of a "divinatory reading" in which one understands the author better than he understood himself, Merleau-Ponty says, "we shall not develop the ideas of the phenomenologists merely according to the texts but according to their intentions. . . . We shall not restrain ourselves from explaining the phenomenological texts by considerations which are not found in their writing" (45).

6. Ricoeur, *Husserl*, 43, 151; Merleau-Ponty, "On the Phenomenology of Language," 84–5, 88. See also "Phenomenology and the Sciences of Man" (1951), where Merleau-Ponty argues for a radical existentializing of language in the last writings, particularly in "The Origin of Geometry," where Husserl sees ideas as "carried into the world of existence by their instruments of expression—books, museums, musical scores, writings" (*Primacy*, 83–84). In the same essay, Merleau-Ponty also argues for Husserl's turn to history in the later writings (85–92).

7. Merleau-Ponty, "On the Phenomenology of Language," 84.

8. Levinas, *Theory of Intuition*, 66.

9. Thao, xxi, 20. Translations from this text are mine.

10. Merleau-Ponty, "Phenomenology and Psychoanalysis," 70.

11. Merleau-Ponty, "Indirect Language and the Voices of Silence," in *Signs*, 39, 43, 45 (italics mine). This 1952 essay specifically uses Saussure as a starting point. Merleau-Ponty read Jakobson as well and wrote extensively on language, not only in *Signs*, but also in *Consciousness and the Acquisition of Language* (1964) and other studies between 1948 and 1959. His discussion of the role of language in "The Origin of Geometry" is in "Phenomenology and the Sciences of Man" (82–83)—lectures that Derrida would likely have heard at the Sorbonne.

12. Bloom, 119.

13. Rapaport, 149, 151.

14. Kristeva, *Revolution*, 140.

15. Habermas, *Modernity*, 248.

16. Derrida, *Points*, 79; Tim Clark, 109. Clark concedes that Derrida's reading of writers is very different from his reading of philosophical figures in terms of a form of "dialectics greatly indebted to Hegel, but refusing to subsume the work of negativity in the universal" (109).

17. Merleau-Ponty, "The Philosopher and Sociology," *Signs*, 98–99, 102.

18. Derrida himself suggests that we take OGr "as a long essay articulated in two parts . . . into *the middle* of which one could staple *Writing and Difference*" (P: 4).

19. It is interesting that here (in 1990) Derrida is once again favorably invoking Sartre and Merleau-Ponty.

20. Thao, 90–97.

21. Ibid., 97.

22. Thao, 97; Gasché, "On Re-presentation," 4.

23. Thao, 96, 98; Ricoeur, *Husserl*, 110.

24. Derrida, *Points*, 261.

25. Thao, 94.

26. Kristeva, *Revolution*, 141.

27. Cumming, 8–11.

28. Ricoeur, *Husserl*, 151.

29. Ibid., 156.

30. Ibid., 155.

31. Norris, *The Truth about Postmodernism*, 54–57.

32. Foucault, "What Is Enlightenment?" 40–43, 36.

33. Derrida, *Aporias*, 44–45, 52, 59.

34. Ibid., 61.

35. Habermas characterizes Foucault's critique of reason as a promising alternative to the one offered by a "temporalized *Ursprungsphilosophie* in Heiddeger and Derrida" (*Modernity*, 248–49). But my point is that Derrida is much closer to Foucault than Habermas concedes.

36. Ibid., 239, 247–49.

37. Jaspers, 145–46.

38. Lyotard, *Phenomenology*, 34.

39. I borrow this word from Schelling's *Ages of the World*, which Derrida cites in connection with the "irony of God" (WD: 68). On the Frankfurt school's relation to Schelling, see Habermas, *Philosophical-Political Profiles*, 63–79.

40. Levinas, *Theory of Intuition*, liv; cf. WD: 118.

41. Derrida could just as well have used Hegel at this point: indeed his reference to the "concept" seems to evoke Hegel. He uses "Heidegger" in part because Levinas uses him as a figure for the tradition he is leaving behind.

42. Derrida translates "Sprachleib" as "la chair linguistique," but "la chair" would necessarily have connotations different from "le corps vécu" with which "Leib" is normally associated.

43. I borrow the phrase from J. Claude Evans, who draws no links with Sartre but argues, in general, that Derrida imposes his own figures on Husserl (66). Evans also comments that Derrida uses a rhetoric of "the inside" (113), which again has more affinities with Sartre than with Husserl or Heidegger.

44. Lyotard, *Heidegger and 'the jews,'* 15–16.

45. Derrida also draws on Sartre in criticizing Levinas's nonpersonal alterity through the concept of an "alter ego": "the other is absolutely other only if he is an ego, that is, in a certain way, if he is the same as I" (WD: 127).

46. Interestingly, however, Derrida admits that he came to Blanchot and Bataille through Sartre (*Points*, 122).

47. Lyotard, *Phenomenology*, 105; *Heidegger and 'the jews,'* 5.

48. Thao, xxv–xxvi.

49. Tim Clark, 5, 9, 18, 109. One could see Yale deconstruction as transposing this dialectic from historiography to literary criticism, thus moving from a broader *epistemic* project to a more narrowly *epistemological* analysis. Indeed Clark quotes Jonathan Culler's statement that Derrida's discussions of literary works are not "*deconstructions* as we have been using the term" and that a "deconstructive literary criticism will be primarily influenced by his readings of philosophical works."

50. Norris, *Derrida*, 142–62.

51. Tim Clark, 9; Carroll, xiv.

52. Butler, *Psychic Life*, 3–4.

53. Heidegger, *Basic Writings*, 217.

54. Habermas, *Modernity*, 414n.

55. Worringer, 18, 16, 37, 23

56. Pavel, 5, 23, 1, 54, 125.

57. Tim Clark, 9.

58. Bourdieu, *Political Ontology*, 100.

59. I am not suggesting that the labels post-Heideggerianism or French Heideggerianism are fully adequate to the work of the theorists they purport to describe—hence my use of the term *field* to suggest an institutional phenomenon that cannot be unequivocally identified with anyone, but that has a performative effect. Jean-Luc Marion's work is probably the simplest case of a post-Heideggerianism that forgets rather than chiasmatically includes Sartre. But Blanchot and Levinas can be read in this way only if one forgets their earlier work, which is increasingly the case (for instance Rapaport, who argues for the seminality of Blanchot to Derrida's Heideggerian turn, nowhere mentions *The Space of Literature*). Nancy is also difficult to place because of the tension in his work between Heidegger and Bataille.

60. Here I am referring not so much to the actual curricular practice of academic departments (which is diverse and conflicted) as to certain, other institutional or marketing practices; for instance theory (not just deconstruction/poststructuralism) is now to be found in the philosophy rather than literature sections of North American bookstores, and it is no longer found in publisher's catalogues under literary studies or as an autonomous category.

61. Rapaport, 16, 19, 112.

62. Renaut and Ferry, *Heidegger and Modernity*, 52.

63. Kristeva, *Revolution*, 141. *The Gift of Death* provides a good example of this retention through deferral and can be contrasted in its extreme obliquity with the way Levinas takes issue with Heidegger's being-toward-death in *God, Death*. Derrida does not criticize Heidegger but marks his distance from the latter by criticizing Patocka, who is said to be different from Heidegger. While Patocka's difference from Heidegger and Derrida's difference from Patocka may be clear, it is hard to say what the difference is between Heidegger and Derrida. Such a difference is insinuated but left obscure; it must somehow be inferred from the difference between Patocka's difference from Heidegger and his resemblance to Heidegger.

64. Rockmore, 56.

65. Bourdieu, *Political Ontology*, 68, 92; Tim Clark, 73.

66. Rockmore, 81–82; Bourdieu, *Political Ontology*, 105.

67. Derrida himself makes this point in "The Ends of Man," which is still highly critical of Heidegger (M: 123–32). Framing Heidegger in terms of his rhetoric of proximity, Derrida argues that "Dasein, though *not* man, is nevertheless

nothing other than man" (127). Nevertheless, as Rapaport points out, Derrida later uses the very rhetoric he criticizes in Heidegger.

68. Levinas, *Theory of Intuition*, 154–56.

69. Binswanger, "Ellen West," 209.

70. Rapaport, 16, 19, 111 and more generally 123–37.

71. See Lycette Nelson, introduction to Blanchot, *The Step Not Beyond*, vii.

CHAPTER 5

1. Foucault, *Politics, Philosophy, Culture*, 22.

2. Megill, 202–4, 225; Dreyfus and Rabinow, 12.

3. This line of argument is also followed by Gary Gutting, who is critical both of the early Foucault's search for an "infrarational truth" and his neglect (from OT to AK) of "non-discursive practices," but who sees him as turning through geneal-ogy to the nondiscursive practices neglected by archaeology and thus as conclud-ing with "an acceptance of reason as the primary means of human liberation" (265–71).

4. Foucault, *Foucault Live*, 58.

5. See Lebrun, "Notes on Phenomenology in *Les mots et les choses*," 20–37; Dreyfus, "On the Ordering of Things," 80–95 (both in *Michel Foucault Philoso-pher*, trans. Armstrong). See also Spanos, *Heidegger and Criticism*, 132–80. Spanos correctly argues for the importance of Heidegger to Foucault's analysis of discipli-nary technology and suggests that Foucault's genealogy needs to be rethought in terms of Heidegger's destruction because the latter "overemphasizes the site of on-tology" while the former overemphasizes the sociopolitical. Spanos, however, deals only with the later Foucault, whereas my argument is that it is precisely this kind of rethinking that we find in the early Foucault.

6. Dreyfus, "Foreword to the California Edition," Foucault, *Mental Illness*, xxxvii–xl; Lebrun, 33.

7. Foucault's principal thesis for the Doctorat d'État, partially translated as *Madness and Civilization*, was already written when he sought Canguilhem's spon-sorhip for it. But, as he admits, Canguilhem's influence on his next work, *The Birth of The Clinic*, was profound (Eribon, 102–3). Canguilhem and Foucault are both discussed but not related in Lecourt's *Marxism and Epistemology*. A brief dis-cussion of the two is provided by Macherey in "De Canguilhem à Canguilhem en passant par Foucault," in *Georges Canguilhem*, 286–94. Macherey emphasizes the absence of the sick person's experience from Foucault's study, and thus opposes Canguilhem's phenomenology to Foucault's archaeology, without allowing for the possibility of a phenomenology of institutions as well as subjects. Finally Canguil-hem is also discussed by Gutting, who sees him as important to an understanding

of archaeology but does not discuss his relationship to phenomenology and does not give detailed attention to Foucault's introduction to Canguilhem's *On the Normal and the Pathological*. Correspondingly he sees the introduction of genealogy in *Discipline and Punish* as the turning point in Foucault's career and subsumes BC and OT into AK, thus criticizing the work up to AK for being too limited to purely discursive practices. My own analysis sees a much larger role for the nondiscursive in the early Foucault while also defining the category very differently from Gutting.

8. I have used the original French title for this book rather than the English title *Death and the Labyrinth*, which has no warrant. However I refer to the study parenthetically as DL.

9. Foucault, introduction, Canguilhem, *Normal*, 24, 8.

10. It is worth noting the last term in Foucault's summary of the opposition between the existentialists and Canguilhem: "It is to this philosophy of meaning, subject and the experienced thing that Canguilhem has opposed a philosophy of error, concept, and *the living being*" (ibid., 24; emphasis mine).

11. I borrow the term from Kristeva, who notes that "every signifying practice is a field of transpositions of various signifying systems (an inter-textuality)" (*Revolution*, 60).

12. Foucault, introduction, Canguilhem, *Normal*, 23

13. Ibid., 23.   14. Ibid., 9.

15. LaCapra, 153.   16. See Chapter 3, n. 60.

17. Dreyfus, "Introduction to the California Edition," Foucault, *Mental Illness*, xix–xxii. Miller, 63; Foucault, *Mental Illness*, 50.

18. Foucault, *Dream*, 31.

19. Ortega y Gasset, 14–21. Ortega specifically discusses "disciplines" and "order[s] of knowledge" (14, 17). Ortega's lectures were given in 1932–33.

20. Dreyfus, "Introduction to the California Edition," Foucault, *Mental Illness*, xxxix. An example of a return to phenomenology in Foucaultian cultural analysis is Scarry's *The Body in Pain*, which analyzes torture as part of the machinery of power but also tries to give voice to pain as something denied access to the order of discourse. Although she does not cite Canguilhem, Scarry's analysis of pain can be compared with his (*Normal*, 96–97).

21. Foucault, *Dream*, 56, 21.

22. Merleau-Ponty, *The Visible*, 218; Foucault, *Dream*, 36; Lyotard, *Phenomenology*, 34.

23. Foucault, *Dream*, 54.

24. Ibid., 38, 42, 34.

25. Kristeva, *La révolte intime*, 223–58; Foucault, *Dream*, 34, 36, 71, 67–68, 45–51, 57–59.

26. Foucault, *Dream*, 43.

27. Ibid., 31, 66, 32–33.

28. Ibid., 31. Spiegelberg distinguishes Binswanger's *"phenomenological* anthropology" from *"philosophical* anthropology": "the former does not claim to determine the essence of man as a whole but confines itself to phenomenological experience—i.e., how human *Dasein* is concretely experienced" (194). This distinction helps to explain the paradox of Foucault's using anthropology in an evidently laudatory way. But it is also worth noting that Foucault does not use *phenomenological* as a qualifier for anthropology but keeps the two terms separate, thus marking his awareness of the fact (a) that Heideggerian phenomenology cannot be an anthropology because Heidegger did not see *Dasein* as human and (b) that Binswanger's inflection of Heidegger towards anthropology is a goal that Foucault shares. In OT Foucault takes account of Heidegger's turning and his critique of Sartre. But what he rejects in Sartre is the latter's inverse Cartesianism and not his anthropology or his deconstruction of being.

29. Heidegger, *Basic Writings*, 131.

30. Foucault, *Foucault Live*, 19.

31. Macey (139) also points out the importance for BC of Bataille's *Histoire de l'oeil* on which Foucault had written in "A Preface to Transgression" (in *Language, Counter-memory*, 29–52).

32. Foucault, *Politics, Philosophy, Culture*, 19–24.

33. Interview in *La quinzaine litteraire* (April 15, 1966), quoted by Eribon, 161. For Foucault's interest in Lacan and psychoanalysis generally during this period and for his auditing of Lacan's seminars, see Eribon (139) and Miller (62). Racevskis discusses in a general way the usefulness of the Lacanian triad of the Symbolic, Imaginary, and Real for understanding archaeology (19, 67–77). His discussion, however, is on the level of content rather than form; he makes no detailed comparisons and does not see Foucault as formally inscribing his work within the transferential structure of the analytic session.

34. See for example Weedon.

35. Lacan, quoted in Marini, 202.

36. Lacan, *Fundamental Concepts*, 89.

37. See the summary of "Séminaire XIII: l'objet de la psychanalyse," in Marini, 199–200.

38. Lacan, *Fundamental Concepts*, 80, 71–2.

39. Ibid., 100, 83. For the contiguities between Heidegger and Lacan, see

Lukacher, 38–46. Lukacher is, however, reading Heidegger against and beyond himself.

40. See Hegel, *Aesthetics*, I.597–98; Schopenhauer, I.197.

41. Lacan, *Fundamental Concepts*, 82, 84.

42. Foucault, *Politics*, 23.

43. Foucault, *Mental Illness*, 50.

44. See Simmel's writings on culture from 1907–18 in *Simmel on Culture*.

45. Canguilhem, *Connaissance*, 13, 102–3; trans. mine.

46. Canguilhem, *Normal*, 101, 111–12.

47. Foucault, introduction, Canguilhem, *Normal*, 9.

48. Ibid., 13.

49. Canguilhem, *Normal*, 40.

50. Ibid., 78, 103, 64, 104

51. Ibid., 93, 97.

52. Ibid., 63, 228–29.

53. Foucault, introduction, Canguilhem, *Normal*, 13–19, 8.

54. Ibid., 9.

55. Ibid., 9, 24.

56. Ibid., 7.

57. Ibid., 17.

58. Sartre, *Sketch*, 25.

59. Canguilhem, *Normal*, 50.

60. Ibid., 87–88.

61. Merleau-Ponty, *Structure*, 64–65; this book, drawing on some of the same sources, had just appeared when Canguilhem published *Normal* (294n29).

62. Canguilhem, *Connaissance*, 116.

63. Ibid., 86.

64. Sartre, *Sketch*, 24.

65. Foucault, introduction, Canguilhem, *Normal*, 8.

66. Merleau-Ponty, *Structure*, 68, 91; see especially 220–24.

67. Foucault, introduction, Canguilhem, *Normal*, 20–21, 22.

68. Foucault, *Politics, Philosophy, Culture*, 23.

69. Foucault, introduction, Canguilhem, *Normal*, 11.

70. Ibid., 23.

71. Canguilhem, *Normal*, 34.

CHAPTER 6

1. There has been little analysis of this text or its place in Foucault's corpus, although Hollier comments briefly on the relationship between BC and DL as both being organized around "death as the key to reading" ("The Word of God: 'I Am Dead,'" in *Michel Foucault Philosopher*, 136–37).

2. The evidence for and against is given by Miller (20–29) and Eribon (324–26). Eribon cites an interview in February 1984 in which Foucault is aware

that doctors suspected he had AIDS; Miller mentions his preoccupation with AIDS in the fall of 1983 and his Nietzschean will to know the truth of death.

3. Lacan uses the term *matheme* to describe such psychoconceptual figures as the Möbius strip and the Klein bottle (Marini, 198). For the fold, see Deleuze, *The Fold*, 73–75; Perniola, *Enigmas*, 10. Deleuze had first used the fold in connection with Foucault's work (*Michel Foucault*, 94–123) but does not deal with any works before AK.

4. Jameson, 29–30.

5. I borrow this term from Gasché, who uses it to elaborate Derrida's deconstruction of a classical reflectionism based on a dialectic of self-confirmation but does not, however, cite Foucault's image (*Tain*, 6).

6. Blanchot, *Space*, 104.

7. Lacan as paraphrased by Marini, 198.

8. Robbe-Grillet, *For a New Novel*, 81, 84, 86.

9. Levinas, *Proper Names*, 137.

10. Foucault, *Mental Illness*, 50, 56.

11. Abraham and Torok argue that a patient's words can be read anagrammatically as concealing certain meanings that are ultimately unreadable, like Lacan's Real. Words are thus swallowed by the patient and "encrypted" as things inside the psyche.

12. Kristeva, *Revolution*, 63–64; "Within the Microcosm of the Talking Cure," in *Interpreting Lacan*, 42–43.

13. In an interview with P. Caruso, Foucault speaks of his difficulty in reconciling the conflicting attractions of literature and the positive social sciences (quoted in Gane, 41). Although the early work is built around a dialogue between the two, literature later disappears from Foucault's work; Gane says that while as an "intellectual personality" he may be aware of a tension, the later Foucault's "writings fall decisively into the positive tradition" (41).

14. De Certeau, 172–73.

15. Foucault, *Dream*, 32.

16. Foucault, *Foucault Live*, 4, 18.

17. Ibid., 4.

18. The distinction is briefly discussed by Megill, who differs from me in seeing OT as largely a structuralist work (208, 204).

19. Foucault, *Foucault Live*, 4.

20. Foucault, introduction, Canguilhem, *Normal*, 13.

21. Foucault, *Foucault Live*, 8–9.

22. See also ibid., 5.

23. Ibid., 7.

24. Eribon, 155.

25. Merleau-Ponty, *Visible*, 74.

26. Ibid., 63, 197. Merleau-Ponty's term "chiasm" (*Visible*, 130–55, 215) connnotes an "intertwining" and can be distinguished from de Man's "aporia," which signifies an "unpassable path" between opposites rather than a process in which they cross, coincide, and differ. In *Visible*, Merleau-Ponty develops the figure of the chiasm in connection with his concept of *la chair* or the flesh, which now replaces his earlier and simpler notion of *Leib* or the lived body (simpler because it suggests an embodiment rather than a (dis)embodiment of spirit in matter). In connection with the flesh, Merleau-Ponty describes the chiasmatic intertwining of subject and object, perception and language, and seeing with what is seen. The chiasm is his version of the fold: indeed he describes the experience of the flesh as a "coiling over of the visible upon the visible" that "traverses me and constitutes me as a seer" without allowing "me" to be a point of origin because "I" am also thereby enfolded into other bodies and spaces (140).

27. Merleau-Ponty, *Visible*, 63, 171, 214.

28. For a reading of Merleau-Ponty that places him between phenomenology and deconstruction (though without foregrounding the latter), see Leder.

29. Merleau-Ponty, *Phenomenology*, viii.

30. I borrow Foucault's account of how Blanchot conceives language in "Language to Infinity" (*Language, Counter-memory*, 58–59).

31. Merleau-Ponty, *Visible*, 52–74.

32. Ibid., 69.

33. Ibid., 69–70.

34. Ibid., 179, 201–2.

35. Ibid., 171.

36. Ibid., xx–xxvii.

37. Ibid., 218.

38. Ibid., 215.

39. Foucault, "A Preface to Transgression," *Language, Counter-memory*, 42.

40. Ibid., 66.

41. According to Heidegger "language is neither expression nor an activity of man" ("Language" [1959], in *Poetry, Language, Thought*, 197). According to Foucault "where there is a sign, there man cannot be" (*Foucault Live*: 8; cf. also OT: 339).

42. Foucault, "Maurice Blanchot," 15, 12.

43. Foucault, "Language to Infinity," 57.

44. Levinas uses the word "murmuring" with reference to Blanchot (*Proper Names*, 131). Foucault uses it in his two essays on Blanchot ("Language to Infinity," 55–56, 60; "Maurice Blanchot," 17, 25) and quotes Blanchot as using the word ("Maurice Blanchot," 22). He also uses it with reference to Renaissance concep-

tions of language and particularly in relation to resemblance in OT (41, 58, 69, 120); finally, he uses it with reference to the unthought and the unconscious as well as with reference to literature (OT: 103, 327). The notion of language as repeating itself to infinity, which is central to "Language to Infinity," is repeated with reference to the Renaissance (OT: 41). Finally the figure of murmuring can also be seen as linked to a highly phenomenological cluster of terms that includes *glittering, shimmering shining*, and *appearing*—the latter two both being rendered by the German word *Schein* (OT: 300, 325, 382, 386; "Maurice Blanchot," 18).

45. Foucault, *Foucault Live*, 22.

46. Foucault, "Maurice Blanchot," 21–22. "A Preface to Transgression" is in *Language, Counter-memory*, 27–52.

47. Foucault, *Maurice Blanchot*, 53, 16.

48. Ibid., 21.

49. "[I]l s'agit d'une étude structurale qui essaie de déchiffrer dans l'épaisseur de l'historique les conditions de l'histoire elle-même" (*Naissance de la clinique*, xv). In the 1972 revision this is changed to "il s'agit d'une étude qui essaie de dégager dans l'épaisseur du discours les conditions de son histoire." The English translation corresponds to neither passage but conflates the two (BC: xix). Bernauer provides a useful account of the differences between the two versions of BC (188–92). Bernauer sees the 1972 revision as attempting to cut Foucault's ties to structuralism. It seems, however, that Foucault is concerned to make the text methodologically consistent with the recently published AK. In the above passage "history" is replaced by "discourse," and history is in fact located *within* discourse. Again, on p.xiii of both French versions (BC: xvii—again a conflation of both versions), Foucault twice introduces the neostructuralist word *discourse*.

50. Foucault, *Foucault Live*, 55.

51. Foucault, " Language to Infinity," 55–57.

52. Ibid., 57.

53. Gasché, *Tain*, 16, 21

54. Bourdieu, *Homo Academicus*, xviii–xxiv.

55. See my article "The University in Crisis: Cultural Studies, Civil Society, and the Place of Theory," pp. 8–25.

CHAPTER 7

1. Sedgwick, 284–85.

2. Derrida, *Points*, 212.

3. Sartre, *Mallarmé*, 136–37. Sartre makes Mallarmé an embodiment of Blanchot's poet as distinct from prose writer, recalling Blanchot's "Literature and

the Right to Death," the essay written in response to his own *What Is Literature?* (133). He also links Mallarmé's *being-towards-failure* with Heidegger's *being-toward-death* (129).

4. Blanchot, *Space*, 85–159. Foucault, OT: 305–6, 383–84; *Language, Counter-memory*, 68–86; BC: 195–98.

5. See Derrida for a discussion of the relationship between psychoanalysis and madness (*Resistances*, 97, 104–7). In OT Foucault's (unstated) interest seems to be in Lacan, as is suggested by his attempt to think psychoanalysis alongside linguistics.

6. Foucault, *Foucault Live*, 45. Lebrun attributes the word *archaeology* to Husserl (33), while Gutting traces it to Merleau-Ponty, who sees psychoanalysis as an archaeology. Gutting (5n) also cites as Foucault's first use of the term a phrase in *Mental Illness* where Foucault describes Freudian neurosis as "a spontaneous archaeology of the libido." *Archaeology* thus seems divided between the two forms of phenomenology already discussed. But as my analysis of OT should have suggested it is precisely this ambiguity in the term that makes it so central to that book. For the term encapsulates what Foucault describes as modernity's "double advance, on the one hand towards formalism in thought and on the other towards the unconscious." In other words archaeology is precisely the place where "structuralism" (already prefigured by Husserl) and "phenomenology find . . . the general space that defines their *common ground*" (OT: 299).

7. Foucault, *Madness and Civilization*, x–xi. I have cited the abridged English edition because the preface was removed from later French editions.

8. Foucault, *Foucault Live*, 40.

9. Ibid., 4.

10. Ibid., 46.

11. Hollier, "The Word of God," 139, 138.

12. Harpham, 223.

13. Frank, "On Foucault's Concept of Discourse," in *Michel Foucault Philosopher*, 109, 102. Frank does not distinguish between OT and AK, assuming that *episteme* in the former is synonymous with *discourse* in the latter. As my previous discussion should suggest, however, Foucault has a purpose in using both terms in OT. In the earlier work *episteme* is a descriptive and *discourse* an evaluative term; in AK *discourse* has become a purely descriptive term. In other words *discourse* in OT is a way of using language that Foucault criticizes, an epistemic choice with which his own later work is complicit. Correspondingly, epistemes in OT are not what Foucault later calls discourses. For while I agree with Frank that discourse is "a symbolic order . . . which makes it possible for all subjects who have been socialised under its authority to speak and act together" (105), epistemes are

"symbolic" in a permeably Lacanian way, whereas discourses are symbolic in a hegemonically Althusserian way.

14. Ricoeur, *Hermeneutics*, 198–203.

15. See Dreyfus and Rabinow (49) who also provide the most helpful account of the "statement" (44–58). Deleuze also discusses the statement at length (*Michel Foucault*, 1–22).

16. Megill, 227. While conceding the importance of Mallarmé and Heidegger to OT (208, 221), Megill sees Foucault's work in the early sixties as essentially structuralist (204, 211–19), though obfuscated by phenomenological residues. AK thus occupies a pivotal position in his narrative in that it renounces these "nostalgic" residues (222) while also providing a critique of science and method, thus moving beyond both phenomenology and structuralism. Megill's reading of the progress of Foucault's career is to some extent reminiscent of Dreyfus and Rabinow's argument that he moves beyond structuralism and hermeneutics, although his reading of the genealogical phase differs from theirs.

17. Harpham, 222–23.

18. Bataille, *Inner Experience*, 21–22.

19. Harland, 1–5. Cf. also Dreyfus and Rabinow's characterization of AK as "semi-structuralist" because of its "claim that discourse has some sort of priority that enables it to 'use' non-discursive relations" (67).

20. I refer to Spanos's 1977 critique of spatial form in *Theory*, "Breaking the Circle: Hermeneutics as Dis-closure," reprinted and revised in *Heidegger and Criticism* (22–52). Spanos's specific targets are structuralism and the New Criticism, but he also sees the work of de Man as complicit with the spatializing tradition (48–51). Although in this essay he sees Derrida as pursuing the same project as himself, he elsewhere complains that both Derrida and de Man interpret Heidegger "through post-Structuralist eyes" ("Heidegger, Kierkegaard, and the Hermeneutic Circle: Towards a Postmodern Theory of Interpretation as Disclosure," in *Martin Heidegger and the Question of Literature*, 148). The implications of Spanos's distinction between a phenomenological "destruction" and a "post-Structuralist" *deconstruction* are elaborated by Leitch (59–86), who sees the latter as setting "writing or language as *ground*" (84; emphasis mine). Spanos and Leitch distinguish between destruction and deconstruction and not between deconstruction and poststructuralism, though Spanos uses the last of these terms to characterize what is wrong with a deconstruction that approaches Heidegger from a structuralist perspective.

21. Lefebvre, *La production de l'espace*, 31; trans. mine. Lefebvre's comment is made in connection with the Hegelian state, which he sees as swallowing up time at the end of history in an "immobile space, the place and milieu of achieved

Reason" (30). But although he does not discuss contemporary theory extensively, it is clear that he sees Derrida and the *Tel Quel* group as complicit with this "flattening" (31) of the social and cultural spheres through an absorption of time into space (12, 74).

22. Deleuze, "What Is a *Dispositif?*" in *Foucault*, 159.

23. Deleuze and Guattari, *Thousand Plateaus*, 381–82.

24. Kristeva, *Revolution*, 141.

25. Deleuze, *Foucault*, 19–21; Paul Bové, "Foreword: The Foucault Phenomenon: The Problematics of Style," ibid., xxi–xxiii.

26. Megill, 215.

27. Kristeva, *Revolution*, 140; Butler, *Psychic Life*, 34, 54–55. As Butler further points out, the libido is thus "not absolutely negated through repression, but rather becomes the instrument of its own subjection (55) in what is also for our purposes a phenomenological return, a return of consciousness at the very site of its effacement.

28. Deleuze, "What Is a *Dispositif?* 160; Shumway, 94–95.

29. Foucault, *Naissance* (1963). The corresponding passage in the English translation occurs on p. xvii, but it is a conflation of the 1963 and 1972 versions.

30. Foucault, *Naissance* (1972), xiii; trans. mine.

31. Blanchot, "Michel Foucault," 68, 70.

32. Foucault, *Mental Illness*, 46.

33. Ibid., 37.

34. Blanchot, *Space*, 42; emphasis mine.

35. I borrow this phrase from Derrida, who uses it to define a similar complicity between Husserl's transcendental idealism and Joyce's radical empiricism or between absolute univocity and absolute equivocity (OG: 103).

36. Dreyfus and Rabinow, 84–85.

37. See Barthes, foreword, Morrisette, 12.

38. Guillory, 232–33, 248, 254–55, 257. See more generally 231–65.

39. Gasché, *Wild Card of Reading*, 3–5, 112.

40. Ibid., 104–5.

41. Ibid., 104.

42. Deleuze, *Foucault*, 117.

43. Gasché, *Wild Card of Reading*, 112.

44. Foucault, *This Is Not a Pipe*, 49, 44.

45. Ibid., 44.

46. Ibid., 44–45.

47. Norris distinguishes between a "deconstruction" committed to the Kantian project of critique and "a heady post-structuralist style of apocalyptic discourse"

(*Derrida*, 222–24). I agree that poststructuralism abandons considerations of ethics; nonetheless, the distinction between deconstruction and poststructuralism is not necessarily one between philosophy and the line of thinkers represented by the "poet-philosophers" (235) that David Carroll defends as "paraesthetic" in arguing for the compatibility of art and critical thinking (xv, 3–4). The point is not that poststructuralism makes use of art but that it trivializes it in a way that deconstruction does not. On the seriously ontological use of the "literary" in Derrida and Blanchot see Tim Clark.

48. Quoted in Bernauer, 2.

49. Foucault, *Power/Knowledge*, 85.

50. Dreyfus and Rabinow, 101–3. Lentricchia, *After the New Criticism*, 189, 349–50. Lentricchia, however, does later note that power is somewhat like a metaphysical substance, though one that has no "predominant direction . . . [or] terminus" ("Reading Foucault," 51).

51. Foucault, *Discipline and Punish*, 35, 43, 45.

52. Carroll, 120, 77; Foucault, *Discipline and Punish*, 131.

53. Hertz, 86.

54. Carroll's claim that "it would be absurd" to suppose that Foucault is proposing torture as an alternative to the present penal system (122) elides the moral ambiguity that distinguishes Foucault's work from Scarry's.

55. Foucault, *Language*, 148.

56. Dreyfus, "On the Ordering of Things," in *Michel Foucault*, 80–82.

57. Foucault, *Discipline and Punish*, 198.

58. Deleuze and Guattari, by contrast, refigure this same force in (post)romantically organic terms. Like disease (BC: 10–11), their rhizome also circulates according to no "particular course" and in the process undergoes "metastases and metamorphoses" (*Thousand Plateaus*, 7, 4).

59. Kristeva, *Revolution*, 141; Rajan, "Trans-Positions of Difference," 220–23.

60. Baudrillard, *Simulacra*, 41

61. Dreyfus, "Introduction to the California Edition," Foucault, *Mental Illness*, xv–xxiii; "Ordering," 82–85.

62. Deleuze, *Foucault*, 110–11.

63. Deleuze speaks of a "return" to Bergson that would extend "his project" in line with developments in "life," "society," and "science" by pursuing the "three directions of . . . intuition as method, philosophy as rigorous science and the new logic as theory of multiplicities." He notes that these motifs occur in phenomenology, which both resembles and differs from the work of Bergson (*Bergsonism*, 115–18). The organicist materialism of Deleuze and Guattari in *A Thousand Plateaus* can be seen as a contemporary continuation of Bergsonian phenomenol-

ogy, which would differ from other forms of phenomenology not in terms of the three directions noted above but in terms of its emphasis on *élan vital* rather than on negativity and the unthought.

64. Deleuze, *Foucault*, 59.

65. Ibid., 64, 109.

66. We can note the many instances in AK where Foucault, in a renunciatory mourning, recalls the phenomenological language of his early work one last time so as to turn away from it; for instance: "Our task is not to give voice to the silence that surrounds [statements]. . . . [W]e are not linking these 'exclusions' to a repression; we do not suppose that beneath manifest statements something remains hidden and subjacent. . . . There is no sub-text. And therefore no plethora" (110; cf. also 28, 47, 62, 76, 125).

67. Butler, *Psychic Life*, 92, 94.

68. De Man, *Aesthetic Ideology*, 59.

69. Ibid., 59.

70. Foucault, *Power/Knowledge*, 87.

71. Deleuze, *Foucault*, 51.

72. Ibid., 109.

CHAPTER 8

1. Dosse, I.38–70, II.17–31.

2. Gasché, *Inventions*, 108; cf. 107–28 generally. Gasché's argument is that deconstruction is not as radical as we think, at least not in the way we think it is inasmuch as "breaks" with the past are quite traditional (59). Though my emphases are different, I sympathize with this view insofar as it separates deconstruction from "postmodernism" (121) and underlines its consistency with earlier analyses of rationality including phenomenology (28–57). Baudrillard, *Mirror*, 113; SED: 126, 144, 146, 152.

3. Dosse, I.38; Lyotard, *Phenomenology*, 105, and more generally 73–132. See also Sartre, "L'Anthropologie" (1972), 282–87.

4. Vattimo, 12–13, 17.

5. Luhmann, 18, 20. Luhmann argues that understood in terms of mediation and the media, "love as a medium is not itself a feeling, but rather a code of communication, according to the rules of which one can express, form and simulate feelings" (19–20).

6. I have provided my own translations of the French edition because the English translation is somewhat free with respect to paragraph breaks and sometimes phrasing. Page references to the French edition are followed, after a semi-colon, by references to Benedict's translation of *The System of Objects*.

7. Vattimo, 14–15, 17.

8. According to Vattimo the mass media do not actually make contemporary society "more 'transparent', but more complex, even chaotic," and it is in this chaos that "our hopes for emancipation lie" (4).

9. The phrase is Charles Levin's in the introduction to Baudrillard's *Political Economy* (11).

10. Pefanis, 62; Gane, *Baudrillard's Bestiary*, 32–33. Gane points to the differences between *System* and Barthes's *Elements of Semiology* and *The Fashion-System* (32–42). But since Barthes had already gone beyond his own structuralism in the latter as well as in "Rhetoric of the Image" (1964, in *Image, Music, Text*), Baudrillard's relationship to Barthes is more complex than Gane suggests.

11. The English translation renders the second occurrence of "essentiel" as "invaluable": "This [structural] analysis is invaluable" (7). Yet it is clear that Baudrillard is not valorizing but dismissing technical analysis: "Cette analyse est essentielle: elle nous donne les éléments d'une cohérence jamais vécue, jamais lisible dans la pratique" [This analysis is essentialist: it gives us the elements of a coherence that is never lived, never readable in practice] (12).

12. In actual fact Bourdieu accuses the book of "masquerading" as a phenomenologico-structural analysis (*Distinction*, 569).

13. Baudrillard, *Ecstasy*, 91. "Phenomeno-structuralism" is Nancy Metzel's term for the work of Eugene Minkowski; see her introduction to her translation of his *Lived Time*, xvii.

14. This is Jeffrey C. Alexander's criticism of Bourdieu's "false polemic" against structuralism, "which while apparently embracing phenomenology actually casts subjectivity in a deterministic antivoluntaristic form." Thus, as Alexander points out, the notion of *habitus* is simply a "subjectification of objective force" and a more pragmatic form of structuralism (131, 136, 140).

15. Baudrillard, *Mirror*, 50–51.

16. As Poster notes, Baudrillard does not adequately theorize the code, which can be defined as "a language or sign system unique to the mode of information, to electronically mediated communication systems" (58). The code is thus the late capitalist equivalent of the discourse that Foucault sees as emerging in the classical period.

17. "Sign, Function, and Class Logic" is considerably more assertive in its use of linguistic-structural terminology as part of a Barthesian "critical structuralism." Here Baudrillard defines his project as based not upon "the inventory but upon the distribution of objects . . . upon formal or functional syntagma, in short, an analysis of the syntax of objects," involving a "'horizontal' topoanalysis . . . accompanied by a 'vertical' semiology"(*Political Economy*, 34–35).

18. Barthes, *Image-Music-Text* (1969), 39–40.

19. Baudrillard, *Mirror*, 21, 17. A more extensive discussion of voluntarism and its contradictions can be found in CS: 69–76.

20. Baudrillard also foregrounds the notion of rhetoric in "Sign, Function, and Class Logic" (*Political Economy*, 34, 40).

21. Barthes, *The Fashion System*, 287.

22. Poster, 62.

23. Barthes, *The Fashion System*, 12.

24. The English word obviously does not capture the double sense of the French term. *Consommation* means "consumption" but also an almost ecstatic and metaphysical "satisfaction."

25. The recent English translation removes, at Baudrillard's request (197n), the statistical tables relating to social expenditures in the section "The Vicious Circle of Growth" (37–48). Presumably this is because these tables are vestiges of the positivist sociology Baudrillard is criticizing.

26. Heidegger, *Being and Time* (1927/1953), 8, 10; *Basic Writings*, 103, 96.

27. Heidegger, *Basic Writings*, 272–78. Heidegger writes of the mathematical: "According to this inner drive, a liberation to a new freedom, the mathematical strives out of itself to establish its own essence as the ground of itself and thus of all knowledge" (296).

28. Ibid., 294.

29. Binswanger, quoted in Frie, 86.

30. Although Baudrillard acknowledges the influence of Sartre on his early work (see later), his comments on Heidegger are confined to the uselessness of arguing over his Nazism in a postpolitical era (*Transparency*, 89–91).

31. Bataille prefaces his major work with a quotation from Blake. He refers to a Bergsonian *élan vital*, and writes that the "human mind reduces operations, in science as in life, to an entity based on typical particular systems . . . with limited ends. . . . Economic science . . . restricts its object to operations carried out with a view to a limited end. It does not take into consideration a play of energy that no particular end limits: the play of *living matter in general*, involved in the movement of light of which it is the result" (*The Accursed Share*, 5, 24, 22–3).

32. Baudrillard, *Political Economy*, 208.

33. Ibid., 206.

34. Baudrillard, *Baudrillard Live*, 59. Though Baudrillard is consistently critical of Freud, his early work draws extensively on Lacan's theories of desire and the Real. In later comments, he praises Lacan for overthrowing psychoanalysis through a focus on the signifier that has much in common with Saussure's theory of anagrams, which Baudrillard, like Foucault and Kristeva, sees as challenging

discourse through a revolution in poetic language (S: 56–59). Yet Lacan's subversion of Freud's "scientism" occurs in a "manner that is itself contaminated by psychoanalysis" (58). For this reason, from *Mirror* onward Baudrillard is engaged in a sustained polemic against Lacan's division of the imaginary from the symbolic and specifically against the economizing of the symbolic within the Law of the Father (*Mirror*, 61; SED: 133).

35. Baudrillard, *Political Economy*, 204; SED: 154.

36. Baudrillard, *Mirror*, 49.

37. Derrida, *Resistances*, 78–79, 100–105.

38. Baudrillard, *Political Economy*, 129.

39. Ibid., 163.

40. Ibid., 129.

41. Baudrillard does not use the Derridean spelling of the term and does not mention Derrida, but he does allude to Derridean *différance* in his analysis of Saussure's anagrams (SED: 208). It would seem that he does not mention Derrida here because by 1970 Derrida had revised his use of *difference* in a more (post)structural direction. For Baudrillard's critique of poststructuralism, see the next chapter.

42. Baudrillard, *Political Economy*, 147, 163. Whereas alienation still keeps man as a subject separate from the objects he produces through his labor (even when this labor is industrially alienated from him), reification makes man a product of his own products. Reification is a concept introduced by Lukács and taken up by Benjamin, to whom Baudrillard often alludes (SED: 55–57; S: 179), thus marking his continuity with the Frankfurt school. Mark Poster also briefly discusses Baudrillard's affinities with the Frankfurt school in his introduction to *Mirror* (11–12).

43. Baudrillard, *Mirror*, 32, 55. The critique of technology will inevitably call to mind Heidegger's essay on the subject. Baudrillard, however, is tacitly critical of Heidegger when he writes, "Science and Technology present themselves as revealing what is inscribed in Nature" (55). For a trenchant critique of Heidegger from this same viewpoint, see Ihde, 103–16.

44. Baudrillard, *Mirror*, 42, 32, 113.

45. Baudrillard, *Political Economy*, 149, 151, 90, 159, 161.

46. Baudrillard, *Mirror*, 122; *Political Economy*, 128.

47. Kristeva, *Revolution*, 141.

48. Baudrillard, *Mirror*, 152, 147–49, 150–51.

49. For a discussion of the three orders of simulacra, see SED: 50–58.

50. See Levinas, *God, Death*, 9–10. Levinas's lectures, given during 1975–76, were contemporaneous with *SED*. Like Baudrillard (SED: 190n) he argues against Heidegger's being-towards-death as a redialecticizing of death.

51. Derrida, *Points*, 212.

52. Derrida, *Resistances*, 76.

53. Derrida, *Points*, 278–82.

54. Hertz, 85–86. On antihumanism and terror, see Chapter 3 of this book.

55. Baudrillard, *Political Economy*, 64–66.

56. Ibid., 67–68. I refer to the pivotal distinction between symbol and allegory in Benjamin's *The Origin of German Tragic Drama*, 159–95, 207–21.

57. Merleau-Ponty, "The Experience of Others," in *Merleau-Ponty and Psychology*, ed. Hoeller, Merleau-Ponty's discussion of habit in this text is an obvious source for Bourdieu—perhaps even more so than Husserl's more abstract treatment of the subject in *Cartesian Meditations*. Habit is not something mechanical or fixed, but is a transferrable "aptitude for responding to a particular type of situation with a particular form of solution. Thus habit as an operation is both bodily and spiritual. It is an *existential operation*" (Merleau-Ponty, "Experience," 52).

58. Baudrillard, *Political Economy*, 64–65.

59. Merleau-Ponty, "Experience," 50.

60. Baudrillard, *Political Economy*, 65.

61. Baudrillard criticizes Jean Starobinski for assuming that Saussure remained loyal to the law of productivity in envisioning a retotalization of the dispersed syllables; he cites Isis's reuniting of "'Orpheus' dismembered body.'" In fact, the diffraction of the "theme word" is the "equivalent of putting God . . . to death in the sacrifice" (SED: 199–200). De Man similarly criticizes Riffaterre in *Semiotics of Poetry* for "re-lexicaliz[ing]" Saussure by making the "matrix word" into the structural center of the text (RT: 39).

62. Baudrillard, *Political Economy*, 65.

63. Ibid., 152.

64. Derrida, *Resistances*, 76.

65. De Man, *Critical Writings*, 13–15. In opposing inwardness to the nostalgia for permanence, in grounding it in history rather than temporality, and in linking it not only to Heidegger but also to Hegel's unhappy consciousness, de Man exemplifies what we have previously discussed as the translation of Heideggerian ontology through French phenomenology.

66. Derrida, *Resistances*, 76, 104. "Cogito and the History of Madness," WD: 31–62.

67. Ibid., 109, 106.

68. Žižek, *Tarrying*, 3–4.

69. Baudrillard later links primitive cultures with an ability to deal with the "inhuman" that is necessary to fatal theory (FS: 183).

70. This of course is Derrida's early reading of Levinas. One could argue that

Levinas's engagement with the work of Ernst Bloch a decade later in *God, Death* is very far from being the extreme thought of the outside that Derrida critiques earlier.

CHAPTER 9

1. Poster, 62–63.
2. Norris, *What's Wrong with Postmodernism*, 164–93, and *Uncritical Theory*, 11–31, 133–34; Kellner, *Jean Baudrillard*, 94–217.
3. Baudrillard, *Silent Majorities*, 106; *Simulacra*, 16, 41.
4. Baudrillard, *Simulacra*, 31, 153; *Forget Foucault*, 86.
5. Baudrillard, *Simulacra*, 6, 16 (trans. mine), 17–18, 41.
6. Baudrillard, *Forget Foucault*, 10, 12; *Simulacra*, 9; *Transparency*, 7.
7. Baudrillard, *Simulacra*, 155–56, 41.
8. Baudrillard, *Simulacra*, 18, 29, 41. Unlike Lyotard and Deleuze, Foucault is not guilty of complicity but of nostalgia. Foucault's writing is the most powerful instance of a "generating spiral that is no longer a despotic architecture but a filiation *en abîme*." But although he "pulverize(s]" power he does not question its "*reality principle*." Foucault is thus Baudrillard in an earlier incarnation: still committed, despite the evidence, to "a possible coherence of politics and discourse" (*Forget Foucault*, 9–12).
9. Baudrillard, *Forget Foucault*, 11–12, 35–36.
10. Ibid., 17–18.
11. Ibid., 75.
12. In making this distinction Baudrillard explicitly draws on the psychoanalytic terminology of separation as well as on the philosophic terminology of transcendence and negativity. Opposing metaphor to metonymy he describes the former as the possibility of "differential fields and distinct objects," whereas "total metonymy," which is "viral by definition (or lack of definition)," is the contamination of everything by everything contiguous to it (*Transparency*, 8). The metonymic or metamorphic body is what Baudrillard also describes as "obese." The obese body, in turn, is "indivisible," "pregnant with all the objects from which" it has "been unable to separate" (FS: 30).
13. Baudrillard, *Transparency*, 7, 24.
14. Ibid, 41; *Forget Foucault*, 17–18.
15. Baudrillard, *Illusion of the End*, 78, 96, 91.
16. Baudrillard, *America*, 47; *Illusion of the End*, 108, 102.
17. Kristeva, *Language*, 17.
18. Baudrillard, *Evil Demon*, 41.
19. Baudrillard, *Transparency*, 7; *Simulacra*, 22.
20. Baudrillard, *Transparency*, 144, 30.

21. Ibid., 8. It is interesting that in *Transparency* (1990) Baudrillard uses the metaphor/metonymy distinction to replace his earlier distinction between metaphor and metamorphosis in a 1984 interview (*Forget Foucault*, 75) and in EC (1987).

22. Baudrillard, *Transparency*, 106. While still using the terminology of the "accursed share" here (106), Baudrillard already concedes Bataille's outmodedness (32), as he does more extensively in *Paroxysm* (26–27).

23. Baudrillard, *Forget Foucault*, 84.

24. Baudrillard, *Baudrillard Live*, 38.

25. Baudrillard, *Illusion of the End*, 52; *Paroxysm*, 40.

26. Baudrillard, *Illusion of the End*, 55, 65.

27. Baudrilard, *Transparency*, 106.

28. Kristeva, *Revolution*, 140–43. See my two articles "Language, Music and the Body: Nietzsche and Deconstruction," 147–69; "Trans-Positions of Difference: Kristeva and Post-Structuralism," 215–37.

29. Baudrillard, *Evil Demon*, 41, 43.

30. Baudrillard, *Paroxysm*, 40.

31. Baudrillard, *Evil Demon*, 51.

32. Baudrillard, *Illusion of the End*, 105. It is worth noting that the normative rather than dismissive evocation of these earlier *topoi* occurs mainly in the more recent work. *Illusion* also returns to what is quite explicitly a form of cultural psychoanalysis (e.g. 11–12, 22).

33. Deleuze and Guattari, *Thousand Plateaus*, 353.

34. Baudrillard, *Paroxysm*, 23.

35. Baudrillard, *Evil Demon*, 52, 40–41.

36. Derrida, *Points*, 212. I refer to Heidegger's characterization of the world-picture as a system (*The Question Concerning Technology*, 129). A deconstruction, however local, is always concerned with the larger metaphysics underwriting the local case.

37. Baudrillard, *Baudrillard Live*, 51.

38. Baudrillard, *Paroxysm*, 47.

39. Baudrillard, *Evil Demon*, 41–42.

40. Baudrillard, *Baudrillard Live*, 143, 160.

41. Baudrillard, *Simulacra*, 22 (trans. mine), 18; *Silent Majorities*, 106.

42. Baudrillard, *Baudrillard Live*, 51.

43. Baudrillard, *Silent Majorities*, 4–5, 108, 6, 2.

44. Baudrillard notes that a game "forms a system with neither contradiction nor internal negativity" (S: 149). Baudrillard's notion of the game can be set against Deleuze and Guattari's discussion of games in the context of "striated" ver-

sus "smooth" space. Chess assumes a striated space; it is "indeed a war, but an institutionalized, regulated coded war." Go assumes a smooth space, " a milieu of exteriority . . . pure strategy" (*Thousand Plateaus*, 353). Baudrillard's assimilation of theory to a game simulates the nomadic tactics of smooth space, but his emphasis on rules betrays his desire for a striated space.

45. Hollier, *Absent without Leave*, 10–31. In contrast to such commentators as Robbe-Grillet, Hollier is unusual in recognizing that existentialism began, at least in literature, as a "radical antinaturalism" committed to a "desubjectivization of consciousness," a "transposition of 'I' into 'there is'" (10, 29). Baudrillard recognizes Sartre as the "dominating influence of the age" and alludes to an early Sartrean influence on his work (*Baudrillard Live*, 20, 203).

46. Robbe-Grillet, "Nature, Humanism, Tragedy," *For a New Novel*, 61–70.

47. Baudrillard, *Transparency*, 3, 14–35.

48. Baudrillard criticizes Deleuze and/or Lyotard at several points, often only by allusion;see SED: 137, 143; S: 138, 144, 146, 149, 174; *Transparency*, 144.

49. Starr, 20. Structural repetition is the view that failure has happened before, while specular doubling holds that the revolution is always already a mirror image of what it seeks to overthrow. (15).

50. 1968 has been discussed as eliciting at least two radically opposite reactions: one neoconservative and the other resulting in the libidinal politics of Deleuze and Guattari, Lyotard (briefly), and to some extent Kristeva. De Man's turn, however, does not occur until the mid-seventies, and his immediate context is not France but the post-Vietnam era in the United States. While de Man's emphasis on rhetoric can be read as an overdetermined (and not a simply neoconservative) response to the waning of the revolutionary sixties, Guillory has read it as a (perhaps related) internalization of technobureaucratization (see Chapter 7 of this book). Others have read de Man's later work—in completely opposite ways—as a response to the much earlier political trauma of Nazism. Thus 1968 can be no more than a metonymy for a deeply unreadable connection between intellectual and material history. In Baudrillard's case, the turn is again one that occurs in the mid-seventies, and the technological changes that he adduces as explanations for fatal theory are more important than 1968 per se (though the two are not unrelated). Baudrillard himself evokes 1968 at several points (e.g. CS: 195; SED: 29, 34; *Forget Foucault*, 108–16). While initially associating it with a turn from production to reproduction in a Bourdieuvian sense (SED: 29), he later concludes that 1968 "remains indecipherable. It was the forerunner of nothing" (*Forget Foucault*, 115).

51. Starr, 60, 22. I would, however, want to use the term *revolution* very broadly.

52. Baudrillard, *Evil Demon*, 47.

53. Sartre sees emotion as having a substitutive structure: what consciousness "is unable to endure in one way it tries to seize in another way"; thus "when the paths before us become too difficult . . . we try to change the world; that is, to live it as though the relations between things and their potentialities were not governed by deterministic processes but by magic" (*Sketch*, 79, 63).

54. One misses the irony of such statements at one's own risk. For as Baudrillard clearly indicates "a war is not any the less heinous for being a mere simulacrum: the flesh suffers just the same" (*Simulations*, 70).

55. Baudrillard, *Baudrillard Live*, 141.

56. Baudrillard, *Transparency*, 41.

57. Baudrillard, *Baudrillard Live*, 58.

58. Baudrillard, *Evil Demon*, 43–44.

59. Baudrillard, *Baudrillard Live*, 139.

60. Baudrillard, *Silent Majorities*, 102.

61. Baudrillard, *Simulacra*, 5.

62. Baudrillard, *Evil Demon*, 46; *Baudrillard Live*, 177.

63. Klossowski's interest in medieval heresies is clearest in his strange novel *The Baphomet* (1965), which provides a Manichean genealogy for his interest in Nietzsche and Sade. On Klossowski, see Jean-Pol Madou. Madou sees Klossowski's corpus (including books on Sade and Nietzsche and works of fiction that combine heresy and pornography) as continuing Bataille's attempt to recover "la part maudite" in the face of an awareness of the economic and commodification that is much more intense than Bataille's (114–16).

64. Madou, 88; trans. mine.

65. Foucault, "The Prose of Actaeon" (1964), xxvi–viii, xxxiii.

66. Baudrillard, *Simulacra*, 40; Perniola, *La società dei simulacri*, 121–22, 127–28. Two chapters of Perniola's book—one on simulacra and one on seduction—were published in *Traverses*, a journal to which Baudrillard frequently contributed and with which he was associated (10 [February, 1978] and 18 [February, 1980]).

67. Perniola, *La società dei simulacri*, 125. Perniola traces this technology back to Loyola and the Jesuits (122–25, 127), as Baudrillard had earlier done (SED: 52–53).

68. Baudrillard, *Simulacra*, 4.

69. Baudrillard, *Paroxysm*, 28.

70. Baudrillard, *Evil Demon*, 29.

71. Perniola, *La società dei simulacri*, 118.

72. Baudrillard, *Paroxysm*, 25, 40; *Evil Demon*, 13–15, 52.

73. Kierkegaard, 278.

74. Baudrillard, *Paroxysm*, 71; *Evil Demon*, 52–53; *Baudrillard Live*, 184.

75. This is the view taken by Scott Durham, who in a recent book distinguishes two versions of the simulacrum. The first is the "negative and privative" version of Baudrillard, who sees it as a "copy of a copy . . . [un]grounded in an original" and thus "as the non-representation of the object or as the non-participation in the Idea." The second is the "histrionic and performative" version of Deleuze, who sees the simulacrum as "in its daemonic aspect, as the positive expression of the metamorphic and creative 'powers of the false.'" In this second version, which can be traced back to Tertullian and which includes Klossowski, the simulacrum is "the mask of an evil *simulator*, a diabolical actor" or daemon, expressing the "inherenetly unstable nature" of the daemon" (7–10). As my analysis suggests, Baudrillard draws on both traditions, specifically evoking the second one in his phrase "the evil demon of images."

76. Baudrillard, *Paroxysm*, 25; *Illusion of the End*, 94.

77. Baudrillard, *Illusion of the End*, 93.

78. Baudrillard, *Evil Demon*, 45–46.   79. Baudrillard, *Paroxysm*, 69–71.

80. Baudrillard, *Evil Demon*, 40–41.   81. Baudrillard, *Paroxysm*, 71.

82. Kierkegaard, 278.   83. Baudrillard, *Paroxysm*, 82, 43.

84. Ionesco, 162–63.

85. Baudrillard, *Illusion of the End*, 40; *Paroxysm*, 47.

86. Baudrillard, *Paroxysm*, 47; *Illusion of the End*, 111. The Deleuzian word *singularity* has become increasingly frequent in Baudrillard's late works, as has "multiplicity." See *Paroxysm*, 63, 67, 69, 94–95.

87. Baudrillard, *Illusion of the End*, 110–12; *Paroxysm*, 71.

88. Baudrillard, *Evil Demon*, 40.

89. Baudrillard, *Illusion of the End*, 90.

90. Ibid.,115.

91. Baudrillard, *America*, 9.

92. Gane, *Critical and Fatal Theory*, 182.

93. Baudrillard, *Paroxysm*, 82.   94. Baudrillard, *America*, 3–6.

95. Ibid., 1, 5, 6.   96. Baudrillard, *America*, 69.

97. Ibid., 51, 5.   98. Baudrillard, *Paroxysm*, 82.

Works Cited

Essays in multiple-essay volumes included in the Works Cited are not listed individually. Their sources are given in parenthetical references or endnotes.

Abraham, Nicholas, and Maria Torok. *The Wolf Man's Magic Word* (1976). Trans. Nicholas Rand. Minneapolis: University of Minnesota Press, 1986.

Agamben, Giorgio. *The Coming Community* (1990). Trans. Michael Hardt. Minneapolis: University of Minnesota Press, 1993.

Alexander, Jeffrey C. *Fin de Siècle Social Theory: Relativism, Reduction, and the Problem of Reason*. London: Verso, 1995.

Arac, Jonathan, Wlad Godzich, and Wallace Martin, eds. *The Yale Critics: Deconstruction in America*. Minneapolis: University of Minnesota Press, 1983.

Armstrong, Timothy, trans. *Michel Foucault Philosopher*. New York: Routledge, 1992.

Barthes, Roland. *Critical Essays* (1964). Trans. Richard Howard. Evanston: Northwestern University Press, 1972.

———. *The Fashion System* (1967). Trans. Matthew Ward and Richard Howard. New York: Hill and Wang, 1983.

———. *Image-Music-Text* (1969). Trans. Richard Howard. New York: Hill and Wang, 1977.

———. *Writing Degree Zero and Elements of Semiology*. Trans. Annette Lavers and Colin Smith. 1967; rpt. Boston: Beacon Press, 1970.

Bataille, Georges. *The Accursed Share: An Essay on General Economy, Vol. I: Consumption* (1967). Trans. Robert Hurley. New York: Zone Books, 1991.

———. *Inner Experience* (1943/1953). Trans. Leslie Anne Boldt. Albany: SUNY Press, 1988.

———. *Visions of Excess: Selected Writings, 1927–1939*. Trans. Allan Stoekl. Minneapolis: University of Minnesota Press, 1985.

Baudrillard, Jean. *America* (1986). Trans. Chris Turner. London: Verso, 1989.

———. *Baudrillard Live: Selected Interviews*. Ed. Mike Gane. London: Routledge, 1993.

———. *The Consumer Society: Myths and Structures* (1970). London: Sage, 1998.

————. *The Ecstasy of Communication* (1987). Trans. B. and C. Schutze. New York: Semiotext(e), 1988.

————. *The Evil Demon of Images*. Sydney: Power Institute, 1987.

————. *Fatal Strategies* (1983). Trans. Philip Beitchman and W. G. J. Niesluchowski. New York: Semiotext(e), 1990.

————. *For a Critique of the Political Economy of the Sign*. Trans. Charles Levin. St. Louis: Telos Press, 1981.

————. *Forget Foucault* (1977). Trans. H. Beitchmann and M. Polizotti. New York: Semiotext(e), 1987.

————. *The Illusion of the End* (1992). Trans. Chris Turner. Stanford: Stanford University Press, 1994.

————. *In the Shadow of the Silent Majorities or, "The End of the Social" and Other Essays* (1978). Trans. Paul Foss et. al. New York: Semiotext(e), 1983.

————. *The Mirror of Production* (1973). Trans. Mark Poster. St. Louis: Telos Press, 1975.

————. *Paroxysm: Interviews with Philippe Petit* (1997). Trans. Chris Turner. London: Verso, 1998.

————. *Seduction* (1979). Trans. Brian Singer. New York: St. Martin's Press, 1990.

————. *Simulacra and Simulations* (1981). Trans. Sheila Faria Glaser. Ann Arbor: University of Michigan Press, 1991.

————. *Simulations*. Trans. Paul Foss, Paul Patton, and Philip Beitchman. New York: Semiotext(e), 1983. [selected from *L'Échange symbolique et la mort* (1976) and *Simulacres et simulation* (1981)].

————. *La société de consommation: ses mythes, ses structures*. Paris: Denoël, 1970.

————. *Symbolic Exchange and Death* (1976). Trans. Iain Hamilton Grant. London: Sage, 1993.

————. *The System of Objects* (1968). Trans. James Benedict. London: Verso, 1996.

————. *The Transparency of Evil: Essays on Extreme Phenomena* (1990). Trans. James Benedict. London: Verso, 1993.

Benjamin, Walter. *The Origin of German Tragic Drama* (1924–25). Trans. John Osborne. London: NLB, 1977.

Bernauer, James. *Michel Foucault's Force of Flight: Toward an Ethics for Thought*. Atlantic Highlands, N.J.: Humanities Press, 1990.

Binswanger, Ludwig. "Ellen West" (1944). *Existence: A New Dimension in Psychiatry and Psychology*. Ed. Rollo May et. al. New York: Basic Books, 1958. 237–364.

Blanchot, Maurice. *The Blanchot Reader*. Ed. Michael Holland. Oxford: Blackwell, 1995.

————. *La communauté inavouable*. Paris: Minuit, 1983.

————. *"The Gaze of Orpheus" and Other Literary Essays*. Trans. Lydia Davis. Barrytown, N.Y.: Station Hill Press, 1981.

————. "Michel Foucault as I Imagine Him" (1986). Trans. Jeffrey Mehlman. *Foucault/Blanchot*. New York: Zone Books, 1987. 63–109.

————. *The Space of Literature* (1955). Trans. Ann Smock. Lincoln: University of Nebraska Press, 1982.

————. *The Step Not Beyond* (1973). Trans. Lycette Nelson. Albany: SUNY Press, 1992.

————. *The Writing of the Disaster* (1980). Trans. Ann Smock. Lincoln: University of Nebraska Press, 1986.

Bloom, Harold. *The Anxiety of Influence: A Theory of Poetry*. New York: Oxford University Press, 1973.

————, ed. *Romanticism and Consciousness*. New York: Norton, 1970.

Bourdieu, Pierre. *Distinction: A Social Critique of the Judgment of Taste* (1979). Trans. Richard Nice. Cambridge: Harvard University Press, 1984.

————. *Homo Academicus* (1984). Trans. Peter Collier. Cambridge, Mass.: Polity, 1988.

————. *The Political Ontology of Martin Heidegger* (1988). Trans. Peter Collier. Stanford: Stanford University Press, 1991.

Butler, Judith. *The Psychic Life of Power: Theories of Subjection*. Stanford: Stanford University Press, 1997.

————. *Subjects of Desire: Hegelian Reflections in Twentieth-Century France*. 1987; rpt. New York: Columbia University Press, 1999.

Canguilhem, Georges. *La connaissance de la vie*. Paris: Vrin, 1967.

————. *On the Normal and the Pathological* (1943; rpt. 1972). Trans. Carolyn R. Fawcett. Intro. Michel Foucault. 1978; rpt. New York: Zone Books, 1991.

Carroll, David. *Paraesthetics: Foucault, Derrida, Lyotard*. New York: Methuen, 1987.

Caws, Peter. *Sartre*. London: Routledge and Kegan Paul, 1979.

Chase, Cynthia. *Decomposing Figures: Rhetorical Readings in the Romantic Tradition*. Baltimore: Johns Hopkins University Press, 1986.

Clark, David. "Monstrosity, Illegibility, Denegation: De Man, bp nichol, and the Resistance to Postmodernism." *Monster Theory: Reading Culture*. Ed. Jeffrey Jerome Cohen. Minneapolis: University of Minnesota Press, 1996. 40–71.

Clark, Tim. *Derrida, Heidegger, Blanchot: Sources of Derrida's Notion and Practice of Literature*. Cambridge: Cambridge University Press, 1992.

Cumming, Robert DeNoon. *Phenomenology and Deconstruction*, Vol. 1: *The Dream Is Over*. Chicago: University of Chicago Press, 1991.

De Certeau, Michel. *Heterologies: Discourse on the Other*. Trans. Brian Massumi. Minneapolis: University of Minnesota Press, 1986.

Deleuze, Gilles. *Bergsonism* (1966). Trans. Hugh Tomlinson and Barbara Habberjam. New York: Zone Books, 1991.

———. *The Fold: Leibniz and the Baroque* (1988). Trans. Tom Conley. Minneapolis: University of Minnesota Press, 1993.

———. *Michel Foucault* (1986). Trans. Séan Hand. Minneapolis: University of Minnesota Press, 1988.

Deleuze, Gilles, and Félix Guattari. *A Thousand Plateaus: Capitalism and Schizophrenia* (1980). Trans. Brian Massumi. Minneapolis: University of Minnesota Press, 1987.

De Man, Paul. *Aesthetic Ideology*. Ed. Andrzej Warminski. Minneapolis: University of Minnesota Press, 1996.

———. *Allegories of Reading: Figural Language in Rousseau, Nietzsche, Rilke, and Proust*. New Haven: Yale University Press, 1979.

———. *Blindness and Insight: Essays in the Rhetoric of Contemporary Criticism* (1971). 2d rev. ed. Minneapolis: University of Minnesota Press, 1983.

———. *Critical Writings 1953–1978*. Ed. Lindsay Waters. Minneapolis: University of Minnesota Press, 1989.

———. *The Resistance to Theory*. Minneapolis: University of Minnesota Press, 1986.

———. *The Rhetoric of Romanticism*. New York: Columbia University Press, 1984.

———. "Structure intentionelle de l'image romantique." *Revue internationale de philosophie* 51 (1960). 68–84.

Derrida, Jacques. *Aporias* (1993). Trans. Thomas Dutoit. Stanford: Stanford University Press, 1993.

———. *Edmund Husserl's "Origin of Geometry": An Introduction* (1962/1974). Trans. John P. Leavey Jr. Stony Brook, N.Y.: Nicolas Hays, 1978.

———. *The Gift of Death* (1992). Trans. David Wills. Stanford: Stanford University Press, 1995.

———. "'Il courait mort:' salut, salut." *Les temps modernes* 587 (1996): 7–54.

———. *Margins of Philosophy* (1972). Trans. Alan Bass. Chicago: University of Chicago Press, 1982.

———. *Memoires for Paul de Man*. Trans. Cecile Lindsay et. al. Rev. ed. New York: Columbia University Press, 1989.

———. *Of Grammatology* (1967). Trans. Gayatri Chakravorty Spivak. Baltimore: Johns Hopkins University Press, 1976.

———. *Of Spirit: Heidegger and the Question* (1987). Trans. Geoffrey Bennington and Rachel Bowlby. Chicago: University of Chicago Press, 1989.

————. *Points . . . Interviews 1974–1994*. Ed. Elisabeth Weber. Trans. Peggy Kamuf et. al. Stanford: Stanford University Press, 1995.

————. *Positions* (1972). Trans. Alan Bass. Chicago: University of Chicago Press, 1981.

————. *Le problème de la genèse dans la philosophie de Husserl*. Paris: Presses Universitaires de France, 1990.

————. *Resistances of Psychoanalysis* (1996). Trans. Peggy Kamuf, Pascale-Anne Brault, and Michael Naas. Stanford: Stanford University Press, 1998.

————. *"Speech and Phenomena" and Other Essays* (1967–68). Trans. David B. Allison. Evanston: Northwestern University Press, 1973.

————. "The Time of a Thesis: Punctuations" (1980). *Philosophy in France Today*. Ed. Alan Montefiore. Cambridge: Cambridge University Press, 1983. 34–49.

————. *Writing and Difference* (1967). Trans. Alan Bass. Chicago: University of Chicago Press, 1978.

Descombes, Vincent. *Modern French Philosophy* (1979). Trans. L. Scott-Fox and J. M. Harding. Cambridge: Cambridge University Press, 1980.

Dews, Peter. *Logics of Disintegration: Post-Structuralist Thought and the Claims of Critical Theory*. London: Verso, 1987.

Dosse, François. *History of Structuralism* (1992). Trans. Deborah Glassman. 2 vols. Minneapolis: University of Minnesota Press, 1997.

Dreyfus, Hubert L., and Paul Rabinow. *Michel Foucault: Beyond Structuralism and Hermeneutics*. 2d ed. Chicago: University of Chicago Press, 1983.

Durham, Scott. *Phantom Communities: The Simulacrum and the Limits of Representation*. Stanford: Stanford University Press, 1998.

Eagleton, Terry. *Literary Theory: An Introduction*. Oxford: Blackwell, 1983.

Eribon, Didier. *Michel Foucault*. Trans. Betsy Wing. Cambridge: Harvard University Press, 1991.

Evans, J. Claude. *Strategies of Deconstruction: Derrida and the Myth of the Voice*. Minneapolis: University of Minnesota Press, 1991.

Fisera, Vladimir, ed. *Writing on the Wall. May 1968: A Documentary Anthology*. Trans. Nicholas Ainsworth et. al. London: Allison and Busby, 1978.

Foucault, Michel. *The Archaeology of Knowledge and "The Discourse on Language"* (1969 and 1971). Trans. A. M. Sheridan Smith. New York: Pantheon, 1972.

————. *The Birth of the Clinic: An Archaeology of Medical Perception* (1963; rev. ed. 1972). Trans. A. M. Sheridan. 1973; rpt. London: Routledge, 1986.

————. *Death and the Labyrinth: The World of Raymond Roussel* (1963). Trans. Charles Ruas. Berkeley: University of California Press, 1986.

————. *Discipline and Punish: The Birth of the Prison* (1975). Trans. Alan Sheridan. New York: Vintage Books, 1979.

————. *Dream, Imagination, and Existence* (1954). Trans. Forrest Williams. In *Dream and Existence.* Ed. Keith Hoeller. Trans. Forrest Williams and Jacob Needleman. 1984–85; rpt. Seattle: Review of Existential Psychology and Psychiatry, 1986.

————. *Foucault Live (Interviews 1966–84).* Trans. John Johnston. Ed. Sylvère Lotringer. New York: Semiotext(e), 1989.

————, ed. *I, Pierre Rivière, Having Slaughtered My Mother, My Sister, and My Brother . . . A Case of Parricide in the Nineteenth Century* (1973). Trans. Frank Jellinek. 1975; rpt. Lincoln: University of Nebraska Press, 1982.

————. *Language, Counter-memory, Practice: Selected Essays and Interviews.* Ed. Donald F. Bouchard. Trans. Donald F. Bouchard and Sherry Simon. Ithaca: Cornell University Press, 1977.

————. *Madness and Civilization: A History of Insanity in the Age of Reason.* Trans. Richard Howard. 1965; rpt. New York: Vintage Books, 1973.

————. *Maladie mentale et personnalité.* Paris: Presses Universitaires de France, 1954.

————. "Maurice Blanchot: The Thought from Outside" (1966). Trans. Brian Massumi. *Foucault/Blanchot.* New York: Zone Books, 1987. 1–58.

————. *Mental Illness and Psychology* (1954; rev. ed. 1962). Trans. Hubert Dreyfus. 1976; rpt. Berkeley: University of California Press, 1987.

————. *Naissance de la clinique. Une archéologie du regard médical.* Paris: Presses Universitaires de France, 1963.

————. *The Order of Things: An Archaeology of the Human Sciences* (1966). Trans. Pub. New York: Vintage, 1973.

————. *Politics, Philosophy, Culture.* Ed. Lawrence D. Kritzman. New York: 1988.

————. *Power/Knowledge: Selected Interviews and Other Writings 1972–1977.* Ed. Colin Gordon. Trans. Colin Gordon et. al. New York: Pantheon, 1980.

————. "The Prose of Actaeon" (1964). In Pierre Klossowski, *The Baphomet* (1965). Trans. Sophie Hawkes and Stephen Sartarelli. New York: Marsilio, 1998. 19–38.

————. *This Is Not a Pipe* (1973). Trans. and ed. James Harkness. Berkeley: University of California Press, 1983.

————. "What Is Enlightenment?" *The Foucault Reader.* Ed. Paul Rabinow. New York: Pantheon, 1986. 32–51.

Frank, Manfred. *What Is Neostructuralism?* (1984). Trans. Sabine Wilke and Richard Gray. Minneapolis: University of Minneosta Press, 1989.

Frie, Roger. *Subjectivity and Intersubjectivity in Modern Philosophy and Psychoanalysis: A Study of Sartre, Binswanger, Lacan, and Habermas.* London: Rowman and Littlefield, 1997.

Gane, Mike. *Baudrillard: Critical and Fatal Theory.* London: Routledge, 1991.

———. *Baudrillard's Bestiary: Baudrillard and Culture*. London: Routledge, 1991.

Gasché, Rodolphe. *Inventions of Difference: On Jacques Derrida*. Cambridge: Harvard University Press, 1994.

———. "On Re-presentation, or Zigzagging with Husserl and Derrida." *Southern Journal of Philosophy*, 32 (1993), Supplement, 4: 1–18.

———. *The Tain of the Mirror: Derrida and the Philosophy of Reflection*. Cambridge: Harvard University Press, 1986.

———. *The Wild Card of Reading: On Paul de Man*. Cambridge: Harvard University Press, 1998.

Gasset, José Ortega y. *Some Lessons in Metaphysics*. Trans. Mildred Adams. New York: Norton, 1969.

Genosko, Gary. *Baudrillard and Signs: Signification Ablaze*. London: Routledge, 1994.

Guillory, John. *Cultural Capital: The Problem of Literary Canon Formation*. Chicago: University of Chicago Press, 1993.

Gutting, Gary. *Michel Foucault's Archaeology of Scientific Reason*. Cambridge: Cambridge University Press, 1989.

Habermas, Jürgen. *Philosophical-Political Profiles* (1971 and 1973). Trans. Frederick G. Lawrence. Cambridge: MIT Press, 1985.

———. *The Philosophical Discourse of Modernity: Twelve Lectures* (1985). Trans. Frederick G. Lawrence. Cambridge: MIT Press, 1987/1995.

Harari, Josué V., ed. *Textual Strategies: Perspectives in Post-Structuralist Criticism*. Ithaca: Cornell University Press, 1979.

Harland, Richard. *Superstructuralism: The Philosophy of Structuralism and Post-Structuralism*. London: Methuen, 1987.

Harpham, Geoffrey Galt. *The Ascetic Imperative in Culture and Criticism*. Chicago: University of Chicago Press, 1987.

Hegel, G. W. F. *Aesthetics: Lectures on Fine Art* (1835). Trans. T. M. Knox. 2 vols. Oxford: Clarendon Press, 1975.

Heidegger, Martin. *Basic Writings*. Ed. David Farrell Krell. New York: HarperCollins, 1993.

———. *Being and Time* (1927/1953). Trans. Joan Stambaugh. Albany: SUNY Press, 1996.

———. "Language" (1959). *Poetry, Language, Thought*. Trans. Albert Hofstadter. New York: Harper and Row, 1975. 187–211.

———. *"The Question Concerning Technology" and Other Essays*. Trans. William Lovitt. New York: Harper and Row, 1977.

Hertz, Neil. "Lurid Figures." *Reading de Man Reading*. Ed. Lindsay Waters and Wlad Godzich. Minneapolis: University of Minnesota Press, 1989. 82–104.

Hollier, Denis. *Absent without Leave: French Literature Under the Threat of War.* Trans. Catherine Porter. Cambridge: Harvard University Press, 1997.

Hollier, Denis, ed. *The College of Sociology 1937–39* (1979). Trans. Betsy Wing. Minneapolis: University of Minnesota Press, 1988.

Howells, Christina. *Derrida: Deconstruction from Phenomenology to Ethics.* Cambridge: Polity Press, 1999.

———. "Derrida and Sartre: Hegel's Death Knell." *Derrida and Deconstruction.* Ed. Hugh Silverman. New York: Routledge, 1989. 169–81.

———. "Sartre and Derrida: Qui perd gagne" (1982). In *Sartre: An Investigation of Some Major Themes.* Ed. Simon Glynn. Aldershot: Avebury, 1987. 146–60.

Husserl, Edmund. *The Crisis of European Sciences and Transcendental Phenomenology: An Introduction to Phenomenological Philosophy* (1934–37). Includes the Vienna Lecture. Trans. David Carr. Evanston: Northwestern University Press, 1970.

———. *Husserl: Shorter Works.* Ed. Peter McCormick and Frederick A. Elliston. Notre Dame: University of Notre Dame Press, 1981.

———. "Philosophy as a Rigorous Science" (1911). In *Phenomenology and the Crisis of Philosophy.*. Trans. Quentin Lauer. New York: Harper and Row, 1965. 71–147.

Hyppolite, Jean. *Genesis and Structure of Hegel's Phenomenology of Spirit* (1946). Trans. John Heckman. Evanston: Northwestern University Press, 1974.

———. *Logic and Existence* (1952). Trans. Leonard Lawlor and Amit Sen. Albany: SUNY Press, 1997.

Ihde, Don. *Postphenomenology: Essays in the Postmodern Context.* Evanston: Northwestern University Press, 1993.

Ionesco, Eugene. *Notes and Counter Notes: Writings on the Theatre.* Trans. Donald Watson. New York: Grove Press, 1964.

Jameson, Fredric. *The Political Unconscious: Narrative as a Socially Symbolic Act.* Ithaca: Cornell University Press, 1981.

Jaspers, Karl. *Kant.* Trans. Ralph Manheim. New York: Harcourt, Brace and World, 1962.

Kant, Immanuel. *Anthropology from a Pragmatic Point of View* (1798). Trans. Victor Lyle Dowdell. Carbondale: Southern Illinois University Press, 1978.

Kellner, Douglas. *Jean Baudrillard: From Marxism to Postmodernism and Beyond.* Stanford: Stanford University Press, 1989.

Kierkegaard, Søren. *The Concept of Irony.* Trans. Lee M. Capel. Bloomington: Indiana University Press, 1972.

Kittler, Friedrich. *Discourse Networks 1800/1900.* Trans. Michael Metteer. Stanford: Stanford University Press, 1990.

Klossowski, Pierre. *The Baphomet* (1965). Trans. Sophie Hawkes and Stephen Sartarelli. New York: Marsilio, 1998.

Kojève, Alexandre. *Introduction to the Reading of Hegel: Lectures on the Phenomenology of Spirit.* Ed. Raymond Queneau (1947). Trans. James H. Nichols Jr. 1969; rpt. Ithaca: Cornell University Press, 1980.

Kristeva, Julia. *Language: The Unknown: An Initiation into Linguistics (1981).* Trans. Anne M. Menke. New York: Columbia University Press, 1989.

———. *La révolte intime: pouvoirs et limites de la psychanalyse II.* Paris: Fayard, 1997.

———. *Revolution in Poetic Language* (1974). Trans. Margaret Waller. New York: Columbia University Press, 1984.

———. "Within the Microcosm of the Talking Cure." Trans. Thomas Gora and Margaret Waller. *Interpreting Lacan.* Eds. Joseph H. Smith and William Kerrigan. New Haven: Yale University Press, 1983. 33–48.

Kurzweil, Edith. *The Age of Structuralism: Lévi-Strauss to Foucault.* New York: Columbia University Press, 1980.

Lacan, Jacques. *The Four Fundamental Concepts of Psychoanalysis* (1973). Trans. Alan Sheridan. London: Penguin, 1977.

———. *Speech and Language in Psychoanalysis.* Trans. and ed. Anthony Wilden. Baltimore: Johns Hopkins University Press, 1968.

LaCapra, Dominick. *A Preface to Sartre.* Ithaca: Cornell University Press, 1978.

Lacoue-Labarthe, Philippe, and Jean-Luc Nancy, *The Literary Absolute: The Theory of Literature in German Romanticism* (1978). Trans. Philip Barnard and Cheryl Lester. Albany: SUNY Press, 1988.

Lawall, Sarah. *Critics of Consciousness: The Existential Structures of Literature.* Cambridge: Harvard University Press, 1968.

Leclaire, Serge. *Psychanalyser: Un essai sur l'ordre de l'inconscient et la pratique de la lettre.* Paris: Seuil, 1968.

Lecourt, Dominique. *Marxism and Epistemology: Bachelard, Canguilhem, and Foucault* (1969). Trans. Ben Brewster. London: NLB, 1975.

Leder, Drew. *The Absent Body.* Chicago: University of Chicago Press, 1990.

Lefebvre, Henri. *Position: contre les technochrates.* Paris: Gonthier, 1967.

———. *La production de l'espace.* Paris: Éditions Anthropos, 1974.

Leitch, Vincent. *Deconstructive Criticism: An Advanced Introduction.* New York: Columbia University Press, 1983.

Lentricchia, Frank. *After the New Criticism.* Chicago: University of Chicago Press, 1980.

———. "Reading Foucault (II)." *Raritan* 4:2 (Summer 1982): 51.

Levinas, Emmanuel. *De l'évasion*. Paris: Fata Morgana, 1982/1997.

——. *De l'existence à l'existant*. Paris: Vrin, 1981.

——. *Discovering Existence with Husserl*. Trans. Richard A. Cohen and Michael B. Smith. Evanston: Northwestern University Press, 1998.

——. *Éthique et infini*. Paris: Fayard, 1982.

——. *Existence and Existents* (1946). Trans. Alphonso Lingis. The Hague: Martinus Nijhoff, 1978.

——. *God, Death, and Time* (1993). Trans. Bettina Bergo. Stanford: Stanford University Press, 2000.

——. *Humanisme de l'autre homme*. Montpellier: Fata Morgana, 1972.

——. *The Levinas Reader*. Ed. Seán Hand. Oxford: Blackwell, 1989.

——. *Proper Names* (1975 and 1976). Trans. Michael B. Smith. Stanford: Stanford University Press, 1996.

——. *The Theory of Intuition in Husserl's Phenomenology* (1930/1963). Trans. André Orianne. Evanston: Northwestern University Press, 1973/1995.

——. *Time and the Other* (1947). Trans. Richard A. Cohen. Pittsburgh: Duquesne University Press, 1987.

Luhmann, Niklas. *Love as Passion: The Codification of Intimacy* (1982). Trans. Jeremy Gaines and Doris L. Jones. 1986; rpt. Stanford: Stanford University Press, 1998.

Lukacher, Ned. *Primal Scenes: Literature, Philosophy, Psychoanalysis*. Ithaca: Cornell University Press, 1986.

Lukács, Georg. *The Meaning of Contemporary Realism* (1957). Trans. John and Necke Mander. London: Merlin Press, 1963.

Lyotard, Jean-François. *The Differend: Phrases in Dispute* (1983). Trans. Georges Van Den Abbeele. Minneapolis: University of Minnesota Press, 1988.

——. *Heidegger and 'the jews'* (1988). Trans. Andreas Michel and Mark Roberts. Minneapolis: University of Minnesota Press, 1990.

——. *Phenomenology* (1953). Trans. Brian Beakley. Albany: SUNY Press, 1991.

Macey, David. *The Lives of Michel Foucault*. London: Hutchinson, 1993.

Macherey, Pierre. "De Canguilhem à Canguilhem en passant par Foucault." *Georges Canguilhem: Philosophe, historien des sciences*. Paris: Albin Michel, 1993. 286–94.

Machin, Richard, and Christopher Norris, eds. *Post-Structuralist Readings of English Poetry*. New York: Cambridge University Press, 1987.

Macksey, Richard, and Eugenio Donato, eds. *The Structuralist Controversy: The Languages of Criticism and the Sciences of Man*. 2d ed. Baltimore: Johns Hopkins University Press, 1972.

Madou, Jean-Pol. *Démons et simulacres dans l'ouevre de Pierre Klossowski*. Paris: Klincksieck, 1987.

Marini, Marcelle. *Jacques Lacan: The French Context*. Trans. Anne Tomiche. New Brunswick: Rutgers University Press, 1992.

May, Todd. *The Political Philosophy of Poststructuralist Anarchism*. University Park: Penn State University Press, 1994.

Megill, Alan. *Prophets of Extremity: Nietzsche, Heidegger, Foucault, Derrida*. Berkeley: University of California Press, 1985.

Melville, Stephen W. *Philosophy beside Itself: On Deconstruction and Modernism*. Minneapolis: University of Minnesota Press, 1986.

Merleau-Ponty, Maurice. "The Experience of Others" (1951–52). Trans. Fred Evans and Hugh J. Silverman. *Merleau-Ponty and Psychology*. Ed. Keith Hoeller. Atlantic Highlands: Humanities Press, 1990. 33–63.

———. *Humanism and Terror: An Essay on the Communist Problem* (1947). Trans. John O'Neill. Boston: Beacon Press, 1969.

———. *Merleau-Ponty à la Sorbonne: résumé de cours 1949–1952*. Paris: Cynara, 1988.

———. "Phenomenology and Psychoanalysis: Preface to Hesnard's *L'Ouevre de Freud*" (1960). Trans. Alden L. Fisher. *Merleau-Ponty and Psychology*. Ed. Keith Hoeller. Atlantic Highlands: Humanities Press, 1990. 67–72.

———. *Phenomenology of Perception* (1945). Trans. Colin Smith. London: Routledge and Kegan Paul, 1962/1974.

———. "Philosophy and Non-philosophy since Hegel." Trans. Hugh J. Silverman. *Philosophy and Non-Philosophy since Merleau-Ponty*. Ed. Hugh J. Silverman. New York: Routledge, 1988. 9–83, 297–315.

———. *The Primacy of Perception*. Ed. James M. Edie. Evanston: Northwestern University Press, 1964.

———. *The Prose of the World* (1969). Ed. Claude Lefort. Trans. John O'Neill. Evanston: Northwestern University Press, 1973.

———. *Signs* (1960). Trans. Richard C. McCleary. Evanston: Northwestern University Press, 1964.

———. *The Structure of Behavior* (1942). Trans. Alden L. Fisher. Pittsburgh: Duquesne University Press, 1983.

———. *The Visible and the Invisible*. Ed. Claude Lefort (1964). Trans. Alphonso Lingis. Evanston: Northwestern University Press, 1968.

Miller, James. *The Passion of Michel Foucault*. New York: Simon and Schuster, 1993.

Minkowski, Eugene. *Lived Time: Phenomenological and Psychopathological Studies*. Evanston: Northwestern University Press, 1970.

Morrisette, Bruce. *The Novels of Robbe-Grillet* (1963). Trans. and rev. by the author. Ithaca: Cornell University Press, 1975.

Mowitt, John. *Text: The Genealogy of an Antidisciplinary Object*. Durham: Duke University Press, 1992.

Nancy, Jean-Luc. *The Birth to Presence*. Trans. Brian Holmes et. al. Stanford: Stanford University Press, 1993.

———. *The Inoperative Community*. Ed. Peter Connor. Trans. Peter Connor et. al. Minneapolis: University of Minnesota Press, 1986.

Nietzsche, Friedrich. *The Birth of Tragedy*. In *The Birth of Tragedy and the Genealogy of Morals*. Trans. Francis Golffing. New York: Doubleday, 1956.

Norris, Christopher. *Deconstruction: Theory and Practice*. London: Methuen, 1982.

———. *Derrida*. London: Fontana, 1987.

———. *Paul de Man: Deconstruction and the Critique of Aesthetic Ideology*. London: Routledge, 1988.

———. *The Truth about Postmodernism*. Oxford: Blackwell, 1993.

———. *Uncritical Theory: Postmodernism, Intellectuals, and the Gulf War*. Amherst: University of Masssachsetts Press, 1992.

———. *What's Wrong with Postmodernism: Critical Theory and the Ends of Philosophy*. Baltimore: Johns Hopkins University Press, 1990.

Pavel, Thomas. *The Feud of Language: A History of Structuralist Thought*. Oxford: Blackwell, 1992.

Pefanis, Julian. *Heterology and the Postmodern: Bataille, Baudrillard, and Lyotard*. Durham: Duke University Press, 1991.

Perniola, Mario. *Enigmas: The Egyptian Moment in Society and Art*. Trans. Christopher Woodall. London, Verso, 1995.

———. *La società dei simulacri*. Bologna: Capelli, 1980.

Piaget, Jean. *Le structuralisme*. Paris: Presses Universitaires de France, 1970.

Plank, William. *Sartre and the Surrealists*. Ann Arbor: UMI Research Press, 1981.

Poster, Mark. *The Mode of Information: Poststructuralism and Social Context*. Chicago: University of Chicago Press, 1990.

Racevskis, Karlis. *Michel Foucault and the Subversion of Intellect*. Ithaca: Cornell University Press, 1983.

Rajan, Tilottama. *Dark Interpreter: The Discourse of Romanticism*. Ithaca: Cornell University Press, 1980.

———. "Displacing Post-Structuralism: Romantic Studies after Paul de Man." *Studies in Romanticism* 24 (1985): 451–74.

———. "The Erasure of Narrative in Post-Structuralist Representations of Wordsworth." *Romantic Revolutions: Criticism and Theory*. Ed. Kenneth Johnston et. al. Bloomington: Indiana University Press, 1990. 350–70.

———. "Language, Music, and the Body: Nietzsche and Deconstruction." *Intersections: Nineteenth-Century Philosophy and Contemporary Theory*. Ed. Tilottama Rajan and David L. Clark. Albany: SUNY Press, 1995. 147–69.

———. "Trans-Positions of Difference: Kristeva and Post-Structuralism." *Ethics, Politics, and Difference in Julia Kristeva's Writing*. Ed. Kelly Oliver. New York: Routledge, 1993. 215–37.

———. "The University in Crisis: Cultural Studies, Civil Society, and the Place of Theory." *Literary Research/Recherche Littéraire* 18:35 (2001): 8–25.

Rajan, Tilottama, and Michael O'Driscoll, eds. *After Poststructualism: Writing the Intellectual History of Theory*. Toronto: University of Toronto Press, 2002.

Rapaport, Herman. *Heidegger and Derrida: Reflections on Time and Language*. Lincoln: University of Nebraska Press, 1989.

Reader, Keith A. *Intellectuals and the Left in France since 1968*. New York: St. Martin's Press, 1987.

Readings, Bill. *The University in Ruins*. Cambridge: Harvard University Press, 1996.

Regan, Charles E. *Paul Ricoeur: His Life and Works*. Chicago: University of Chicago Press, 1996.

Renaut, Alain, and Luc Ferry. *French Philosophy of the Sixties: An Essay on Antihumanism* (1985). Trans. Mary H. S. Cattani. Amherst: University of Massachusetts Press, 1990.

———. *Heidegger and Modernity* (1988). Trans. Franklin Philip. Chicago: University of Chicago Press, 1990.

Richter, David. *The Critical Tradition: Classic Texts and Contemporary Trends*. New York: St. Martin's, 1989.

Ricoeur, Paul. "The Antinomy of Human Reality and the Problem of Philosophical Anthropology" (1960). *The Philosophy of Paul Ricoeur: An Anthology of His Work*. Ed. Charles E. Regan and David Stewart. Boston: Beacon Press, 1978. 20–35.

———. "Hegel and Husserl on Intersubjectivity." *From Text to Action*. Evanston: Northwestern University Press, 1991. 227–45.

———. *Hermeneutics and the Human Sciences*. Ed. and trans. John B. Thompson. Cambridge: Cambridge University Press, 1981.

———. *Husserl: An Analysis of His Phenomenology* (1949–57). Trans. Edward G. Ballard and Lester E. Embree. Evanston: Northwestern University Press, 1967.

Robbe-Grillet, Alain. *For a New Novel: Essays on Fiction* (1963). Trans. Richard Howard. New York: Grove Press, 1963.

Rockmore, Tom. *Heidegger and French Philosophy: Humanism, Antihumanism, and Being*. New York: Routledge, 1995.

Roustang, François. *Dire Mastery: Discipleship from Freud to Lacan.* Trans. Ned
    Lukacher. Baltimore: Johns Hopkins University Press, 1976.

Ryan, Michael. *Marxism and Deconstruction: A Critical Articulation.* Baltimore:
    Johns Hopkins University Press, 1982.

Sartre, Jean-Paul. "L'Anthropologie" (1972). *Situations philosophiques.* Paris: Galli-
    mard, 1990.

———. *Being and Nothingness: An Essay on Phenomenological Ontology* (1943).
    Trans. Hazel E. Barnes. New York: Washington Square, 1956.

———. *Critique of Dialectical Reason* (1960). Trans. Alan Sheridan-Smith.
    London: Verso/NLB, 1976.

———. *Imagination: A Psychological Critique* (1936). Trans. Forrest Williams. Ann
    Arbor: University of Michigan Press, 1972.

———. *Mallarmé, or the Poet of Nothingness* (1986). Trans. Ernest Sturm. Univer-
    sity Park: Pennsylvania State University Press, 1991.

———. *Nausea* (1938). Trans. Robert Baldick. Harmondsworth: Penguin, 1965.

———. *The Psychology of Imagination* (1940). Trans. Bernard Frechtman. New
    York: Washington Square, 1966.

———. *Sketch for a Theory of the Emotions* (1939). Trans. Philip Mairet. London:
    Methuen, 1962.

———. *The Wartime Diaries of Jean-Paul Sartre: November 1939–March 1940.*
    Trans. Quintin Hoare. New York: Pantheon, 1984.

———. *What Is Literature?* (1947). Trans Bernard Frechtman. Gloucester, Mass.:
    Peter Smith, 1978.

Scarry, Elaine. *The Body in Pain: The Making and Unmaking of the World.* New
    York: Oxford University Press, 1985.

Schopenhauer, Arthur. *The World as Will and Representation* (1818 and 1850). Trans.
    E. F. J. Payne. 2 vols. New York: Dover, 1969.

Sedgwick, Eve. "Gender Criticism." In *Redrawing the Boundaries: The Transforma-
    tion of English and American Literary Studies.* Ed. Stephen Greenblatt and Giles
    Gunn. New York: MLA, 1992. 271–302.

Shumway, David R. *Michel Foucault.* Charlottesville: University Press of Virginia,
    1989.

Simmel, Georg. *Simmel on Culture.* Ed. David Frisby and Mike Featherstone.
    London: Sage, 1997.

Simpson, David. *The Academic Postmodern and the Rule of Literature.* Chicago:
    University of Chicago Press, 1995.

Spanos, William. *Heidegger and Criticism: Retrieving the Cultural Politics of De-
    struction.* Minnesota: University of Minnesota Press, 1993.

————. (ed.) *Martin Heidegger and the Question of Literature*. Bloomington: Indiana University Press, 1979.

Spiegelberg, Herbert. *Phenomenology in Psychology and Psychiatry: A Historical Introduction*. Evanston: Northwestern University Press, 1972.

Starr, Peter. *Logics of Failed Revolt: French Theory after May '68*. Stanford: Stanford University Press, 1995.

Sturrock, John, ed. *Structuralism and Since: From Lévi-Strauss to Derrida*. New York: Oxford University Press, 1979.

Thao, Trân Duc. *Phenomenology and Dialectical Materialism* (1951). Trans. Daniel J. Herman and Donald V. Morano. Dordrecht: Reidel, 1986.

Touraine, Alain. *The May Movement: Revolt and Reform* (1968). Trans. Leonard Mayhew. New York: Random House, 1971.

Turkle, Sherry. *Psychoanalytic Politics*. New York: Guilford Press, 1992.

Ulmer, Gregory L. *Applied Grammatology: Post(e)-Pedagogy from Jacques Derrida to Joseph Beuys*. Baltimore: Johns Hopkins University Press, 1985.

Vattimo, Gianni. *The Transparent Society* (1989). Trans. David Webb. Baltimore: Johns Hopkins University Press, 1992.

Wahl, Jean. *Le malheur de la conscience dans la philosophie de Hegel* (1929). 2d ed. Paris: PUF, 1951.

————. *Mots, mythes, et réalité dans la pensée de Heidegger*. Paris: Les cours de la Sorbonne, 1962.

————. *Philosophies of Existence: An Introduction to the Basic Thought of Kierkegaard, Jaspers, Marcel, Sartre* (1959). Trans. F. M. Lory. London: Routledge and Kegan Paul, 1969.

Wang, Orrin. "De Man, Marx, Rousseau, and the Machine." *After Poststructuralism: Writing the Intellectual History of Theory*. Ed. Tilottama Rajan and Michael O'Driscoll. Toronto: University of Toronto Press, 2002. 310–32.

Weedon, Chris. *Feminist Practice and Poststructuralist Theory*. Oxford: Blackwell, 1987.

Wolin, Richard. *The Terms of Cultural Criticism: The Frankfurt School, Existentialism, Poststructuralism*. New York: Columbia University Press, 1992.

Worringer, Wilhelm. *Abstraction and Empathy: A Contribution to the Psychology of Style* (1910). Trans. Michael Bullock. New York: Meridian, 1967.

Young, Robert, ed. *Untying the Text: A Post-Structuralist Reader*. Boston: Routledge and Kegan Paul, 1981.

Žižek, Slavoj. *Looking Awry: An Introduction to Jacques Lacan Through Popular Culture*. Cambridge: MIT Press, 1992.

————. *Tarrying with the Negative: Kant, Hegel, and the Critique of Ideology*. Durham: Duke University Press, 1993.

Index

In this index "f" after a number indicates a separate reference on the next page, and "ff" indicates separate references on the next two pages. A continuous discussion over two or more pages is indicated by a span of numbers. "Passim" is used for a cluster of references in close but not consecutive sequence.